Advances in

ARCHAEOLOGICAL
METHOD AND THEORY

Volume 2

Advisory Board

Advances in
ARCHAEOLOGICAL
METHOD AND THEORY

Volume 2

Edited by

MICHAEL B. SCHIFFER

Department of Anthropology
University of Arizona
Tucson, Arizona

ACADEMIC PRESS   **New York**   **San Francisco**   **London**   **1979**

A Subsidiary of Harcourt Brace Jovanovich, Publishers

ACADEMIC PRESS, INC.
111 Fifth Avenue, New York, New York 10003

United Kingdom Edition published by
ACADEMIC PRESS, INC. (LONDON) LTD.
24/28 Oval Road, London NW1 7DX

ISSN 0162-8003

ISBN 0-12-003102-7

PRINTED IN THE UNITED STATES OF AMERICA

79 80 81 82   9 8 7 6 5 4 3 2 1

Contents

v

7 On the Quantification of Vertebrate Archaeofaunas
DONALD K. GRAYSON

8 The Role of Archaeometry in American Archaeology: Approaches to the Evaluation of the Antiquity of *Homo sapiens* in California
R. E. TAYLOR and LOUIS A. PAYEN

9 Paleoethnobotany in American Archaeology
RICHARD I. FORD

List of Contributors

Numbers in parentheses indicate the pages on which the authors' contributions begin.

Carole L. Crumley (141), Department of Anthropology, University of North Carolina, Chapel Hill, North Carolina 27514

Richard I. Ford (285), Museum of Anthropology, The University of Michigan, Ann Arbor, Michigan 48109

Donald K. Grayson (199), Department of Anthropology, University of Washington, Seattle, Washington 98195

Michael A. Jochim (77), Department of Anthropology, University of California, Santa Barbara, California 93106

Charles W. McNett, Jr. (39), Department of Anthropology, The American University, Washington, D.C. 20016

Stanley J. Olsen (175), Department of Anthropology, University of Arizona, Tucson, Arizona 85721

Louis A. Payen (239), Radiocarbon Laboratory, Department of Anthropology, University of California, Riverside, California 92521

William L. Rathje (1), Department of Anthropology, University of Arizona, Tucson, Arizona 85721

Donna C. Roper (119), Department of Anthropology, University of Missouri-Columbia, Columbia, Missouri 65211

R. E. Taylor (239), Department of Anthropology, University of California, Riverside, California 92521

Contents of Volume 1

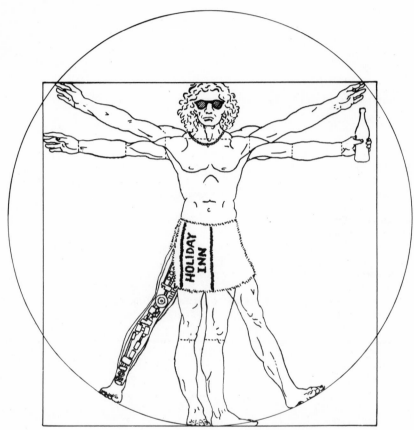

MODERN MATERIAL CULTURE STUDIES

Modern Material Culture Studies

WILLIAM L. RATHJE

AN ARCHAEOLOGICAL INTRODUCTION TO MODERN
MATERIAL CULTURE

"Everytime I run across an article relating how archaeologists are excavating and interpreting a new dig, I can't help but wonder what would happen should our civilization be abruptly extinguished." Thus wrote Nancy Stahl in a UPS article (Stahl 1975), which concluded that archaeologists in A.D. 3075 would reconstruct 1975 society "based on the contents of our basements." Upon finding empty boxes "archaeologists would undoubtedly jump to the conclusion that we were a race of box worshippers." Halloween costumes would become "sacred garments" and a wedding dress a "sacrificial robe," both used in "pagan rituals." If archaeologists "inadvertently" chose Disneyland as their excavation site, they would conclude that we were a "race of giant threefingered mice." This amazing article is only one of many that pit archaeologists against everything from Ebbet's Field to laundromats [*The Weans* (Nathan 1960), Tell-el-New York III (Greenberg 1953), Report on Grand Central Terminal (Szilard 1961), and the Archaeologicus segment of Saturday Night Live (NBC-TV, April 15, 1978)]. This genre of popular archaeology asks the question—what if archaeologists studied us? The answer is almost always the same—they would be unabashedly moronic.

This is a dismal prospect. Luckily, most of the descriptions of archaeology in the future are based on distorted views of (*a*) how sites are formed and the selective nature of archaeological preservation, (*b*) how

1

archaeologists choose sites for excavation, and (c) the nature of archaeological interpretation and hypothesis testing. Luckily also, this misunderstanding has not robbed archaeologists of their sense of humor nor repressed their curiosity.

Most of us have played the game, what will an archaeologist learn about us in 1000 years? A few archaeologists have decided not to wait a millenium for the answer and are taking the question seriously now. Some are working on salvage operations to preserve data on the social context of our material culture. Others are recording similar data to test theories about the relation between human behavior and material culture. Still others are studying modern settings to evaluate and expand the repertoire of method and theory used to reconstruct past societies. The implication of these activities is clear. Archaeologists are now doing the archaeology of us.

The first part of this chapter will describe the kinds of studies of modern material culture that archaeologists are doing and their reasons for doing them. There is little published literature at present, and many research reports are undergraduate term papers with their attendant weaknesses. Therefore, this first section of the chapter is an overview, not a critical review, of the dealings of archaeologists with our material culture. The second part of this chapter describes the broader context of studies of modern material culture in current behavioral science research.

THE ROLE OF MODERN MATERIAL CULTURE STUDIES IN ARCHAEOLOGY

The archaeological study of modern material culture traces its theoretical foundation to recent changes in what archaeologists perceive as their research domain. During the last decade, a number of archaeologists have independently rejected two traditional aspects of the definition of archaeology: (a) that archaeologists must dig for their data, and (b) that archaeological data must be old (Fontana 1970; Deetz 1970, 1977a,b; Salwen 1973; Leone 1973; Ascher 1974; Reid et al. 1974; Ferguson 1977; and others). This bold action left archaeology with a single defining characteristic: *a focus on the interaction between material culture and human behavior and ideas, regardless of time or space.*

The bulwark of this view of archaeology runs to the roots of the discipline. Archaeology developed as the behavioral science of the past. Because informant interviews and documentary data were usually unavailable, archaeologists had to examine physical evidence as a source of information about related human behavior. As a result, archaeologists developed a unique appreciation for the critical role material culture plays in social behavior. It is this insight that is the organizing principle of archaeology. It is also this insight that has led to a series of recent expansions in the domain of archaeological research. Archaeological excavations and investigations of documents made important contributions to knowledge of our recent past, and *historic-sites archaeology* and *industrial archaeology* were given their pedigrees. Other archaeologists found that in order to use material culture to reconstruct past behavior, it was helpful to observe the way people use material culture today, and *ethnoarchaeology* and *experimental archaeology* became legitimate offspring. Through this expansion process, the subject matter of archaeology has grown to include artifacts both below and above ground level.

In the latest phase of this developmental process, archaeologists are now studying modern America. They are seeking recognition within the domain of archaeology by (*a*) making contributions to the process of building archaeology's conceptual tools, and (*b*) providing the insights into our society and our relation to past societies that are unique to an archaeological perspective. Their basic subject matter is material culture, usually defined broadly enough to include not only typical "artifacts" but also plowed fields, polluted rivers, and other physical entities modified by human behavior (Deetz 1977a,b). Their studies quantitatively record and analyze the relationship between material culture and human behaviors and beliefs in a modern industrial setting, and include studies that compare the past to the present within a long-term perspective.

Cultural anthropology, sociology, cultural and urban geography, environmental psychology, and a variety of other behavioral sciences study recent and contemporary society. However, few record the same kinds of data an archaeologist would collect on the social context of material culture. Archaeological modern material culture studies are designed not to replace the work of other disciplines, but to supplement them. Archaeology is a behavioral science with its own particular methods, theories, and viewpoints.

The archaeologist's exploitation of modern data does have precedents. The most legendary is A. V. Kidder's excavation of the town dump of Andover, Massachusetts, in the 1920s. This research is preserved only in archaeological folklore; the results were never reported. All too often this has been the fate of similar studies. Nevertheless, enough studies of our society by archaeologists have been formally and informally reported to outline the general research avenues they are pioneering. I have gathered the archaeological studies of modern material culture into four catagories based on their rationales and potential contributions to archaeology: (*a*) teaching archaeological principles, (*b*) testing archaeological principles,

(c) doing the archaeology of today, (d) relating our society to those of the past.

Contribution 1: Teaching Archaeological Principles

The most obvious characteristic of modern material culture studies is their usefulness in teaching archaeology. Completed studies can be valuable learning aids. Gilborn (1968), for example, designed a typological analysis of Coke bottles primarily as a tool for explaining seriation. Rather than read the reports of others, however, the main advantage of studies of modern material culture is that students can be asked to do their own. Involving undergraduates as archaeological investigators of their own society has a variety of useful benefits: (a) an analytical perspective of an ongoing society makes students aware of the systematic relation between material culture and behavior; (b) students can most easily learn the strengths and weaknesses of archaeological methods and theories by applying them in a familiar setting; (c) data for study are available locally in an unending supply, and there is no destruction of older, scarcer sites; (d) during their studies of material culture, undergraduates gain practical experience in the research process, including project design, data recording, analysis, and reporting; (e) this approach generates a great deal of enthusiasm among students, which will surely not be overlooked in an era of declining anthropology enrollments.

Archaeology students at a number of universities have benefited from these advantages. Nevertheless, there are only a few published reports on the instructional implications of studies of our material culture (McVicker 1972, 1973; Salwen 1973; Ascher 1974; Rathje 1974; Kavanaugh 1978; Wilk and Schiffer 1978, n.d.). To illustrate the extent of the unreported use of student projects, I shall draw upon experience in the department where I teach.

Students began doing studies of modern material culture in archaeology classes at the University of Arizona in 1971. At that time, the majority of projects were straightforward tests of archaeology's basic premise: that behavior and material culture are related in a systematic manner. These papers begin with the assumption, based on personal experience in our society, that a specific pattern of behaviors is known. Associated patterns in the use and disposal of material culture are then postulated; finally, actual activity loci are checked to determine whether observed patterns reflect expectations of use and deposition.

John Hohman (1975), for example, selected as his topic behaviors at isolated road ends and carefully recorded the surface remains at the ends of two dirt roads in the Tucson desert. The resulting maps show two concentric rings of materials at both road ends. The ring closest to the road was composed of broken beer bottles; the larger ring consisted of beer cans, presumably tossed away rather than dropped. In areas secluded from the lights of approaching cars, a number of sex-related items were encountered. Thus, the material remains at both road ends showed patterns that conformed to the activities that were assumed to occur at road ends. As so many modern material culture studies do, this project also produced an unexpected discovery. Behind each road end were dumps for stolen cars and property, such as wallets—an unanticipated correlate of road end behavior.

Over the past five years, the direction of student projects has expanded from tests of general premises to include tests of a variety of specific techniques and principles. At present, undergraduates in method and theory courses participate in modern material culture class exercises that involve students in seriation, chronology building, soil analysis, use–wear analysis, identification of patterning in the behavioral and natural factors that affect site formation, and the field testing of hypotheses (Wilk and Schiffer 1978, n.d.).

Students have also begun to examine more complex archaeological problems in their independent term papers. Many studies at the University of Arizona, as elsewhere, have centered on traditional archaeological concerns with burial ritual and cemeteries (see also McVicker 1972 for a description of similar studies done by Loyola students in Chicago); a few examples will illustrate the potential value of these student studies.

Several students have examined the relation between grave markers and socioeconomic stratification. One compared the size and decoration on gravestones of males and females at cemeteries in Philadelphia and Tucson over the last thirty years. Results showed no difference between males and females on the East Coast, but larger gravestones for males in Tucson (Franey 1977). Another student identified a clear tendency for markers of similar sizes to cluster in a cemetery (Fahey 1975). The possibility that this pattern represented the clustering of burials of individuals of similar socioeconomic status was tested by a particularly industrious student. Goodoff (1972) recorded a sample of markers, searched for relevant obituaries, and found a correlation between job and general pay scale and size and form of grave marker.

This result lends credence to the common archaeological assumption that the energy invested in grave goods, grave construction, and the act of interment is usually commensurate with the deceased's position within a community (Tainter 1978). Although this assumption may be valid as a rule, some papers have begun to explore exceptions. One study of a mortuary that served Mexican-American families concluded that in certain cases cause of death overrides socioeconomic position as the major influence on funeral expenditures (Moosman 1975). In the case of breast cancer deaths, networks of relatives mobilize well beyond normal bounds to finance extremely elaborate funerals. Regardless of family status, little expenditure beyond basic necessity is provided for drug overdose victims. Because of a small sample size, the distortions represented by these types of exceptions have not yet been evaluated.

Some cemetery studies have implications for the archaeological interpretation of changes in a society's economic viability and internal social structure. Bartholomeu (1977) proposed that local fluctuations in funerary equipment may reflect fluctuations in regional economics. Test data indicated that as personal income in the United States rose and fell, so did expenditures on grave markers in Tucson. Goldman (1972) expected to find that during periods of economic and political stress the recording of family ties and religious affiliation on grave markers would increase. Data from the last fifty years in Tucson indicated a marked increase in both types of inscriptions during World War II. As these types of findings are rigorously tested and analyses are further expanded, they may have important implications for traditional archaeological burial studies.

Although the student papers I have mentioned and hundreds like them are all interesting, none of these reports are published. This is a pattern the University of Arizona shares with other anthropology departments that emphasize student analyses of modern material culture (Salwen 1973:162). It is partly because term papers in undergraduate classes lack the energy investment and concern for detail necessary to be considered for journal publication. It is also partly because there are few clear publishing opportunities. As more professional archaeologists publish their modern material culture studies, more students will find the motivation and the publication outlets to follow suit.

In the meantime, the student papers that have been written are an invaluable research and development reservoir of ideas for large-scale projects. Arizona's Le Projet du Garbáge, an archaeological study of modern household garbage, began in 1971 as undergraduate term papers by Allen (1971) and Araiza (1971). Arizona's Reuse Project, concerned with the acquisition and disposal of household furniture and appliances, drew upon a number of student papers in its development process (Schiffer and McCarthy 1978).

The students who have done modern archaeology projects are themselves an even more valuable resource than their papers (S. South, personal communication 1978). The archaeology of modern settings has no rules or traditional ways of doing things. The field is open. The creative challenge is to give it form and substance. In the process, students are free to develop innovative approaches and attitudes. Students fresh from their own modern material culture projects are likely to approach traditional data from productive new directions. Some of these directions will probably include using modern material culture to develop the method and theory components of the discipline of archaeology; enter contribution 2.

Contribution 2: Testing Archaeological Principles

The potential of modern material culture studies to develop and validate archaeological principles provides the rationale for current ethnoarchaeological analyses of small communities in nonindustrial societies (Gould 1978). Although these studies are useful in interpreting hunter–gatherer campsites and farming villages, both Salwen (1973) and Ascher (1974) point out that archaeologists excavate large urban centers as well. Modern cities are the progeny of ancient urban centers, just as modern bushmen are descended from hunter–gatherers of the past. Neither setting can be considered pure, untainted by modern technologies and beliefs. Because of the monolithic nature of the present global economy, industrial and nonindustrial communities are related through multinational production–distribution systems, tourism, and aid in health, education, and "development." Thus, modern hunter–gatherers in Australia hunt with shotguns from the deck of pickup trucks, and rural farmers in Buganda wear wristwatches and listen to Linda Ronstadt on transistor radios. Given the industrial impurities in all modern settings, assumptions about ancient urban societies may be more appropriately tested in modern urban centers than in rural areas of the third world.

Salwen (1973) has proposed several research areas where studies of modern material culture could make contributions to the archaeology of ancient urban centers, including (*a*) analyzing vandalism as a process of site formation and an indicator of social values, (*b*) determining the material correlates of ethnic differentiation through the use of archaeological typologies, and (*c*) identifying patterns of the use of space within buildings and generally within cities. In a recent paper on this latter topic, Wilk and Schiffer (n.d.) have identified several patterns in behavior and material remains associated with vacant lots in Tucson. Testing these patterns in traditional archaeological sites may lead to new interpretations of the functions of the "vacant" portions of ancient cities.

Identifying those locations in archaeological sites used for periodic markets is a major theoretical and practical concern of the archaeologists of complex societies, especially in the Near East and Mesoamerica.

Nevertheless, little progress in this direction has been made. Schiffer and Schaefer (n.d.) are attacking the problem from a new perspective with (a) a cross-cultural survey of ethnohistoric and modern data on periodic markets and (b) a detailed analysis of swap meets and their material correlates in Tucson. As the correlates accumulate, so do the chances that this study of modern behaviors will have a major practical impact on traditional archaeology. In a similar study, Morenon (1978) is investigating the material correlates of the link between organizational complexity and increasing task specialization in auto service garages in Portales, New Mexico.

At least one new archaeological technique has been tested using modern material culture data. Historic sites often produce numbers of rusted tin cans devoid of labels identifying their original contents. McCarthy has developed a technique that uses can sizes, the historic records of national food packers, and a Monte Carlo simulation to assign food types and nutritive values to old cans. As a test, McCarthy's technique was tried out on can size data collected by the Garbage Project in Tucson. When simulated can contents were compared to known can contents, the match added considerable credibility to the technique as a new tool of historic-sites archaeology (Rathje and McCarthy 1977).

Many techniques and principles tested in modern settings are not limited in application to historic or urban sites. Time depth and cultural diversity are keystone characteristics of archaeological data. A large number of methods and models used in archaeological interpretation cross-cut these dimensions and must therefore be based on general principles that relate behavior and ideas to material culture. Seriation, for example, is based on general propositions about behavior patterns in the invention, adoption, production, distribution, and discard of material culture. Often archaeological models of behavior–material change are based on general propositions about the way people move goods, form bureaucracies, or respond to economic stress. Such general archaeological principles can be applied and tested in any society, including our own. This assertion was amply justified in the mid-1960s, when Deetz and Dethlefsen (1966; Dethlefsen and Deetz 1967) began to explore the principles behind seriation, using historic gravestones from Boston and vicinity. Not only did these data provide eloquent confirmation of the basic accuracy of the technique, but they led to further refinement of the technique by introducing the "Doppler effect" (Deetz and Dethlefsen 1965). In addition, Deetz and Dethlefsen (1966) documented an interesting model of cultural innovation that tied together ideology and material culture (see also Eighmy 1977).

One University of Arizona student paper that applied seriation in a modern setting is an interesting offspring of the Deetz and Dethlefsen research. Feldman and Hughes (1972) selected a sample of 100 cars from a used car lot. A set of ten stylistic and ten functional attributes were recorded for each. First the cars were seriated on the basis of style alone, then just on the basis of function. The results were surprising. Archaeologists usually assume that stylistic attributes are the best for seriations. Modern cars, however, show considerable stylistic variability at any one time (compare a Cadillac with a Volkswagen or a Datsun 240z). In contrast, functional attributes, such as amber turn signals, seat belts, and ignition locks, are usually adopted by all manufacturers at more or less the same time. Thus in this one test case, functional attributes served as useful horizon markers and produced a more accurate seriation than did the stylistic attributes.

A number of other student papers have used modern data from Tucson to evaluate general propositions of archaeological relevance (see also Schiffer 1976, 1978 for a description of additional student papers of this sort). One hypothesis states that the distance an object may be moved for repair is a function of the object's size and the number of such items in a given vicinity. A positive test was obtained using clock repair data (Nettles 1972). The proposition that the distance between an object's use area and storage area is directly related to the frequency of the object's use was studied and tentatively confirmed in modern kitchens (Hughes 1972). Another study used sales data on washing machines and other appliances to derive a model of status symbol replacement which related changes in an item's status value to changes in replacement costs and the quantity in circulation (Swan 1972).

The general cross-cultural and cross-temporal applicability of some archaeological principles is now being evaluated with modern material culture from our society as one of the test cases. One example is Ascher's (1968) description of archaeological site formation which includes data from an auto junk yard in Ithaca, New York, and a Seri Indian village in Mexico.

Another archaeological proposition with cross-cultural and cross-temporal implications was offered by McKellar's (1973) paper on litter on the University of Arizona campus, which indicated that there was a critical size factor in litter disposal patterns. Items above 4 inches (about 9 cm) in size were consistently found in trash cans; objects smaller than 4 inches were left behind as litter. A world away, Jim O'Connell was studying site formation processes among modern Australian Aborigines. His research showed that when regular activity areas were cleared and swept, the size of the leftovers was 9 cm or less. After considering McKellar's research, O'Connell is intrigued by the possibility of a general

McKellar Principle of disposal, with obvious implications for both past and present (J. O'Connell, personal communication 1977).

As a recipient of old principles to test and as a donor of new and tested principles, modern material culture studies are likely to develop in tandem with the pulse of archaeological method and theory. In addition, it is clear that the more we use our society as a place to apply archaeological techniques, the more information we shall retrieve about our own society from archaeology's unique perspective; enter contribution 3.

Contribution 3: Recording the Archaeology of Today

We are immensely egotistical. Somehow we must feel that things will stay the same as they are. Otherwise we would realize that what future archaeologists will say about us is not really a game. Continual change is one of the defining characteristics of modern civilization. Decades from now historians and archaeologists will be trying to reconstruct the culture history and lifestyles of the 1970s. Decades from now relevant archaeological data will not be easy to find.

One of the classic folktales of archaeology is Tell-el-New York III (Greenberg 1953), an account of an archaeologist's attempt to interpret the ruins of Ebbets Field, the home stadium of the Brooklyn Dodgers. It is more than ironic that the Dodgers are now in Los Angeles and that in the mid-1960s Ebbets Field was completely razed and replaced by an apartment complex. The material remains of the stadium were sold to memorabilia collectors, reused in other old buildings, recycled into new items, or dumped in various New York landfills.

The behavioral contexts of these and a myriad other data we take for granted are being discarded. This is an important theme for justifying modern material culture studies in archaeology. Without such research, a major portion of our cultural heritage will be irretrievably lost—lost through biases in recording and preservation methods or lost because no attempt is made to record or preserve it at all.

Scholars who deal with ancient literate civilizations have noted that the printed work often lies about events and is incomplete in its picture of human behaviors, focusing mainly on the doings of powerful individuals. Archaeologists echo these sentiments, but for some reason such complaints have rarely been raised in our own society, where distortions and gaps in the written records of our behavior clearly exist (Glassie 1977; Carson 1978).

Most *distortions* are the product of human bias in the data on behavior that enter written records. First, few behavioral scientists or government record keepers collect data on the social context of our material culture in any systematic, quantitative manner. Second, when they do, their "objective" data are usually collected by using methods with built-in biases. For example, the majority of their data are obtained by asking informants to describe their behavior. Informants responding to questionnaires or interview–surveys may intentionally misrepresent behaviors, such as beer drinking, which have positive or negative cultural connotations. Unintentional inaccuracies in informant accounts of behaviors also arise because of problems of recalling detailed quantitative data (Webb *et al.* 1966; Adams 1973; Brittin and Zinn 1977).

Most *gaps* in written records are due to biases in which records are preserved for study. As historic-sites archaeologists and historians of technology have found from experience, owing to a narrow conception of history, many data relevant to understanding our lifestyles are not acquired by libraries. Old Sears and Roebuck catalogues are hard to locate, yet they hold important data on items that touched the daily lives of almost everyone in America. In fact, the basic documents on our material culture, the patents, repair manuals, and mail advertisements, are not even valued (Fontana 1968; Gideon 1948).

Equal to the failure to preserve literature and printed matter is a paucity of artifacts saved from daily life. Because of the way we value material possessions and the role of antiques in our society, some items are preserved. Just as libraries usually seek outstanding pieces of literature, however, "old" items are often considered worthy of "antique" status because they possess unique features. In fact, it sometimes seems that the more abundant and persistent an item is during its period of use, the fewer examples are intentionally preserved (Michael B. Schiffer, personal communication 1976).

The preservation of common artifacts has fallen to enthusiastic private collectors of memorabilia, such as the members of London's Ephemera Society, which is devoted to saving anything printed or written that was intended for purely short-term use: railway timetables, laundry lists, school report cards, and Christmas cards. The fad of collecting today includes almost every kind of common artifact—beer cans, can openers, box tops, hub caps. This type of acquisition has been institutionalized in the form of curators of modern material culture at some museums and a general increase in concern over what should be collected and how it should be documented and displayed (Sturtevant 1969; Harris 1978; Stramstad 1978, Palmer 1978).

To archaeologists of the future, private collections will most closely resemble those of today's looters, which are a series of items ripped out of context and devoid of behavioral meaning. Actual contextual analyses of our material products will be extremely difficult for future archaeologists.

The flow of goods and materials from context to context has become increasingly rapid through recycling, second-hand organizations, garage sales, swap meets, and other forms of reuse (Schiffer 1976). In addition, our society takes pains to destroy the past context of materials, which are finally discarded. For example, almost every disposal site in urban America has a bulldozer that spends its day running back and forth through newly dumped debris and thoroughly mixing garbage collection units together. Our unparalleled success at eradicating archaeological contexts is an example of what seems to be a general rule: as societies develop in complexity, garbage disposal becomes more systematic and energy-intensive—trash compactors, regular garbage collection, specialized demolition organizations, specialized recycling, resource recovery, and disposal sites.

On the basis of these patterns of preservation, or more accurately the lack of preservation, Fontana (1968), Ascher (1974), Glassie (1977), and Hume (1978:27) have all argued for a contemporary study of material culture in use in our everyday life. Common artifacts, their patterns of use, and their effects on our social, economic, religious, and political behaviors are as important to American history as the transcripts of the Watergate hearings.

Many of the studies that intentionally make a contribution to our culture history focus on material culture as an important component in our belief systems. Leone has carried this aspect of modern material culture studies to its most sophisticated form in (*a*) analyzing the role of fences in Mormon life (Leone 1973) and (*b*) discussing the implications of the differences between the Mormon Temple in Washington and the Catholic and the Episcopal National Cathedrals (Leone 1977).

Another type of study that records our current lifestyles and culture history does so in a context of "relevance." The Garbage Project is an example. Begun in 1972 as a training exercise for archaeology students, the project soon found that its quantitative data record of the contents of modern household garbage cans was useful to a variety of scholars and government policymakers. Specifically, refuse data on beer consumption have been used to (*a*) supplement informant interview data and (*b*) define the direction of biases in reporting so that correction factors can be applied to informant responses (Rathje 1978; Rathje and McCarthy 1977). Other Garbage Project studies have focused on (*a*) the behavioral correlates of food waste at the household level (Harrison *et al.* 1975; Harrison 1976; Rathje and Hughes 1977) and (*b*) the effects of inflation on the food purchasing strategies of specific population segments, especially low-income households (Rathje and Harrison 1978). Current research includes work for the Environmental Protection Agency on identifying the responses over a year of specific population segments to ads promoting recycling. A second endeavor is a pilot Garbage Project in Milwaukee to compare the consumer behaviors of matched as well as dissimilar population groups between Milwaukee and Tucson. Based on this background, the Garbage Project represents an archaeological contribution to data gathering techniques employed by behavioral scientists and others studying our society (Rathje and Hughes 1975).

Every archaeological study of modern material culture, whether done in the name of teaching or testing or relevance or cognitive studies, preserves important data on the current conditions of our society. These behavior–material descriptions of our society are important for understanding ourselves today and, in addition, our relation to the past; enter contribution 4.

Contribution 4: Relating Our Society to Past Societies

A final rationale for doing the archaeology of today is that it provides an opportunity for communicating the results of more traditional archaeology to the public. For us really to understand how we are similar to, or different from, our ancestors, we must be able to look at ourselves in ways that are comparable to the way we look at the past. Material culture provides an unbroken record that reaches from the first discarded tool to the contents of our garbage cans. Although material culture has yet to be fully exploited as a link from past to present, some archaeologists are being drawn in this direction.

Historic-sites archaeologists such as South (1978), Schuyler (1977), and Hume (1978), among others, are finding their data literally and figuratively lying closer and closer to the present. In addition, many cultural resource management (CRM) archaeologists, especially in urban centers, are finding themselves surveying and digging through their own living surfaces (Dickins and Bowen 1978a). The law, in fact, requires the CRM archaeologist to evaluate all cultural resources in an impact area. CRM, therefore, provides a special impetus for long-term studies that relate us to our ancestors (Cotter 1974; Hosmer 1978). Often this opportunity leads to the construction of chronologies that connect past and present. One example is the glass chronology used by Ellis and Grange (1978), which extends from early Egypt to the Alcoa lip of 1976: but potential contributions extend beyond histories of technology. The archaeological record can be used as an "explanatory bridge" connecting past and present (Carson 1978).

One example of an attempt to relate historic sites to the present through an archaeological perspective is Daniel Ingersoll's investigations at the

Strawberry Bank Site, located in the city of Portsmouth, New Hampshire. The physical excavations centered on Puddle Dock, a filled waterway and wharf structure built between 1830 and 1840. Besides the archaeological material retrieved, Ingersoll used a wide range of historic sources. The problems investigated all related to the genesis of modern cities: solid waste disposal, land use patterns, immigration, slum development, and absentee landlordism (Ingersoll 1971:67). Perhaps the most significant bridge to the present resulted from the dock fill data:

> The industrial revolution . . . was supplying the consumer with hundreds of dispos-able containers and materials by the end of the nineteenth century. The estimated 25,000 cubic yards of fill deposited in the upper portion of Puddle Dock show that the age of the throw-away world began not in the twentieth century but during the 19th [Ingersoll 1971:70].

Ingersoll's background includes work with James Deetz. A second past–present study also derived inspiration from Deetz. During the last five years, W. H. Adams and colleagues have been doing the ethnoar-chaeology of a rural American community, Silcott, Washington (1900–1930). The remains of the town will soon be buried by the reservoir behind Lower Granite Dam. In a major step toward legitimizing the archaeology of our recent past, this study is a "salvage" component of the Alpawa Project. Adams, like Ingersoll, exploits a wide range of historic sources; but Adams went one step further—he added an archivist/ethnographer, in part to talk to individuals who had once lived in Silcott. Because of major deficiencies in historic records and materials, Adams believes that his combination of ethnography and archaeology at Silcott is a significant contribution to the accurate reconstruction of a rural American lifestyle. This contribution is especially important because Adams (1973, 1975) maintains that the recorded behavior–material data are so different that the Silcott of only one or two generations ago represents a culture totally different from that of modern America.

These and similar studies all point toward erasing the dividing line between past and present. As yet, however, this line is still in place, maintained to some degree by archaeologists themselves. They have often failed to explore questions raised in historic sites in modern society. Ingersoll says that the "throw-away age" began in the nineteenth cen-tury. But what are the actual differences between modern solid wastes and those discarded in the mid-1800s? For this comparison, Ingersoll seems to rely on his stereotype of modern refuse. Adams maintains that the material inventory of Silcott is vastly different from that of today; but where are those differences quantified? In these and other cases, ar-chaeologists draw a line between the material commodities that are the traditional domain of their discipline and the material culture that shapes every day of their lives. As a result of this dividing line, most studies have fallen short of realizing a quantitative view of the major changes in America which transformed us from a folk to a truly urban society within the last 50 years (Dickens and Bowen 1978b). Nevertheless, the feasibility of such studies is illustrated by one of the first modern material culture studies in anthropology, which is still one of the best (Richardson and Kroeber 1940). Jane Richardson and A. L. Kroeber recorded six stylistic attributes of formal dresses pictured in a sample of fashion journals from 1787 to 1936 (their present). Analyses demonstrated that fashion was not capricious, but that each of the six attributes followed cycles of 70 to 100 years' periodicity.

We are always in the process of becoming the past. In fact, we can often catch ourselves in the act of continuing the long-term trends that archaeologists identify in their studies of change. The linking of past to present in an archaeological perspective is a natural by-product of using modern material culture studies to teach archaeological principles, to test archaeological principles, and to record our current culture history. Each such study contributes to the preservation of archaeological data that will otherwise be lost. Each study, therefore, potentially has relevance for comparing our society to past societies and contributes new dimensions to the archaeology of us.

Contributions: Potentials and Realities

Few comprehensive archaeological studies of modern material culture have yet to be undertaken and published. This is largely because their contribution to traditional archaeological interests has yet to be demonstrated. The value of the archaeology of our society has yet to be demonstrated because of the tempting sirens archaeologists find waiting in modern settings to lure them into other pursuits.

The first bait that subverts archaeologists is encountering living informants. W. H. Adams hired an ethnographer to collect material culture data from Silcott informants. Within a short time, Adam's colleague had turned into a "full-fledged ethnographer," and the archaeologist was left on his own to collect what material–behavior data he could (Adams 1975:344). This same transformation into ethnographer has befallen other analyzers of modern material culture.

With the potential to talk to people comes an interest in what people say, in "meanings" and "values" (see Deetz 1977a; Leone 1973, 1977; Ascher 1974; Fontana 1970, among others). Often, rather than produce materialist ethnographies that focus on behavioral correlates of material culture, archaeologists turn to "mentalist archaeology," using material culture as one key to belief systems. This view can separate the archaeologist of modern society from the research of the majority of his archaeological colleagues—dusting sand from broken pots. But mentalist archaeology does have potential relevance to dirt archaeologists.

The first value of mentalist archaeology is sensitizing archaeologists to the importance of belief systems in human behavior. As outlined by Leone (1977), it is possible to see how dependent the powerful socioeconomic framework of the Mormon Church is upon its carefully structured belief system. As intricate as the interplay among beliefs, behavior, and material culture is, archaeologists might find this realization depressing if not for mentalist archaeology studies, which include quantitative data and hold out the potential of identifying cognitive correlates of material culture.

In his study of folk houses in Middle Virginia, Henry Glassie (1975) collected his data in a rigorous quantitative format and identified changes in house construction patterns during the economic and political upheavals of the nineteenth century. Similar patterns of change were identified in Ireland and England. Most behavioral studies would likely have stopped there or would perhaps have related changes to trade patterns or local economics. Glassie, however, went on by attempting to understand the relation between house forms and mental systems in eighteenth-century Middle Virginia. He concluded, among other things, that the architectural designs seemed to "accurately reflect the conflict in a society that is schizophrenically attracted at once—as American society is—to hierarchical social classification and to egalitarian activity" (Glassie 1975:181). Heady stuff for an archaeologist to attempt, but it speaks of a potential to identify the cognitive correlates of material culture. A similar potential is evident in Dethlefsen and Deetz' (1967) concern for the symbolic meanings of the carvings on their historic gravestones.

The other element of modern material culture that can subvert archaeologists is relevance. The Garbage Project, for example, has made relatively few direct contributions to dirt archaeology. As with mentalist archaeology, however, there are indirect benefits to traditional archaeology. Archaeologists have often waxed eloquent about the amount of information that can be gleaned from material data. If an archaeological approach to modern material culture cannot tell us something useful about ourselves today, those words might be called into question. The most important aspect of "relevant" studies is that an archaeological perspective and methodology are making contributions to useful knowledge about the present, further legitimizing the ability of archaeologists to learn about the past.

These indirect benefits aside, the ideal "archaeological" study of modern material culture contributes not only to the present, but also directly to knowledge of the past. The first real modern material culture breakthroughs in archaeology await those purists who will shun the temptations of mental systems and relevance and walk the straight and narrow of testing archaeological principles for the past in the present.

The traditions of modern material culture studies in archaeology are only beginning to be set. Nevertheless, it is clear that if they are well done, each individual archaeological study in a modern setting can contribute to (a) teaching archaeological principles, (b) testing archaeological principles, (c) recording culture history, and (d) recording the archaeological data for quantitative cross-cultural comparisons. Any good dirt archaeology project performs these functions. The creative challenge for the archaeologists studying modern material culture is translating the potential of good archaeology into action in our own society.

Realizing the full potential of archaeological research in modern civilizations requires understanding the function of modern material culture studies in contemporary behavioral science, as well as in the discipline of archaeology. The next section of this paper considers archaeological modern material culture studies in this broader context.

THE SOCIAL CONTEXT OF TECHNOLOGY

It is now no joke when Union Carbide claims that "something we do today will touch your life" or when Eaton states that "we're as much a part of the car as the car is a part of your life." Over the past few years, we, as individuals, have become increasingly aware of the part material culture plays in our daily activities. A claustrophobic realization of our encapsulation by material culture was one of the sources of "pop art" as it emerged in the early 1960s and developed into a fascination with the "popular culture" of the 1970s. This avant-garde concern for the sociocultural impact of material culture is paralleled by a scholarly interest. During the past decade, the behavioral sciences and humanities have begun to focus attention on our articulation with our artificial environment. Analyses of technology are nothing new, but putting technology in a social context is.

Modern material culture studies have, in fact, become a recognized research endeavor in a variety of disciplines. Sociologists increasingly turn to observations and measures of behavior–material interactions because of increasing difficulties with obtaining interviews and evaluating informant bias. Environmental psychologists, urban geographers, and urban planners are studying the impact of material environments on behaviors and attitudes, and vice versa. Market researchers and consumer educators have long focused on behavior–material studies because the relationship between commodities, attitudes, and behaviors is a key to selling products and concepts efficiently. Architectural theorists are studying the way people use forms and space out of a need to make artificial environments useful for the kinds of things people actually do. Government policy planners and specialists in resource management and technological development have begun to make assessments of the behavioral implications of technology because simple technological solutions to problems often backfire, owing to unexpected human reactions. Even cultural anthropologists are recording the social context of technology because of the devastating effects of introducing new technologies in "primitive" communities.

The development of modern material culture studies in most disciplines, including archaeology, seems to have followed similar courses. This shared evolution process is worth outlining, as it seems to be leading to a new research focus in the behavioral sciences.

Phase 1: The "Popular Culture" Phase

The first gropings toward a focus on the social context of material culture have been forms of play, such as the Tell-el-New York III tales, which pit bumbling future archaeologists against the contents of basements and Disneyland. Mania collectors of art deco, old baseball cards, and Superman comics are another symptom of a new awareness of common material things. From the same roots rose Robert Rauschenberg, Andy Warhol, and Larry Poons, who focused their "pop" art on the artifacts of our everyday lives. It is no accident that many of their early works that received critical acclaim depicted Coke bottles, an American "super-artifact" (e.g., Warhol 1962; Fairbanks 1967). Other artists, such as author Tom Wolfe, have proclaimed themselves as chroniclers of the wave of material culture as it breaks over us. In this role, Wolfe records the ever-increasing numbers of people who drop out of traditional leisure and social activities and drop into the material culture tide of cars, bikes, boats, television, stereos and the "new social etiquette." Wolfe also documents the individuals who become a literal part of the wave, such as Carol Doda, who "blew up her breasts with emulsified silicone, the main ingredient of Silly Putty" (Wolfe 1968:i, 65–74).

This kind of interest in the humanistic context of material culture seems to be the basis for "popular culture" departments in academia. The first and largest was founded by an English literature specialist, Ray B. Browne, in the late 1960s at Bowling Green. In 1974 the department had a

$500,000 library, 4 professors, 43 graduate students, and 600 undergraduates each quarter. It also publishes a "more or less scholarly" quarterly (*Time,* Dec. 30, 1974, p. 42); *The Journal of Popular Culture* contains articles on carnivals, women's magazines, the social significance of T-shirts, and the architecture of McDonald's hamburger stands. The specific rationale for "popular culture" studies in the humanities is based on the concept that material culture is so much a part of our everyday lives that understanding our relation to it will help us to better understand ourselves, to better cope with our environment, and even to answer some of the more profound questions of meaning in life (Glassie 1977; Fishwick and Browne 1970; Kavanaugh 1978). Whatever their ultimate purpose, the substance of humanistic studies struck a responsive chord among behavioral scientists who began to do their own analyses.

Phase 2: The "Measurement" or "Reflexive" Phase

Serious behavior–material studies are based on three factors: (*a*) the ubiquity of material culture, (*b*) the unique possibilities material culture offers for recording data using standardized scales and measures, and (*c*) the assumption that material culture and behavior are interrelated in a systematic manner. Within most disciplines modern material culture studies were developed primarily to use material culture as a passive indicator or mirror of attitudes and/or behaviors. This type of utilization is typical of archaeological studies, but it is best illustrated by the past uses of material culture in sociological research.

The move in sociology toward adding material culture to attitude and behavior studies is exemplified in the literature of social stratification and has most often taken the form of indices based on house types or living-room furniture. Other items, such as magazines and clothing, have also been used. The format was set in the 1940s by Warner's studies (Warner *et al.* 1960). In his work, most of the material indices were considered of peripheral value, and the methodology was not sophisticated. Little concern was spent on developing internally consistent classifications or even standardized measures. The result is that many early studies are not well documented or not replicable.

In the last two decades, the role of material culture in sociology has expanded. Over the last decade, interview and questionnaire methods have been subjected to more and more criticism concerning the effect of the measuring device on informants. This led to the plea by Eugene Webb and his colleagues for sociologists to attempt to develop "unobtrusive" measures of behaviors and attitudes:

> Interviewers and questionnaires intrude as a foreign element into the social setting
> they would describe, they create as well as measure attitudes, they elicit atypical roles
> and responses, they are limited to those who are accessible and will cooperate . . . but
> the principle objection is that they are used alone [Webb *et al.* 1966:1].

Webb's classic book itself is a good example of the result of this call. Although eloquent in its rationale for developing new, unobtrusive measures, it is mundane in its practical suggestions. The level of sophistication is illustrated by the example cited most often: determining the popularity of a museum display by the rate at which the floor tiles in front of it are replaced. The matter has rested at this level until recently. Owing to increasing informant refusal rates for interviews and questionnaires, sociologists are again talking seriously about using observations of material culture to record behaviors; but a decade after Webb's book, their new analysis techniques still lack the sophistication of the rationale for using them (Sinaiko and Broedling 1975).

There are exceptions (e.g., Roach and Eicher 1965). More rigorous studies have begun to appear and with them new quantitative and methodological concerns. In a study of living-room furniture, Laumann and House express distress over their "failure to carefully select and differentiate" within material attributes and over the "fundamental crudity" of the resulting categories (1970:338). These same authors also express a new awareness of the value of material culture as components of behavioral systems: "Certainly [material items] afford a means of examining some of the more subtle hypotheses regarding peoples' lifestyles with greater objectivity and precision than hitherto has been possible." The implication they draw from their data, however, is still based on an assumed isomorphism of material culture and attitudes and actions: "people with traditional decor are also more traditional in their behavior and attitudes" (Laumann and House 1970:337).

Many material culture studies by professional and student archaeologists alike have followed this format—a search for material correlates of specific social and ideological characteristics. Studies have sought isomorphisms between: cost of house and lawn furnishings (Rosenberg 1976), sociodemographic characteristics and reuse alternatives (Banes 1977; Larich 1977), types of litter and types of films shown at drive-in theaters (Schlessman 1977), fashions and the women's liberation movement (Ackerman 1975), the purchase of over-the-counter drugs and marital status (Snyder 1972), bathroom decoration and the use of hallucinogenic drugs (Motz 1972), and the way people dress and the way they put ketchup on hamburgers (Thomas 1971).

These are studies in search of stereotypes. The basic goal is to construct a neatly organized world in which material culture is isomorphic with attitudes and behaviors. This approach derives from our own personal relations to material culture. Because material culture is so pervasive in our society, we, as individuals, develop clear stereotypes and shorthands, and such normative methods obscure variety.

As a result, students are often frustrated when a specific type of material culture does not fit into neat patterns with behavior. The "reflexive" studies, which have sought direct correlations between behavior and material items, have found much more variety than predicted. This result itself is indicative of two conclusions: (*a*) that our behavior–material stereotypes drastically oversimplify the real world, and (*b*) that in many cases expected correlates may not exist because our society is in continual flux and material culture–behavior relationships are constantly changing. These propositions are part of a transformation, not only in the way behavioral scientists view material culture, but also in the way Americans view their everyday world. An American mythology itself is changing.

American Mythology in Flux

The characteristically human, and especially American, response to problems is technology. From the start, technology was awarded a prime role in the American Dream, in which "wilderness [transformed by] science and technology [results in] abundance" (Garretson 1976:12). The same myth is in evidence today. Not enough food? Produce more fertilizer and machinery and invent new forms of processing. Poor quality of life in "less developed countries?" Model economic development on United States energy-intensive systems. In the American Dream the relationship between technology and behavior is assumed to be direct and understandable. Increasingly, however, this basic premise is being contradicted in the real world.

Reality has become an ever-accelerating parade of technological foulups: medicines that cause disease, food processing that radically decreases food value, cleaning products that pollute, toys that harm children, urban renewal projects that create slums. Technological–behavioral backfires have become so expectable in our society that a new mythology of mistrust of technology is replacing the old supertechnology myth (Coates 1974). In the "old mythology," technology was our champion whatever the problem. In a grim "new mythology," bred in energy crises, environmental disasters, and other technological foul-ups, technology is the problem.

We are currently caught between these myths of technology as super hero and technology as supervillain. Our schizophrenia is evident in the popular media. It is clear on television screens, where the ultimate technology superhero, the "six million dollar man," appears alongside the Waltons, a "new myth" family happy in their material poverty. It is clear in movies. The classic "2001" (1968) is an archetypal enactment of the transition from old to new mythologies, documenting humanity's struggle with technology gone berserk—in this case a paranoid computer named Hal. It is clear in written materials, where *Popular Mechanics* and the *Whole Earth Catalogue* are sold on the same newsstands. It is clear in songs, especially those about cars. Americans seem attached to cars through an invisible umbilical cord (Botkin 1970; Hammond 1970). Cars have always been a source of pride, our most multipurpose status symbol and the subject of adulation in songs such as "Little Deuce Coupe" (Jan and Dean), "409" (The Beachboys), and "Hot Rod Lincoln" (Chuck Berry). More recently, however, these same machines have been derided for lack of safety, poor gas economy, pollution, and massive factory recalls. Some new songs are now less charitable, such as "Oh Lord, Mr. Ford" (Jerry Reed):

> It seems your contribution to man
> To say the least got a little out of hand
> Oh Lord, Mr. Ford, what have you done?

Our transition in mythologies is most explicitly documented in books such as *The Wastemakers* (Packard 1963), *The Greening of America* (Reich 1970), *Future Shock* (Toffler 1971), *Limits to Growth* (Meadows *et al.* 1972), *Small Is Beautiful* (Schumacher 1973), and *Diet for a Small Planet* (Lappe 1971). These technological doomsday texts attempt to lay out the scope of our struggle with material bounty and material disaster. Their focus is not technology, but how it changes behavior and lifestyles. In effect, technology is viewed not as a passive servant of human wishes, but as an active component of societies with both positive and negative effects on behavior. This change in public perspective holds implications for modern material culture studies.

The study of material culture as a passive reflection of particular behaviors and cognitive structures was in tune with our "old" mythology—material culture is under control and essentially passive. The "new" mythology of technology's active role in society is emerging as a strong rationale for a new behavioral science based on behavior–material studies. Increasingly the popular media stress the need to anticipate the effect of a technology on behavior before it is introduced. Thus, what were once only technological problems are now also behavioral science problems; enter phase 3.

Phase 3: The "Social Context of Technology" Phase

Every new discipline, as well as many older ones, searches for an organizational principle that integrates and provides a point of view for all its research. Few find this nirvana, even after decades of looking. Modern material culture studies have had their point of view forced upon them. In fact, it is a common point of view that is actually assembling a field of study out of the fringes of other disciplines. The nucleus of this new perspective is clear:

Technology was developed to cope with our environment. Ultimately, however, it has replaced our natural surroundings as the source of our challenge. As material culture has increased in quantity, so have its unplanned side effects, transforming human societies in wholly unexpected ways. In fact, it seems that change often comes as the result of coping with the unanticipated consequences of planned behaviors. If we are to achieve any control over our technology and the form of our society, we need to be able to understand our present condition and anticipate future changes. Systematic efforts must be made to understand how we function in our manufactured environment. Studies that focus on defining the basic principles of the interaction between behavior and technology will provide a basis for evaluating our current condition, anticipating directions of change, and, as a result, making planning and policy decisions with fewer unexpected side effects.

The first fruits of this new perspective are studies of the *social context of technology* (SCTs). Two types of SCT have been implemented: (*a*) evaluations of the "current" social context of technology, and (*b*) projections of "future" social effects of proposed technologies. Current SCTs have focused on a wide range of issues: (*a*) Social issues, such as the effect of toys and books on the development of adult role models among minorities; or the behavioral implications of urban renewal projects. (*b*) Health issues, such as the relation between toys, children, and accidents; or studies of the effect of food processing and delivery systems on consumer nutrition. (*c*) Resource management issues, such as consumer reactions to the gasoline shortage and the energy crisis; or the effect of national brand advertising on the purchases made by the poor. Many of these studies are undertaken by or for government agencies; others are done by urban planners, consumer educators, market researchers, sociologists, economists, and civil engineers.

The second type of SCT is a form of futurism called "technological assessment" and is a new component of congressional policymaking in Washington. Technological assessment is defined as the analysis of the total impact of a technology on society:

> To be useful, a technology assessment must go far beyond conventional engineering and cost studies to look at what else may happen in achieving an immediate goal, to the range of social costs, the impacts on the family, on legal, political, and social institutions, on the environment, on international relations, on land-use planning, on the structure of cities, and on the makeup of populations [Coates 1974:30–32].

Futuristic SCTs may be as specific as forecasting the local effects of a new highway or factory—a process in which archaeologists now participate—or the national effects of another oil embargo. Marshall McLuhan's (1966) insights into the "global village" and models of global systems such as those developed in *The Limits to Growth* (Meadows *et al.* 1972) and its sequel, *Mankind at the Turning Point* (Mesarovic and Pastel 1976), are futuristic SCTs at a more abstract level.

From both types of SCT, there do seem to be the beginnings of two themes of analysis. The first and most important theme in SCTs is that material culture is treated as a dynamic component impinging on our behavior and cognition. This means the addition of a material component to traditional behavior–cognition studies. Thus, the second theme of SCTs is their holistic perspective based on the premise that human actions are not made up of discrete, independent components. Actions are composed of a complicated integration of cognitive, material, and behavioral elements. In any systematic analysis, all three must be considered. *Cognitive elements* are (*a*) general cultural rules elicited from informants and (*b*) informant perceptions of what behavior actually occurs as a result of these rules. *Behavioral elements* are (*c*) records of direct observations of actions and (*d*) common behavioral shorthand concepts (income level, ethnicity, demography, education level) used to classify people in groups that are assumed to have behavioral significance. Material elements are quantitative data in the form of standardized measures of (*e*) the material culture environment and (*f*) the natural environment affecting human actions. These are not separable components. They are all involved in a total description and understanding of human actions (Shimada n.d.).

Current and futuristic SCTs are linked together by more than shared themes. The ability to anticipate changes depends upon being able to define (*a*) the present state of all relevant variables, and (*b*) how these variables will interact with each other and with new variables. Thus, futuristic SCTs are dependent on current SCTs (*a*) for information on current situations as a base point, and (*b*) for data on the past interactions of specific variables as a basis for projections. Defining future impacts must, therefore, rely upon studies of past and present technology–behavior interactions.

The most important component in this process is building a coherent set of valid general principles to be tested in current SCTs and applied in futuristic SCTs. These principles will likely become the basis of a new discipline focused on defining the relationship of technology to society. The simulations and computer modeling exemplified by Forrester (1975) in studies that emphasize the counter-intuitive behaviors of social systems are in the forefront of this crystallizing discipline.

Archaeology is relevant to this developing field. In a very real sense, all futurism must be based on the past. Archaeology can provide methodologies for studying material culture as well as backup data and general principles for current and futuristic SCTs to draw upon.

Contribution 1: Long-Term Background Studies

Traditional archaeological studies should be the foundation of many SCTs. As Dickins and Bowen (1978b) have found in urban CRM, "many of our modern problems—such as overcrowding, impersonalization, and pollution—have considerable historical depth, with clear manifestations in the archaeological record." To use this archaeological record efficiently, however, comparable modern data must also be recorded from an archaeological perspective.

Contribution 2: Material Culture Methodologies and Data

The process of doing the archaeology of our society can be valuable to SCTs in its own right. Although there is, in theory, a new focus on material culture in a behavioral context, at present there are few useful data. In fact, in studies of contemporary social systems, a holistic perspective has rarely been achieved. *Cognitive* elements are sometimes ignored or inadequately defined. Many types of *behavior* are not directly observed, but are described only through interview–surveys—which are more relevant to a study of informant perceptions than to actual events. But the greatest problem is the lack of quantitative data on the *material* environment as it impinges upon human cognition and behavior. As our society has become more and more dependent upon technology and directed by its products, the fact that this element is missing has become increasingly obvious.

Archaeology's second contribution to SCTs is providing modern material–behavior data and new methods for data collection. Archaeologists have over one hundred years of experience in studying material culture in a behavioral context. All the modern material culture data collected by archaeologists fall either wholly or in large part outside the purview of standard methodologies used to record material culture in our society. The result is that archaeological data represent a unique information source that (*a*) supplements information collected by traditional means, (*b*) describes the current status of particular behavior-material patterns, and (c) provides a data bank for developing and testing general behavior–material principles. Many archaeological modern material culture studies concentrate on the acquisition and disposal of material culture by specific population segments. These data can be useful for SCTs.

Disposal Data: Site Formation Processes. The disposal of garbage, or solid wastes, in both legal and illegal forms is one of the most important problems facing industrial societies. This process of site formation, which includes both the behavioral and natural factors working on depositing and modifying material culture, is also a major concern of archaeologists. Studies of modern site formation can be beneficial to both SCT and traditional archaeological interests.

The behavioral aspect of the legal disposal of solid wastes involves determining the broad socioeconomic correlates of household discard behavior, including variation in solid wastes relative to household demographic composition and social strata, time of year, and general state of the economy. A number of civil engineers and solid waste managers have recently begun to conduct such studies. Their research examines one or two sociodemographic dimensions of discarding households, such as income or ethnicity, in relation to solid wastes recorded in gross material composition categories, such as paper, ferrous metal, and plastic (Resource Planning Associates 1972; Winkler and Wilson 1973; Winfield 1974; Tolley *et al.* 1978). These data have not been sufficient, however, to explain the variability in the household-level solid waste stream. An understanding of household discard patterns must be based on data describing the use-lives of specific products and the consumption patterns of specific population segments. Obtaining these data, in turn, requires recording the sociodemographics of discarding households in more detail as well as recording the solid wastes by particular type and brand name. There is a clear opening for archaeological expertise in describing complex behavior patterns in the procurement, consumption, and discard of household commodities (Rathje and Hughes 1975). The resulting behavior–material correlates can be used in modeling the future composition of the solid waste stream as well as in reconstructing past behaviors from older solid wastes.

Once garbage is in a disposal location, there are more opportunities for site formation research. Although biochemists have the empirical results of laboratory simulations, they have few field data on the generation of leachate, the potentially hazardous runoff from disposal sites that can contaminate groundwater (Dunlap *et al.* 1976). Studies of the biodegradation process through the excavation of actual landfills and dumps would provide material culture sequences and decay rate information useful to historic-site archaeologists and, in addition, actual test data including specified solid wastes and environmental conditions for leachate scientists.

The excavation and recording of recent garbage disposal sites is not a hypothetical archaeological problem; it is faced every day by urban CRM archaeologists. As Dickins and Bowen observed, dumps have changed considerably in the past few decades, and documenting this change is relevant to traditional archaeology and SCTs:

> It is probable that once we have elicited what these dumps have to tell us about their formation, the life span of various artifacts, decomposition rates of various materials, and human attitudes about the pathological by-products of urban behavior, we can proceed to generate some hypotheses about the solid waste problem and other seemingly maladaptive aspects of urban life [1978b].

Similar studies of patterns in littering activities, illegal dumping, and related material culture decay rates are being increasingly undertaken by federal and local government agencies (Federal Highway Administration 1974; Samtur n.d.). Here, too, archaeologists can participate. The McKellar Principle was based on a study of littering behavior. Another relevant student paper identified 1774 illegal dumps and patterns in their distribution around Tucson relative to specific socioeconomic neighborhoods (Clifford 1977). Both South (n.d.) and Morenon *et al.* (1976) have used poptops in archaeological studies. Morenon *et al.* (1976), for example, conducted surface surveys of modern refuse to determine the rate of utilization of specific sites in a national forest and estimate the potential impact of forest visitors on cultural resources. This study illustrates the synergistic value of collecting modern SCT data on littering behavior for traditional archaeological and CRM purposes.

Acquisition Data: The Relation between Behavior, Material Culture, and Cognition. Defining disposal patterns requires studying patterns of acquisition. As archaeologists define the sociodemographic correlates of household procurement patterns (Rathje and Harrison 1978; Schiffer and McCarthy 1978), more subtle variables can be added for analysis. One area of interest is the effect of cognitive structures on the acquisition of material culture, and, vice versa, the effect of material culture acquisition on cognitive structures. For example, Oscar Lewis' (1969) study of the possessions of poor families in a barrio of Mexico City illustrates the effect of religion on the way money is allocated to acquire material culture.

A related area of research is the role of material culture in maintaining or breaking down ethnic boundaries (Newton 1974; Tumin 1952:84–98). This issue is especially important because many CRM and other urban archaeological projects involve work in ethnic neighborhoods—Blacks (Schuyler 1974; Fleming 1971), Spanish-Americans (Ellis and Grange 1978), and Chinese (Ayres 1973). A number of material culture studies have also been done in Native American communities (Brown 1974; Katz 1974; Fontana 1978), and Salwen (1973) has suggested doing similar studies of ethnic groups in modern cities. The potential of documenting the material aspects of enculturation, the ability to procure food and other resources, and the maintenance of ethnic patterns can be significant data for theoretical archaeological analyses and practical SCTs. A considerable amount of research remains to be done to document systematically the cumulative effect that material culture and cognitive structures have on behavior and each other. Archaeological participation in this research may provide valuable insights for interpreting the past as well as the present. The use of modern data for interpreting the past, however, will require that archaeologists participate in the additional step of theory building.

Contribution 3: Theory Building

Archaeologists can play a role in building the theoretical structure of SCT research. The dramatic new format of SCTs, especially futuristic SCTs, is for the moment an elaborate facade. The ability to understand current and future behavior–material consequences must be based on empirically tested principles. Documented principles are essential for any attempts to control, mitigate, foresee, or simply understand the sociocultural effects of technology. At present there are few such principles. It is in this area that archaeology can make a significant contribution with its interests in nomothetic principles of behavior–material relations.

General material–behavior principles are as relevant to the study of the past as they are to the present and the future. Thus, archaeologists who explore modern societies in search of general principles of behavior can make a contribution to the study of the past. Likewise, those who choose traditional areas to explore general principles can make useful contributions to understanding the social context of technology and the impact of future technologies on future societies. Archaeology can be limited to the reconstruction of past behavior by using artifacts as passive reflections of ancient lifeways. On the other hand, from the same data base, archaeology can expand to develop a theory of the relations between people and things.

ARCHAEOLOGY'S ROLE IN MODERN MATERIAL CULTURE STUDIES

If archaeologists could speak with the ancient Maya of Tikal, would they stop recording the material data in their tombs and caches? Would they stop looking at the arrangements of spaces and rooms in palaces or attempting to quantify trade patterns? No. These material elements are important and legitimate components in a study of ancient Maya civilization. Material items are no less important in our twentieth-century civilization. In fact, the social context of technology has rarely been a more significant issue.

Modern material culture offers a unique source of knowledge about ourselves and our ties to the past. Modern material culture shapes our lives in many ways, and understanding how it does this is important to learning about our past and anticipating the future. Modern material culture studies represent a final step in the transformation of archaeology into a unified, holistic approach to the study of society and its material products. The challenge of doing the archaeology of our own constantly changing society may be a little frightening to archaeologists accustomed to carefully exhuming the remnants of dead civilizations. But we need not worry. At the very worst, we are bound to do better than finding a race of giant three-fingered mice worshipping boxes in our basements.

REFERENCES

Ackerman, K.
  1975 A change is gonna come . . . Paper prepared for Anthropology 136. Manuscript on deposit, Arizona State Museum Library, University of Arizona, Tucson.
Adams, W. H.
  1973 An ethnoarchaeological study of a rural American community: Silcott, Washington, 1900–1930. *Ethnohistory* **20**(No. 4):335–346.
  1975 Archaeology and the recent past: Silcott, Washington, 1900–1930. *Northwest Anthropological Research Notes* **9**(No. 1):156–165.
Allen, S.
  1971 A comparison of garbage. Paper prepared for Anthropology 35b. Manuscript on deposit, Garbage Project Files, University of Arizona, Tucson.
Araiza, F.
  1971 Skyline vs. a Chicano barrio garbage. Paper prepared for Anthropology 35b. Manuscript on deposit, Garbage Project Files, University of Arizona, Tucson.
Ascher, R.
  1968 Time's arrow and the archaeology of a contemporary community. In *Settlement archaeology*, edited by K. C. Chang. Palo Alto: National Press Books, Pp. 43–52.
  1974 Tin can archaeology. *Historical Archaeology* **8**:7–16.
Ayres, J. E.
  1973 The Chinese in Tucson. Paper presented at the Arizona Historical Convention, Tucson.
Banes, M.
  1977 Reuse activities: Book disposal in metropolitan Tucson. Paper prepared for Anthropology 136. Manuscript on deposit, Arizona State Museum Library, University of Arizona, Tucson.

Bartholomeu, M.
  1977 A study of gravestones and their relationship to economic prosperity and economic depression. Paper prepared for Anthropology 136. Manuscript on deposit, Arizona State Museum Library, University of Arizona, Tucson.
Botkin, B. A.
  1970 Icon on wheels: Supericon of popular culture. In *Icons of popular culture,* edited by M. Fishwick and R. B. Browne. Bowling Green: Bowling Green University Popular Press. Pp. 47–62.
Brittin, H. C., and R. J. Zinn
  1977 Meat-buying by Whites, Mexican-Americans, and Blacks. *Journal of the American Dietetic Association* **71**:623–628.
Brown, D.
  1974 Social structure as reflected in architectural units at Picuris Pueblo. In *The human mirror,* edited by M. Richardson. Baton Rouge: Louisiana State University Press. Pp. 317–338.
Carson, C.
  1978 Doing history with material. In *Material culture and the study of American life*, edited by I. M. G. Quimby. New York: Norton. Pp. 41–64.
Clifford, S.
  1977 An analysis of illegal dumping patterns in the Tucson area. Paper prepared for Anthropology 298m. Manuscript on deposit, Garbage Project Files, University of Arizona, Tucson.
Coates, J. F.
  1974 Technological assessment; how will it all work? *ASTM Standardization News* **2**:30–32.
Cotter, J.
  1974 Above ground archaeology. *American Quarterly* **26**(No. 3):266–280.
Deetz, J.
  1970 Archaeology as a social science. *Bulletin of the American Anthropological Association* **3**(No. 3, Part 2):115–125.
  1977a Material culture and archaeology—what's the difference? In Historical archaeology and the importance of material things, edited by L. Ferguson. *Society for Historical Archaeology, Special Publication Series* No. 2, 9–12.
  1977b *In small things forgotten: The archaeology of early American life.* Garden City, N.Y.: Anchor Doubleday.
Deetz, J., and E. Dethlefsen
  1965 The Doppler Effect and archaeology: A consideration of the special aspects of seriation. *Southwestern Journal of Anthropology* **21**:196–206.
  1966 Death's heads, cherubs and willow trees: Experimental archaeology in colonial cemeteries. *American Antiquity* **31**:502–510.
Dethlefsen, E., and J. Deetz
  1967 Eighteenth century cemeteries: A demographic view. *Historical Archaeology* 1967, 66–68.
Dickins, R. S., and W. R. Bowen (organizers)
  1978a Symposium on Urban Archaeology. Presented at the 43rd annual meeting of the Society for American Archaeology, Tucson.
  1978b Problems and promises in urban historical archaeology: The MARTA Project. Paper presented at the 43rd annual meeting of the Society for American Archaeology, Tucson.
Dunlap, W. J., D. C. Shew, J. M. Robertson, and C. R. Toussaint
  1976 Organic pollutants contributed to groundwater by a landfill. In *Gas and leachate*

from landfills, edited by E. J. Genetelli and J. Cirello. Cincinnati: U.S. Environmental Protection Agency. Pp. 96–110.

Eighmy, J.
> 1977 Mennonite architecture: Diachronic evidence for rapid diffusion in rural communities. Ph.D. dissertation, Department of Anthropology, University of Arizona. Ann Arbor: University Microfilms.

Ellis, G., and R. T. Grange
> 1978 Excavations at Ybor City, Tampa, Florida. Paper presented at the 43rd annual meeting of the Society for American Archaeology, Tucson.

Fahey, A.
> 1975 Gravestone design and inscription—have they changed with time? Paper prepared for Anthropology 136. Manuscript on deposit, Arizona State Museum Library, University of Arizona, Tucson.

Fairbanks, J.
> 1967 Coke bottle and egg. Painting in the Craig Gilborn Collection, Winterthur, Delaware.

Federal Highway Administration
> 1974 *Highway litter survey: Report to Congress.* Washington, D.C.: U.S. Department of Transportation.

Feldman, C., and W. W. Hughes
> 1972 A brief study of seriation using functional and stylistic attributes of automobiles. Paper prepared for Anthropology 136. Manuscript on deposit, Arizona State Museum Library, University of Arizona, Tucson.

Ferguson, L.
> 1977 Historical archaeology and the importance of material things. In Historical archaeology and the importance of material things, edited by L. Ferguson. *Society for Historical Archaeology, Special Publication Series* No. 2, 5–8.

Fishwick, M., and R. B. Browne (editors)
> 1970 *Icons of popular culture.* Bowling Green: Bowling Green University Popular Press.

Fleming, R. L.
> 1971 After the report, what?: The uses of historical archaeology, a planner's view. *Historical Archaeology* **5**:49–61.

Fontana, B. L.
> 1968 Bottles, buckets, and horseshoes: The unrespectable in American archaeology. *Keystone Folklore Quarterly.*
> 1970 In search of us. *Historical Archaeology* **4**:1–2.
> 1978 Artifacts of the Indians of the Southwest. In *Material culture and the study of American life,* edited by I. M. G. Quimby. New York: Norton. Pp. 75–108.

Forrester, J. W.
> 1975 Counterintuitive behavior of social systems. In *Collected papers of Jay W. Forrester.* Cambridge: Wright-Allen Press. Pp. 61–76.

Franey, M.
> 1977 The war between the sexes: Do they fight it to the grave? Paper prepared for Anthropology 198m. Manuscript on deposit, Arizona State Museum Library, University of Arizona, Tucson.

Garretson, L. R.
> 1976 *American culture: An anthropological perspective.* Dubuque: W. C. Brown.

Gideon, S.
> 1948 *Mechanization takes command: A contribution to anonymous history.* New York: Norton.

Gilborn, C.
    1968   Pop pedagogy. *Museum News* **47**:12–18.
Glassie, H.
    1975   *Folk housing in Middle Virginia: A structural analysis of historic artifacts.* Knoxville: University of Tennessee Press.
    1977   Archaeology and folklore: Common anxieties, common hopes. In Historical archaeology and the importance of material things, edited by L. Ferguson. *Society for Historical Archaeology, Special Publication Series* No. 2, 23–35.
Goldman, R.
    1972   Family and religion: A graveyard study. Paper prepared for Anthropology 1A. Manuscript on deposit, Arizona State Museum Library, University of Arizona, Tucson.
Goodoff, W. A.
    1972   Graves and status. Paper prepared for Anthropology 136. Manuscript on deposit, Arizona State Museum Library, University of Arizona, Tucson.
Gould, R. A., ed.
    1978   *Explorations in ethnoarchaeology.* Albuquerque: University of New Mexico Press.
Greenberg, J. H.
    1953   A new interpretation of the so-called "Violence Texts" based on the new discoveries from Upper Tell-El-New York III. Manuscript on deposit, Arizona State Museum Library, University of Arizona, Tucson.
Hammond, H.
    1970   The image of American life: Volkswagen. In *Icons of popular culture*, edited by M. Fishwick and R. B. Browne. Bowling Green: Bowling Green University Popular Press. Pp. 63–71.
Harris, N.
    1978   Museums, merchandising, and popular taste: The struggle for influence. In *Material culture and the study of American life*, edited by I. M. G. Quimby. New York: Norton. Pp. 140–174.
Harrison, G. G.
    1976   Socio-cultural correlates of food utilization and waste in a sample of urban households. Ph.D. dissertation, Department of Anthropology, University of Arizona. Ann Arbor: University Microfilms.
Harrison, G. G., W. L. Rathje, and W. W. Hughes
    1975   Food waste behavior in an urban population. *Journal of Nutrition Education* **7**(No. 1):13–16.
Hohman, J.
    1975   Road end behavior. Paper prepared for Anthropology 136. Manuscript on deposit, Arizona State Museum Library, University of Arizona, Tucson.
Homser, C. B.
    1978   The broadening view of the historical preservation movement. In *Material culture and the study of American life*, edited by I. M. G. Quimby. New York: Norton. Pp. 121–139.
Hughes, W. W.
    1972   A brief study of the relationship between storage facilities and their related preparation and assembly sites. Paper prepared for Anthropology 136. Manuscript on deposit, Arizona State Museum Library, University of Arizona, Tucson.
Hume, I. N.
    1978   Material culture with the dirt on it: A Virginia perspective. In *Material culture*

and the study of American life, edited by I. M. G. Quimby. New York: Norton.
Pp. 21–40.

Ingersoll, D. W.
1971 Problems of urban historical archaeology. *Man in the Northeast* 1(No. 2):66–74.

Katz, P.
1974 Adaptations to crowded space: The case of Taos Pueblo. In *The human mirror,* edited by M. Richardson. Baton Rouge: Louisiana State University Press. Pp. 300–316.

Kavanaugh, J. V.
1978 The artifact in American Culture: The development of an undergraduate program in American studies. In *Material culture and the study of American life*, edited by I. M. G. Quimby. New York: Norton. Pp. 65–74.

Lappe, F. M.
1971 *Diet for a small planet.* New York: Ballantine Books.

Larich, P.
1977 The Reuse Project. Paper prepared for Anthropology 136. Manuscript on deposit, Arizona State Museum Library, University of Arizona, Tucson.

Laumann, E. O., and J. S. House
1970 Living room styles and social attributes: The patterning of material artifacts in a modern urban community. *Sociology and Social Research* **54**:321–342.

Leone, M. P.
1973 Archaeology as the science of technology: Mormon town plans and fences. In *Research and theory in current archaeology,* edited by C. L. Redman. New York: Wiley, Pp. 125–150.
1977 The new Mormon Temple in Washington, D.C. In Historical archaeology and the importance of material things, edited by L. Ferguson. *Society for Historical Archaeology, Special Publication Series* No. 2, 43–61.

Lewis, O.
1969 The possessions of the poor. *Scientific American* **221**(No. 4):114–125.

McKellar, J.
1973 Correlations and the explanation of distributions. Paper prepared for Anthropology 136. Manuscript on deposit, Arizona State Museum Library, University of Arizona, Tucson.

McLuhan, M.
1966 *Understanding media.* New York: Signet Books.

McVicker, D.
1972 The cemetery seminar: Exploring the research and learning potential of the "New Archaeology." Paper presented at the 37th annual meeting of the Society for American Archaeology, Miami.
1973 Pots—Past and present. Paper presented at the 38th annual meeting of the Society for American Archaeology, San Francisco.

Meadows, D. H., D. L. Meadows, J. Randers, and W. Behrens, III
1972 *The limits to growth: A report of the Club of Rome's project on the predicament of mankind.* New York: Universe Books.

Mesarovic, M., and E. Pastel
1976 *Mankind at the turning point.* New York: Dutton.

Moosman, J. E.
1975 Ethnographic funerals and archaeological burials: A view from the mortuary. Manuscript on deposit, Arizona State Museum Library, University of Arizona, Tucson.

Morenon, E. P.
1978   Garages, task groups and functional variability: Torque wrenching the present and side-scraping the past. Paper presented at the 77th annual meeting of the American Anthropological Association, Los Angeles.

Morenon, E. P., M. Henderson, and J. Nielsen
1976   *The development of conservation techniques and a land use study conducted near Ranchos de Taos, New Mexico.* Dallas: Fort Burgwin Research Center, Southern Methodist University.

Motz, A.
1972   Individual bathroom decoration coordinated with educational level and drug use. Paper prepared for Anthropology 136. Manuscript on deposit, Arizona State Museum Library, University of Arizona, Tucson.

Nathan, R.
1960   *The Weans.* New York: Knopf.

Nettles, I.
1972   The effect of mass on distance to repair using time mechanisms as an example. Paper prepared for Anthropology 136. Manuscript on deposit, Arizona State Museum Library, University of Arizona, Tucson.

Newton, D.
1974   The Timbira hammock as a cultural indicator of social boundaries. In *The human mirror,* edited by M. Richardson. Baton Rouge: Lousiana State University Press. Pp. 231–251.

Packard, V.
1963   *The waste makers.* New York: Pocket Books.

Palmer, A. M.
1978   Through the glass case: The curator and the object. In *Material culture and the study of American life,* edited by I. M. G. Quimby. New York: Norton. Pp. 219–244.

Rathje, W. L.
1974   The Garbage Project: A new way to look at the problems of archaeology. *Archaeology* **27**(No. 4):236–241.
1978   Archaeological ethnography. In *Explorations in ethnoarchaeology,* edited by R. A. Gould. Albuquerque: University of New Mexico Press. Pp. 49–76.

Rathje, W. L., and G. G. Harrison
1978   Monitoring trends in food utilization. *Proceedings, Federation of Experimental Biologists* **37**:9–14.

Rathje, W. L., and W. W. Hughes
1975   The Garbage Project as a nonreactive approach. In *Perspectives on attitude assessment: Surveys and their alternatives,* edited by H. W. Sinaiko and L. A. Broedling (Technical Report No. 2). Washington, D.C.: Manpower Research and Advisory Services, Smithsonian Institution. Pp. 151–167.
1977   Food loss at the household level: A perspective from household residuals analysis. *RANN 2, Proceedings of the Second Symposium on Research Applied to National Needs, National Science Foundation, Washington, D.C.* **2**:32–35.

Rathje, W. L., and M. McCarthy
1977   Regularity and variability in contemporary garbage. In *Research strategies in historical archaeology,* edited by S. South. New York: Academic Press. Pp. 261–286.

Reich, C. A.
1970   *The greening of America.* New York: Random House.

Reid, J. J., W. L. Rathje, and M. B. Schiffer
    1974   Expanding archaeology. *American Antiquity* **39**:125–126.
Resource Planning Associates
    1972   *Potential economic value of the municipal solid waste stream.* Washington, D.C.: National Center for Resource Recovery.
Richardson, J., and A. L. Kroeber
    1940   Three centuries of women's dress fashions: A quantitative analysis. *Anthropological Records* **5**(No. 2):
Roach, M. E., and J. B. Eicher (editors)
    1965   *Dress, adornment and the social order.* New York: Wiley.
Rosenberg, R.
    1976   The variability of non-living objects found on the front property of households. Paper prepared for Anthropology 136. Manuscript on deposit, Arizona State Museum Library, University of Arizona, Tucson.
Salwen, B.
    1973   Archeology in Megalopolis. In *Research and theory in current archeology,* edited by C. L. Redman. New York: Wiley. Pp. 151–163.
Samtur, H.
    n.d.   Litter control strategies: An analysis of litter, littering behavior and litter control programs. Environmental Protection Agency, Office of Solid Waste Management Programs, Washington.
Schiffer, M. B.
    1976   *Behavioral archeology.* New York: Academic Press.
    1978   Methodological issues in ethnoarchaeology. In *Explorations in ethnoarchaeology,* edited by Richard A. Gould. Albuquerque: University of New Mexico Press. Pp. 229–247.
Schiffer, M. B., and M. McCarthy
    1978   Results of the Reuse Project pilot study. Paper presented at the 77th annual meeting of the American Anthropological Association, Los Angeles.
Schiffer, M. B., and J. Schaefer
    n.d.   The ethnoarchaeology of periodic markets (in preparation).
Schlessman, A.
    1977   No-tell drive-in. Paper prepared for Anthropology 136. Manuscript on deposit, Arizona State Museum, University of Arizona, Tucson.
Schumacher, E. F.
    1973   *Small is beautiful: Economics as if people mattered.* New York: Harper.
Schuyler, R. L.
    1974   Sandy Ground: Archaeological sampling in a Black community in metropolitan New York. *Conference on Historic Sites Archaeology Papers, 1972* **7**:13–51.
    1977   Archaeology of the New York metropolis. *Bulletin of the New York State Archaeological Association* No. 69, 1–19.
Shimada, I.
    n.d.   A three-fold approach to prehistoric construction behavior: A case study (in press).
Sinaiko, H. W., and L. A. Broedling (editors)
    1975   *Perspectives on attitude assessment: Surveys and their alternatives* (Technical Report No. 2). Washington, D.C.: Manpower Research and Advisory Services, Smithsonian Institution.
Skramstad, Jr., H. K.
    1978   Interpreting material culture: A view from the other side of the glass. In *Material*

culture and the study of American life, edited by I. M. G. Quimby. New York: Norton. Pp. 175–200.

Snyder, D.
  1972   Are married men really that healthy? Paper prepared for Anthropology 136. Manuscript on deposit, Arizona State Museum Library, University of Arizona, Tucson.

South, S.
  n.d.   Historic site content, structure and function. *American Antiquity* (in press).

Stahl, N.
  1975   Jelly side down: Questions soon beyond a mother. Universal Press Syndicate.

Sturtevant, W. C.
  1969   Does anthropology need museums? *Proceedings of the Biological Society of Washington* **82:**619–650.

Swan, L. R.
  1972   Testing for status symbol changes in modern material culture. Paper prepared for Anthropology 136. Manuscript on deposit, Arizona State Museum Library, University of Arizona, Tucson.

Szilard, L.
  1961   Report on Grand Central Terminal. In *The voice of the dolphins*. New York: Simon & Schuster. Pp. 115–122.

Tainter, J. A.
  1978   Mortuary practices and the study of prehistoric social systems. In *Advances in archaeological method and theory*. edited by M. B. Schiffer (Vol. 1). New York: Academic Press. Pp. 106–143.

Thomas, S.
  1971   Pass the ketchup, please! Paper prepared for Anthropology 136. Manuscript on deposit, Arizona State Museum Library, University of Arizona, Tucson.

Toffler, A.
  1971   *Future shock*. New York: Random House.

Tolley, G. S., V. S. Hastings, and G. Rudzitis
  1978   *Economics of municipal solid waste management: The Chicago case* (EPA-600/8-78-013). Cincinnati: Muncipal Environmental Research Laboratory, U.S. Environmental Protection Agency.

Tumin, M. M.
  1952   *Caste in a peasant society: A case study in the dynamics of caste*. Princeton: Princeton University Press.

Warhol, A.
  1962   Coca-cola bottles. Painting in the Henry N. Abrams Family Collection, New York.

Warner, W. L., M. Meeker, and K. Eells
  1960   *Social class in America: A manual of procedure for measurement of social status*. New York: Harper.

Webb, E. J., D. T. Campbell, R. D. Schwarts, and L. Sechrest
  1966   *Unobtrusive measures: Nonreactive research in the social sciences*. Chicago: Rand McNally.

Wilk, R. and M. B. Schiffer
  1978   The modern material culture field school. Paper presented at the 77th annual meeting of the American Anthropological Association, Los Angeles.
  n.d.   The archaeology of vacant lots in Tucson, Arizona. *American Antlquity* (in press).

Winfield, G. L.
    1974   *Solid waste sampling: Baltimore City*. Baltimore: Department of Public Works.
Winkler, F. P., and D. G. Wilson
    1973   Size characteristics of municipal solid waste. *Compost Science* **14**(No. 5):6–11.
Wolf, T.
    1968   *The pump house gang*. New York: Farrar, Straus.

The Cross-Cultural Method in Archaeology

CHARLES W. McNETT, JR.

INTRODUCTION

The cross-cultural or comparative method has a broad and a narrow definition, both of which are of interest to archaeologists. In the broad sense, whenever two cultures are compared, the cross-cultural method has been used. Defined in this way, the cross-cultural method is commonly used by archaeologists whenever they compare two or more site components, either through space or through time or through both.

There is, however, a narrower and more specialized definition of the term, which involves gathering data on a relatively large number of units. This aspect of the cross-cultural study has, in its turn, two subdivisions. One uses data on a large number of cultures within a region or on regions within a larger area. These are then compared statistically in order to group similar cultures (or regions, if the larger approach is taken) together. This so-called California approach to the cross-cultural study will be discussed in historical perspective below. It is clearly related to many regional comparisons done by archaeologists, although probably it is more rigorous methodologically.

The other aspect of the cross-cultural study in the narrower sense is now called the hologeistic (whole world) method, defined by Naroll *et al.* as

a method for the empirical testing of theories which attempt to explain some general

ADVANCES IN ARCHAEOLOGICAL METHOD AND THEORY, VOL. 2
Copyright © 1979 by Academic Press, Inc.
All rights of reproduction in any form reserved.
ISBN 0-12-003102-7

characteristics of human existence. The method measures theoretical variables in a large, worldwide sample of human cultures and examines statistical correlations among those variables to determine whether the intervariable relationships are as predicted by the theory [1974:121].

They go on to point out that the hologeistic method may also be used to develop "insights"—that is, hypotheses to be tested against the data. They clearly feel, however, that the hologeistic method is best applied toward theory testing because it is "the second-best method known to science for testing to see whether insights are right or wrong. The best method . . . is controlled experiment" (Naroll *et al.* 1974:122).

The modern hologeistic study may take four different forms, according to Naroll and Naroll (1973), depending upon the units used for analysis. These have been named holohistorical, holonational, holocultural, and holoarchaeological. Although all four forms may be of interest to archaeologists, the holocultural (using ethnographic cultures) and the holoarchaeological (using archaeologically known cultures but possibly including the ethnographic culture as the most recent time stratum) are particularly interesting.

Holocultural studies have already been used by archaeologists and ethnologists to develop insights suitable for testing with archaeological data, to develop proxy measures with which the archaeologist can measure social phonemena such as residence rules for which there is often no obvious material evidence, and to test theories of interest to archaeologists, such as the theory of cultural evolution. So far only one holoarchaeological study has been done, and that by an ethnologist (Schaefer 1977a and discussion below).

In addition to the archaeologically useful results that can be produced by hologeistic studies, the method is also appealing philosophically to the archaeologist. Most modern archaeologists now seem agreed that the scientific method can and should be applied to archaeological data. Hologeistic scholars are also agreed upon the use of the scientific method and, in fact, cite the same philosophers of science used by the modern archaeologist.

Given the proven results of interest to the archaeologist produced by the hologeistic method, and given the similar philosophical bias of archaeologists and ethnologists conducting hologeistic studies, one is rather at a loss to explain why this method has not been used more for archaeological purposes. This chapter will examine all the archaeologically oriented hologeistic studies known to the author, the editor, and the referees of this paper. They consist of a mere handful.

One possible explanation is that, even in ethnology, the method has, for historical reasons, had its vicissitudes, although the production of hologeistic studies is now growing at an exponential rate, not only in anthropology but in related disciplines as well (Schaefer 1977b). A second possible reason is that many archaeologists seem to be unaware of the usefulness of the hologeistic method. This review is designed to introduce the hologeistic method to the archaeologist unfamiliar with it.

HISTORY OF HOLOGEISTIC STUDIES

Beginnings

The cross-cultural or comparative method was first systematically applied in anthropology by Edward B. Tylor (1889) in a study of marriage and descent presented to the Royal Anthropological Society. In this study Tylor used a worldwide sample of cultures to study the "adhesions" between various traits. These trait comparisons were cast into something very similar to the modern 2×2 contingency table, and comparisons between the expected and the observed numbers of cells were used, although statistical tests of significance had yet to be developed. During the discussion that followed, the eminent scientist Sir Francis Galton rose to inquire how many of the traits were independent and how many were due to diffusion. In the stilted language of the time, according to the account of the discussion (Tylor 1889:24), "Dr. Tylor congratulated himself on having been able to place the present method before investigators whose criticism was of such importance, from their thorough appreciation of the points in which such a method has inherent weakness." Translated, Galton had him stumped!

Despite the criticism, Tylor had made a real advance on previous efforts, such as those of many other early evolutionists who unsystematically compared cultures from around the world, or the attempts at codification made by Spencer, for Tylor had deliberately looked for evidence of association (adhesion, in his words) between traits. Later, the sociologists Hobhouse *et al.* (1930, originally 1915) made a monumental effort at compiling and cross-tabulating huge quantities of data. However, the climate of the times was both antievolutionary and antistatistical, and the majority of social scientists, including anthropologists, chose to ignore this work. Cross-cultural studies were undertaken, but given the historical–particularist bent of the times, these efforts were restricted to regional studies, mostly involved with the problem of empirically defining cultural relationships such as the culture area.

The California School

Alfred Kroeber was a leader in these attempts, as he was in so much of the anthropology of the time. As used by the so-called California school of cross-cultural method, data were gathered on as many traits as possible for every culture within a region. A variety of coefficients were then used to measure intercultural (Q-type) relationships. The resulting symmetrical matrix was inspected and/or manipulated by hand in order to define clusters of closely related cultures. The ultimate aim, of course, was the reconstruction of the history of the cultures involved. Driver and Kroeber (1932) is the classic work from this school. In addition to Kroeber and his students (e.g., Harold Driver), a second group working along the same lines was composed of the scholars Czekanowski, Klimek, Milke, and others using the *Kulturkreis* concept. Driver (1965:323–326, 1970) provides an interesting history of all these efforts.

Although the California school invented a large number of similarity coefficients and collected copious quantities of data, very few results were published. Even Kroeber himself used the data for only two short papers in the early 1940s, which were without statistics (Driver 1965:326), and Naroll *et al.* (1974:141) point out that "Driver's pioneer work on the reliability of ethnographic data [resulting from his research under Kroeber] was ignored for an entire generation." What had happened, apparently, was that in the years it took to collect and analyze the data, the answers forthcoming were for questions anthropologists were no longer asking in the early 1940s.

The Yale School

By the 1940s, many researchers in the discipline were more interested in the functional relationships of the parts of specific cultures than in their history, although there was significant concern on the part of some for larger cultural regularities. This latter concern motivated the founding of the Cross-Cultural Survey by George Peter Murdock in 1937 (Murdock 1940). Murdock was then situated at the Institute of Human Relations at Yale University (whence the title Yale school), where his first efforts consisted in attempting to code data on a large corpus of ethnographic reports and culminated (beginning in 1953) in the Human Relations Area Files. The first important anthropological publication that resulted from this work was the seminal *Social Structure* (Murdock 1949), which was soon followed by a number of other important and innovative works. Driver (1965:324–325), in summing up the approach of the California and Yale schools, states: "The California method was largely empirical in that it was not bolstered by formal postulates, theorems, or propositions,'' whereas ''the Yale school, on the other hand, was largely postulational, in that considerable functional or psychological theory was formulated in advance, and only the data relevant to the theory collected.'' In short, the California school was in the best Boasian tradition, whereas the Yale school was scientific in its orientation.

In fact, Naroll (1970a) and Cohen (1970) make a powerful plea for the use of the scientific method, which sounds for all the world like most of the methodological writing that has taken place in archaeology in the past 15 years; indeed, they cite the same sources. Kroeber would have made much of this case of independent invention. In applying the scientific method to his data, what Murdock had done was to predict relationships between social structure variables from theory, collect data from a worldwide sample of cultures, and test the association with various statistical measures. As Driver (1965:325) points out, however, the predictions were sometimes modified on the basis of the collected evidence before the tests were run.

Despite the methodological importance of Murdock's work, a storm of protest ensued. In the first place, Murdock was proposing causal sequences on the basis of the relationships he demonstrated, and this was called ''evolutionary''—certainly a pejorative comment at the time. In the second place, by using statistical tests, Murdock had opened up a Pandora's box of problems because of the mathematical assumptions underlying their use.

Human Relations Area Files

At the same time that he was putting the data to use, Murdock was continuing to collect and codify data. This took two different directions: the development of the Human Relations Area Files, and the development of tabular coded data, which later proved suitable for computer processing. With regard to the first line of effort, the Human Relations Area Files (HRAF) was set up as a precomputer data storage and retrieval system. Each reference for a culture chosen for inclusion in the files is read by one or more coders, who enter a code number for each and every trait discussed in the text directly on the page. The standardized code numbers are taken from the *Outline of Cultural Materials* (Murdock *et al.* 1971), which lists 631 different index categories for cultural material, each cross-indexed to similar categories. Of particular interest to archaeologists would be such categories as 221—Annual Cycle, 226—Fishing, 243—Cereal Agriculture, 301—Ornaments, 324—Stone Industry, and many others. A copy of the page is made for each code number appearing on it, and all the resulting slips are filed numerically under the culture. To use the file, the researcher determines the code numbers of interest, goes to the file for the culture(s) desired (over 200 have been coded), and pulls the pages containing the data sought.

The result is a manual Key Word in Context index that has proved extremely valuable to researchers in many fields, but there are two major difficulties. Although HRAF has made every effort to ensure consistency in assigning the code numbers for traits, it is possible to find data of interest under several different code numbers. Second, the sheer manual labor of the librarian in refiling slips is considerable if there is heavy use of the "paper" files. As a result, there is a microfiche version, which requires little refiling, is cheaper for a library to secure, but is less easy to use. The ideal solution would be to convert the entire file to a computerized storage and retrieval system, but the cost would be prohibitive and the file would be so large as to be extremely costly to process.

Coded Data

However, the tabular coded files also developed by Murdock have proved more amenable to computer processing, although they sacrifice the specific detail of the regular files. The first effort along these lines was the World Ethnographic Sample (Murdock 1957), which included coded data arranged in 15 columns. Allowing for subcodes, about 30 variables were coded for 565 cultures in addition to latitude and longitude. For instance, Column 1 contains information on cultivated plants and domesticated animals; Column 2 on agriculture (a major code for its importance, and a minor code for division of labor by sex). Other columns that might interest an archaeologist include other forms of subsistence, settlement pattern, and social stratification.

Whereas many of the codes are ordinal (contain rankable data), others are purely nominal (unrankable categories), which limits the options for statistical tests in some cases. In using this sort of tabular data, in addition, the researcher is one step removed from the raw data and must depend upon the expertise of the coder (often Murdock himself) for the validity of the data.

Murdock then left Yale for Pittsburgh, where he founded the journal *Ethnology*. Over the next several years, installments of the Ethnographic Atlas appeared at intervals in this journal. The Atlas was an expansion of the World Ethnographic Sample, and a collation of the installments appeared as Murdock (1967). In addition, Murdock's colleague at Pittsburgh, Herbert Barry III, prepared a computerized version of the bulk of the information in both an original alphabetically coded set and a numerically coded set more easily manipulated by computer. Comprising information on 96 traits for 1170 cultures, these data are available from HRAF. The present writer has prepared the control cards necessary to use the numerical version as a fully labeled Statistical Package for the Social Sciences SAVE FILE, which is now available from HRAF.

Subsequently, Murdock and White's (1969) Standard Cross-Cultural Sample was developed to solve some of the sampling problems in hologeistic research discussed below. The SC-CS contains data on 186 cultures selected by Murdock to represent all the major culture types of the world and a largely augmented set of coded data. Barry once again has prepared punched cards for computer analysis. In addition to the two data cards for the Ethnographic Atlas, there are ten other cards for each culture, containing data on cultural complexity, subsistence economy, and settlement pattern (of particular interest to archaeologists) as well as a host of other variables.

The Indiana School

During this time Driver had temporarily retired (Jorgensen 1974), but he returned to teach and do research at Indiana University. Still essentially inductive in approach, Driver's more recent work until his retirement has enough differences from the research he conducted under Kroeber to be dubbed the Indiana school. His recent writings contain both advances in mainstream cross-cultural methodology (Naroll *et al.* 1974:141) and ground-breaking research in the application of factor analysis to worldwide and continent-wide data matrices. His first effort in this direction (Driver 1956) applied precomputer cluster analysis much in the old California school way but used a data matrix of 280 tribes from North America. That same year (Schuessler and Driver 1956; Driver and Schuessler 1957), he came out with a factor analysis of the intercorrelations of 16 Indian tribes, using 2500 traits for each. Certainly one of the first factor analyses done by an anthropologist, it was followed by the Driver and Schuessler (1967) factor analysis of the World Ethnographic Sample. The procedure followed was to dichotomize the 15 variables and intercorrelate them. Then the correlation matrix was factored. This worldwide factoring was followed by factoring by continent in order to compare differences. Throughout his work, Driver has continually stressed the importance of diffusion within geographic areas, along with the possibility of functional associations.

This brief and incomplete history of the cross-cultural method has of necessity omitted many important studies and contributions. Its intent is to demonstrate the long history of the method in anthropology and to indicate the massive amounts of data pertinent to anthropological, including archaeological, questions that have been collected and codified. That the method has not had more general acceptance among anthropologists as a whole until recently rests upon an apparent misconception and some very intractable statistical problems. Although the misconception can be cleared up, the successful solution of the statistical problems has resulted only in the very recent past in the modern cross-cultural method to be discussed below.

PROBLEMS

The Functionalist Argument

The misconception about the cross-cultural method common in anthropology has been termed the functionalist argument, and it goes something like this: "Traits in my culture are integrated into a functional whole so that matrilineality, say, *means* something quite different in this culture than in any other. Moreover, my culture itself is in no way comparable to any other culture; it is a unique, functional whole. The cross-cultural method is trying to compare apples and oranges." As Leach (1964:299) put it, "It is not that Murdock's tabulators misread their sources; it is simply that the ethnographic facts of the case will not fit tidily into tabulated categories. I believe that this is true of all human societies." Ember answered this argument definitively, and his comment is cited at length:

> In cross-cultural research, we are not interested in global comparisons of cultures as was the old "comparative method." Rather we are concerned with examining relationships between specific variables—e.g., degree of economic and degree of political development—in a sample of societies. The definition of a sample unit [or a trait] depends solely upon the purpose of the study. To put the issue simply, if our intent is to examine the relationship between volume and weight in "fruit," it does not matter one whit that we are dealing with "apples" and "pears" or even "watermelons" [1964:296].

If the functionalist argument does seem to be tilting at windmills, there are some very real and intractable problems faced by the cross-cultural method. The following discussion depends upon Naroll *et al.* (1974, 1976) and the author's own experience in conducting cross-cultural surveys.

Sampling

A most rigorous method of testing theories involves the use of measures of association along with statistical tests of significance—that is, ones that give the exact probability that chance alone could have caused the level of association found. All such tests assume that the sample is random, which demands that all items in the sample have an equal probability of being included in the sample, and that the selection of one item in no way influences the selection of any other (all items are independent). The latter is, of course, the question raised by Galton in 1888 and described above.

In the simplest form of random sample, both conditions are met by enumerating the population of interest, numbering it, and going to a table of random numbers to draw the sample. Such a procedure is impossible when one is dealing with human cultures. In the first place, according to Naroll *et al.* (1974:122) "there are some four thousand human languages spoken today," and there are usually many local cultural variants among the speakers of each language. If to these are added all the cultures that have existed and no longer do, the magnitude of the problem becomes evident. Second, even if all cultures were known, the term "culture" is not adequately defined. This can be termed Flower's problem, and it is a problem that was also raised in 1888 (Michael B. Schiffer, personal communication 1978).

Although various definitions of unit have been offered (Naroll 1964 is an example), the pragmatic approach most researchers take is to insist that all cultures in the sample speak mutually unintelligible languages. What is desired for analysis is a functional whole at whatever level of abstraction. Since whole cultures seldom, if ever, cross linguistic boundaries, different cultures rather than two variants of the same culture will necessarily be in the sample.

Moreover, "focused" ethnographic reports may also help. These are defined (Naroll *et al.* 1976:13–20) as one or more reports that apply to the same community and the same time period. Rules of thumb here are that the ethnographies for a given culture should all apply to a period of ten years or less, since cultures change over time, and that they should be based upon the same community. If this fails, the data are considered unfocused and may be biased.

A simple test of whether lack of focus is producing spurious correlations is to compute measures of association separately in the focused and unfocused data. If the focused data have a higher value, the lack of focus obviously has no effect; if, on the other hand, the unfocused data show a higher association, then the lack of focus *may* be causing a problem. There are, however, a number of other tests that can be run to verify this (Naroll *et al.* 1976:44–50). Divale (1975) has shown that a lack of focus will actually *lower* correlations, thus making the test of theory conservative.

If the language boundary rule and the use of focused data help assure functional wholes for analysis, they do not solve the problem of statistical requirements for sampling. Murdock and White (1969) sought a solution in the Standard Cross-Cultural Sample when they analyzed all the cultures in the Ethnographic Atlas and divided them into "clusters" of obviously very closely related cultures. Groups of similar and usually contiguous clusters were then divided into 200 sampling provinces. Then a culture was selected from each province to represent it, usually on the basis of an adequate bibliography. Allowing for a few problems, and the dropping of one of a pair of provinces when the pair was too similar to include both, 186 cultures remain.

The Standard Cross-Cultural Sample (SC-CS) is not random, but the intent is obvious—to assure that each major cultural type is represented in the sample. As a result, it certainly represents the cultural universe and is, in fact, a universe of sorts itself in that all known cultural types are represented. It seems reasonable that a test of a cultural hypothesis that can be generalized to all cultural types would be just as valid and useful to anthropology as one that can be generalized to all cultures. In fact, there are two main difficulties with the SC-CS that are due not to sampling but to the fact that traits of interest to the researcher may not be coded, and to the lack of information on data quality control factors.

The present writer, working with a professional statistician (McNett and Kirk 1968), took a different approach. The reasoning was rather simple—if we cannot take a random sample of all the cultures of the world, why not randomly sample the *space* the cultures occupy? Archaeologists do this all the time. As originally developed, the method involved using a table of random numbers to pick latitude and longitude coordinates defining a set of sample points. A block ten degrees to a side was then drawn about each point, and the culture closest to the point was picked to represent it. The method originally used a Mercator projection, and Harold Driver (personal communication 1967) quickly pointed out that the method was not random, since in the far north and south degrees were much smaller; therefore areas there had a higher probability of selection. Actually, this resulted in the blocks being smaller, so that there was less chance that these blocks would contain a culture, in part canceling out the greater probability. However, as published, Driver's advice was followed, and it was recommended that an equal area projection be used with a regular grid overlaid on it. Random grid points would then be selected. This introduced problems, since equal area projections usually resemble strips of orange peel at the north and south, and this raises the problem of incomplete blocks. It seems likely at this point that to use this spatial method of sampling one ought to go back to using latitude and longitude but do it on a computer where the probabilities of all points could be equalized. The method, apparently using a Mercator projection, has been computerized for use by the Dartmouth College anthropology instructional programs. Possible modifications are unknown.

Although the method obviously produces a random sample of space, one of its major problems is that it heavily overrepresents Oceania, which is a giant area occupied by very similar cultures, each separated by large amounts of open sea.

Naroll's approach has been similar to that of Murdock and White, although there are subtle and important differences. He proposes (Naroll 1967) a "stratified random sample of a bibliographically defined universe." One such sample is the Standard Ethnographic Sample (Naroll *et al.* 1970; Naroll and Sipes 1973), in which the bibliographic criteria for inclusion of a society are that the ethnographer lived in a culture lacking a written language for at least a year, with a working knowledge of the language spoken, and published at least 40 pages on his work covering certain specified subjects. The bibliographic universe is arranged by the 60 culture areas of the world and lists a total of 535 publications on 226 cultures. To use it, the researcher randomly draws one culture from each culture area to form the sample and goes to the works listed in the bibliography for each. Although the cultures in the list do not all have equal probability of selection for the sample, they do have known probabilities of selection, and the sample is representative of all culture areas of the world. By extension, then, it should also represent all the cultures of the world.

Naroll also drew the HRAF Quality Control Sample using essentially the same procedure, although criteria for inclusion were much less rigorous. After Murdock had stratified the HRAF cultures that were already coded into 60 culture areas, a list was prepared of a-1 cultures from each area described by at least one professional anthropologist. "A" cultures were those described by two or more anthropologists; "B" cultures are those described only by one. A culture was drawn randomly from the cultures on the "A" list for each culture area. If there were no "A" cultures, a "B" culture was drawn instead.

Subsequently, some additional coding was done by the HRAF staff to improve the quality of the data. A set of Probability Sample Files based on these cultures is now available at those institutions having the HRAF paper files. Lagacé (1977) offers a description of the 60 cultures and a wealth of other data. One of the chief advantages of this sample, in addition to the fact that the data are indexed in the HRAF files, is that the data quality control variables discussed below are already coded for analysis.

Otterbein (1976) provides a thorough discussion of all the samples and coded data sets currently available, along with a critical evaluation of each, as well as his own view on the procedures to be followed in drawing a holocultural sample.

To reiterate, none of these approaches to sampling produces a sample that strictly meets the requirement of equal probabilities, but all do produce a sample that represents the cultural universe. Many are suitable for use with statistical tests without unduly damaging the assumption of equal probability underlying the tests.

Obviously, sampling procedures will be determined in part by the hypothesis being tested. Indeed, in some cases it may be possible to use known biases in the sample to advantage in testing a hypothesis (Michael B. Schiffer, personal communication 1978).

Galton's Problem

The problem of independence (Galton's Problem) does arise in these samples, however, for diffused traits are obviously not independent. To clear up a common misapprehension immediately, it is well-known that many traits have diffused markedly, and the cross-cultural study is not trying to prove otherwise. But for the application of inferential statistics, it is necessary to prove for each trait that *diffusion has not taken place in the sample used* in order to prove independence of cases. Of course, the purpose of the study is to demonstrate that two or more traits occur together, whether diffused or independently invented. There is a large literature concerning this problem (Naroll *et al.* 1974:127–129 for a summary), but the most common solution seems to be the linked-pair method (Naroll's fifth test). To perform a linked-pair test, all the cultures in the sample are aligned according to propinquity, and then each adjacent pair is compared in turn for the possession of the trait being tested. If the trait is diffused in the sample, adjacent pairs will have a high occurrence of common presence and common absence, which may be measured by calculating phi or a similar association coefficient that can be evaluated by means of a chi-squared test. Lack of independence is a problem only if both traits in a particular association are affected, and in this case it may be removed by the use of measures of partial association (Naroll *et al.* 1974:128).

Tests for Galton's Problem have demonstrated themselves to be quite effective. In a cross-cultural study conducted by the author (McNett 1970a), 30 traits were tested by the linked-pair method, and one was found to have a significant association between adjacent pairs (phi = .50 or more). The trait coded was the presence or absence of a written calendar. On inspection of the data, it was found that the modern calendar was the only kind that could occur in the societies in the sample, and its spread, of course, is the product of diffusion.

Actually, some writers tend to discount Galton's Problem (Straus and Orans 1978; Ember 1971). In fact, empirical research reported by Ember (1971) seems to indicate that Galton's Problem, when it occurs, tends to *deflate* associations. Moreover, the small size of cross-cultural samples is, in itself, a safeguard against Galton's Problem, since the cultures in a sample tend to be widely separated from each other. Many researchers use the "three-degree rule"—all cultures in the sample must be three degrees of latitude or longitude from each other. Observing this rule also helps to ensure that two variations on the same culture do not appear in the same sample.

All in all, modern hologeistic samples seem to be remarkably representative, a conclusion that can be bolstered by other work by the author. For instance, in McNett (1970a), there is a comparison of three ordinal scales of cultural evolution developed independently and using different cross-cultural samples. Although the basis of the statistical comparison consisted in only the five cultures that occurred in all three of the studies compared, there was a significant Kendall's Coefficient of Concordance of .69 between them. Moreover, the scientific method has a built-in safeguard against less than perfect methods, including sampling techniques: all results must be replicable by others. The present writer knows of no replication of a hologeistic study in which the second author came to diametrically opposed conclusions to the first. Such conflicts are, of course, rather common in other anthropological studies, including archaeological ones where case studies or more limited, nonverifiable comparisons are made.

Error and Bias

The most perfect sample in the world of science will yield incorrect results if the data collected from it are subject to error. There are two types of error possible. The first, random error, usually results in varying degrees of imprecision, which tend to cancel each other out. It produces, in effect, more variability than actually obtains in the data. As a result, tests of significance are liable to be conservative, and significant results can be viewed with confidence (Naroll *et al.* 1974:125). On the other hand, systematic error, or bias, can be extremely destructive. In fact, much of the concern expressed above about sampling can be seen as an effort to prevent bias.

The first step in an effort to eliminate systematic (and, as a corollary, random) error is to operationally define the variables involved (Pelto

1970). In a manual for use in doing hologeistic studies with the HRAF Probability Sample Files (Naroll *et al.* 1976:8–12), several examples of this approach are given, and the suggestion is made to try to cast all scales for the measurement of the variable into an ordinal (ranked data) form because of the information preserved. Such an ordinal scale may be as simple as: no information, trait absent, trait present; or it may represent the relative ranking of a series of interval measurements such as population size. It should be pointed out that use of precoded data such as the Standard Cross-Cultural Sample may introduce problems, since many of those scales are, in fact, nominal. Some manipulation will usually produce an ordinal scale, however.

Once the scales for the relevant variables are developed, they should be pretested and revised, if necessary. For instance, in McNett (1967) two traits—presence of status differentiation and presence of social classes—had been defined in such a way that both were in fact measuring the same thing, and one was dropped from further analysis.

Proxy Measures and Coding

Once coding begins, another problem may emerge—paucity of data. It is frequently found that even with operational definitions, the ethnographers had not provided sufficient information to make a decision. In such a case, the use of a proxy measure may be possible (Naroll *et al.* 1976:11–12). For instance, they cite the case of frequency of suicide, which had been carefully defined but for which only 20 of the 60 societies had sufficient information. A proxy measure was defined, which consisted of the number of lines in the ethnography devoted to suicide divided by the total number of lines in the ethnography. As a result, they were able to code 33 societies for the trait. Of course, it is up to the researcher to argue convincingly that the proxy is actually measuring the trait of interest.

Once the measures are defined and tested, data collection can begin in earnest. Unfortunately, the researcher is aware of the proposition being tested, and this may affect the coding of the traits, consciously or unconsciously. The solution to the possible introduction of bias here is to have a naïve coder (one who does not know anything except how to code and where to find the data) recode all the data (Naroll *et al.* 1976:17–79). The two sets of data are correlated and, if substantially in agreement, they may be averaged for the final data. If not, the definitions of the traits must be redefined and the data recoded using a new naïve coder (the old one is no longer naïve in the sense that the coder has prior experience with the data). Another method, used by the present writer (McNett 1967), is to compare the researcher's codes with those from some set of precoded data. For instance, 7 of the 30 traits used in the study cited were also coded by Murdock in the World Ethnographic Sample for a substantial number of the cultures used. Correlation between Murdock's naïve coding (he obviously did not know the proposition being tested) and those used in the study produced a highly significant phi of .81. It was concluded that either the coding for these traits was not biased and, by extension, the remaining traits were unlikely to be either, or both Murdock and the author were biased in the same way. However, this bias could not be caused by Murdock's favoritism toward the author's hypothesis, which is what the test is designed to prevent.

Data Quality Control

Once the data are coded, other sources of bias must also be considered. Naroll has been an important figure in data quality control, and his *Data Quality Control: A New Research Technique* (Naroll 1962a) is the seminal work in the field. Currently recommended for consideration (Naroll *et al.* 1976:20) are the following five factors, any one of which produce bias:

1. Systematic observation by fieldworkers (as opposed to traveler's reports)
2. Use of native language by the fieldworker
3. Length of stay in the field
4. Number of fieldworkers times months in the field
5. Time between fieldwork and actual existence of the culture (informants versus actual observation)

These factors are coded and correlated with each trait used in the study. High correlations between the quality control factor and a trait indicate the possibility of systematic error. This bias can be removed, however, by running a partial correlation which holds the quality control factor constant, in effect preventing it from causing bias. For a study using the Standard Ethnographic Sample, these factors have, in the main, already been controlled by the method of selection of the bibliographic entries.

Testing the Proposition

Assuming that all the data problems are insignificant or have been solved, the researcher can now proceed to a test of the proposition of interest. Several factors relating to interpretation remain to be discussed. In the first place, following up on Driver's work, it may be that the correlations obtained are not worldwide, but regional. To test for this, the sample is subdivided regionally, and the correlations are rerun for each region. It may turn out that a particular functional relationship holds in one region, but not in another. For the Probability Sample Files (Naroll *et al.* 1976:47–49), owing to the small size, it is recommended that the regions be the Old and New Worlds. The same course would be taken when using the Standard Ethnographic Sample, which also results in a small sample. For the Standard Cross-Cultural Sample, on the other hand, recomputing over continents would provide adequate sample size in each.

Second, what about deviant cases—that is, those cultures that do not express the relationship as predicted? As Köbben (1967) asks: "Why exceptions?" Such an analysis may reveal important new information, which needs to be considered. Basically, seven possible causes of exceptions may be found (Naroll *et al.* 1976:55):

1. Error
2. Multicausality
3. Parallel causality
4. The existence of functional equivalents
5. An intervening variable
6. Culture lag
7. A charismatic individual leader (a "great man")

Examination of the deviant cases may reveal some or all of these factors at work. As Naroll *et al.* (1976:54) observe, "For an explanation to be sufficient, it must be applicable to all the societies that were examined."

Another aspect of interpretation is causal analysis, the ultimate aim of scientific research. It is by now well-known that significant correlations do not necessarily prove causality, but recent work on causality has produced a number of methods of analysis when correlations are high enough to indicate its possibility. For instance, HRAF now has a computer program available that will help in evaluating a number of groups of possible causal models among three variables of interest (Naroll *et al.* 1976:52–54).

A last problem should be mentioned. A statistical level of significance of a coefficient of, say, .05 indicates that chance alone will produce the results obtained 5 times out of 100 trials. The conclusion is that this is so unlikely that one may believe with confidence that the correlation is real. On the other hand, for a large number of correlations, one may believe with equal confidence that some high correlations *are not real*—5 out of 100 are expected to be due to chance alone. HRAF now offers a computer program that will test whether the correlations obtained could be in error owing to this group risk factor (Naroll *et al.* 1974:126–127).

THE MODERN HOLOGEISTIC METHOD

Conducting a holocultural study is relatively easy. Rohner *et al.* (1978) even provide a check list of methodological steps for both "quick and dirty" and rigorous cross-cultural studies. For example, the researcher could go to the Probability Sample Files and code the data of interest, except for the data quality control variables that have already been coded by HRAF. The data sheets, indicating the tests to be run, are sent to HRAF, which will run them and return the results. Alternatively, the HRAFLIB computer programs can be obtained for a nominal sum and installed at the user's computer facility. Naroll *et al.* (1976:29) estimate that a "typical study" will cost "$5000 to $10,000 of your own time and that of your staff," whereas the cost of computer processing by HRAF will run "a few hundred dollars." They suggest (Naroll *et al.* 1976:2) that a really rigorous study will take 50–100 hours of coding by the researchers, the same amount of time by the naïve coder, and the performance of all the tests mentioned above. All in all, the researcher can expect to work half-time for two or three years, and the result could be a "splendid doctoral thesis." On the other hand, a pilot study involves little more than coding the data and running correlations and would make a "good proposal for a Ph.D dissertation." Obviously, if the pilot study pans out, then one picks up with the naïve coder in the rigorous procedure. In fact, if the data are coded in the Ethnographic Atlas or the Standard Cross-Cultural Sample, a pilot study can be run in a few minutes. Such studies are a valuable source of insights for full-blown and rigorous hypothesis testing.

Lest this paper sound like a commerical for the Human Relations Area Files, one should hasten to point out that an equally rigorous study can be done almost anywhere with a decent library and computer center. For instance, the data could be collected from a sample chosen from the Standard Ethnographic Sample, and the relevant tests (omitting the data quality control tests for a pilot or insightful study) can be run using any of a number of statistical routines such as the Statistical Package for the Social Sciences. The coded data submitted to CROSSTABS in SPSS will produce the required Tau B or gamma coefficients suitable for ordinal data. If Galton's Problem or other possible sources of bias are evident, the necessary partial correlations can be computed by PARTIAL CORR using the original Tau B coefficients. Deviant case analysis can take place by using WRITE CASES to get the data and locate the cultures in the relevant deviant cells from CROSSTABS. In addition, there are some causal analysis routines in SPSS with which the present writer is not familiar. No estimate of the effect of the level of significance for larger numbers of variables (group risk) is available, however. The chief advantage of using HRAF will be seen to be the savings in time (money) provided by the fact that the data are indexed for easy retrieval and the HRAFLIB programs form an integral package. However done, hologeistic studies offer a rigorous, scientific method of testing propositions of interest to anthropologists.

RESULTS

Have these studies produced any useful results? Naroll (1970b) contains a summary of 150 cross-cultural studies and includes a rating of the methodological rigor of each. Naroll and Naroll (1977) present a general summary of the current state of cultural anthropology, which includes review papers by Witkowski (1977) on kinship, Otterbein (1977) on warfare, Erickson (1977) on cultural evolution, and Levinson (1977a) on "What have we learned from cross-cultural surveys?" that are pertinent to a discussion of the success of the cross-cultural method.

Kinship and Warfare

In summarizing modern cross-cultural findings relating to kinship, Witkowski (1977:660) points out that although unilocal kinship is a necessary condition for unilineal descent, it is not a sufficient condition; that is, many unilocal societies do not have unilineal descent. From the archaeologist's point of view, this means that forms of unilocal residence will not serve as a proxy measure for unilineal descent systems.

At the same time, patrilocality is the norm for human societies, and these societies tend "to have high rates of feuding and internal warfare and to constantly expand at the expense of their neighbors," whereas matrilocal residence arises from "severe competition for resources due to migration, external war, and relatively small population size" (Witkowski 1977:664). Matrilocality breaks up the male interest groups and thus promotes group solidarity.

Patrilocality is, however, an apparently good proxy measure for polygyny, which is, after all, virtually impossible in a matrilocal situation (Witkowski 1977:665). Polygyny comes about because the quarrelsomeness of patrilocal societies reduces the number of marriageable males. In addition, in strongly polygynous societies, the supply of marriageable females may be increased by delaying marriage for males until a relatively late age.

Witkowski (1977:665) concludes: "Patrilocality, warfare, polygyny and delayed marriage form a feedback network in which an increase in one variable reverberates through the system, causing an increase in other variables." Since archaeologists now have a verified proxy measure for patrilocality (see below), they are also in a position to be able to deal with the rest of the social traits that make up this subsystem.

In a closely related paper by Otterbein the point is made that

warfare [is] related to a number of important variables: level of sociocultural complexity, history (migration and territorial expansion), demography (societal size, population density, female infanticide, and sex ratios), social structure (residence, descent, form of marriage, and exogamy) [1977:693].

Table 2.1 summarizes Otterbein's synthesis of cross-cultural warfare studies. Quite clearly, archaeologists can frequently determine migration and degree of political centralization. When they can, the rest of the traits summarized in the table become predictable. In short, migration and political centralization become proxy measures for the rest of the traits in the table.

TABLE 2.1

Relationships between Centralization and Migration in Studies of Warfare[a]

Variable	Nonmigration or migration into unoccupied land		Migration into occupied land or occupation of land by invaders	
	Uncentralized Political Community	Centralized Political Community	Uncentralized Political Community	Centralized Political Community
Residence	Patrilocal, avunculocal	Patrilocal	Matrilocal	Multilocal, neolocal, patrilocal
Form of marriage	General polygyny	General polygyny	Limited polygyny, monogamy	Limited polygyny, monogamy
Degree of military	Low	High	High (for invaders), Low (for defenders)	High (for invaders), Low (for defenders)
Feuding	Present	Absent	Absent	Absent
Internal war	Frequent	Frequent	Infrequent	Frequent
External war	Infrequent	Infrequent	Frequent	Frequent
Goals of war	Defense–revenge, glory	Political	Economic	Political
Peacemaking mechanisms	Present	Present	Absent	Present

[a] After Otterbein (1977) with permission.

Cultural Evolution

The theory of cultural evolution that underlies much of anthropological thought, including recent efforts in archaeology [the seminal paper for the "new archaeology" (Binford 1962) is explicitly evolutionary in orientation], has received much attention in cross-cultural studies. Naroll (1970b), in summarizing such studies to 1970, points out that there is strong evidence for a regular progression of a worldwide nature from generalists to occupational specialization, from simple organization to complex organization, from rural to urban settlement, from wealth-sharing to wealth-hoarding, from consensual leadership to authoritative leadership, from responsible elite to exploitative elite, and from vengeance war to political war. Moreover, such apparently distantly removed aspects of culture as perception, art styles, games, song and dance styles, theology, and deference patterns are also believed to be related to cultural evolution.

Both Erickson (1977) and Levinson (1977a) update Naroll's (1970b) summary. The former points out that cultural evolutionary studies using the cross-cultural method tend to stress the universal model of White and that relatively little work has been done on Steward's multi-linear concept. In addition, and of specific interest to archaeologists, Erickson (1977:676) calls attention to R. Naroll's contention in Naroll and Naroll (1973) "that peaceful diffusion has been a significant factor of evolution." Erickson sees corroborative evidence in the studies of nuclear areas and the processes of urbanization conducted by many archaeologists in both the New and Old Worlds.

Finally, a number of researchers have chosen to focus on factor analysis of matrices derived from cross-cultural surveys. Comparing a number of these, Naroll defines four main factors (dimensions) of culture:

> These four main factors are: (1) agriculture, and related characteristics of technology and settlement, (2) sociopolitical complexity, and related authority patterns, (3) patrilineality, and related patterns of residence and kin terms, and (4) matrilineality, and related patterns of residence and kin terms [1970b:1257].

This review has been all too brief and is intended to indicate the wide range of topics of archaeological interest to which cross-cultural surveys have been applied. It is important to point out that virtually all of them have involved hypothesis testing in one form or another. This is seen very clearly in a project undertaken by HRAF to update the Naroll paper in which more than 1300 propositions from more than 300 cross-cultural surveys were described (Levinson 1977b). The data included in the compendium are the proposition tested, the sample used, data quality control and other safeguards, and the results of the test of the proposition.

The propositions are indexed by main subject, Outline of Cultural Materials trait number, key words, and author. For instance, under the key word "stoneworking" appears an entry for "sex allocation of stoneworking," which refers to Proposition 548. In the body of the work, Proposition 548 lists the hypothesis tested as follows:

> The probability that any activity will be assigned to males is increased to the extent that it has features which give males a definite advantage, and/or females a definite disadvantage, in its performance, regardless of whether the distinction is innate or socio-cultural [Murdock and Provost 1973:210–211].

The variables tested were hunting large aquatic fauna, smelting of ores, metalworking, lumbering, hunting large land fauna, woodworking, fowling, trapping small land fauna, boatbuilding, stoneworking, mining and quarrying, and land clearance. The hypothesis was supported, and a factor analysis of the variables was also undertaken. Four factors were found: masculine advantage, feminine advantage, "nomadic/sedentary differences in allocation of housebuilding and processing of animal products," and a factor relating to increasing task specialization of intensity of agriculture (Levinson 1977b:565). In addition, these traits, along with another 38 relating to division of labor by sex, appear in the Standard Cross-Cultural Sample on Card 7.

Not only does this proposition contribute directly to archaeological interpretation, but it opens up all sorts of interesting possibilities with regard to other possible data combinations within the Standard Cross-Cultural Sample, such as the distribution of stoneworking by sex on a worldwide basis. Thus, the proposition may be used as a starting point for a number of studies that could produce very interesting insights.

CROSS-CULTURAL ARCHAEOLOGY

What follows is a topical review of the use of the cross-cultural method for archaeological purposes. Although probably not exhaustive, it certainly covers most of the papers that have been published using this method.

Proxy Measures

One of the most fertile fields for the use of the cross-cultural survey applied to archaeological ends is the development of the proxy measure. Fritz (1972), who calls proxy measures "instruments for indirect observation of the past," has made the use of such measures in archaeology both methodologically and theoretically rigorous, although he appears not to be aware of the hologeistic method. As he points out (Fritz 1972:136), "All remote phenomena must be observed indirectly," whether galactic events or past human behavior. Although the common view of such instruments tends to be mechanical—telescopes, for instance—instruments can be verbal as well. All that is required is that "an instrument must be so constructed that when a particular past phenomenon is observed, the instrument used gives a distinctive reading or takes on a particular value" (Fritz 1972:136–137).

Such an instrument can be constructed by following three procedural steps:

1. A plausible instrument must be devised. This will usually take the form of some datum from the archaeological record that can logically or theoretically be predicted to occur along with some other datum of interest not normally found preserved in the archaeological record in a form suitable for direct observation. The argument linking the instrument and the past phenomenon to be measured must be a demonstrable one.

2. Plausible tests for the validation of the instrument must be constructed and performed. These tests depend upon empirical support for the theoretical linkage postulated between the instrument and the past phenomenon it is assumed to measure. According to Fritz (1972:153), "This empirical support normally is derived from the analysis of present or historically documented societies."

3. Finally, the results of the test must be evaluated. If the instrument is confirmed, it may be used to measure past phenomena; if not, it must be reformulated or a new instrument devised and tested in its turn.

Actually, a number of such instruments have already been defined and confirmed for archaeologists through the use of cross-cultural surveys. Apparently the first of these was Naroll's (1962b) work on an instrument to measure population size. Using a grab sample of 18 societies for which data were available, he was able to demonstrate a positive allometric (log–log regression) relationship between dwelling area of the largest settlement and population. The largest settlement is defined "as the most populous cluster of dwellings enclosable by a circle of 6-km radius at any time in the regular annual cycle" and dwelling area as "the total area under roof of dwellings" (Naroll 1962b:588). He concluded that a rough approximation of population would be one-tenth the dwelling area in square meters. Although this study was done prior to modern quality control development and with a nonrandom sample, it was important in demonstrating the effectiveness of the cross-cultural survey in developing archaeological instruments.

Somewhat later Cook and Heizer (1968) did a California school survey investigating the same relationship with regional data. Although the details of their study differed from Naroll's, Cook and Heizer concluded that

> a close correlation between floor space and population can be demonstrated over a wide range of territory, irrespective of local variation. This relationship appears to be stable, generally valid, and applicable throughout the entire province [1968:115].

At about the same time, Robbins (1966:3), inspired by the work of Beardsley and others cited below, set out to develop an instrument to measure the "relative permanence of settlement patterns." On the basis of a review of ethnographic literature, Robbins predicted that

> circular ground plans will tend to be associated with relatively impermanent or mobile settlement patterns, and that rectangular house ground plans will tend to be associated with more permanent or sedentary community settlement patterns [1966:7].

The sample used consisted of a random sample of the Ethnographic Atlas for which information was coded on both house plan and settlement pattern. The 50 societies in the sample that also occurred on a diffusion arc proposed by Naroll for testing for Galton's Problem were then analyzed. All statistical tests of the hypotheses were significant beyond the .001 level. In addition, a test was run comparing ground plan and community size which was significant beyond the .05 level, while a test comparing ground plan and intensity of agriculture was significant beyond the .001 level. He also tested for Galton's Problem and found it not to be a factor in his results. Consequently, he concluded (Robbins 1966:15), "In general, all postulates and predictions were confirmed."

Shortly thereafter, Whiting and Ayres (1968) prepared a study which showed that a wide range of culture traits could be measured with floor plan as the instrument. A subsample of the Ethnographic Atlas was used, which attempted to meet the criteria for sampling discussed above while minimizing Galton's Problem, so the sample was not specifically tested for diffusion. Comparing for associations between floor plan (curvilinear and rectilinear) and various construction features, it was found that curvilinear houses have curved roofs, whereas rectilinear houses have roofs made up of planes. Furthermore, as might be expected, curvilinear houses tend to use flexible building materials, both in walls and in roofs. To continue with their comparisons, rectilinear houses (median 300 square feet) are more likely to be multi-roomed, whereas curvilinear (median 100 square feet) are more likely to be single-roomed.

When floor plan was compared with other aspects of culture, similar striking verifications of floor plan as an instrument of indirect observation were found. Thus, "societies in our sample with multiple-roomed dwellings usually have extended families, status differentiations, or both"

(Whiting and Ayres 1968:123), although the converse does not hold. The same relationship held with floor area alone. They also confirmed Robbin's results cited above that nomads have curvilinear houses, whereas permanent settlements tend to have rectilinear houses, and showed that ecological factors (availability of building materials) do not markedly enter into this relationship. Finally, "societies with curvilinear houses tend to be polygynous, and those with rectilinear houses tend to be monogamous (Whiting and Ayres 1968:130)." In addition to the methodological safeguards mentioned, the researchers also broke down the data into a regional analysis (New World versus Old World) and showed that whereas the measurements made by the instruments were more reliable in either the New or the Old World, all were reasonably reliable on a worldwide basis.

The present writer (McNett 1970b) has attempted to demonstrate that community pattern is a reliable instrument to measure 23 different traits that can be shown to be the products of cultural evolution. On the basis of the Beardsley *et al.* (1956) community pattern scheme discussed below, the lambda coefficient was used to assess the improvement in prediction produced by knowing the community pattern, over simple guessing based upon knowing only the odds for the given trait. Overall, knowing the community pattern improved prediction by 50%, and individual traits ranged from an improvement high of 83% for presence–absence of religious hierarchy to a low of 13% for presence–absence of a standing army. It was found that trait patterns in the middle of the scale are highly variable and that the instrument measures most accurately for very simple and very complex cultures. It is not known if this variability is inherent in the data, or if it is the result of the number of Oceanic societies in the sample, discussed above, that might be subject to special ecological pressures.

Ember (1972) has developed an instrument that archaeologically measures matrilocal versus patrilocal residence. As an extension of his research on residence rules based on the hologeistic method, Ember drew a sample using a table of random numbers from the societies in the HRAF paper files that were also in the Ethnographic Atlas. Of 63 societies drawn, 22 were prevailingly matrilocal or patrilocal and also had data on living house floor areas. Neolocal societies were not included, because Ember had already shown that this form of residence is associated with commercial exchange, especially a money economy. He therefore suggests coins or other standardized currency as a suitable instrument to measure neolocality. He has also shown that bilocality is the result of recent depopulation and suggests that prior to European contact it may not have existed. The 18 patrilocal societies in the sample had a mean of

326 square feet of floor area per living house with a standard deviation of 547 square feet. The Nootka with a house size of 2450 square feet undoubtedly contributed to the large standard deviation and inflated the mean as well. On the other hand, the four matrilocal societies had a mean of 868 square feet and a standard deviation of only 179. Actually, with the exception of the Nootka *the two groups did not overlap at all.*

In the same paper, Ember reports that he immediately replicated the study, which is one way of compensating for a lack of data quality-control tests. His primary motivation, however, was that the results were too good. With a sample of 15 drawn in the same manner as the first, the results were that patrilocal societies had a mean of 232 square feet and a standard deviation of 140, while matrilocal societies had 1236 square feet with a standard deviation of 814. There was one overlap between the two, with the patrilocal Marquesans at 485 square feet and the matrilocal Warrau at 484. In sum then, only the Nootka of the patrilocal group from both samples have a floor area of more than 511 square feet, while only the Warrau of the matrilocal group have an area of less than 672. The rubicon between the two, Ember suggests, is in the area of 550–600 square feet. Ember states, following Murdock, that in cases of sororal polygyny, the sisters always live together, but this does not hold for cultures with nonsororal polygyny. As an extension, sisters also ought to be better able to live together when married to different men. Therefore, matrilocal societies ought to have larger houses to accommodate the several nuclear families. Conversely, in patrilocal societies, each different wife—not being related—will require a separate and smaller house.

Divale (1977), as part of a research project on matrilocality, replicated Ember's two studies. He drew his sample by randomly selecting 57 cultures from the Standard Cross-Cultural Sample, which was reduced to include only matrilocal and patrilocal societies. Of the 57, only 32 had information on floor area. Using square meters, he found that the patrilocal societies had a mean floor area of 28.2 square meters, while the matrilocal averaged 188.4. A *t*-test of the difference was highly significant. There were three deviant patrilocal cases—Armenians, Japanese, and Manus. The former two are much more complex than others in the sample, while the last also has double descent, which is usually found in a culture that used to be matrilineal–matrilocal. The two deviant matrilocal cultures were the Chiricahua Apache and Paiute—both nomadic hunters.

Divale (1977:114) then combined all three samples (dropping common cases) and recalculated both means and standard error of the mean. He concluded that a prediction of patrilocal residence for any culture where the average house floor area was between 14.5 and 42.7 square meters (plus and minus two standard errors from the mean of 28.6) would be right

95% of the time. A prediction of matrilocality could be made with the same confidence level between 79.2 and 270.8 square meters with a mean of 175.9.

Disagreeing with Ember's explanation for this regularity, Divale (1977:114–115) suggests that matrilocal societies have a complex of traits including "recent migration to their locales, a purely external warfare pattern, frequent warfare, an absence of feuding within the local community, an absence of peacemaking mechanisms, the presence of men's houses, and local exogamy for males." They are cultures that had been patrilocal but changed to matrilocal in order to change warfare patterns. Since the males are all strangers, living in a matrilocal arrangement leads to solidarity, as does the men's house if the culture uses one.

This analysis fits well with recent work on kinship and the causes of warfare patterns cited above. While a few proxy measures have been developed so far for use in archaeology, this application of the cross-cultural method seems to be most fruitful and holds great promise for the future development of archaeology. "Redundant" measures may be especially important, for the more independent instruments there are to measure any one trait, the more confidence there may be in the validity of the measurement.

Producing Insights

Although it is only one of a number of ways of producing insights suitable for testing, the "quick and dirty" cross-cultural study can be used on a worldwide or even a regional basis with a fair degree of assurance that the hypothesis produced will be verifiable. However, most archaeological use of cross-cultural data for this purpose has been relatively unsystematic. For instance, Jochim (1976) developed a set of models by reference to the ethnographic literature and the work of researchers such as Murdock. In so doing, he used primarily selected individual case studies. This is not to say that he is doing bad archaeology, for he proceeds to test the models against the archaeological data; it suggests, rather, that cross-cultural methodology might have been more appropriate and produced better models.

For other examples, Wilmsen (1973) used worldwide ethnographic data, mostly in the form of maps, to develop a mathematical model of the spacing of hunting bands, and Tuggle (1970) used both Coult and Habenstein's (1965) cross-tabulation of the World Ethnographic Sample and also the Ethnographic Atlas to gain insights about exogamy for the purpose of model building. Although it is not a carefully done hologeistic study, Tuggle's use of precoded data is a fairly rigorous method of gaining insights. It seems likely that the Ethnographic Atlas alone would produce enough hypotheses to keep a whole generation of archaeologists busy testing them.

A fairly rigorous use of the cross-cultural method to develop insights occurred in 1955, when a group of archaeologists met at a seminar to consider the functional and evolutionary aspects of community patterning (Beardsley *et al.* 1956). From a grab sample of ethnographic cultures, they were able to define six evolutionary community patterns ranging from nomadic to fully sedentary with an associated set of patterns for pastoral nomads. Each pattern was seen as the result of the interplay of environment and available technology. In a daring statement for the time, they showed that functionalism and evolution are different aspects of the same reality. Synchronically, each community pattern had certain traits with which it formed a functional whole; diachronically, the patterns would be arrranged into an evolutionary sequence.

Finally, Chang (1958) used a worldwide cross-cultural sample (excluding North America) to develop analytic insights regarding community and settlement patterns and some social correlates. These insights are then applied to North American archaeological sequences. Although his data base is more systematic than the seminar's, his results are presented more tentatively.

Testing Propositions

Such insightful studies grade into archaeological research using the holocultural method to test propositions. Thus Binford (1971), in studying the archaeological potential of mortuary rites, sets up a number of propositions concerning burial practices, deduces hypotheses from them, and tests the hypotheses with a sample of 40 societies drawn from HRAF's regular files. His basic comparative variable was the complexity of the status structure. Apparently unaware of Naroll's (1956) index of social complexity, he was forced to use subsistence form as a proxy, a practice with which he was not very happy. With the data coded in the World Ethnographic Sample on subsistence, information on a set of propositional related variables was gathered from HRAF. These were whether burial distinctions were made on the basis of conditions of death, location of death, age, sex, social position, or social affiliation, and whether the distinctions were made in body preparation, treatment, and disposition, grave form, orientation and location, furniture form, quantity, or form and quantity.

According to Binford (1971:18), the proposition "that there should be a direct correlation between the structural complexity of mortuary ritual and status systems within socio-cultural systems" was confirmed. He also tested the proposition that age and sex should be more important distinctions among less complex peoples, whereas differential burial should be based on social position among more complex cultures. This was confirmed, although the caution was made that the measures were crude and the sample was not random. A cross-tabulation of differential burial practices and body, grave, and furniture variables also proved enlightening to Binford in the analysis of burials.

Murray (1978) set about testing a proposition based on the work of Schiffer, which stated that increasing site size or population, or both, would result in less correspondence between artifact use and discard locations. Murray formulated hypotheses from this proposition and tested them with a worldwide cross-cultural sample drawn from about 50% of the available HRAF files. It was necessary to use proxy measures, and a deviant case analysis was undertaken. In general, the hypotheses derived from the proposition were confirmed, and additional insights were gained. She concludes, "Element discard location will equal use location at only one type of habitation site—that occupied by a migratory population" (Murray 1978:12).

Finally, the present writer tested the Beardsley seminar's formulation cited above using a worldwide cross-cultural sample (McNett 1967, 1970a). The community pattern scheme was confirmed by the research, although the patterns could be redefined slightly to fit the ethnographic data better. This redefinition was even more highly significant statistically.

All three of the uses of the cross-cultural method in archaeology—gaining insights, developing proxy measures, and testing archaeologically relevant propositions—may be viewed as a part of the larger whole now called ethnoarchaeology and defined by Schiffer (1978:2) as "the study of material culture in systemic context for the purpose of acquiring information, both specific and general, useful in archaeological investigation." Although only holocultural studies have been done to date for these purposes, both holonational and holohistorical (including holoethnohistorical) studies may become important in the future. As Schiffer (1978:3) states, "It should also be noted at the outset that ethnoarchaeologists are not limited to studying primitive, nonliterate or nonindustrial societies. All living socio-cultural systems are within the province of ethnoarchaeology."

ARCHAEOLOGY IN THE SERVICE OF ANTHROPOLOGY

The discussion so far has centered on what the cross-cultural method can do for archaeology. The converse—What can archaeology do for the cross-cultural method?—also needs to be considered. As Ember (1972:181–182) put it, "The possibility of using archaeological data to test causal hypotheses will supplement the limited tests we can now make using documentary data." He continues, "Indeed, the archaeological record will probably continue indefinitely to be more useful than the ethnohistorical record for the testing of causal hypotheses." Fritz (1972:153) has made somewhat the same point when he observes, "The outcome of an indirect test of an instrument for observing a past phenomenon necessarily adds to or subtracts from the credibility of, for example, anthropological theory." Archaeology, if it is to be anthropology, must make its data available to the whole discipline.

Consider, then, the following fascinating scenario presented by Thomas:

> A massive compilation of archaeological data would first have to be synthesized into a central data bank; present archaeologists are probably operating at the level of Tylor in 1888. Perhaps some dogged archaeologist will pattern these files after HRAF (Human Relations Area Files). In fact, archaeologists could even dream up a catchy acronym such as the ARF (Archaeological Relations File), or perhaps WARP (World Archaeological Record Project), or maybe even SHARD (Sample of Holocultural Archaeological Research Data). The major prehistoric cultures of the world could then be coded into objective categories for future statistical analysis. Consider the Cochise culture, for example. *Cochise,* a prehistoric manifestation of the generalized Desert culture, flourished in southern Arizona from about 7000 BC to about 1 AD. The Cochise peoples could be treated as any society of the Ethnographic Atlas, and coded upon many of the Atlas' variables. The Cochise culture, for example, practiced little or no agriculture (col. 12), hunted a great deal (col. 8), lived in semi-nomadic bands (col. 30), lived in communities of less than 50 people (col. 31), lacked metallurgy (col. 42), lacked pottery manufacture (col. 48), and lacked class stratification (col. 68). Although some of the Atlas codings could not be applied to archaeological culture—especially categories of kinship terminology, religion, sexual practices, and linguistic affiliation—these variables are more than compensated by relevant ecological and material cultural categories. Many problems will arise with specific codings, of course, but ethnographic cross-cultural coding is at present still not without such difficulty.
>
> Once the data files had been established, investigators could follow the lead of their current cross-cultural brethren and test a variety of hypotheses upon randomly selected prehistoric societies. Specific aspects of interest could be the role of ecological factors in shaping cultural practices, the relationship between population size and productivity, the reasons for migration and warfare, the evolution of the state. In fact, many of the objectives of modern cross-cultural analysis could fruitfully be explored upon the archaeological samples, since only archaeological data posses suitable time depth to test many of the underlying mechanisms of cultural change and social process [1976:454–455].

Independently of Thomas' scenario, Naroll had asked the present writer in 1973 to prepare a proposal for funding for HRAF to set up exactly such a file. As described in the proposal, the HRAF–ARCH file would be coded from an Outline of Archaeological Materials based on the Outline of Cultural Materials. Experts in each of the 60 culture areas in the HRAF Quality Control File would be asked to pick one archaeologically known culture for each of four sampling strata in each culture area—preferably in the same geographic location as the culture picked for the Probability Sample File. These strata were defined as follows:

1. Cultures lacking bifacially flaked projectile points
2. Prepottery and preagricultural cultures, using bifacial projectile points or microliths
3. Societies employing horticulture and/or pottery hollowware
4. Civilizations with monumental architecture and/or writing and the calendar
5. The ethnographic culture in the HRAF files

Data quality control factors to be considered in picking the sample cultures were as follows:

1. Carbon-14 or other solid dating available
2. Site boundaries known
3. More than 50% of site excavated. (Today one might substitute an adequate random sampling design.)
4. Community pattern known
5. Structure of individual site known
6. Ecological data available
7. Report written by professional or well-qualified amateur

Funding was sought for an initial round of coding of the 20 best known areas, the sale of which was expected to finance the second round of coding, and so on. Despite the attractiveness of such a file as that outlined by Thomas, the proposal received a very unfavorable reception and was not funded. HRAF retains its interest in archaeological data, however, and is currently preparing a worldwide set of archaeological bibliographies.

Although Naroll and Naroll (1973) proposed holoarchaeological studies such as those that the HRAF–ARCH file would have made possible, only one such study seems ever to have been done (Schaefer 1977a)—and that by a cultural anthropologist interested in cross-cultural studies.

Schaefer and his associates drew a judgmental sample of 31 archaeological site components around the world. According to Schaefer (1977a:80), "We were interested in testing the relationship between settlement growth and technological specialization." Settlement size was chosen as the proxy measure for the former, and number of artifact types for the latter. Artifact types as reported by the archaeologist were a problem, since "a question might be raised as to the intercomparability of their types'' (Schaefer 1977a:81), so "etic level" judgments were used to prepare a master type list.

Data quality control variables used in the study were report length, length of stay in the field, crew size, number of illustrations, and quality of illustrations. The last was used as a proxy measure for care used in excavation, sloppy illustrations being viewed as a possible indicator of sloppy excavation.

Schaefer (1977a:80) reports a gamma of .40 with an associated probability of less than 2%. There is a significant, albeit somewhat small, relationship between settlement size and number of artifact types. In addition, Schaefer computed partial correlations in which the effect of each of the data quality control variables was removed. On the basis of these tests Schaefer (1977a:81) states that "the quality of archaeological site reports as measured by our group does not significantly diminish the ordinal scale correlation found between occupation size and the number of artifact types."

From an archaeologist's point of view, Schaefer's pioneering work has two apparent faults. In the first place, some of the sites are open-air or even surface sites, whereas others are in caves. It seems quite likely that differential preservation of bone and wooden artifacts may have seriously skewed his type counts. In the second place, the judgmental sample seems to have a disproportionately high number of early man and simple hunter sites, a few complex cultures, and hardly any simple horticulturalists. As Schaefer (1977a:80) points out, no list of sites suitable for sampling such as the Ethnographic Atlas or Standard Ethnographic Sample exists.

These caveats should not be taken to detract from Schaefer's innovative work; he seized the initiative when archaeologists, including the present writer, would not. There is quite clearly a felt need for holoarchaeological studies to which archaeologists should respond.

CONCLUSIONS

The use of the cross-cultural method in archaeology will undoubtedly increase in the future as more archaeologists become aware of the method and its power to solve archaeological problems.

For the archaeologist interested in gaining insights that may be tested against either archaeological or cross-cultural data, a pilot study may be simply done using the Ethnographic Atlas or the Standard Cross-Cultural Sample if the data are already coded. Such a study is literally quick and probably not very dirty. As an example, Figure 2.1 shows an example of

EXAMPLE OF ETHNOA CROSSTABS

FILE   ETHNOA   (CREATION DATE = 01/27/78)

* *
   SUBSIST2   HUNTING   C R O S S T A B U L A T I O N   O F
* BY MARRES2 PREVAILING MARITAL RESIDENCE
* PAGE 1 OF 2

MARRES2

Each cell: COUNT / ROW PCT / COL PCT / TOT PCT

SUBSIST2	IPATRILOC IAL 1.	VIRILOCA L 2.	AMBI,BI OR UTROL 3.	AMBI,PAT RI, AVUN 4.	NEOLOCAL 5.	MATRILOC AL 6.	AVUNCULO CAL 7.	UXORILOC AL 8.	AMBI-UXO R OR AVU 9.	NO COMMO N OR NO 10.	ROW TOTAL
0. 0-5%	215 / 64.6 / 37.0 / 18.7	50 / 15.0 / 20.9 / 4.3	17 / 5.1 / 21.0 / 1.5	1 / 0.3 / 9.1 / 0.1	14 / 4.2 / 31.8 / 1.2	15 / 4.5 / 30.0 / 1.3	8 / 2.4 / 15.7 / 0.7	9 / 2.7 / 10.8 / 0.8	1 / 0.3 / 20.0 / 0.1	3 / 0.9 / 42.9 / 0.3	333 / 28.9
1. 6-15%	265 / 63.9 / 45.6 / 23.0	53 / 12.8 / 22.2 / 4.6	9 / 2.2 / 11.1 / 0.8	9 / 2.2 / 81.8 / 0.8	20 / 4.8 / 45.5 / 1.7	18 / 4.3 / 36.0 / 1.6	26 / 6.3 / 51.0 / 2.3	9 / 2.2 / 10.8 / 0.8	3 / 0.7 / 60.0 / 0.3	3 / 0.7 / 42.9 / 0.3	415 / 36.0
2. 16-25%	62 / 38.8 / 10.7 / 5.4	41 / 25.6 / 17.2 / 3.6	11 / 6.9 / 13.6 / 1.0	1 / 0.6 / 9.1 / 0.1	8 / 5.0 / 18.2 / 0.7	8 / 5.0 / 16.0 / 0.7	11 / 6.9 / 21.6 / 1.0	16 / 10.0 / 19.3 / 1.4	1 / 0.6 / 20.0 / 0.1	1 / 0.6 / 14.3 / 0.1	160 / 13.9
3. 26-35%	21 / 16.3 / 3.6 / 1.8	56 / 43.4 / 23.4 / 4.9	27 / 20.9 / 33.3 / 2.3	0 / 0.0 / 0.0 / 0.0	0 / 0.0 / 0.0 / 0.0	4 / 3.1 / 8.0 / 0.3	5 / 3.9 / 9.8 / 0.4	16 / 12.4 / 19.3 / 1.4	0 / 0.0 / 0.0 / 0.0	0 / 0.0 / 0.0 / 0.0	129 / 11.2
4. 36-45%	12 / 19.7 / 2.1 / 1.0	17 / 27.9 / 7.1 / 1.5	11 / 18.0 / 13.6 / 1.0	0 / 0.0 / 0.0 / 0.0	1 / 1.6 / 2.3 / 0.1	4 / 6.6 / 8.0 / 0.3	0 / 0.0 / 0.0 / 0.0	16 / 26.2 / 19.3 / 1.4	0 / 0.0 / 0.0 / 0.0	0 / 0.0 / 0.0 / 0.0	61 / 5.3
5. 46-55%	5 / 18.5 / 0.9 / 0.4	6 / 22.2 / 2.5 / 0.5	2 / 7.4 / 2.5 / 0.2	0 / 0.0 / 0.0 / 0.0	0 / 0.0 / 0.0 / 0.0	1 / 3.7 / 2.0 / 0.1	1 / 3.7 / 2.0 / 0.1	12 / 44.4 / 14.5 / 1.0	0 / 0.0 / 0.0 / 0.0	0 / 0.0 / 0.0 / 0.0	27 / 2.3
6. 56-65%	1 / 10.0 / 0.2 / 0.1	5 / 50.0 / 2.1 / 0.4	1 / 10.0 / 1.2 / 0.1	0 / 0.0 / 0.0 / 0.0	1 / 10.0 / 2.3 / 0.1	0 / 0.0 / 0.0 / 0.0	0 / 0.0 / 0.0 / 0.0	2 / 20.0 / 2.4 / 0.2	0 / 0.0 / 0.0 / 0.0	0 / 0.0 / 0.0 / 0.0	10 / 0.9
COLUMN TOTAL	581 / 50.4	239 / 20.7	81 / 7.0	11 / 1.0	44 / 3.8	50 / 4.3	51 / 4.4	83 / 7.2	5 / 0.4	7 / 0.6	1152 / 100.0

70

(CONTINUED)

```
              COUNT  I
              ROW PCT IPATRILOC VIRILOCA AMBI,BI  AMBI,PAT NEOLOCAL MATRILOC AVUNCULO UXORILOC AMBI-UXO NO COMMO   ROW
              COL PCT IAL       L        OR UTROL RI, AVUN           AL       CAL      AL       R OR AVU N OR NO   TOTAL
              TOT PCT I     1.I      2.I      3.I      4.I      5.I      6.I      7.I      8.I      9.I     10.I
SUBSIST2      --------I--------I--------I--------I--------I--------I--------I--------I--------I--------I--------I
                      I    0   I    3   I    2   I    0   I    0   I    0   I    0   I    0   I    0   I    0   I    5
55-75%          7.    I  0.0   I 60.0   I 40.0   I  0.0   I  0.0   I  0.0   I  0.0   I  0.0   I  0.0   I  0.0   I  0.4
                      I  0.0   I  1.3   I  2.5   I  0.0   I  0.0   I  0.0   I  0.0   I  0.0   I  0.0   I  0.0   I
                      I  0.0   I  0.3   I  0.2   I  0.0   I  0.0   I  0.0   I  0.0   I  0.0   I  0.0   I  0.0   I
                      I--------I--------I--------I--------I--------I--------I--------I--------I--------I--------I
                      I    0   I    6   I    0   I    0   I    0   I    0   I    3   I    0   I    0   I    0   I    9
76-85%          8.    I  0.0   I 66.7   I  0.0   I  0.0   I  0.0   I  0.0   I 33.3   I  0.0   I  0.0   I  0.0   I  0.8
                      I  0.0   I  2.5   I  0.0   I  0.0   I  0.0   I  0.0   I  3.6   I  0.0   I  0.0   I  0.0   I
                      I  0.0   I  0.5   I  0.0   I  0.0   I  0.0   I  0.0   I  0.3   I  0.0   I  0.0   I  0.0   I
                      I--------I--------I--------I--------I--------I--------I--------I--------I--------I--------I
                      I    0   I    2   I    1   I    0   I    0   I    0   I    0   I    0   I    0   I    0   I    3
86-100%         9.    I  0.0   I 66.7   I 33.3   I  0.0   I  0.0   I  0.0   I  0.0   I  0.0   I  0.0   I  0.0   I  0.3
                      I  0.0   I  0.8   I  1.2   I  0.0   I  0.0   I  0.0   I  0.0   I  0.0   I  0.0   I  0.0   I
                      I  0.0   I  0.2   I  0.1   I  0.0   I  0.0   I  0.0   I  0.0   I  0.0   I  0.0   I  0.0   I
                      I--------I--------I--------I--------I--------I--------I--------I--------I--------I--------I
              COLUMN      581      239       81       11       44       50       51       83        5        7       1152
              TOTAL      50.4     20.7      7.0      1.0      3.8      4.3      4.4      7.2      0.4      0.6      100.0
```

CHI SQUARE = 401.56396 WITH 81 DEGREES OF FREEDOM   SIGNIFICANCE = 0.0000
CRAMER'S V =   0.19680
CONTINGENCY COEFFICIENT =   0.50841
LAMBDA (ASYMMETRIC) = 0.03799 WITH SUBSIST2 DEPENDENT.   = 0.10858 WITH MARRES2 DEPENDENT.
LAMBDA (SYMMETRIC) = 0.06881
UNCERTAINTY COEFFICIENT (ASYMMETRIC) =   0.10146 WITH SUBSIST2 DEPENDENT.   = 0.10553 WITH MARRES2 DEPENDENT.
UNCERTAINTY COEFFICIENT (SYMMETRIC) =   0.10345
KENDALL'S TAU B =   0.26774   SIGNIFICANCE =   0.0000
KENDALL'S TAU C =   0.21373   SIGNIFICANCE =   0.0000
GAMMA =   0.35559
SOMERS'S D (ASYMMETRIC) =   0.27999 WITH SUBSIST2 DEPENDENT.   = 0.25603 WITH MARRES2 DEPENDENT.
SOMERS'S D (SYMMETRIC) = 0.26747
ETA = 0.45482 WITH SUBSIST2 DEPENDENT.   = 0.26737 WITH MARRES2 DEPENDENT.
PEARSON'S R = 0.22958 SIGNIFICANCE =   0.0000

NUMBER OF MISSING OBSERVATIONS =   18

71

the initial stages of an insightful cross-cultural study. The archaeologist, for instance, might want to know what kind of marital residence patterns simple hunters could be expected to have. Interestingly, only (17) 1.5% of the 1152 cultures for which both variables were coded depend on hunting for more than 65% of their subsistence. Of these, 11 are virilocal defined by Murdock (1967) as "without localized unilineal kin groups," three are defined as living "optionally with or near either parents," and three are uxorilocal ("without matrilocal and matrilineal kin groups"). The next step in such an insightful study would involve a computer run to get the names of these cultures, followed, perhaps, by a check of the original ethnographies to determine possible functional relationships that would lead to such arrangements of residence. Based upon this research, hypotheses could be developed and tested using the hologeistic method and attendant methodological safeguards. On the other hand, when some of the desired variables are not precoded, a workable procedure would seem to be to randomly draw 10 cultures from each of the six continental areas in either the EA or SC-CS, and to look up the uncoded variables in the bibliographic sources cited for each culture in the sample. However, if no variables of interest are precoded, then one must go either to the Probability Sample Files if a set is available, or to the Standard Ethnographic Sample bibliography, drawing a culture at random from each culture area. In this case, the study will still be relatively dirty, but it could scarcely be called quick. Depending on funds, a subset of culture areas might be chosen. In any case, data quality control and other tests are not performed.

Both the development of proxy measures and the testing of propositions demand the use of the full, rigorous hologeistic method. Although the sample of 60 cultures would be the same as the last of the insightful studies discussed, all data quality control factors and other safeguards would be applied. In the case of the Standard Ethnographic Sample, data quality control variables were taken into account in defining the bibliography, whereas these are precoded for the Probability Sample Files, providing a savings of time and money, which gives the edge to the use of these two samples.

The full modern hologeistic method as outlined here will probably be used more and more by archaeologists if research into proxy measures in archaeology increases as it should. These instruments for indirect observation have a particular importance to archaeology—not only will they allow archaeologists to deal more fully with the whole cultural system, but they will also provide data that the cultural anthropologist needs. Students in introductory archaeology courses universally learn that archaeology provides time depth to anthropology. With the exception of the development of urbanism, much of what archaeologists have discovered is either unknown or ignored by the rest of the discipline. The cross-cultural method offers both a method to rectify this situation and a means to take full advantage of the data that archaeology can supply.

REFERENCES

Beardsley, R. K., P. Holder, A. D. Krieger, B. J. Meggers, and J. B. Rinaldo
  1956   Functional and evolutionary implications of community patterning. In Seminars in archaeology: 1955, edited by R. Wauchope. *Memoirs of the Society for American Archaeology* **11**:129–157.
Binford, L. A.
  1962   Archaeology as anthropology. *American Antiquity* **28**:217–225.
  1971   Mortuary practices; their study and their potential. In Approaches to the social dimensions of mortuary practices, edited by J. A. Brown. *Memoirs of the Society for American Archaeology* **25**:6–29.
Chang, K. C
  1958   Study of the neolithic social grouping: Examples from the New World. *American Anthropologist* **60**:298–334.
Cohen, R.
  1970   Generalizations in ethnology. In *Handbook of method in cultural anthropology,* edited by R. Naroll and R. Cohen. Garden City, N.Y.: Natural History Press. Pp. 31–50.
Cook, S., and R. Heizer
  1968   Relationships among houses, settlement areas, and population in aboriginal California. In *Settlement archaeology,* edited by K. C. Chang. Palo Alto: National Press. Pp. 79–116.
Coult, A. D., and R. W. Habenstein
  1965   *Cross tabulations of Murdock's world ethnographic sample.* Columbia: University of Missouri Press.
Divale, W. T.
  1975   Temporal focus and random error in cross-cultural hypotheses tests. *Behavior Science Research* **10**:19–36.
  1977   Living floor area and marital residence: A replication. *Behavior Science Research* **12**:109–116.
Driver, H.
  1956   An integration of functional, evolutionary, and historical theory by means of correlations. *Indiana University Publications in Anthropology and Linguistics* **12**:1–36.
  1965   Survey of numerical classification in anthropology. In *The use of computers in anthropology,* edited by D. Hymes. The Hague: Mouton. Pp. 302–344.
  1970   Statistical studies of continuous geographical distributions. In *Handbook of method in cultural anthropology,* edited by R. Naroll and R. Cohen. Garden City: Natural History Press. Pp. 620–639.
Driver, H., and A. E. Kroeber
  1932   Qualitative expression of cultural relationships. *University of California Publications in American Archaeology and Ethnology* **31**:211–256.

Driver, H., and K. F. Schuessler
　1957　Factor analysis of ethnographic data. *American Anthropologist* **59**:655–663.
　1967　Correlational analysis of Murdock's 1957 ethnographic sample. *American Anthropologist* **69**:332–352.

Ember, M.
　1964　Comment on Naroll: On ethnic unit classification. *Current Anthropology* **5**:296.
　1971　An empirical test of Galton's problem. *Ethnology* **10**:98–106.
　1972　An archaeological indicator of matrilocal versus patrilocal residence. *American Antiquity* **38**:177–182.

Erickson, E. E.
　1977　Cultural evolution. *American Behavioral Scientist* **20**:669–680.

Fritz, J. M.
　1972　Archaeological systems for indirect observation of the past. In *Contemporary archaeology*, edited by M. Leone. Carbondale: Southern Illinois University Press. Pp. 135–157.

Hobhouse, L. T., G. C. Wheeler, and M. Ginsberg
　1930　*The material culture and social distributions of the simpler peoples* (Monographs on Sociology, No. 3). London: London School of Economics and Political Science.

Jochim, M. A.
　1976　*Hunter–gatherer subsistence and settlement: A predictive model.* New York: Academic Press.

Jorgensen, J. (editor)
　1974　*Comparative studies by Harold E. Driver and essays in his honor.* New Haven: HRAF Press.

Köbben, A.
　1967　Why exceptions? The logic of cross-cultural analysis. *Current Anthropology* **8**:3–34.

Lagacé, R.
　1977　*Sixty cultures.* New Haven: HRAF Press.

Leach, E.
　1964　Comment on Naroll: On ethnic unit classification. *Current Anthropology* **4**:299.

Levinson, D.
　1977a　What have we learned from cross-cultural surveys? *American Behavior Science* **20**:757–792.
　1977b　*Guide to social theory* (5 vols.). New Haven: HRAF Press.

McNett, C. W., Jr.
　1967　The inference of socio-cultural traits in archaeology: A statistical approach. Ph.D. dissertation, Tulane University. Ann Arbor: University Microfilm.
　1970a　A settlement pattern scale of cultural complexity. In *Handbook of method in cultural anthropology*, edited by R. Naroll and R. Cohen. Garden City, N.Y.: Natural History Press. Pp. 872–888.
　1970b　A cross-cultural method for predicting nonmaterial traits in archaeology. *Behavior Science Notes* **5**:195–212.

McNett, C. W., Jr., and R. E. Kirk
　1968　A suggested method of drawing random samples in cross-cultural surveys. *American Anthropologist* **70**:50–55.

Murdock, G. P.
　1940　The cross-cultural survey. *American Sociological Review* **5**:361–370.

1949   *Social structure*. Macmillan, New York.

1957   World ethnographic sample. *American Anthropologist* **59**:664–687.

1967   *Ethnographic atlas*. Pittsburgh: University of Pittsburgh Press.

Murdock, G. P., C. S. Ford, A. E. Hudson, R. Kennedy, L. W. Simmons, and J. W. M. Whiting

1971   *Outline of cultural materials* (4th rev. ed., 5th printing with modifications). New Haven: HRAF Press.

Murdock, G. P., and C. Provost

1973   Factors in the division of labor by sex: A cross-cultural analysis. *Ethnology* **12**:379–392.

Murdock, G. P., and D. White

1969   Standard cross-cultural sample. *Ethnology* **8**:329–369.

Murray, P.

1978   Discard location: The ethnographic data. Manuscript on deposit, University of Arizona, Tucson.

Naroll, R.

1956   A preliminary index of social development. *American Anthropologist* **58**:687–715.

1962a *Data quality control: A new research technique. Prolegomena to a cross-cultural study of culture stress*. Glencoe, Ill.: Free Press.

1962b Floor area and settlement population. *American Antiquity* **27**:587–589.

1964   On ethnic unit classification. *Current Anthropology* **5**:283–312.

1967   The proposed HRAF probability sample. *Behavior Science Notes* **2**:70–80.

1970a Epistemology. In *Handbook of method in cultural anthropology*, edited by R. Naroll and R. Cohen. Garden City, N.Y.: Natural History Press. Pp. 25–30.

1970b What have we learned from cross-cultural surveys? *American Anthropologist* **72**:1227–1288.

Naroll, R., W. Alnot, J. Caplan, J. F. Hansen, J. Maxant, and N. Schmidt

1970   A standard ethnographic sample: Preliminary edition. *Current Anthropology* **11**:235–248.

Naroll, R., G. Michik, and F. Naroll

1974   Hologeistic theory testing. In *Comparative studies by Harold E. Driver and essays in his honor*, edited by J. Jorgensen. New Haven: HRAF Press. Pp. 121–148.

1976   *World-wide theory testing*. New Haven: HRAF Press.

Naroll, R., and F. Naroll (editors)

1973   *Main currents in cultural anthropology*. New York: Appleton.

1977   Issue devoted to cultural anthropology. *American Behavioral Scientist* **20**:619–792.

Naroll, R., and R. Sipes

1973   A standard ethnographic sample: Second edition. *Current Anthropology* **14**:111–140.

Otterbein, K.

1976   Sampling and samples in cross-cultural studies. *Behavior Science Research* **11**:107–122.

1977   Warfare: A hitherto unrecognized critical variable. *American Behavioral Scientist* **20**:693–710.

Pelto, P.

1970   *Anthropological research: The structure of inquiry*. New York: Harper.

Robbins, M.
  1966 House types and settlement patterns: An application of ethnology to archaeological interpretation. *Minnesota Archaeologist* **28**:3–35.
Rohner, R., R. Naroll, H. Barry, III, W. T. Divale, E. E. Erickson, J. M. Schaefer, and R. G. Sipes
  1978 Guidelines for holocultural research. *Current Anthropology* **19**:128–129.
Schaefer, J. M.
  1977a The growth and development of hologeistic cross-cultural research. *Annals of the New York Academy of Sciences* **285**:75–89.
  1977b (with the collaboration of David Levinson) The growth of hologeistic studies. *Behavior Science Research* **12**:71–108.
Schiffer, M. B.
  1978 Methodological issues in ethnoarchaeology. In *Explorations in ethnoarchaeology*, edited by R. Gould. Albuquerque: University of New Mexico Press.
Schuessler, K. F., and H. Driver
  1956 A factor analysis of 16 primitive societies. *American Sociological Review* **21**:493–499.
Straus, D., and M. Orans
  1978 Residence and descent is hyperdiffusional? *Behavior Science Research* **13**:1–24.
Thomas, D. H.
  1976 *Figuring anthropology: First principles of probability and statistics*. New York: Holt.
Tuggle, H.
  1970 Prehistoric community relationships in east central Arizona. Unpublished Ph.D. dissertation, University of Arizona.
Tylor, E. B.
  1889 On a method of investigating the development of institutions: Applied to laws of marriage and descent. *Journal of the Royal Anthropological Institute* **18**:245–272.
Whiting, J. W. M., and B. Ayres
  1968 Inferences from the shape of dwellings. In *Settlement archaeology*, edited by K. C. Chang. Palo Alto: National Press. Pp. 117–133.
Wilmsen, E. N.
  1973 Interaction, spacing behavior, and the organization of hunting bands. *Journal of Anthropological Research* **29**:1–31.
Witkowski, S. R.
  1977 Kinship. *American Behavioral Scientist* **20**:657–668.

Breaking Down the System: Recent Ecological Approaches in Archaeology

MICHAEL A. JOCHIM

INTRODUCTION

Ecological research is thriving in archaeology. The field has seen a proliferation of new techniques for gathering information about past environments, an increasing research emphasis on the nature of human interaction with these environments, and the adoption of generalizations, concepts, and jargon from biological ecology. A survey and synthesis of all these developments is beyond the scope of this paper; a completely objective treatment of the topic is beyond the powers of this author, who has his own ideas about what ecological approaches in archaeology should be. The following, therefore, represents an overview of selected trends in ecological archaeology with an emphasis on certain theoretical issues.

ECOLOGY, CULTURE, AND ADAPTATION

The first responsibility in such an overview is to define the topic, or at least this author's understanding of the topic. Ecological anthropology is the study of cultural behavior in its natural and social environment, in

ADVANCES IN ARCHAEOLOGICAL METHOD AND THEORY, VOL. 2

terms of its relationship to this environment. Ideally, practitioners of this approach subscribe to a holistic view of the determinants and ramifications of human behavior, and thus attempt to widen the viewpoint of anthropology so as to understand more fully the complexity of human culture.

An underlying theoretical basis for ecological studies is evolution, with its concepts of adaptation and fitness. When we examine the behavior of any organism, we try to understand it, to see the sense in it. Such an attempt implies that some fundamental end is being served by the behavior. Evolutionary theory provides not only such an end, but also the means of assessing performance. The end is *adaptation* to the environment, measured by relative *fitness*, or the genetic contribution to the next generation. Consequently, explanations of patterns of animal behavior are usually phrased in terms of their adaptive significance, their contribution to fitness.

A similar attempt to make sense of human goals and behavior has led many anthropologists to view a particular activity not as the solution to a problem, which is the view taken here, but rather as one step toward the realization of an ultimate goal. The distinction is important, because in the context of problem solving, numerous, often conflicting, and sometimes capricious goals may guide an individual's decisions, whereas in the context of a single, unifying goal, the decisions seem to be more harmonious and comprehensible. In recognition of the fact that humans are part of the biological world, in which "only one process, natural selection for individual adaptation, ordinarily produces goal-seeking behavior" (Richerson 1977:2), "adaptation" is assumed to be this basic underlying goal:

> [Human and nonhuman behavior] both function to effect adaptation to the environment and . . . are subject to a kind of selection resulting, *inter alia*, from the fact that individuals or populations behaving in certain different ways have different degrees of success in survival and reproduction and, consequently, in the transmission of their ways of behaving from generation to generation [Vayda and Rappaport 1968:493].

Here we have a direct analogy drawn between the behavior of humans and that of other animals: both are seen as means to the same ends. In view of the many clear differences separating humans from the rest of the animal world, this analogy is startling. It is also very appealing in that (*a*) the diversity of human activities can be brought together within a common framework of understanding: (*b*) these activities can be analyzed by using concepts and methods developed in evolutionary ecology; and (*c*) human evolution can be studied as a continuation of known processes without recourse to concepts of a qualitative leap or a threshold of human consciousness. Humans are different, but perhaps we are only doing many of the same things in different ways.

One discussion of biological adaptation that is quite suitable for the framework used here is the following:

> It is self-evident that any living species, at least any species not about to become extinct, has a valid set of solutions for certain basic ecological, or biological problems. It must secure food to replenish its energy store, must have a place to live, and a method to reproduce and thus to perpetuate its genes in succeeding generations. Possession of a valid set of such solutions is called adaptedness [Dobzhansky 1974:323].

Clearly, the same definition might be applied to humans, with perpetuation of genes as the ultimate criterion of success. Is such a definition sufficient, however? Can human adaptation be reduced ultimately to genetic survival? Many people think so, or at least believe that this may be a valuable working assumption (Durham 1976). On the other hand, many others believe that human adaptation must be defined in a broader manner, to allow for the perpetuation not only of genes but also of culture, of "ways of behaving" (Vayda and Rappaport 1968:493). Humans live in groups and share common commitments to a way of life, which many of their activities seek to perpetuate. "Better Dead Than Red" is a slogan not easily reconciled with genetic fitness.

Once we admit this broader definition of adaptation, however, we face serious problems. If culture be defined as the extrasomatic means of adaptation (White 1949), and adaptation as the perpetuation of culture, then culture becomes a means of perpetuating itself! Perhaps some rewording can help to reduce this apparent circularity. Living humans have a valid set of solutions for survival and genetic perpetuation. Culture consists in the extrasomatic (behavioral and ideological) components of these solutions, the chosen motives, and the resulting strategies for survival. Human adaptation, then, might involve the perpetuation not simply of genes, but also of a particular set of solutions based on certain goals. Culture does indeed tend to perpetuate itself, and an assumption of cultural conservatism becomes analogous to the observed conservatism of biological evolution:

> The class of possible evolutionary futures is highly restricted by the properties of the evolutionary present and the conservatism of evolution. Not only is there a tendency to do nothing, but if anything does occur, it does so in the smallest possible steps [Slobodkin 1977:333].

Additional problems with this definition of human adaptation derive from the difficulties of measuring the persistence of cultural behavior and of reconciling such persistence with the continuous changes in behavior that we can observe. What is to persist? Not the people themselves: births and deaths constantly alter their identity. Not the size of the cultural group, for population growth should be genetically adaptive. The type of economy, the political structure, or the religion? If so, then we cannot say that humans ever have been adapted except for a frozen instant of time. Can we more easily approach this problem, perhaps, through a systems framework and examine the persistence of the systemic relationships? We could talk of certain variables in our cultural systems being maintained within ranges that permit the continued existence of the system, for example (Rappaport 1968). Yet one of the major criticisms of the systems ecological approach has been that it overemphasizes the stability or equilibrium of cultural systems, to the neglect of disequilibrium or change (Vayda and McCay 1975).

Here, again, a rephrasing of the problem may help to suggest a useful approach to the dilemma. People solve problems of survival in their own terms. They choose solutions to the perceived problems that satisfy their goals by using available means. Problems, means, and goals that are widely shared may lead to widely shared solutions as well. Problems may change directly through environmental changes; their perception may be altered through communication and experience; the available means may change through accident, invention, or contact; and the goals may change through education or coercion. It is no wonder that behavior is so frequently changing. What may persist in adaptation, then, is simply the possession of any valid set of solutions, together with the *acceptance of their validity*. The observed conservatism of behavior or the impression of equilibrium of cultural systems may reflect either a temporary stability of problems, means, and goals or the fact that changes must build on the "evolutionary present," must come about in the context of ongoing solutions.

If human adaptation involves more than biological fitness, it is likely that the mechanisms of human adaptation also differ from those of biological evolution. In an excellent analysis of the evolution of cultural behavior, Durham (1976) discusses some of the problems inherent in a theory of cultural evolution. For any such theory to be complementary to biological evolution, it must incorporate "(1) sources of variation, (2) selection criteria, and (3) mechanisms for the retention of positively selected variants" (Durham 1976:94). Durham goes on to suggest "invention, diffusion, and accident" as sources of variation, and inclusive biological fitness as the major selection criterion. The mechanisms for retention are given less attention, but are suggested to include experiences, socialization, and teaching. Yet if theories of cultural evolution are to be more than grand analogies, it is essential that we understand these mechanisms. Darwin's evolutionary theory assumed its greatest potential only with the discovery of the genetic basis—the mechanism of the process. The same is true of any theory of cultural evolution: until we understand the mechanisms involved, we are limited to description and analogy.

As Durham states, "Biological theories of adaptation do not yet make adequate allowance for learning and nongenetic inheritance" (1976:90). Learning is the basis of cultural behavior; in order to understand the mechanism of cultural selection, we must investigate the process by which new behaviors are taught, learned, and retained. We must understand the relationship between adaptation and learning. A behavioral approach to learning, which promises greatest utility in comprehending this relationship, has been suggested by Harner among others: "It seems unlikely that cultural institutions and traits can be successfully passed on through centuries and millennia without having some regular reinforcement for their maintenance" (1973:152). Our focus should perhaps be on the specific reinforcers for each behavior if we would seek to understand the continuation of that behavior. By examining learning and reinforcement, we may be better able to deal with some of the unique characteristics of cultural evolution: the selective retention or diffusion of single ideas, the potential rapidity of change, and the opportunity for deliberate change by rational strategizing (Richerson 1977:15).

A final consideration in this section is the predictability of behavior—whether we can predict the course of evolution, the direction of sequential adaptations. Biologists who stress the existence of general trends in evolution argue that we can, at least on the macroscopic level (Margalef 1968:30); those who deny such trends or their significance suggest otherwise (Colinvaux 1973:497). Some of the factors affecting the predictability of evolution are summarized by the following statement:

> The complexity of the situation is, however, so overwhelming that we cannot predict whether or not an environmental challenge will evoke an adaptive evolutionary response in concrete cases. A response will not occur if genetic raw materials for it are unavailable . . . The response to changing environments may be too slow to save a species from extinction . . . Finally, a coherent adaptive response to a given environment may be achieved by quite different means [Dobzhansky 1974:318].

One aspect of evolutionary change does, at least, seem to be predictable: "Evolution will proceed according to the principle of adaptive modifications along the lines of least resistance" (Stebbins 1974:303). This is the evolutionary conservatism stressed by Slobodkin cited earlier.

How predictable, then, is human behavior? By analogy with biological evolution as currently understood, the answer would have to be very poorly, except for a vague tendency for "cultural inertia" (Durham

1976:99). But there are some promising factors. Terrell quotes Kluckhohn to the effect that "all cultures constitute so many somewhat distinct answers to essentially the same questions posed by human biology and by the generalities of the human situation," and emphasizes the relative constancy of human biology and the variability of the situation (Terrell 1977:245). It is to this situation, to the environment in the broadest sense, that we must look for the questions or problems. It may be possible to analyze and characterize different environments according to their "common problems for life" (Colinvaux 1973:51), and to relate these to biogeographical distributions. Furthermore, it then may be possible to "elucidate general features of hazards and responses and to develop generalizations in terms of such variables as the magnitude, duration, and novelty of hazards, the magnitude and reversibility of responses to them, the temporal order in which responses of different magnitudes occur, and the persistence or nonpersistence of response processes" (Vayda and McCay 1975:297).

ECOLOGICAL RESEARCH IN ANTHROPOLOGY

Despite its holistic ideal, much of ecological anthropology seems to have rather narrow focuses. On the one hand, the "environment" examined has been frequently limited to the natural environment, and the human interaction to the realm of subsistence behavior. This represents a restriction on the variables investigated, and although such restrictions have been previously recognized and criticized (Flannery 1972; Vayda and McCay 1975), it will be argued here that they may be necessary and fruitful components of ecological research as long as the imposed limitations are viewed as temporary.

On the other hand, there appears to be a trend to impose a very different sort of restriction on ecological work: an emphasis on the behavior or sociocultural systems to the neglect of the behavior of humans themselves. This approach represents a restriction on the units or levels of complexity examined; although it may be heuristically valuable and intellectually gratifying, such a limitation may be more difficult to overcome in the long run. It is not a systems framework per se that is at issue, but rather the very nature of an ecological approach. Some see the goal of ecological anthropology as being the understanding of human behavior in terms of the structure, function, and processes of maintenance and change of sociocultural systems:

> Since early pristine state formations appear in the context of agriculture, it becomes important to explore the conditions under which a more hierarchical system, contain-

ing more specialization, might emerge and prosper at the expense of less complex systems . . . In order to do this, the state sociocultural system must be treated as a whole unit—a system—the systemic behavior of which is being selected for as a whole [Gall and Saxe 1977:257].

Others, including this author, would argue for the reverse: the understanding of the dynamics of sociocultural systems must be in terms of human behavior. This is not simply a matter of semantics; the orientation determines the organization of research, the framing of hypotheses, and the acceptability of explanations. The change in a system from state A to state B can certainly be *described* in terms applicable to the system as a whole—for example, as an increase in subsystem specialization and hierarchical organization of decision making. Certain implications of such a change for the functioning of the entire system can also be examined by treating the system as a whole unit. I seriously doubt, however, that this framework promotes the *understanding and explanation* of the change, which, after all, involves various groups and individuals pursuing different advantages and options with a variety of constraints and goals and in a variety of natural and social environments. The major challenge of this viewpoint is to account for any observed regularities of system "behavior" in terms of individual or group decisions and actions.

ECOLOGICAL ARCHAEOLOGY

The complexity of ecosystems demands that they be broken down into components that can more easily be studied. A review of ecological work in archaeology can profitably examine: (*a*) the enormous variety of ways in which such systems are broken down for investigation, (*b*) the methods of measuring the relevant variables, (*c*) the procedures for determining the structure and underlying processes of variable relationships, and (*d*) attempts to relate such work to the larger, more complex systems.

Research Organization

Behavioral Subsystems

Ecological studies in archaeology can be organized along several dimensions. The most common approach has been to break down human ecosystems into subsystems that represent the traditional subdivisions of anthropological study examined in a systems framework. A significant trend of recent ecological applications of this approach is the inclusion of environmental variables in each of the component subsystems—in other words, the explicit assumption that any aspect of human behavior can involve *direct* interaction with the environment.

Subsistence. Relationships between humans and their environments are most obvious in the realm of food procurement. This fact, together with the relatively great archaeological visibility of food-getting behavior, has led to an overwhelming predominance of subsistence studies in ecological archaeology. Archaeology has always sought to reconstruct prehistoric economies, and many new developments are seeking to increase the variety of information collected. For example, prehistoric use of plants can be examined through the use of various new flotation techniques (Dennell 1978; Jarman *et al.* 1972; Struever 1968; Watson 1976). Faunal remains are yielding greater information on the seasonality of procurement through studies of dental eruption, epiphyseal closure, antler loss, and antler density (Casteel 1972a; Clark 1972; Sturdy 1975), dental banding (Bourque *et al.* 1978), fish scale morphology (Casteel 1974), shellfish dimensions (Moreau 1977), and relative proportions of different species (Jochim 1976; Speth and Davis 1976). New information about human diets may be obtained through analyses of coprolites (Bryant and Williams-Dean 1975) and of bone strontium (Brown 1973).

The wealth of new information so obtained has rendered the study of prehistoric subsistence all the more complicated, with the result that many investigators are profitably breaking down subsistence behavior further into components, either as microenvironments utilized (Coe and Flannery 1964) or as individual resource procurement systems (Cordell 1977; Flannery 1968a; Goodyear 1975; Thomas 1972). In fact, many valuable ecological studies have surprisingly narrow focus: musk oxen (Wilkinson 1975), reindeer (Burch 1972; Sturdy 1975), shellfish (Braun 1974), salmon (Schalk 1977), and root crops (Bronson 1966). The value of such studies derives precisely from their narrow scope: by limiting the number of interrelated variables, it is much easier to examine their interaction and reaction to change. Such studies can be viewed as building blocks in the construction of an understanding of a total subsistence economy.

Archaeologists concerned with the dynamics of prehistoric behavior cannot continue to ignore the dynamics of the environment and its resources. Soils, water sources, plants, and animals are not simply static factors to be selected or exploited; they show patterns of behavior themselves, which condition the timing, magnitude, and techniques of their use and their reaction to this use. Many of the above studies are valuable in their explicit discussion of resource attributes such as spatial and temporal distribution and variability, which affect energy costs, yields, and reliability. As a result, not only can various resources be compared in similar terms, but also the subsistence economy of a group can then be examined in light of general ecological work on feeding strategies. Such recent work, by analyzing such resource characteristics as search and pursuit times and patchiness of distribution, has been able to suggest optimal strategies (for example, specialization versus generalization, clumping versus dispersal) under a variety of assumptions (such as risk minimization, time minimization, energy maximization) in a number of situations related to resource size, density, distribution, and variability, and to degree of competition and predation (Covich 1976; MacArthur 1972; Schoener 1971). The description and understanding of human subsistence change through time or variation in space can be approached in a similar manner (see, e.g., Hardesty 1977; Jochim 1976; Wilmsen 1973).

Technology. Technology has usually been investigated along with subsistence, either as a dependent reflection of past activities, or as an independent stimulus of subsistence change. In a number of recent works, however, technology has been studied without assumptions of dependence or independence, but rather as a set of components potentially related to a wide range of variables in various ways. Again, a common approach has been to focus on one aspect of technology in order to investigate its role in past behavior: canal irrigation (Jacobsen and Adams 1958; Lees 1974), floodwater management (Butzer 1976), sunken fields (Parsons and Psuty 1975), storage facilities (Day 1974; Puleston 1971), land clearance (Boserup 1965; Sanders 1973, 1976), construction (Erasmus 1965; Mendelssohn 1971; Renfrew 1973), and manufacture of ceramics (Van der Leeuw 1976).

In many of these studies it is the emphasis on the *strategic* aspects of technology that may prove most useful. Various technologies can be compared in terms of costs in energy, materials, and personnel, of requirements of special knowledge or coordination, of effects on the natural environment, of implications for competition and work organization, and of relative benefits in different natural environments. Models of strategic choice can then be constructed, based on one or several criteria, such as maximization of security, net productivity, or gross yield. Such models could provide baselines of expectations for comparison with the archaeological record. Sanders' investigations of agricultural techniques in the Maya Lowlands (Sanders 1973) and the Basin of Mexico (Sanders 1976) clearly demonstrate the archaeological applicability of such detailed assessments of technological strategies.

Settlement. Settlement behavior is increasingly analyzed in its environmental context in an effort to determine not simply the pattern but also the system of settlement (Flannery 1976b). The environment of individual sites has usually been examined for its subsistence potential

(Jarman 1972; Rossman 1976; Vita-Finzi and Miggs 1970). Some regional studies have sought environmental regularities in site placement (Chartkoff and Chartkoff 1975; Flannery 1976a,d; Jochim 1976; Larson 1971; Madsen and Berry 1975; Sielmann 1971; Zarky 1976), whereas others have focused on site spacing (Reynolds 1976) and the relationship to elements of the social and political environment (Earle 1976; Johnson 1972; Marcus 1973). Surveys now frequently include a stratification of the area according to features of the natural environment (Bettinger 1977; Dickson 1975; Lovis 1976; Thomas 1972), with the assumption that people will have shown different patterns of interaction with these various strata.

Johnson (1977) has written an excellent review of various techniques of regional analysis in archaeology, highlighting the behavioral assumptions and goals underlying these techniques. A consideration of such goals allows settlement and spatial behavior to be viewed as the outcome of strategic decisions aimed at realizing certain ends. The minimization of both movement and risk emerge as two of the most common assumptions underlying current archaeological techniques of spatial analysis, paralleling an emphasis in general ecological studies of spacing behavior (Pianka 1974; Wiens 1976). An analysis of settlement strategies in this framework must consequently examine both the reliability and the distribution of resources and personnel as these relate to costs of production, transport, and distribution in order to investigate behavior related to territoriality, sedentarization, and agglomeration (Dyson-Hudson and Smith 1978; Johnson 1977; Wilmsen 1973).

Demography. Demographic studies have assumed a central position in current archaeology, focusing primarily on the ratio of population to resources. Despite tremendous problems of definition and measurement (see, e.g., Brush 1975; Mayden 1975), the concept of "carrying capacity" or some type of (dynamic) upper limit to this ratio for a given technology is widely held. As a result, much work has been devoted to determining this limit and to exploring how populations have been maintained in an equilibrium below such a limit (Casteel 1972b; Divale 1972; Dumond 1975; Mayden 1972; Sanders 1976; Zubrow 1975). Alternatively, studies of prehistoric change are giving increasing causal priority to processes of "population pressure" in which this limit or threshold is exceeded (Adams 1977; Binford 1968; Carneiro 1970; Cohen 1977; Harris 1977; Smith 1972; Spooner 1972). Certainly the relationship between populations and resources is central to ecological studies, and some of the many approaches to understanding this relationship will be discussed below. A different emphasis in demographic studies is exemplified by the provocative work of Wobst (1974, 1975), who focuses on demography in a spatial context, including the relationship of mating systems to topography and to population density and distribution.

There has been some consideration of population size and density as reflecting the outcome of strategizing choices. Dumond (1972), for example, assumes a constant tendency on the part of human populations to increase, with the resulting threat of resource shortages requiring decisions involving population regulation, migration, or expansion of subsistence techniques and resources. Although he ignores the questions of the locus of decision making or the implementation and enforcement of such decisions, this is an extremely valuable approach because it serves to link behavioral processes to population patterns; demography is not consigned to a position of passive dependence upon resources. Cowgill (1975a,b), in addition, rightly points out that different strategies may be selected by different sectors of the same society.

Social Organization, Trade, Warfare, and Religion. Numerous studies of prehistoric sociopolitical organization now view the environment in a dynamic context rather than as a static setting. Much of the current work on both the rise and fall of complex societies, for example, gives some attention to the processes of adaptation to such conditions as the differential distribution of resources (Flannery *et al.* 1967; Rathje 1971, 1973; Renfrew 1972; Sanders 1968, 1973, 1976), geographic circumscription by natural or social factors (Carneiro 1970; Webster 1975), or meteorological fluctuations (Athens 1977; Bell 1971; Jorde 1977; Peebles and Kus 1977). Similarly, two collections of articles on prehistoric trade and exchange show a tendency to treat the environment not simply as a source of goods, but rather as a set of factors directly influencing demand, procurement, and distribution (Earle and Ericson 1977b; Sabloff and Lamberg-Karlovsky 1975). Warfare has been examined both as a manifestation of competition for resources (Larson 1972) and as a process having certain organizational requirements and thereby constituting a component of the social environment (Peebles and Kus 1977; Webster 1975). And finally, when religion and ideology have been included in explicitly ecological work, it has been along the lines suggested by Rappaport (1971), in institutional form as a regulator of system relationships (Drennan 1976), although some suggestions for the incorporation of value systems into ecological work have appeared (Cowgill 1975a,b; Dumond 1972; Jochim 1976; Shimkin 1973).

Underlying many of these studies, either implicitly or explicitly, is an emphasis on the strategies of coping with differential access to resources and on the management of these coping strategies. Patchy resource distributions or techniques such as irrigation, for example, are frequently stated to engender economic and, ultimately, sociopolitical differences among individuals or groups according to their access rights. It should certainly be possible to measure relative abundance (and hence potential accessibility) of various resources, and to evaluate resources according to their suitability for permanent ownership and defense (based on distribution, productivity, and predictability—see, e.g., Dyson-Hudson and Smith 1978). It is not at all clear, however, just why, when, and how the potential for limited access and control is converted into formalized inequalities among individuals. Surely, even the most egalitarian of hunter–gatherer societies experience some resources in relatively short supply. There seems, in fact, to be a concept of some (unquantified) *threshold* of resource scarcity lurking in many of these formulations.

Similarly, redistribution, trade, and warfare have been viewed as mechanisms for coping with relative resource scarcity—mechanisms with certain managerial requirements leading to inequalities of authority and rank. For example, Dumond (1972:297) states that "no society in which basic productive resources must be carefully allocated is without formalized rank." No suggestions are offered, however, about how to quantify "carefully allocated," although some threshold of managerial requirements seems implied. In a similar argument, Logan and Sanders (1976:49) and Sanders *et al.* (1976:164) imply that the needs for coordination of specialists, redistribution of goods, and resolution of conflicts may reach certain levels requiring institutional adjustments, without a specification of how to determine these critical levels. Rappaport (1971) has suggested some valuable criteria for assessing the performance of different managing institutions (for example, according to speed, flexibility, and cost of upkeep), yet no such quantitative comparison has appeared to my knowledge; much less has any particular managing institution been linked to a particular, quantified level of "needs."

Geographic Extent

Another dimension along which ecological approaches may be organized is geographic: according to the spatial extent of the behavior examined. Human behavior tends to assume the structure of a nested hierarchy in space, and different types of interaction may require study areas of different sizes. Although no clear boundaries may be set, it is convenient to group various approaches into three categories: those focusing on the site and its catchment, the larger sustaining region for a group, and broader areas containing several groups or larger societal units. With each of these approaches there is a growing tendency to break down the monolithic concept of environment into a number of microenvironments or variables of potential relevance.

Site and Catchment.   Virtually every site report has directed some attention to the site's setting or hinterland, and recently such attention has often been described as the site's "ecology." Usually it is no such thing. Rather, such discussions tend to consist largely in a description of nearby vegetational zones together with the subsistence contribution of each. To be sure, these descriptions convey some information about human–environmental interactions, but only very little. An ecological interest demands, for example, exploration of the resources used in relation to those available, the constraints on the organization of procurement, the spatiotemporal variability of the environment, and the environmental effects of exploitation. Catchment analysis (Vita-Finzi and Higgs 1970) provides a framework for investigating the distribution of potential and actual resources and the effects on procurement costs; detailed palynological and paleontological studies may be used to supplement information provided by on-site food remains. Reconstructed subsistence potential under certain technological assumptions can be evaluated in relation to independent estimates of food needs, with possible implications for the organization of procurement and the potential for environmental degradation (Culbert 1973b: Sanders 1976). Nonutilization of accessible resources may suggest the underlying determinants of food selection (Klein 1977) or the existence of sociopolitical limits to procurement (Flannery 1968b).

Small Regions. Archaeologists interested in the subsistence of nomadic societies, especially hunter–gatherers, utilize a regional focus in order to investigate the seasonal movements and activities of such groups (Bettinger 1977; Jochim 1976; MacNeish 1971; Thomas 1973; Winters 1969). In addition, most questions about subsistence diversity and interdependence, social interaction, and political dominance of more sedentary and organizationally complex societies require such a regional approach. In such studies, emphasis is placed upon the differential location of settlements, their differing component activities, and their relationships with one another as elements of the total environment. Spatial distributions can be examined in light of subsistence requirements in order to assess the role of nonsubsistence factors (Blanton 1975b; Charlton 1973, 1975; Flannery 1976a; Parsons 1970). Various levels of spatial settlement hierarchies may be investigated for diversity within and between clusters (Peebles and Kus 1977; Renfrew 1973), or for their distortion from ideal geometric configurations by environmental factors (Earle 1976; Reynolds 1976).

Larger Areas. Larger areas of investigation are most frequently utilized in archaeology when the research emphasis is placed on the processes of change. Meteorological changes affecting rainfall patterns, sea level, temperature ranges, or ecological processes such as soil erosion or exhaustion may have widespread effects; their role as causal factors of change in any one site or region can be clarified only through an examination of their ramifications throughout their distribution (Andrews 1973; Braun 1974; Fitzhugh 1976; Grabert and Larsen 1975; Madsen and Berry 1975; Winter 1976). Population changes may be interpreted as absolute increases or decreases, or as spatial redistributions depending on the size of the region under study, and the explanatory requirements would be different in each case (Adams 1972; Andrews 1973; Parsons 1969; Sanders 1973). In a study of the population history of the Valley of Mexico, for example, the Tula region is included during Second Intermediate and Late Horizon times, on the basis of ethnohistoric evidence of close ties between the two areas (Sanders *et al.* 1976:177). It is not clear how purely archaeological evidence would indicate the need for an expansion of the study area during these periods.

The analysis of long-distance interaction, by definition, requires an areal focus; much current work emphasizes the role of trade and economic symbiosis and thus the significance of large-scale environmental differences (Rathje 1971; Sanders and Price 1968) or of the volume and selectivity of interaction with resource sources (Ericson 1977; Flannery 1968b; Rathje 1975; Renfrew 1977). Common to many of these studies are concepts of demands stimulated either by environmental deficiencies of "necessary" items (Rathje 1971) or by prestige requirements for exotic materials (Flannery 1968b). The identification of "necessities," however, must involve the question of cultural preferences, which may be only partially explicable by empirical study. The import of obsidian into the Maya Lowlands, for example, might appear "rational" and "necessary" after a detailed comparison of technological attributes of obsidian with any local materials and a cost–benefit analysis of their respective procurement systems—but only with some assumptions regarding desirable technical qualities and energy conservation.

Transaction Currencies

A third organizational dimension of ecological work might be according to the currency of transactions investigated. The tasks of measuring and comparing human behavior in relation to the environment require that some common dimensions or scales be used. The ecological view of interactions as exchanges of energy, matter, and information suggests some common currencies to which many transactions may be reduced (Flannery 1972). Ecological archaeology has shown a tendency through time to shift emphasis from matter to energy exchanges, with information-processing as an emerging focus.

Energy. The current primacy of energy as a currency stems in part from its wide applicability in that other currencies can potentially be reduced to energetic equivalents; foods, for example, can be measured for their caloric equivalents. Even information has been expressed as the degree of organization of matter or energy caused by doing work (Margalef 1968). Consequently, energy as an ecological currency has gained wide acceptance and, in addition, is valuable to cross-cultural studies because of its freedom from cultural context (Odend'hal 1972). Studies of energy contents, energy flow, and energetic costs and benefits form an important part of ecological research (Athens 1977; Blanton 1975a; Gall and Saxe 1977; Hayden 1975; Schalk 1977; Shawcross 1972; Wilkinson 1972).

Implicit in many of these studies is the concept of an energy budget, in which energy (or time, or personnel) is a limited resource requiring decisions regarding its allotment. Yet the upper limit of this budget, and how this limit is altered by technological or organizational changes, has not been quantified. Furthermore, energy is too often regarded as the only currency, and a goal of maximum energetic efficiency to put this budget in the black is considered the overriding aim of all decisions.

Matter and Information.   The focus on energetics, however, is not sufficient. People use and exchange many materials for their content other than calories, including nutrients such as protein (Gross 1975; Marner 1977; Lange 1971; Sanders 1973; Shimkin 1973). Other substances are important as raw materials: the technological usefulness of obsidian, clay, and copper ore is not defined by the caloric equivalents of these materials, so that although the energetics of their procurement may be a valuable focus, there are many other factors requiring examination. Furthermore, the information contained in objects is not limited to the degree of organization of their molecules but, more important, includes the meaning assigned to this organization. Studies of archaeological provenience may aid interpretations in this respect (Flannery 1968b, 1976c; Paulsen 1974; Pires-Ferreira 1976; Pyne 1976; Sidrys 1977). Similarly, Millon (1976:244–247) has stressed that the understanding of the role of sites (such as Teotihuacan) in a settlement system requires an analysis not only of economic activities, but also of religious functions as well.

Flannery (1972) has called for a direction of attention to the flow of information and the processes of decision-making as necessary to ecological studies, particularly those dealing with more complex societies, and several works document the growing concern with these factors (Blanton 1976b; Peebles and Kus 1977; Rathje 1975; Renfrew 1975; Wright and Johnson 1975). Again, a threshold concept seems to be involved here, relating complexity of decisions to the structure of decision-making institutions. If one could indeed measure the "channel capacity" for information flow of various institutions, together with the volume of information flow in various cultural systems, this approach could be a powerful research framework. These problems of measurement notwithstanding, it can provide a valuable guide to the formulation of hypotheses.

Level of Organizational Complexity

Regional Populations. Ecological studies might also be viewed along a fourth dimension—that of the level of organizational complexity investigated. That is, systems can be constructed with different degrees of inclusiveness, and the behavioral patterns detected will vary according to the level of organization examined. By analogy with the biological emphasis on populations, most archaeological research focuses on local or regional groups or societies as the units of behavior. If these units can be identified in the archaeological record, then their structure can be described in terms of such properties as density, birth and death rates, age distribution, growth form, and spatial distribution, and their aggregate behavior in terms of population regulation, energy flow, dispersal, competition, and mutualism. Such patterned aggregate behavior is usually analyzed for its adaptive significance through its contribution to group maintenance or expansion.

Major criticisms of such approaches point out that groups are rarely the units of behavior or of adaptation, and that the research focus should be placed upon subgroups, classes, and individuals (Chang 1975; Cowgill 1975a,b; Shimkin 1973; Vayda and McCay 1975). Certainly there exist group characteristics; these may be examined as part of the context of individual or class behavior. Also, there may be varying degrees of group cohesion, depending upon the processes of concensus, cooperation, coaxing, and coercion, but this property must be investigated and treated as yet another group characteristic, not assumed to underlie behavior. A similar problem of units of analysis exists in the field of biological ecology, and as Orians (1973:1239) states, "Perhaps the greatest challenge for contemporary ecology is the development of theories about the properties of communities on the basis of selection for the attributes of their component individuals." Ecological archaeology faces this challenge as well.

Cultural Systems. On a different level of complexity, some recent work has emphasized the study of whole cultural systems (Gall and Saxe 1977; Peebles and Kus 1977; Rathje 1973, 1975; Sabloff and Lamberg-Karlovsky 1974; Tainter 1977). Characteristics of the entire system so examined find their analogy in the macroecological properties of community ecology (for example, stability, homeostasis, diversity, and maturity). Studies on this level offer fascinating comparisons among systems of various types, but the value of such general systems approaches has been questioned (Spaulding 1973). Too often, analogies are drawn between cultural systems and biological communities and ecosystems in order to draw upon supposed regularities or laws of biological succession or evolution.

Such temporal patterns in group or system properties have been a principal concern of many ecologists. Relatively short-term studies of species replacement in a community have described patterned trends of succession leading to a climax. Longer-term studies have depicted temporal patterns in the evolution of ecosystems:

> Succession is in progress everywhere and evolution follows, encased in succession's frame. As a consequence, we expect to find a parallel trend in several phylogenetic lines which can also be recognized as a trend realized in succession [Margalef 1968:81].

Among the trends postulated have been increase in biomass, stability, stratification, complexity, diversity, efficiency of production, and information (Margalef 1968:28–29). Some of these suggested changes have since been found not to occur in every case (Colinvaux 1973:549; Margalef 1968:30–32; Slobodkin 1977:334). Others do seem to take place, but the fact has been suggested to be trivial: for example, an increase in complexity and diversity of life through time is inevitable in the evolution of life from nonliving matter or in the colonization by plants and animals of an empty landscape (Colinvaux 1973:550–563). Other than a general direction, from simple to complex, there seem to be no consistent trends in evolution or succession (Dobzhansky 1974; Sauer 1977; Slobodkin 1977; Stebbins 1974). And even this general direction is observable only in retrospect: "It does not follow that the evolution is being directed by some outside agency, or that it has been programmed beforehand" (Dobzhansky 1974:311). In a concurring view, Colinvaux states:

> In the proper Darwinian view of ecology there is no organizing principle behind succession. Successions are not directed by some holistic process of the superorganism. Nor, and this is much more important to modern ecology, are they directed by negative feedbacks of ever-refining ecosystems [1973:571].

Changes in macroscopic cultural characteristics through time have similarly been described as showing general directions or trends. Among those suggested have been increased complexity and diversification, efficiency of energy use, size of social group, carrying capacity, and stability (Durham 1976:95). In the definition and analysis of these trends, many have relied on analogies between societies and organisms, communities, or ecosystems. If such general biological, successional, or evolutionary trends might now be lacking or trivial, then the value of any analogies is dubious. Certainly we can identify temporal trends in cultural behavior and its complexity—in retrospect. Much of this directionality derives from the simple fact that the present builds upon the past, that present solutions have been constructed in the context of previous decisions. Additional complications, incidentally, derive from the mixing of analogies by simultaneously conferring properties of biological populations (predation) and communities (maturity) on cultural systems (Gall and Saxe 1977).

Such analogies are often provocative and may suggest characteristics worthy of further investigation. Their great danger, however, derives from their tendency to lead to discussions of system behavior, system strategies, and system goals. As shorthand descriptions these discussions may be heuristically valuable, but they may lead to an acceptance of behavioral interpretations at this level. If a wide theoretical gap separates individual and group behavior, then a chasm divides the behavior of individuals and their cultural systems. Systems approaches have great value; explanations of system behavior pose tremendous problems of translation into human terms.

Systemic Property

Homeostasis.   A fifth dimension along which ecological studies might be examined is the nature of the dominant system property or process emphasized. On the one hand, ecological work has shown great preoccupation with stability, maintenance, and homeostatic regulation (Clark 1975; Drennan 1976; Hayden 1975; Odner 1972; Wilkinson 1972). Such studies often focus on short time ranges, may explicitly seek various proximate limiting factors in the environment, and attempt to determine negative feedback processes in a systems framework. Here, again, the ratio between population and resources is a central concern. Too frequently there has been a tendency to assume a stable ratio to be the normal state of most systems; the current preoccupation with population pressure as a causal agent of cultural change, therefore, prompts a search for the special conditions leading to this abnormal development. Dumond (1972) and others, on the other hand, take the opposite view: that population growth is the normal situation and any equilibrium is abnormal, requiring work to maintain. Although it may be neither possible nor valuable to determine any generally "normal" state of cultural systems, both extreme views are useful in constructing models and developing hypotheses and their implications.

Change.   By contrast, there is an equal ecological devotion to change, evolution, and adaptive processes (Athens 1977; Blanton 1975a; Braun 1974; Earle 1977; Fitzhugh 1976; Grabert and Larsen 1975; Tainter 1977; Webster 1975; Winter 1976). These studies usually utilize longer time ranges and seek to define processes of positive feedback. Criticisms of ecological work have pointed out problems of reconciling these two approaches, of accounting for change once an equilibrium state has been demonstrated (summarized in Vayda and McCay 1975). Some work has posited the need for extra-systemic "kicks" such as sea level changes and plant mutations for the origins of agriculture (Binford 1968; Flannery 1968a). In later work, explanatory emphasis has been given to the dynamic nature of any equilibrium (Ammerman 1975; Dumond 1972, 1975; Harpending and Bertram 1975), so that the relationship between humans and their environment is viewed as constantly in flux. Dumond's (1972) work has the additional advantage of being organized within a decision-making framework, allowing for either stability or change as possible outcomes.

The emphases on stability or change, therefore, might be viewed as stressing adjustments to small perturbations on the one hand, or responses to large perturbations on the other. The dividing line between "small" and "large" is, of course, undefined, but its implicit assumption in many works again raises the problem of thresholds—in this case separating stability from change in a system. Following Rappaport (1968), such thresholds might be viewed as points where accumulated quantitative factors are transformed through some "switch" into qualitative changes. The neatness of this mechanical model is appealing, yet our inability so far to quantify such points suggests that the model system is too highly structured and coherent to correspond to cultural systems. How many female complaints and garden invasions among the Tsembaga are necessary to trigger the pig festival?

We might more profitably view the "switches" as choices that, given their underlying goals, might occur with varying probabilties in different situations. Tsembaga pig festivals *could* be held at almost any time, although they become increasingly likely, the more frequent the complaints and garden invasions. Such quantitative factors, which may increase the probability of a particular choice, could be identified. Furthermore, it is necessary to realize that a decision could be made whatever its statistical probability, but that only certain situations will support it and amplify its effects through positive feedback. Rather than expecting some fixed mechanical threshold for cultural change, consequently—whether this is in terms of number of complaints, volume of trade, or length of irrigation canals—it may be more valuable to seek factors influencing the probability and reinforcement of particular choices.

Problem

A sixth and final method of breaking down human ecosystems—one that has been frequently advocated but only sporadically applied—is to focus on various problems, hazards, stresses, or demands. The most explicit archaeological statement of this approach is that by Sanders (1968:120): "Each biological and physical environment offers certain problems to human utilization." More recent work has enlarged the realm of relevant problems to include technological, demographic, and sociopolitical factors as well, and thus to approach the holistic ideal of ecology (Vayda and McCay 1975). If problems become a central focus, then the relevant variables can be specified and examined and their implications for human responses assessed. Research can be directed toward investigating the frequency and magnitude of the problem, the means available for solutions, the goals guiding solutions, the conflicting demands of different problems, and the secondary effects of different solutions.

Problems, means, and solutions can be identified within any of the traditional categories of anthropological concern and at any level of spatial complexity. The perception and context of each individual's problems may be unique or widely shared. Choices of solutions may be numerous or strictly limited by the recognized available means. Solutions may be consciously chosen or the product of habit and tradition. The choices may be made by each individual or by designated authorities. The goals guiding these solutions may be culturally or individually specific.

Similar problems may have been faced by other animal species, and numerous viable solutions in the form of morphology and behavior would have been attained in the course of evolution through natural selection. The nature of these solutions and their relationship to the species' environmental interactions form the subject of ecology. Any general ecological techniques and principles, consequently, that describe common features of such solutions may be potentially applicable to humans, and this is the thesis of cultural ecology.

A focus on behavior as problem solving makes any distinction between the "cognized" and "objective" environments less troublesome (Rappaport 1968). The perceived environment is crucial to understanding the decisions and solutions; it allows investigation of the recognition of problems, the awareness of potential solutions, and the evaluation of realized benefits. A more objective appraisal of the environment, by contrast, allows an evaluation of long-term impact and secondary ramifications of solutions. Furthermore, such an objective view can be defined in terms applicable to many areas, which can be measured cross-culturally.

Ecological investigations could, in part, be focused on the constraints on choices of responses, such as technological capabilities, institutionalized demands, sanctioned options, and the activities of other individuals. Equally important, and only recently stressed in ecological anthropology (Cowgill 1975a,b; Dumond 1972; Logan and Sanders 1976;

Rutz 1977; Shimkin 1973), are the goals guiding the choices among various alternatives. Value systems have frequently been excluded from discussion by ecological anthropolotists because they are nonmaterial and not reducible to caloric equivalents. In a view of behavior as problem solving requiring choices, a framework exists for incorporating this aspect of ideology into an ecological system. No decision is made in a vacuum, but it is made to attain preferred ends, and these preferences may vary among individuals, classes, and societies. It must be realized, too, that decisions or goals themselves may be in conflict: each individual must make multiple choices involving numerous aspects of behavior, each demanding time and energy, and each perhaps guided by a different set of preferences or norms. The result may be that the actual behavior of an individual represents a compromise solution to these competing demands. No single factor such as energetic efficiency or risk minimization may be maximized.

Dumond (1972:288) for example, has suggested that decisions affecting the relationship between population and resources will "involve a balance among three components—the satisfaction of material wants, the satisfaction of affective relationships (including purely symbolic ones, as with gods), and the expenditure of least effort." He goes on to postulate that none of these is maximized; rather, relative deprivation is minimized, which in turn depends upon cultural standards and individual experience. Logan and Sanders (1976:37) discuss agricultural strategies in the Basin of Mexico in terms of effort minimization and security of crop yield. Jochim (1976) investigates hunter–gatherer subsistence choices as compromises between goals of maximization of security and efficiency. Few archaeologists, however, have discussed the mechanisms whereby such goals are translated into decisions in specific situations. Here the techniques of game theory (Shimkin and Lowe 1977) and linear programming (Reidhead 1977) will prove valuable simulation devices.

A focus on individual behavior does not deny the existence of group characteristics, nor the value of their study. Populations may be compared in terms of their age and sex structure and spatial distribution, communities or systems in terms of their diversity, stability, and structure. Such emergent, macroecological properties may be viewed in several ways: as the aggregate of various individual decisions and activities, as the result of cooperation by individuals to attain solutions, and as part of the context of such individual behavior. An individual of a widely dispersed population in a highly fluctuating environment faces different problems and is likely to behave in a manner different from one in a crowded, stable environment. A comparison of populations in terms of their aggregate or cooperative behavior or structure of decision making may help to explain differential adaptive success. Changes in group characteristics through time may suggest changing strategies of individual adaptation.

An emphasis on problems seems to be emerging in the ecological literature. Many stimulating studies are working "from the ground up," examining specific environments, habitat types, or resource bases for their implications for human use. Andrews (1973), Rathje (1971) and Sanders (1968), for example, are quite explicit in their discussions of the problems inherent in the Maya Lowlands, as is Flannery (1969) about the oak woodlands of the Near East, and Butzer (1976) regarding the Nile Valley. General problematic characteristics of arid lands (Day 1974; Harpending and Bertram 1975; Plog 1975), cold archipelagoes (McCartney 1975), arctic marine environments (Fitzhugh 1975, 1976; Tuck 1976), anadromous fish resources (Schalk 1977), and big game species (Burch 1972; Wilkinson 1975) have been similarly investigated with a focus on their potential implications for exploitation. Various aspects of technology and resource procurement are increasingly being examined, not simply as examples of human–environmental interaction, but as solutions to subsistence problems and as potential sources of additional problems themselves. The *implications* of swidden agriculture (Brush 1975, Carneiro 1956; Willey and Shimkin 1973), irrigation farming (Jacobsen and Adams 1958), and sunken fields (Parsons and Psuty 1975) in terms of soil depletion, erosion, grass invasion, and salt build-up are stressed. The scheduling problems of mixed economies and the risks of monocropping are receiving increased attention (Athens 1977; Ford 1974; Gall and Saxe 1977; Peebles and Kus 1977). The import of food and other raw materials is being analyzed both as a solution to shortages and demands and as a source of additional problems requiring organizational responses (Culbert 1973b; Rathje 1973). Allocation systems of sharing and redistribution are questioned in terms of their relationship to problems of environmental diversity and in light of their inherent properties and problems (Earle 1977; Peebles and Kus 1977; Shimkin 1973; Webb 1973).

As mentioned earlier, overpopulation or population pressure plays a prominent role as a widespread problem in interpretations of prehistoric change (but see Blanton 1976a; Cowgill 1975a,b for critiques of explanations based mainly on "population pressure"). Solutions are seen in subsistence change and intensification, technological development, organizational restructuring, population movements, and warfare. The problem of *under*population or shortages of labor or skills has received less attention but may be equally significant (Shimkin 1973). It might be valuable to investigate the ratio not only of population to resources, but also of producers to consumers, or of production to the demands of the elite. The spatial distribution of people as well as of resources may be problematic in terms of their interaction or integration (Sanders 1973; Wobst 1974, 1975).

Variable Measurement

One requirement of both a systems framework and an interest in archaeological comparisons is the development of quantitative techniques of measuring relevant variables (Fitzhugh 1975). This need for measuring devices is underscored by the disagreements in the literature over various environmental characteristics of significance to human adaptations. For example, the Northwest Coast of North America has been described as both uniform and rich (Drucker 1965) and as variable and periodically poor (Piddocke 1965; Suttles 1962). Braun (1974) and Ritchie (1969) disagree over the visibility and ease of collection of certain Atlantic coastal shellfish. The agricultural potential of various regions has been debated for the Valley of Mexico (Blanton 1975b; Charlton 1975) as well as for other parts of the world (Ferdon 1959; Meggers 1954). Clearly, any discussion of environmental constraints, problems, or potential requires some objective measures.

Many studies have presented refinements of such measuring techniques—for example, of climatological variables (Baerreis *et al.* 1976), faunal seasonality (Bourque *et al.* 1978), site populations (Longacre 1976; Marcus 1976), site exploitation zones and their productivity (Flannery 1976a,e; Jarman 1972; Rossman 1976; Zarky 1976), raw material sources and distribution (Earle and Ericson 1977a; Hammond *et al.* 1977; Weigand *et al.* 1977), and even social mobility and complexity (Rathje 1973; Tainter 1977). Reliability of various measures has come under scrutiny (Moore *et al.* 1975; Plog 1975), and suggestions for improving accuracy have included the use of several measures simultaneously (Ammerman *et al.* 1976; Birdsell 1975).

In most cases the archaeological materials available for measurement reflect only indirectly the variables sought. Thus, Cohen (1975) seeks evidence for population pressure among hunter–gatherers in measures of various behavioral shifts, such as increased geographic range of exploitation and increased sedentism, greater dietary variety and reduced dietary variety. Beyond the fact that these measures are mutually contradictory, this approach is problematic. If population pressure is to be used to explain behavioral changes, then such changes cannot be used to measure population pressure in the first place.

A more direct approach is taken by Brumfiel (1976), who investigates the mathematical relationship between measures of site population and catchment productivity; this approach is promising, although its value, of course, depends on the reliability of the component measurements (see also Sanders 1976). Hayden (1975) discusses various types of evidence to be derived from skeletal material to detect nutritional stress and hence resource overexploitation, but before this evidence is taken to indicate population pressure, other potential determinants such as socially limited access to food must be considered. In a similar vein, Fitzhugh (1976) points out that the only direct evidence of the effects of climatic change on animal populations would be in the skeletal material of the animals themselves. Madsen and Berry (1975) criticize assumptions of pinyon nut exploitation in the prehistoric Great Basin because of the lack of direct evidence in the form of nut hulls, although Thomas (1973) has provided much indirect evidence in the form of settlement and artifact distributions. DeBoer (1975) has pointed out the dangers of inferring manioc cultivation from the presence of ceramic platters and obsidian chips. Investigators of the relationship between artifacts and their functions through analyses of wear and spatial distribution have been cautioned on the role of other determinants of variability (Brose 1975).

Some general attributes of environmental problems that are receiving increasing attention in archaeological research include spatiotemporal variability and uncertainty (Adams 1975; Peebles and Kus 1977), and an emphasis on these attributes is profoundly influencing the techniques of variable measurement. Sanders (1973:331) stresses the need for "good ecological surveys that break down the Maya Lowlands into smaller ecological zones that may have played an important role in the distribution of Maya population." He then discusses evidence for great soil variability in the Peten, while the variability in annual precipitation within the same area is emphasized by Shimkin (1973). Goodyear (1975) has produced a detailed, quantitative mapping of vegetation in the Papaguaria region of Arizona as a necessary part of investigations into Desert Hohokam subsistence and settlement. Fitzhugh (1976) and Taylor (1975) have given detailed consideration to variability in ice conditions in their work on Canadian coastal environments. Many workers stratify survey regions according to topography, in order to accommodate regional variability in subsistence potential, although Plog (1975) has cautioned against the assumption of the automatic importance of such strata to prehistoric subsistence. A related trend is the emphasis on the predictability of variation, in which cycles of different frequencies and the role of stochastic fluctuation are stressed (Fitzhugh 1976; Harpending and Bertram 1975; Hayden 1975; Shimkin 1973; Thomas 1972). The importance of uncertainty as a factor related to many problems is increasingly being recognized, whether in the context of individual decisions or system regulation.

Variable Relationships

Once a complex human ecosystem is broken down and certain variables are isolated for study, archaeologists must develop techniques for determining patterns of variable relationships, hypotheses about the underlying processes of interaction, and methods of testing these hypotheses. Spatial distributions are an important component of ecological studies, and much recent work has been directed toward their analysis. Such work included methods of detecting patterns of artifacts (Schiffer 1975; Vierra and Taylor 1977; Whallon 1973, 1974), settlements (Earle 1977; Johnson 1975; Reynolds 1976), and trade items (Ericson 1977; Renfrew 1975, 1977; Sidrys 1977). Increasingly, there is a departure from intuitive assessments and assumptions of simple linear relationships among variables and the attempt to develop methods of detecting nonlinear relationships (including the concept of thresholds), of examining the multiple interrelationships that characterize systems, and of including the effects of random processes in the analysis.

Many sources are drawn upon for hypotheses about the processes underlying such patterns. Ethnographic studies still play a large part (Ericson 1977; Peebles and Kus 1977), as does economics (Renfrew 1975, 1977), and ecological generalizations are finding increased use (Athens 1977; Gall and Saxe 1977; Schalk 1977; Wilkinson 1972). A recent development is the growing use of ethnoarchaeology and ethnohistory on the one hand (Binford and Bertram 1975; Binford and Chasko 1976; Taylor 1975; Yellen 1977) and of modeling procedures on the other (Flannery 1976d; Harpending and Bertram 1975; Longacre 1976; Thomas 1972; Wobst 1974; Zubrow 1976b). The former has the advantage of allowing observation of interaction processes, the latter of their simulation. Each constitutes an invaluable source of hypotheses and their test implications.

In light of the widespread borrowing by ecological archaeologists of generalizations from other disciplines, there must be a clear recognition of their hypothetical nature. In ecological archaeology, as in other approaches, there is a general concern for the formulation and testing of hypotheses. Unfortunately, most testing is currently at the stage of demonstrating correlations among variable distributions in time or space, which, as many writers state, may be suggestive but do not constitute proof of underlying relationships. A common focus of much ecological work, for example, is the demonstration of a temporal correlation between changes in environment and subsistence and settlement (Braun 1974; Dumond 1975; Grabert and Larsen 1975; Madsen and Berry 1975; Winter 1976), environment and sociopolitical organization (Bell 1971), the volume of trade goods and their distribution (Sidrys 1977), or subsistence practices and social complexity (Fitzhugh 1975; Peebles and Kus 1977). Such correlations are a necessary part of establishing the nature of systemic relationships, but are in no way sufficient.

Other ecological studies deal with spatial correlations in an attempt to understand processes. The concentration of modern ramon trees around Maya sites is suggestive of prehistoric subsistence (Puleston 1971). The pattern of trade items in relation to trails or waterways may indicate transport methods (Ericson 1977; Sidrys 1977). Differential densities of artifacts and sites in various environmental zones may suggest subsistence patterns and site functions (Bettinger 1977; Goodyear 1975; Thomas 1973), and site size and density in relation to environmental productivity may constitute evidence for the nature of population growth and regulation (Brumfiel 1976; Sanders 1973; Zubrow 1976b). The suggestion by Logan and Sanders (1976:51) that the development of craft specialization may be related to a lack of suitable local agricultural land might be supported by the demonstration of a spatial correlation between these two factors. In any single study, the correlations are indeed suggestive, but the reality of the underlying processual complexity becomes clear when the huge number of variables that are correlated cross-culturally is examined (see, e.g., Zubrow 1976a:10–11).

The approach of human biogeography (see *World Archaeology* **8**, 1977) seeks to demonstrate similarities between the spatial behavior of humans and that of other organisms, in an attempt to explain this behavior in relation to environmental factors. Similar patterns of colonization of unoccupied land by humans and birds, for example, might suggest similarities of problems faced and solutions attained by the two populations. Nevertheless, the means by which these solutions are reached would clearly differ, so that the processes underlying decisions are not revealed. The principal value of such studies would seem to be to highlight problems and the environmental factors relevant to their solution.

Much rarer in the literature, but perhaps more informative, are demonstrations of a lack of correlation where one might be expected. Ericson (1977), for example, has described the absence of a spatial correlation between the distribution of obsidian and ethnolinguistic boundaries in California, which seems to contradict certain models of reciprocity and social interaction. Andrews (1973) has criticized various theories on the Maya collapse because they do not adequately account for events in the Central and Northern Lowlands; that is, the proposed causal processes do not show a spatial correlation with their supposed effects. McGhee (1976) has pointed out the lack of temporal correlation between Paleoeskimo occupation of Arctic fringe regions and climatic events, thus urging the abandonment of simple causal explanations. In each case, the absence of a correlation would seem to constitute a more significant test than its presence. Archaeology might profit more at this stage from a systematic refutation of hypotheses than from the progressive accumulation of positive correlations.

A serious problem that has yet to be resolved is that similar patterns of variable relationships can be produced by different underlying processes (Hodder and Orton 1976). Adams (1975), for example, has suggested that religious factors as well as processes of administered trade could have produced the settlement patterns of Lower Mesopotamia studied by Johnson (1975). A variety of processes that could lead to centralized grain storage have been proposed by Chang (1975). Renfrew (1975) has demonstrated that two different models of exchange can produce similar distributions of materials. Plog (1975) has pointed out that a random distribution of sites in the Hay Hollow Valley could produce a pattern that is attributed by Zubrow (1975) to factors of environmental productivity. In fact, it has recently been asserted for many spatial distributions that "Different spatial processes can produce the same spatial form" (Clark 1978). Similar problems exist with the interpretation of the patterns of demographic life tables (Moore *et al.* 1975).

In the face of these problems, archaeology must not, of course, abandon the examination of patterns or the search for processes. Rather, research might more profitably proceed from process to pattern, rather than the reverse. That is, the multiple implications of a single hypothesized process could be explored. If shrine maintenance and trade administration, for example, could produce a similar pattern of specialized settlements in Lower Mesopotamia, then surely these two processes can be differentiated by their implications for other aspects of the archaeological record. Johnson (1975) has, in fact, considered multiple lines of evidence in his studies, so perhaps in this case the competing hypothesis should be operationalized and tested against these classes of materials as well. Only through such multiple testing can interpretations of reasonable probability be reached.

System Reassembly

If most ecological archaeology proceeds by initially focusing on limited subsystems of human behavior, then a primary responsibility of this approach is to reassemble these subsystems in order to achieve the ideally holistic explanations of human–environmental interactions. A legitimate doubt might be raised, of course, about the value of trying to construct any intelligible explanations out of such poorly understood parts. Yet the attempts will proceed regardless of such doubts, and certainly some major trends and hopes can be outlined.

Research that is organized at the level of cultural systems finds no need for such reassembly. Its scope is broad, its processes general. However, as has been argued above, this generality may, in fact, hinder understanding of human behavior. Such work is valuable, but perhaps primarily as an organizational framework for detecting patterns that can lead to hypotheses. The understanding of these patterns, the tests of these hypotheses, must involve translation into human actions. This may be simply a personal bias, but this author finds discussions of "systemic strategies of increased hierarchical complexity" quite unilluminating as explanations. Again, it is not a systems framework that is criticized, nor the use of ecosystemic models, but the acceptance of explanations involving behavior on this level.

One solution to the problem of reassembling human ecosystems has been to assign one subsystem causal priority, thereby placing other components in a dependent position. Steward's (1955) pioneering work on cultural ecology has been criticized for his adoption of this solution when he assigned causal priority to subsistence and technology (Vayda and Rappaport 1968). Yet much of recent ecological work seems to have chosen this solution as well, with its causal emphasis on population growth and pressure. Boserup (1965) notwithstanding, there is no evidence to indicate the independence of population growth; its proponents simply minimize its dependent relationships, and this emphasis has been justly criticized. "It seriously hinders our understanding to think of population growth as a relatively autonomous 'prime mover' which in turn stimulates other changes" (Cowgill 1975b:129).

The focus on the problem-solving aspects of behavior, on the other hand, should allow the organization and assembling of diverse approaches without subordinating so many aspects of behavior to a position of simplistic dependence. Natural and social environments may be examined as sources of problems and of the means to their solution. Budgets of energy, nutrients, materials, and special knowledge may be constructed in order to assess options and competing demands. Different individual or group contexts may be evaluated in relation to the goals guiding the choice of solutions. The adequacy of solutions must be analyzed in light of the difficulties of perceiving different problems, the inability to foresee all the implications of solutions, the competing demands of simultaneously solving several problems, and the possible inflexibility of learning and behavior in response to changing problems.

The fact that more than one solution is possible for a given problem must be realized, but such apparent functional alternatives should be examined for their specific differences: their relative costs, speed, and flexibility (Rappaport 1971), as well as their secondary implications. In addition, different problems might be solved by the same solutions; the adequacy of the solution in each case might be investigated. Finally, solutions may affect or constrain one another, and may pose problems of their own. To what extent the archaeological record of cultural evolution represents a chain of solutions and secondary problems is an intriguing question.

REFERENCES

Adams, R. E. W. (editor)
1977   *The origins of Maya civilization*. Albuquerque: University of New Mexico Press.
Adams, R. McC.
1972   Patterns of urbanization in early southern Mesopotamia. In *Man, settlement and urbanism*, edited by P. J. Ucko, R. Tringham, and G. W. Dimbleby. London: Duckworth. Pp. 735–750.
1975   The emerging place of trade in civilizational studies. In *Ancient civilization and trade*, edited by J. A. Sabloff and C. C. Lamberg-Karlovsky. Albuquerque: University of New Mexico Press. Pp. 451–466.
Ammerman, A. J.
1975   Late Pleistocene population dynamics: An alternative view. *Human Ecology* **3**:219–234.
Ammerman, A. J., L. L. Cavalli-Sforza, and D. K. Wagener
1976   Toward the estimation of population growth in Old World prehistory. In *Demographic anthropology*, edited by E. B. W. Zubrow. Albuquerque: University of New Mexico Press. Pp. 27–62.
Andrews, E. W. IV
1973   The development of Maya civilization after abandonment of the southern cities. In *The Classic Maya collapse*, edited by T. P. Culbert. Albuquerque: University of New Mexico Press. Pp. 243–268.
Athens, J. S.
1977   Theory building and the study of evolutionary process in complex societies. In *For theory building in archaeology*, edited by L. R. Bindord. New York: Academic Press. Pp. 353–384.
Baerreis, D. A., R. A. Bryson, and J. E. Kutzbach
1976   Climate and culture in the Western Great Lakes region. *Mid-Continental Journal of Archaeology* **1**:39–58.
Bell, B.
1971   The Dark Ages in ancient history. *American Journal of Archaeology* **75**:1–26.

Bettinger, R. L.
   1977   Aboriginal human ecology in Owens Valley: Prehistoric change in the Great
          Basin. *American Antiquity* **42:**3–17.
Binford, L. R.
   1968   Post-Pleistocene adaptations. In *New perspectives in archaeology,* edited by
          L. R. Binford and S. R. Binford. Chicago: Aldine. Pp. 313–340.
Binford, L. R., and J. B. Bertram
   1977   Bone frequencies—And attritional processes. In *For theory building in ar-
          chaeology,* edited by L. R. Binford. New York: Academic Press. Pp. 77–156.
Binford, L. R., and W. J. Chasko, Jr.
   1976   Nunamiut demographic history: A provocative case. In *Demographic an-
          thropology,* edited by E. B. W. Zubrow. Albuquerque: University of New
          Mexico Press. Pp. 63–144.
Birdsell, J. B.
   1975   A preliminary report on new research on man–land relations in Aboriginal
          Australia. *Society for American Archaeology, Memoirs* **30:**34–37.
Blanton, R. E.
   1975a The cybernetic analysis of human population growth. *Society for American
          Archaeology, Memoirs* **30:**116–126.
   1975b Texcoco Region archaeology. *American Antiquity* **40:**227–230.
   1976a Comment on Sanders, Parsons, and Logan. In *The Valley of Mexico*, edited by
          E. R. Wolf. Albuquerque: University of New Mexico Press. Pp. 179–180.
   1976b The role of symbiosis in adaptation and sociocultural change in the Valley of
          Mexico. In *The Valley of Mexico,* edited by E. R. Wolf. Albuquerque: Univer-
          sity of New Mexico Press. Pp. 181–202.
Boserup, E.
   1965   *The conditions of agricultural growth.* Chicago: Aldine.
Bourque, B. J., K. Morris, and A. Spiess
   1978   Determining the season of death of mammal teeth from archaeological sites: A
          new sectioning technique. *Science* **199:**530–531.
Braun, D. P.
   1974   Explanatory models for the evolution of coastal adaptation in prehistoric east-
          ern New England. *American Antiquity* **39:**582–596.
Bronson, B.
   1966   Roots and the subsistence of the ancient Maya. *Southwestern Journal of An-
          thropology* **22:**251–279.
Brose, D. S.
   1975   Functional analysis of stone tools: A cautionary note on the role of animal fats.
          American Antiquity **40:**86–93.
Brown, A. F. B.
   1973   Bone strontium content as a dietary indicator in human skeletal populations.
          Ph.D. dissertation, University of Michigan, Ann Arbor.
Brumfiel, E.
   1976   Regional growth in the Eastern Valley of Mexico: A test of the "population
          pressure" hypothesis. In *The early Mesoamerican village*, edited by K. V.
          Flannery. New York: Academic Press. Pp. 234–247.
Brush, S. B.
   1975   The concept of carrying capacity for systems of shifting cultivation. *American
          Anthropologist* **77:**799–811.

Bryant, V. M., Jr., and G. Williams-Dean
    1975   The coprolites of Man. In *Avenues to antiquity,* edited by B. M. Fagan. San Francisco: Freeman. Pp. 257–266.
Burch, E. S.
    1972   The caribou/wild reindeer as a human resource. *American Antiquity* **37**:339–368.
Butzer, K. W.
    1976   *Early hydraulic civilization in Egypt.* Chicago: University of Chicago Press.
Carneiro, R. L.
    1956   Slash-and-burn agriculture: A closer look at its implications for settlement patterns. In *Men and cultures,* edited by A. F. C. Wallace (Selected Papers of the Fifth International Congress of Anthropological and Ethnological Sciences). Philadelphia: University of Pennsylvania Press. Pp. 229–234.
    1970   A theory on the origin of the State. *Science* **169**:733–738.
Casteel, R. W.
    1972a Some archaeological uses of fish remains. *American Antiquity* **37**:404–419.
    1972b Two static maximum population-density models for hunter–gatherers: A first approximation. *World Archaeology* **4**:19–40.
    1974   On the remains of fish scales from archaeological sites. *American Antiquity* **39**:557–581.
Chang, K. C.
    1975   Ancient trade as economics or as ecology. In *Ancient civilization and trade,* edited by J. A. Sabloff and C. C. Lamberg-Karlovsky. Albuquerque: University of New Mexico Press. Pp. 211–224.
Charlton, T. M.
    1973   Texcoco region archaeology and the *Codex Xolotl. American Antiquity* **38**:412–422.
    1975   From Teotihuacan to Tenochtitlan: The Early Period revisited. *American Antiquity* **40**:231–234.
Chartkoff, J. L., and K. K. Chartkoff
    1975   Late Period settlement of the Middle Klamath River of northwest California. *American Antiquity* **40**:172–179.
Clark, D. W.
    1975   Technological continuity and change within a persistent maritime adaptation: Kodiak Island, Alaska. In *Prehistoric maritime adaptations of the circumpolar zone,* edited by W. Fitzhugh. The Hague: Mouton. Pp. 203–228.
Clark, G. A.
    1978   Review of *Spatial analysis in archaeology,* by I. Hodder and C. Orton. *American Antiquity* **43**:132–135.
Clark, J. G. D.
    1972   *Star Carr: A case study in bioarchaeology. Addison-Wesley Modular Publications in Anthropology* No. 10.
Coe, M. D., and K. V. Flannery
    1864   Microenvironments and Mesoamerican prehistory. *Science* **143**:650–654.
Cohen, M. N.
    1975   Archaeological evidence for population pressure in pre-agricultural societies. *American Antiquity* **40**:471–474.
    1977   *The food crisis in prehistory.* New Haven: Yale University Press.

Colinvaux, P.
    1973   *Introduction to ecology*. New York: Wiley.
Cordell, L. S.
    1977   Late Anasazi farming and hunting strategies: One example of a problem in congruence. *American Antiquity* **42**:449–461.
Covich, A. P.
    1976   Analyzing shapes of foraging areas: Some ecological and economic theories. *Annual Review of Ecology and Systematics* **7**:235–257.
Cowgill, G. L.
    1975a On causes and consequences of ancient and modern population changes. *American Anthropologist* **77**:505–525.
    1975b Population pressure as a non-explanation. *Society for American Archaeology, Memoirs* **30**:127–131.
Culbert, T. P.
    1973a Introduction: A prologue to Classic Maya culture and the problem of its collapse, In *The Classic Maya collapse*, edited by T. P. Culbert. Albuquerque: University of New Mexico Press. Pp. 3–20.
    1973b The Maya downfall at Tikal. In *The Classic Maya collapse*, edited by T. P. Culbert. Albuquerque: University of New Mexico Press. Pp. 63–92.
Day, K. C.
    1974   Walk-in wells and water management at Chanchan, Peru. In *The rise and fall of civilizations*, edited by J. A. Sabloff and C. C. Lamberg-Karlovsky. Menlo Park, Calif.: Cummings. Pp. 182–190.
DeBoer, W. R.
    1975   The archaeological evidence for manioc cultivation: A cautionary note. *American Antiquity* **40**:419–432.
Dennell, R. W.
    1978   Archaeobotany and early farming in Europe. *Archaeology* **31**:8–13.
Dickson, D. B.
    1975   Settlement pattern stability and change in the Middle Northern Rio Grande Region, New Mexico. *American Antiquity* **40**:159–171.
Divale, W. T.
    1972   Systematic population control in the Middle and Upper Palaeolithic: Inferences based on contemporary hunter–gatherers. *World Archaeology* **4**:222–237.
Dobzhansky, T.
    1974   Chance and creativity in evolution. In *Studies in the philosophy of biology*, edited by F. J. Ayala and T. Dobzhansky. Berkeley: University of California Press. Pp. 309–344.
Drennan, R. D.
    1976   Religion and social evolution in formative Mesoamerica. In *The early Mesoamerican village*, edited by K. V. Flannery. New York: Academic Press. Pp. 345–368.
Drucker, P.
    1965   *Cultures of the North Pacific Coast*. San Francisco: Chandler.
Dumond, D. E.
    1972   Population growth and political centralization. In *Population growth: Anthropological implications*, edited by B. Spooner. Cambridge, Mass.: MIT Press. Pp. 286–310.
    1975   The limitation of human population: A natural history. *Science* **187**:713–721.

Durham, W. H.
    1976   The adaptive significance of cultural behavior. *Human Ecology* **4**:89–121.
Dyson-Hudson, R., and R. Smith
    1978   Human territoriality: An ecological reassessment. *American Anthropologist* **80**:21–41.
Earle, T. K.
    1976   A nearest-neighbor analysis of two formative settlement systems. In *The early Mesoamerican village,* edited by K. V. Flannery. New York: Academic Press. Pp. 196–224.
    1977   A reappraisal of redistribution: Complex Hawaiian chiefdoms. In *Exchange systems in prehistory,* edited by T. K. Earle and J. E. Ericson. New York: Academic Press. Pp. 213–232.
Earle, T. K., and J. E. Ericson
    1977a Exchange systems in archaeological perspective. In *Exchange systems in prehistory.* edited by T. K. Earle and J. E. Ericson. New York: Academic Press. Pp. 3–14.
    1977b *Exchange systems in prehistory.* New York: Academic Press.
Erasmus, C. J.
    1965   Monument building: Some field experiments. *Southwestern Journal of Anthropology* **21**:277–301.
Ericson, J. E.
    1977   Egalitarian exchange systems in California: A preliminary view. In *Exchange systems in prehistory,* edited by T. K. Earle and J. E. Ericson. New York: Academic Press. Pp. 109–126.
Ferdon, E. N., Jr.
    1959   Agricultural potential and the development of cultures. *Southwestern Journal of Anthropology* **15**:1–19.
Fitzhugh, W.
    1975   A comparative approach to northern maritime adaptations. In *Prehistoric maritime adaptations of the circumpolar zone,* edited by W. Fitzhugh. The Hague: Mouton. Pp. 339–386.
    1976   Environmental factors in the evolution of Dorset culture: A marginal proposal for Hudson Bay. *Society for American Archaeology, Memoirs* **31**:139–149.
Flannery, K. V.
    1968a Archaeological systems theory and early Mesoamerica. In *Anthropological archaeology in the Americas,* edited by B. J. Meggers. Washington, D.C.: Anthropological Society of Washington. Pp. 67–87.
    1968b The Olmec and the Valley of Oaxaca: A model for inter-regional interaction in formative times. In *Dumbarton Oaks Conference on the Olmec,* edited by E. P. Benson. Washington, D.C.: Dumbarton Oaks. Pp. 79–110.
    1969   Origins and ecological effects of early domestication in Iran and the Near East. In *The rise and fall of civilization,* edited by J. A. Sabloff and C. C. Lamberg-Karlovsky. Menlo Park, Calif.: Cummings. Pp. 245–268.
    1972   The cultural civilizations. *Annual Review of Ecology and Systematics* **3**:399–426.
    1976a Empirical determination of site catchments in Oaxaca and Tehuacan. In *The early Mesoamerican village,* edited by K. V. Flannery. New York: Academic Press. Pp. 103–116.
    1976b Evolution of complex settlement systems. In *The early Mesoamerican village,* edited by K. V. Flannery. New York: Academic Press. Pp. 162–172.

1976c Interregional religious networks: Contextual analysis of ritual paraphernalia from formative Oaxaca. In *The early Mesoamerican village*, edited by K. V. Flannery. New York: Academic Press. Pp. 329–344.

1976d Linear stream patterns and Riverside settlement rules. In *The early Mesoamerican village*, edited by K. V. Flannery. New York: Academic Press. Pp. 173–179.

1976e The village and its catchment area. In *The early Mesoamerican village*, edited by K. V. Flannery. New York: Academic Press. Pp. 91–94.

Flannery, K. V., A. V. Kirkby, M. J. Kirkby, and A. W. Williams, Jr.
1967 Farming systems and political growth in ancient Oaxaca. *Science* **158**:445–454.

Ford, R. I.
1974 Northeastern archaeology: Past and future directions. *Annual Review of Anthropology* **4**:385–414.

Gall, P. L., and A. A. Saxe
1977 The ecological evolution of culture: The State as predator in succession theory. In *Exchange systems in prehistory*, edited by T. K. Earle and J. E. Ericson. New York: Academic Press. Pp. 255–268.

Goodyear, A. C. III
1975 Hecla II and III: An interpretive study of archaeological remains from the Lakeshore Project, South Central Arizona. *Arizona State University, Anthropological Research Paper* No. 9.

Grabert, G. F., and C. E. Larsen
1975 Marine transgressions and cultural adaptation: Preliminary tests of an environmental model. In *Prehistoric maritime adaptations of the circumpolar zone*, edited by W. Fitzhugh. The Hague: Mouton. Pp. 229–254.

Gross, D. R.
1975 Protein capture and cultural development in the Amazon Basin. *American Anthropologist* **77**:526–549.

Hammond, N., A. Aspinall, S. Feather, J. Hazelden, T. Gazard, and S. Agrell
1977 Maya jade: Source location and analysis. In *Exchange systems in prehistory*, edited by T. K. Earle and J. E. Ericson. New York: Academic Press. Pp. 35–70.

Hardesty, D. C.
1977 *Ecological anthropology*. New York: Wiley.

Harner, M. J.
1973 *Hallucinogens and shamanism*, New York: London and Oxford Press.
1977 The ecological basis of Aztec sacrifice. *American Ethnologist* **4**:65–75.

Harpending, H., and J. Bertram
1975 Human population dynamics in archaeological time: Some simple models. *Society for American Archaeology, Memoirs* **30**:82–91.

Harris, M.
1977 *Cannibals and kings*. New York: Random House.

Hayden, B.
1972 Population control among hunter/gatherers. *World Archaeology* **4**:205–221.
1975 The carrying capacity dilemma. *Society for American Archaeology, Memoirs* **30**:11–21.

Hodder, I. R., and C. Orton
1976 *Spatial analysis in archaeology*. London and New York: Cambridge University Press.

Jacobsen, T., and R. M. Adams
1958 Salt and silt in ancient Mesopotamian agriculture. *Science* **128**:1251–1258.

Jarman, H. N., A. J. Legge, and J. A. Charles
1972   Retrieval of plant remains from archaeological sites by froth flotation. In *Papers in economic prehistory,* edited by E. S. Higgs. London and New York: Cambridge University Press. Pp. 39–48.

Jarman, M. R.
1972   A territorial model for archaeology: A behavioral and geographic approach. In *Models in archaeology,* edited by D. L. Clarke. London: Methuen. Pp. 705–734.

Jochim, M. A.
1976   *Hunter–gatherer subsistence and settlement: A predictive model.* New York: Academic Press.

Johnson, G. A.
1972   A test of the utility of central place theory in archaeology. In *Man, settlement, and urbanism,* edited by P. J. Ucko, R. Tringham, and G. W. Dimbleby. London: Duckworth. Pp. 769–786.
1975   Locational analysis and the investigation of Uruk local exchange systems. In *Ancient civilization and trade,* edited by J. A. Sabloff and C. C. Lamberg-Karlovsky. Albuquerque: University of New Mexico Press. Pp. 285–340.
1977   Aspects of regional analysis in archaeology. *Annual Review of Anthropology* **6:**479–508.

Jorde, L. B.
1977   Precipitation cycles and cultural buffering in the prehistoric Southwest. In *For theory building in archaeology,* edited by L. R. Binford. New York: Academic Press. Pp. 385–396.

Klein, R. G.
1977   The ecology of early Man in Southern Africa. *Science* **197:**115–126.

Lange, F. W.
1971   Marine resources: A viable subsistence alternative for the prehistoric Lowland Maya. *American Anthropologist* **73:**619–639.

Larson, L. H., Jr.
1971   Settlement distribution during the Mississippian Period. *Southeastern Archaeological Conference Bulletin* **13:**19–25.
1972   Functional considerations of warfare in the Southeast during the Mississippian Period. *American Antiquity* **37:**383–392.

Lees, S.
1974   Hydraulic development as a process of response. *Human Ecology* **2:**159–175.

Logan, M. H., and W. T. Sanders
1976   The model. In *The Valley of Mexico,* edited by E. R. Wolf. Albuquerque: University of New Mexico Press. Pp. 31–58.

Longacre, W. A.
1976   Population dynamics at the Grasshopper Pueblo, Arizona. In *Demographic anthropology,* edited by E. B. W. Zubrow. Albuquerque: University of New Mexico Press. Pp. 169–184.

Lovis, W. A.
1976   Quarter sections and forests: An example of probability sampling in the Northeastern Woodlands. *American Antiquity* **41:**364–372.

MacArthur, R. H.
1972   *Geographical Ecology.* New York: Harper.

McCartney, A. P.
1975   Maritime adaptations in cold archipelagoes: An analysis of environment and

culture in the Aleutian and other island chains. In *Prehistoric maritime adaptations of the circumpolar zone*, edited by W. Fitzhugh. The Hague: Mouton. Pp. 281–338.

McGhee, R.
1976 Paleoeskimo occupations of Central and High Arctic Canada. *Society for American Archaeology, Memoirs* **31:**15–39.

MacNeish, R. S.
1971 Speculation about how and why food production and village life developed in the Tehuacan Valley, Mexico. *Archaeology* **24:**307–315.

Madsen, D. B., and M. S. Berry
1975 A reassessment of Northeastern Great Basin prehistory. *American Antiquity* **40:**391–405.

Marcus, J.
1973 Territorial organization of the Lowland Classic Maya. *Science* **180:**911–916.
1976 The size of the early Mesoamerican village. In *The early Mesoamerican village*, edited by K. V. Flannery. New York: Academic Press. Pp. 79–90.

Margalef, R.
1968 *Perspectives in ecological theory*. Chicago: University of Chicago Press.

Meggers, B. J.
1954 Environmental limitation on the development of culture. *American Anthropologist* **56:**801–824.

Mendelssohn, K.
1971 A scientist looks at the Pyramids. *American Scientist* **59:**210–220.

Millon, R.
1976 Social relations in ancient Teotihuacan. In *The Valley of Mexico*, edited by E. R. Wolf. Albuquerque: University of New Mexico Press. Pp. 205–248.

Moore, J. A., A. C. Swedlund, and G. J. Armelagos
1975 The use of life tablets in paleodemography. *Society for American Archaeology, Memoirs* **30:**57–70.

Moreau, J. F.
1977 A biological approach to site seasonality: Shell analysis of two Costa Rican inland shell middens. Paper presented at the 42nd annual meeting of the Society for American Archaeology, New Orleans.

Odend'hal, S.
1972 The energetics of Indian cattle in their environment. *Human Ecology* **1:**1-21.

Odner, K.
1972 Ethno-historic and ecological settings for economic and social models of an Iron Age society: Valldalen, Norway. In *Models in Archaeology*, edited by D. L. Clarke. London: Methuen. Pp. 623–652.

Orians, G. H.
1973 A diversity of textbooks: Ecology comes of age. *Science* **181:**1238–1239.

Parsons, J. R.
1969 Prehispanic settlement patterns in the Texcoco region, Mexico: Preliminary conclusions. Museum of Anthropology, University of Michigan (mimeographed).
1970 An archaeological evaluation of the Codice Xolotl. *American Antiquity* **35:**431–440.

Parsons, J. R., and N. P. Psuty
1975 Sunken fields and prehispanic subsistence on the Peruvian coast. *American Antiquity* **40:**259–282.

Paulsen, A. C.
  1974   The thorny oyster and the voice of God: *Spondylus* and *Strombus* in Andean prehistory. *American Antiquity* **39**:597–607.
Peebles, and C. S., and S. M. Kus
  1977   Some archaeological correlates of ranked societies. *American Antiquity* **42**:421–448.
Pianka, E. R.
  1974   *Evolutionary ecology.* New York: Harper.
Piddocke, S.
  1965   The potlatch system of the Southern Kwakiutl: A new perspective. *Southwestern Journal of Anthropology* **21**:244–264.
Pires-Ferreira, J. W.
  1976   Shell and iron-ore mirror exchange in formative Mesoamerica, with comments on other commodities. In *The early Mesoamerican village,* edited by K. V. Flannery. New York: Academic Press. Pp. 311–328.
Plog, F.
  1975   Demographic studies in Southwestern prehistory. *Society for American Archaeology, Memoirs* **30**:94–103.
Puleston, D. W.
  1971   An experimental approach to the function of Maya chultuns. *American Antiquity* **36**:322–335.
Pyne, N.
  1976   The fire-serpent and were-jaguar in formative Oaxaca: A contingency table analysis. In *The early Mesoamerican village,* edited by K. V. Flannery. New York: Academic Press. Pp. 272–282.
Rappaport, R. A.
  1968   *Pigs for the ancestors.* New Haven: Yale University Press.
  1971   The Sacred in human evolution. *Annual Review of Ecology and Systematics* **2**:23–44.
Rathje, W. L.
  1971   The origin and development of Lowland Classic Maya civilization. *American Antiquity* **36**:275–285.
  1973   Classic Maya development and denouement: A research design. In *The Classic Maya collapse,* edited by T. P. Culbert. Albuquerque: University of New Mexico Press. Pp. 405–456.
  1975   The last tango in Mayapan: A tentative trajectory of production–distribution systems. In *Ancient civilization and trade,* edited by J. A. Sabloff and C. C. Lamberg-Karlovsky. Albuquerque: University of New Mexico Press. Pp. 409–448.
Reidhead, V. A.
  1977   Labor and nutrition in food procurement: Did prehistoric people optimize? Paper presented at the 42nd annual meeting of the Society for American Archaeology, New Orleans.
Renfrew, C.
  1972   *The emergence of civilization.* London: Methuen.
  1973   *Before civilization.* New York: Knopf.
  1975   Trade as action at a distance: Questions of integration and communication. In *Ancient civilization and trade,* edited by J. A. Sabloff and C. C. Lamberg-Karlovsky. Albuquerque: University of New Mexico Press. Pp. 3–60.
  1977   Alternative models for exchange and spatial distribution. In *Exchange systems*

in prehistory, edited by T. K. Earle and J. E. Ericson. New York: Academic Press. Pp. 71–90.

Reynolds, R. G. D.
1976 Linear settlement systems on the Upper Grijalva River: The application of a Markovian model. In *The early Mesoamerican village,* edited by K. V. Flannery. New York: Academic Press. Pp. 180–194.

Richerson, P. J.
1977 Ecology and human ecology: A comparison of theories in the biological and social sciences. *American Ethnologist* **4:**1–26.

Ritchie, W.
1969 *The archaeology of Martha's Vineyard.* Garden City, N.Y.: Natural History Press.

Rossman, D. L.
1976 A site catchment analysis of San Lorenzo, Veracruz. In *The early Mesoamerican village,* edited by K. V. Flannery. New York: Academic Press. Pp. 95–102.

Rutz, H. J.
1977 Individual decisions and functional systems: Economic rationality and environmental adaptation. *American Ethnologist* **4:**94–112.

Sabloff, J. A., and C. C. Lamberg-Karlovsky
1974 Introductory remarks. In *The rise and fall of civilizations,* edited by J. A. Sabloff and C. C. Lamberg-Karlovsky. Menlo Park, Calif.: Cummings. Pp. 1–4.
1975 (editors) *Ancient civilization and trade.* Albuquerque: University of New Mexico Press.

Sanders, W. T.
1968 Hydraulic agriculture, economic symbiosis, and the evolution of states in central Mexico. In *Anthropological archaeology in the Americas,* edited by B. Meggers. Washington, D.C.: Anthropological Society of Washington. Pp. 88–107.
1973 The cultural ecology of the Lowland Maya: A reevaluation. In *The Classic Maya collapse,* edited by T. P. Culbert. Albuquerque: University of New Mexico Press. Pp. 325–366.
1976 The agricultural history of the Basin of Mexico. In *The Valley of Mexico,* edited by E. R. Wolf. Albuquerque: University of New Mexico Press. Pp. 101–160.

Sanders, W. T., J. R. Parsons, and M. H. Logan
1976 Summary and conclusions. In *The Valley of Mexico,* edited by E. R. Wolf. Albuquerque: University of New Mexico Press. Pp. 161–178.

Sanders, W. T., and B. J. Price
1968 *Mesoamerica: The evolution of a civilization.* New York: Random House.

Sauer, J. D.
1977 The structure of an anadromous fish resource. In *For theory building in archaeology,* edited by L. R. Binford. New York: Academic Press. Pp. 207–250.

Schiffer, M. M. B.
1975 The effects of occupation span on site content. In The Cache River Archeological Project: An experiment in contract archeology, assembled by M. B. Schiffer and J. H. House. *Arkansas Archeological Survey, Research Series* No. 8, 265–269.

Schoener, T. W.
1971 Theory of feeding strategies. *Annual Review of Ecology and Systematics* **1:**369–404.

Shawcross, W.
1972   Energy and ecology: Thermodynamic models in archaeology. In *Models in archaeology,* edited by D. L. Clarke. London: Methuen. Pp. 577–622.
Shimkin, D. B.
1973   Models for the downfall: Some ecological and culture-historical considerations. In *The Classic Maya collapse,* edited by T. P. Culbert. Albuquerque: University of New Mexico Press. Pp. 269–300.
Shimkin, D. B., and J. W. G. Lowe
1977   Formal theory building in human ecology: A report of prospects, progress, and problems. Paper presented at the World Anthropology Meeting, Houston.
Sidrys, R.
1977   Mass–distance measures for the Maya obsidian trade. In *Exchange systems in prehistory,* edited by T. K. Earle and J. E. Ericson. New York: Academic Press. Pp. 91–108.
Sielmann, B.
1971   Der Einfluss der 'Umwelt auf die Neolithische Besiedlung Südwestdeutschlands unter Besondere Berücksichtigung der Verhältnisse am Nördlichen Oberrhein. *Acta Praehistorica et Archaeologica* **2.**
Slobodkin, L. B.
1977   Evolution is no help. *World Archaeology* **8:**332–343.
Smith, P. E. L.
1972   Changes in population pressure in archaeological explanation. *World Archaeology* **4:**5–18.
Spaulding, A. C.
1973   Archaeology in the active voice: the new anthropology. In *Research and theory in current archaeology,* edited by C. L. Redman. New York: Wiley. Pp. 337–354.
Speth, J. D., and D. D. Davis
1976   Seasonal variability in Early Hominid predation. *Science* **192:**441–446.
Spooner, B. (editor)
1972   *Population growth: Anthropological implications.* Cambridge, Mass.: MIT Press.
Stebbins, G. L.
1974   Adaptive shifts and evolutionary novelty: A compositionist approach. In *Studies in the philosophy of biology,* edited by F. J. Ayala and T. Dobzhansky. Berkeley: University of California Press. Pp. 285–309.
Steward, J.
1955   *Theory of culture change.* Urbana: University of Illinois Press.
Struever, S.
1968   Flotation techniques for the recovery of small-scale archaeological remains. *American Antiquity* **33:**353–362.
Sturdy, D. A.
1975   Some reindeer economies in prehistoric Europe. In *Paleoeconomy,* edited by E. S. Higgs. London and New York: Cambridge University Press. Pp. 55–95.
Suttles, W.
1962   Variation in habitat and culture in the Northwest Coast. *Akten des 34 Internationalen Amerikanistenkongresses, Wien* pp. 522–537.
Tainter, J. A.
1977   Modeling change in prehistoric social systems. In *For theory building in archaeology,* edited by L. R. Binford. New York: Academic Press. Pp. 327–352.

Taylor, J. G.
1975 Demography and adaptations of eighteenth-century Eskimo groups in northern Labrador and Ungava. In *Prehistoric maritime adaptations of the circumpolar zone,* edited by W. Fitzhugh. The Hague: Mouton. Pp. 269–280.

Terrell, J.
1977 Biology, biogeography and Man. *World Archaeology* **8:**237–248.

Thomas, D. H.
1972 A computer simulation model of Great Basin Shoshonean subsistence and settlement patterns. In *Models in archaeology,* edited by D. L. Clarke. London: Methuen. Pp. 671–704.

1973 An empirical test for Steward's model of Great Basin settlement patterns. *American Antiquity* **38:**155–176.

Tuck, J. A.
1976 Paleoeskimo cultures of northern Labrador. *Society for American Archaeology, Memoirs* **31:**89–102.

Van der Leeuw, S. E.
1976 *Studies in the technology of ancient pottery.* Amsterdam: University of Amsterdam Press.

Vayda, A. P., and B. J. McCay
1975 New directions in ecology and ecological anthropology. *Annual Review of Anthropology* **4:**293–305.

Vayda, A. P., and R. A. Rappaport
1968 Ecology, cultural and non-cultural. In *Introduction to cultural anthropology,* edited by J. A. Clifton. Boston: Houghton. Pp. 477–497.

Vierra, R. K., and R. L. Taylor
1977 Dummy data distributions and quantitative methods: An example applied to overlapping spatial distributions. In *For theory building in archaeology,* edited by L. R. Binford. New York: Academic Press. Pp. 317–326.

Vita-Finzi, C., and E. S. Higgs
1970 Prehistoric economy in the Mount Carmel area of Palestine: Site catchment analysis. *Proceedings of the Prehistoric Society* **36:**1–37.

Watson, P. J.
1976 In pursuit of prehistoric subsistence: A comparative account of some contemporary flotation techniques. *Mid-Continental Journal of Archaeology* **1:**77–100.

Webb, M. C.
1973 The Peten Maya decline viewed in the perspective of state formation. In *The Classic Maya collapse,* edited by T. P. Culbert. Albuquerque: University of New Mexico Press. Pp. 367–404.

Webster, D.
1975 Warfare and the evolution of the State: A reconsideration. *American Antiquity* **40:**464–470.

Weigand, P. C., G. Harbottle, and E. V. Sayre
1977 Turquoise sources and source analysis: Mesoamerica and the southwestern U.S.A. In *Exchange systems in prehistory,* edited by T. K. Earle and J. E. Ericson. New York: Academic Press. Pp. 15–34.

Whallon, R., Jr.
1973 Spatial analysis of occupation floors. I: Application of dimensional analysis of variance. *American Antiquity* **38:**266–278.

1974   Spatial analysis of occupation floors. II: The application of nearest neighbor analysis. *American Antiquity* **39**:16–34.

White, L. A.
1949   *The science of culture*. New York: Farrar, Straus.

Wiens, J. A.
1976   Population responses to patchy environments. *Annual Review of Ecology and Systematics* **7**:81–120.

Wilkinson, P. F.
1972   Ecosystem models and demographic hypotheses: Predation and prehistory in North America. In *Models in archaeology*, edited by D. L. Clarke. London: Methuen. Pp. 543–576.
1975   The relevance of musk ox exploitation to the study of prehistoric animal economies. In *Paleoeconomy*, edited by E. S. Higgs. London and New York: Cambridge University Press. Pp. 96–132.

Willey, G. R., and D. B. Shimkin
1973   The Maya collapse: A summary view. In *The Classic Maya collapse,* edited by T. P. Culbert. Albuquerque: University of New Mexico Press. Pp. 457–502.

Wilmsen, E. N.
1973   Interaction, spacing behavior, and the organization of hunting bands. *Journal of Anthropological Research* **29**:1–31.

Winter, J. C.
1976   The Processes of farming diffusion in the Southwest and Great Basin. *American Antiquity* **41**:421–429.

Winters, H. D.
1969   The Riverton culture. *Illinois State Museum Reports of Investigations* No. 13.

Wobst, H. M.
1974   Boundary conditions for Paleolithic social systems: A simulation approach. *American Antiquity* **39**:147–178.
1975   The demography of finite populations and the origins of the incest taboo. *Society for American Archaeology, Memoirs* **30**:75–81.

Wright, H. T., and G. A. Johnson
1975   Population, exchange, and early state formation in southwestern Iran. *American Anthropologist* **77**:267–289.

Yellen, J.
1977   *Archaeological approaches to the present*. New York: Academic Press.

Zarky, A.
1976   Statistical analysis of site catchments at Ocos, Guatemala. In *The early Mesoamerican village*, edited by K. V. Flannery. New York: Academic Press. Pp. 117–130.

Zubrow, E. B. W.
1975   *Prehistoric carrying capacity: A model*. Menlo Park, Calif.: Cummings.
1976a   Demographic anthropology: An introductory analysis. In *Demographic anthropology*, edited by E. B. W. Zubrow. Albuquerque: University of New Mexico Press. Pp. 1–26.
1976b   Stability and instability: A problem in long-term regional growth. In *Demographic anthropology*, edited by E. B. W. Zubrow. Albuquerque: University of New Mexico Press. Pp. 245–274.

The Method and Theory of Site Catchment Analysis: A Review

DONNA C. ROPER

The spatial distribution of cultural phenomena is a basic theme in archaeology. The culture area concept (Kroeber 1939), the concept of horizon (Willey and Phillips 1958:33), and the notion of a settlement pattern (Willey 1953:1) are but three ways in which archaeologists have ordered space. The current interest of archaeologists in the description and explanation of site location using methods drawn from geography and related disciplines can perhaps be viewed as simply the latest variation on this basic theme. The recent publication of two books on the topic (Hodder and Orton 1976; Clarke 1977b) and the inclusion of two papers on various aspects of locational analysis in this volume should certainly be seen as some indicator of the status of locational analysis in archaeology in the second half of the 1970s.

Even cursory examination of the locational analysis literature (or one of the recent syntheses of this literature, see especially Hodder and Orton 1976; or Hodder 1977) reveals a broad diversity in approach and technique. One characterization of this literature would roughly distinguish two sets of approaches. The first set emphasizes the importance of man–man relationships in structuring a community's ordering of space. Central place theory, the rank–size rule, and gravity models, among others, would be included in this set of locational approaches. Three such models are discussed by Crumley elsewhere in this volume.

Locational approaches in the second group assume the primacy of

ADVANCES IN ARCHAEOLOGICAL METHOD AND THEORY, VOL. 2

man–land relationships in determining site locations. Site catchment analysis belongs with this latter group. It offers an alternative approach to models based on central place theory (for example) in that it shows less concern with band spacing and population density, etc. (e.g., Wilmsen 1973; Schiffer 1975), as determinants of site location, and instead emphasizes such considerations as the availability, abundance, spacing, and seasonality of plant, animal, and mineral resources as important in determining site location. However, it is distinguished from other man–land approaches by the assessment of those resources within a demarcated area surrounding a site. That is, sites are conceived of as points at the focus of an area throughout which economic activities were performed. The characteristics of this entire area, not just the immediate locus of the site, are considered in inferring locational processes.

It is essentially this basic distinction and the assumptions on which it is based that unites the various studies that have been termed site catchment analysis. Examination of the literature reveals a rather wide diversity of purpose, scope, and technique used in site catchment analysis. It is the purpose of this chapter to review the basis of site catchment analysis, the techniques employed in its implementation, and the kinds of uses to which it has been put.

WHAT IS SITE CATCHMENT ANALYSIS?

In proposing the term site catchment analysis, Vita-Finzi and Higgs (1970:5) defined it as "the study of the relationships between technology and those natural resources lying within economic range of individual sites." The term catchment is drawn from the literature of geomorphology where it is synonomous with drainage basin or watershed and denotes the area from which a stream draws its water. Similarly, the catchment of an archaeological site is that area from which a site (or more properly, the inhabitants of a site) derived its resources (see Vita-Finzi 1969a:106— which seems to be the first, albeit indirect, application of the term to the archaeological case). Unlike drainage basins, the size, shape, and location of a site's catchment may not be known in advance, frequently making it necessary to use an initial estimate or approximation of the catchment based on principles of settlement and land use, or some other knowledge.

It is assumed that, in general, the farther one moves from an inhabited locus, the greater the amount of energy that must be expended for procurement of resources. Therefore, as one moves away from that locus, it is assumed that the intensity of exploitation of the surrounding territory decreases, eventually reaching a point beyond which exploitation is unprofitable. Support for this assumption by users of site catchment analysis is drawn largely from the observation by Lee (1969:61) that the !Kung do not normally go more than 6 miles (10 km) from their camps to procure resources, and the studies cited by Chisholm (1968:131) suggesting that agriculturalists do not normally go even this far to tend their fields. Other references could also be cited to illustrate the same point. It is further assumed that prehistoric peoples were aware of this decrease in cost/benefit ratio and located sites, moved their locations, and generally played out a settlement strategy that minimized the ratio of energy expended to energy procured.

It is further assumed that the site's inhabitants were willing to pay a higher price (that is, expend more energy) for some resources than they were for others. Some resources, such as water, are so basic and so vital that the distance to obtain them must be minimized; others are less immediate, are "worth" more, and may therefore be gathered from farther away. Because of this "hierarchy of importance of resources" (Jochim 1976:54; see also Clarke 1968:506; Chisholm 1968:102–104), a differentiation of use, or zonation, of the territory surrounding a settlement occurred. Both Jochim (1976:55) and Flannery (1976a:117) have described this situation in the archaeological literature—Jochim in theory, and Flannery empirically—and Chisholm (1968:101–110) used this assumption to quantify the relative cost of settling at alternative locations.

The biophysical environment is not uniform, however, either spatially or seasonally. The size, shape, and location of an individual site's catchment are therefore largely a function of the zonation, spacing, and seasonal differentials of resource zones exploited from the site. Decisions as to whether or not the community should move to exploit seasonal differentials more economically will also be influenced by the structure of the environment. Although many studies could be cited to support this assumption, the most dramatic example is to be found in Steward's (1938) analysis, "Basin–Plateau Aboriginal Socio-Political Groups." Careful consideration and contrasting of Steward's descriptions of the environmental zonation and settlement patterns of Great Basin tribes well illustrates how major differences in environmental zonation correlate with very different settlement strategies. Site catchment analysis was originally developed as a response to the realization that at different times or places the biophysical environment may offer very different possibilities for exploitation, given that there is a finite distance people are willing to travel to exploit their environment. It is therefore a basic premise of site catchment analysis that site function and site location are correlated, and that inferences can be made about function from knowledge of location.

The rationale for site catchment analysis is therefore relatively simple.

It assumes no more than that human beings are refuging animals, rhythmically dispersing from and returning to a central place (Hamilton and Watt 1970:263), differentially using a seasonally and spatially variable landscape in a manner that generally is conservative of energy, but conservative relative to a relative scale of values placed on needs and wants.

Although site catchment analysis relies largely on anthropological observations, such as those cited above, for its theoretical justification, the basic argument is not entirely without precedent in the literature of economic geography. Both J. H. von Thünen and A. Weber considered location relative to availibility of resources, although in opposing fashions. Von Thünen was concerned with general land use patterns that developed around an isolated place and the balance between costs and returns accruing to performance of various activities at a given distance from this place. Weber reversed the procedure and directed his analysis toward finding an optimum location, given resource distribution and mode of production (Clarke 1977a:21–23; Chisholm 1968:20–41 for discussion and comparison of von Thünen and Weber's work).

HOW IS SITE CATCHMENT ANALYSIS DONE?

In broad outline, site catchment analysis delimits a territory or set of concentric territories surrounding a site and assesses the resource potential contained within that area. The territory assessed is that postulated to be the area from which the greatest quantity of resources was derived.

Higgs et al. (1967), in their study of Paleolithic sites in Epirus, Greece, were the first to apply this form of analysis (although in a general form) when they sought to interpret the function of Kastritsa and its position in the Advanced Paleolithic settlement system of Greece. They recognized the unequal seasonal and spatial distribution of resources, including the animals represented by archaeological remains, and postulated seasonal movements by the human populations that exploited these animals. Their analysis then attempted to ascertain to what extent the Kastritsa site would have been satisfactory for year-round occupation (Higgs et al. 1967:13). Although major interest was with interpretation of Kastritsa, its location was also compared and contrasted with several other nearby sites. Summer and winter hunting conditions in Epirus were reconstructed, and rings 10 km in radius were drawn around each site. Resources within these 10-km radii were not quantified, but visual impressions from inspection of maps conveyed the very different economic potentials of the sites. Advanced Paleolithic sites of Epirus were then grouped, based, in part, on inferences from seasonal potential (Higgs *et al.* 1967:18).

The study by Vita-Finzi and Higgs (1970) of Upper Paleolithic and Neolithic sites in Palestine was actually the first to use the term site catchment analysis, but, more important, it was also the first to discuss some of the assumptions and principles of the type of analysis proposed. Vita-Finzi and Higgs (1970) were interested in evaluating whether their sites necessarily represented sedentary economies, or whether transhumance may have been practiced. The analysis worked from the premise "that attempts to solve this problem must take into account not only artifacts but also the possibilities inherent in the site situations themselves" (Vita-Finzi and Higgs 1970:4).

The "exploitation territory" of a site was defined as "the territory surrounding the site which is exploited habitually" (Vita-Finzi and Higgs 1970:7). This territory was then used as an analytic device for examining the resources immediately accessible to a site's inhabitants.

Higgs *et al.*'s (1967) use of a 10-km radius had not accounted for sharp terrain differentials and thus did not fully account for energy expenditure differentials necessary to procure resources from different places within the immediate vicinity of the site. Vita-Finzi and Higgs (1970) therefore substituted time contours for circular radii, using 2-hour walks from a site for hunter–gatherers, and 1-hour walks for agriculturalists. Using percentages of land types within these time contours, they analyzed the potential for occupation of their sites by comparison of the resource potential of the exploitation territories of the sites. The result was what they called "a very speculative possibility of a pattern of seasonal movement" (Vita-Finzi and Higgs 1970:22–26). In essence, it was a very general, yet testable, hypothesis about seasonal movements of Natufian populations. The Vita-Finzi and Higgs study therefore established site catchment analysis as an inductive method for derivation of hypotheses about settlement system morphology.

The studies of Higgs *et al.* (1967) and Vita-Finzi and Higgs (1970) exemplify the two techniques most commonly used for delimiting the territory to be examined in a site catchment analysis—namely, the use of circular territories of fixed radii and the use of time contours. Both means of determining the area to be studied have since been widely used. Walking 1 hour from agricultural sites and 2 hours from nonagricultural sites has been used by a number of European historians (Webley 1972; Barker 1972, 1973, 1975b; Jarman and Webley 1975; Davidson 1976; Jarman 1976), although circles of fixed radii are more commonly used, especially by Americanists but also by Europeans (Barker 1975a; Fagan

1976; Moore *et al.* 1975; Noy *et al.* 1973; Clark 1972; Higgs and Webley 1971; Ellison and Harriss 1972; Clarke 1972; Dennell and Webley 1975; Rossman 1976; Zarky 1976; Roper 1974, 1975; Peebles 1978). Possibly one reason for the predominance of the latter technique is the fact that circles are more readily employed when data are taken from available maps rather than collected from actual walks taken in the field.

The uncritical acceptance of the Lee and Chisholm distance figures and the mechanical use of these figures expressed as circular radii or time contours are major problems with site catchment analysis as it is currently practiced. Relieving this sterility in approach can perhaps best be initiated by clarifying the catchment concept and explicitly stating its behavioral referent. Very early in the development of site catchment analysis the terms *territory* and *catchment* were distinguished—the former as the area immediately accessible to a site's inhabitants, which was habitually exploited, the latter as the total area from which the contents of a site were derived (Higgs 1975:*ix*). A territory as defined therefore became an analytic device whose size was determined by ethnographic analogy. A catchment, on the other hand, became a behavioral unit whose referent must be inferred from comparative knowledge of site territories, resource distribution, site contents, and settlement system morphology. Obviously, the better the analytic device approximates the behavioral unit, the better the analysis of the catchment itself. Much of the site catchment analysis literature has, however, tended to confuse and merge the two terms. Thus, 2-hour or 10-km (or whatever) territories have been treated as if they were actual catchments; time or distance contours as if the site's inhabitants were on a 10-km-long leash. Several studies have attempted to deal with this problem, however, and it is worth describing them briefly.

Findlow and DeAtley (1974:4–5) explicitly noted the problem with catchment approximation ("most catchment–hinterland types of analyses have failed to produce either a theoretical basis or empirical data to support the use of some particular catchment size or shape") and have attempted to resolve it. Their analysis of sites in the Animas Valley of New Mexico formulated two site types and examined spacing along and across drainages and between sites of the same type as well as different types of sites (Findlow and DeAtley 1974:38–40). Radiocarbon and obsidian hydration dates were used to demonstrate contemporaneity of sites. Observed spacings were taken as an estimate of the size and shape of catchments of different types of sites "as a preliminary step to examining the relative uses and placement of sites within each catchment" (Findlow and DeAtley 1974:54). Browman (1976) similarly calculated the linear spacing of sites to interpret catchment size in Peru.

Cassels (1972b) attempted to determine the actual field (the term he uses in place of catchment) of sites in the Waikato area of New Zealand by constructing Thiessen polygons (Haggett 1965:247–248) around each site. His assumption was that "the most likely boundary between the two sites is a line equidistant between them" (Cassels 1972b:215). Such a means of determining catchments assumes that all sites were contemporary, an assumption of which Cassels is aware and which he accepts unless the contrary is proved (Cassels 1972b:216). Strangely enough, however, once he determined the size of the polygons, he used a set of concentric circles to evaluate resource content and merely presented a frequency distribution of size of polygons.

Dennell and Webley (1975:102) eliminated overlaps of territories, probably by a similar technique, and examined spacing. They too, however, used complete circles (2 km) to evaluate resources (Dennell and Webley 1975:105). Rossman (1976) and Brumfiel (1976) both truncated the overlapping territories by drawing a straight line between the points of intersection of the circles drawn around their sites. In both cases, the truncated territories were used to evaluate resources.

Linear spacing (or some other measure of spacing) and Thiessen polygons are both realistic approaches to estimation of catchment size and shape. Their utility, however, is limited by several considerations. First, they *do* assume contemporaneity of sites, and unless one can demonstrate this to be so, the results could be highly misleading. Second, they assume a comprehensive listing of the sites whose spacing is being examined. This could be a problem if analysis is being done of sites in an area that has not been systematically surveyed or where a survey was done using quadrats, transects, or some other technique yielding an areally discontinuous sample of sites. Third, use of either approach assumes no overlap of actually exploited area, no trade, and no importation of resources—that is, it assumes that the area within the polygon is the sole area exploited.

The problem is, therefore, how do we approximate catchment size and shape with anything but time or distance contours when the site sample is nonsystematic, areally discontinuous, or noncontemporaneous? So far, no one has approached this problem directly. Flannery (1976a) dispensed with analytic devices altogether and attempted to determine site catchments empirically by starting with empirical data on plant, animal, and mineral resources and asking from how far away they must have come (Flannery 1976a:103). It would seem reasonable that some data should be available for most regions as to what resources were utilized, and such data could be used to formulate approximations of catchments of specific sites. Use of ethnographic or ethnohistoric data should also be useful in some areas.

Once an approximation of a catchment is made, the kinds of resources evaluated, the way they are analyzed, and the detail to which they are analyzed also vary. Most analyses employ general land classifications of some kind. For example, Vita-Finzi and Higgs (1970) used a series of "land use capability classes" which are based on modern land uses. These include irrigated land, arable, rough grazing, good grazing/ potentially arable, seasonal marsh, sand dunes, and irrigated crops (Vita-Finzi and Higgs 1970:17). Within the time contours drawn around each site, they evaluated the acreage of the enclosed territory and the percentage of it occupied by each land type. Many other studies have been similarly performed.

Some analyses are explicitly based largely on one kind of resource, such as soil or vegetation. For example, Webley's (1972) analysis of Tell Gezer and several other sites in Palestine was based entirely on analysis of soils and their potential productivity. Peebles' (n.d.) study of Mound-ville, Alabama, was similarly conceived. Adams (1977) was largely concerned with plant potential, and Roper (1974) also relied heavily on floral zones.

Two problems may arise with resource availability estimation: (a) Should inference about important factors in site location be based on a site's relation to a single type of resource? (b) How reliable are the recent or modern distributions?

Even the simplest models of site location specify location as being determined by the interaction of several variables. For example, Chisholm (1968:102–103) has listed water, arable land, grazing land, fuel, and building materials as "the five basic elements of . . . a settler community's economy: with none can the settlement dispense." Jochim (1976:50) has listed as primary goals in settlement placement among hunter–gatherers: "1. Proximity of economic resources. 2. Shelter and protection from the elements. 3. View from observation of game and strangers." Hill (1971:56) has diagrammed a multivariable model of the determinants of site locations, including critical resources, their proximity and spacing, population density, and other variables. The use of single resource types such as soil or vegetation may therefore be unfairly limiting. It may not necessarily allow inference about why a site is located where it is or how it may have functioned in a settlement system. It does, of course, permit description of how sites are located relative to soils or vegetation, and a comparison among sites of their potential for certain economic activities. If this is the goal of a specific study, then use of only a few resource types is fine. More complete modeling of settlement location and the settlement system, however, requires the use of a wider variety of resource types.

Site catchment analysis would be virtually impossible if it were based on anything but modern or recent resource distributions, since maps of past resource distributions are seldom available. However, for a variety of reasons, including geomorphic change, climatic change, fluctuations in sea level, and drastic changes in resource distribution with the introduction of modern land use practices, modern data may be highly unreliable.

The problem cannot be adequately treated here, except to say that it will be necessary to evaluate the case for each area. For example, Higgs and Vita-Finzi (1966:28) refer specifically to changing potentials for exploitation of certain areas in Epirus, Greece. Vita-Finzi's (1969b) study, *The Mediterranean Valleys* is a consideration of how the streams feeding the Mediterranean have modified their courses in the last two millenia (Vita-Finzi 1969b:1) and concludes with a summary of the implications of geomorphic change for available exploitable area (Vita-Finzi 1969b:118). Adams (1977) employs a "grazing filter" for attempting to assess changes in plant food potential surrounding sites in the Rio Puerco Valley in New Mexico. Many archaeologists in the Midwestern United States have used (for site catchment analysis or other purposes) vegetation reconstructions based on the Government Land Office surveys. These were done in the public land states of the United States at about the time of Euro-American settlement. Although they provide reasonable estimates of major vegetation zones, they must be used with caution, for they too were done under varying climatic conditions and other conditions that may affect their utility for prehistoric resource estimation (Wood 1976; King 1978). In some places, and for some time periods, their use could be completely misleading.

The techniques for analysis of site catchment data also vary. Many studies have evaluated the data by inspection of tables or drawings of resource zones surrounding sites (see Barker 1975b for the most exhaustive example of this approach). Sometimes, particularly if a number of sites are being evaluated, this interpretation is graphically assisted with pie diagrams (e.g., Vita-Finzi and Higgs 1970) or histograms (e.g., Ellison and Harriss 1972; Barker 1972) of land type proportions. Roper (1974, 1975) and Baumler (1976) both used multivariate statistical techniques (factor analysis, multidimensional scaling, and cluster analysis) for describing and comparing site territories and their resource potential.

Flannery (1976b:92–93) has suggested, however, that the relevant question may indeed not be what percent of a particular land use type falls within the territory, but rather whether or not this is sufficient land for the needs of the site's inhabitants and whether or not it is significantly more than could be expected by chance. The answer to the former question, he says, requires estimation of both site population and available land. Rossman (1976:102), Flannery (1976a:107), and Zarky (1976:122) all address such estimates in their analyses of site catchments in Formative Mesoamerica. The latter question requires the use of inferential statistics for an answer. Zarky's (1976) analysis of site catchments at Ocós in Guatemala used percentage point differences, chi-squared tests, and binomial tests for evaluating which environmental zones were represented in higher proportions immediately surrounding a site than they were in the total study area.

Common to many site catchment studies is the evaluation of all land types as if they were of equal value for what they produce. This simply is not true, however. Seasonal and spatial disparities in potential is one of the reasons site catchment analysis was originally developed, but few studies actually quantify this potential. A number of exceptions should be discussed.

The simplest and oldest means of accounting for differentials is that used by Vita-Finzi and Higgs (1970:30). In their study, land at greater distances from agricultural sites was weighted proportionally less than was that close to the site, to compensate for the increased travel time required. The area within 1 km was weighted 100%; 1–2 km, 50%; 2–3 km, 33%; 3–4 km, 25%; and 4–5 km, 20%; and the figures were tabled and graphed accordingly (Vita-Finzi and Higgs 1970:28–31). Rossman (1976:100–101) used these same weighting figures in his analysis of exploitation territories in the San Lorenzo area in Mesoamerica. Cassels (1972a:209) adjusted them only slightly (and only because he used a different set of radii) for his analysis in the Waikato area of New Zealand.

Flannery's (1976b) suggestion that population and yield estimates may be used to evaluate the sufficiency of land to support the population has already been mentioned. A number of other studies have been even more specific about producing some estimate of yield of the resource zones within the catchment rings of the sites, without necessarily relating the figures to population density. Peebles' (1978) study of Moundville Phase settlement in Alabama measured areas of different soil types within 1 and 2 km of Moundville Phase sites, and estimated "gross median productivity" of each ring. This was done by multiplying "the midpoints of the range of the average yields of bushels of corn for each soil type in the catchment" and summing the products (Peebles 1978). Webley (1972:178), using soil types, similarly estimated barley yields and goat potentials for a single site in Palestine.

In all these cases, however, estimates have been made for only one or two resources—albeit important ones. Two studies have attempted to quantify a larger number of resources and to incorporate the seasonally different potential as well. Cassels (1972a:209–213) corrected not only for distance from a site, but also for seasonal difference in potential of each zone.

Adams (1977) attempted to assess differential wild plant resource potential for five sites in the Rio Puerco Valley of New Mexico. She developed a set of scores using parts of a plant, the season or seasons of the year when the plant is available, its dependability, and a rough estimate of the work necessary for its procurement and preparation. Seventy-five plants scored included those documented ethnographically for the Southwest and archaeologically for the Rio Puerco. Plant scores were then summed to determine a total tally for the land lying within an arbitrary radius of each site. This technique has the obvious advantage of estimating potential only for those plants most likely employed by the inhabitants of the area. Although seasonal considerations enter the calculation of plant scores, they do not produce an estimate of seasonal fluctuations in resource potential, as does Cassels' (1972a) analysis; rather, they estimate the *total* annual potential within the arbitrary radius of each site.

Adams' study is not unlike a study by Munson *et al.* (1971) in which the yields of several plant and animal species of major economic importance within 1.78 miles (10 square miles) of the Scovill site in Illinois were estimated and the figures compared with actual remains to evaluate whether or not animals and plants were being taken in proportion to their availability. Munson and associates conclude that there was *no* selection for plant species, but that there *was* a selection for animal species (Munson *et al.* 1971:426). An alternative explanation, however, could simply be that plants were collected from the immediate environs of the site, whereas animals were not. In other words, if it is assumed that the samples were good, the observed disparities could simply be a result of zonation of exploitation of resources.

Two studies stand apart from most site catchment studies in not confining themselves to a small, circumscribed area surrounding a site. Foley (1977) developed an ecological model accounting for differential productivity in an area. This model was free of specific loci, instead using quadrats superimposed on a general resource zone map of an area in which some sites were assumed to be located. This approach would then analyze the energy balance by subtracting the value of the energy necessary to exploit an area from a given locus from the extracted energy (Foley 1977:164–165, 177–181). The approach is interesting, but unfortunately it is illustrated with a hypothetical example.

Flannery's (1976a) study, "Empirical Determination of Site Catchments in Oaxaca and Tehuacán," although tied to specific sites, is likewise free of an arbitrary analytic territory. Instead of evaluating what resources were available to a site's inhabitants within some arbitrarily (and perhaps unrealistically) demarcated area, Flannery reversed the procedure, started with data on the plant, animal, and mineral resources found at sites, and asked, "From how far away must they have come?"

(Flannery 1976a:103). The analysis considered all kinds of resources, from the commonest plants to the most exotic trade items. It obviously avoided the problem of arbitrarily superimposing a territory; it also required good faunal and floral preservation, detailed study of those remains, and comprehensive knowledge of resource distributions. Flannery's conclusions expectably suggest a zonation of resource use (1976a:117), but also document a *total* catchment area *far larger* than the analytic territory used in most studies. Most basic plant and mineral needs were satisfied within 5 km of the site, but animals, wood, and exotic materials came from farther away. It is still a documentation of the fact that resources reflected at a site may come from a far broader area than the small analytic territories used by most site catchment analyses.

With the exception of the Foley (1977) and Flannery (1976a) papers, therefore, procedures for site catchment analysis can be summarized as follows. First, define the analytic territory. To do so, use a circle or circles centered on the site or an irregularly shaped territory defined by time contours, or infer the territory by the site's relation to its neighbors. If the latter is done, be prepared to justify the assumption of site contemporaneity. Then, measure the area of each resource zone within each site's territory. Table these figures, or graph them, or use them in a statistical analysis of site territories. Differential weighting of more distant resources, estimates of yields, and accounting for differential seasonal potentials may be used at this point. The exact procedure chosen and the use made of the results of the analysis will depend on the purpose of the analysis. It is to the purpose of site catchment analysis, therefore, that we now turn.

WHY HAS SITE CATCHMENT ANALYSIS BEEN DONE?

The literature on site catchment analysis contains numerous contributions from both British and American researchers. To assess the diversity of site catchment applications, however, it is necessary to appreciate the fact that it is set within quite different contexts in Europe and the Americas.

European Studies

British archaeology has often been seen as largely concerned with artifacts and historical reconstructions of their development. In the late 1960s, however, a new theme entered the British practice of archaeology—that cultural phenomena were not be be explained by culture alone, but also by other factors, including economy. Higgs and Jarman stated this theme quite explicitly at the conclusion of their essay reconsidering the origins of agriculture:

> The cultural model has dominated thought and speculation in European archaeology for many decades . . . . The study of economy, the major selective force in prehistory has, until now, largely been ignored. With its development, . . . the whims, fashions, and freedom of choice associated with cultures may become of less importance to archaeology than the study in man's past of natural mechanisms as the true causes of human behavior [1969:40].

The study of economies has long had a place in British archaeology, particularly following Clark's (1952) major synthesis of the economy of prehistoric Europe. However:

> In spite of Clark's admonition that many archaeologists were too artefactually oriented, the field has continued to be dominated by the consideration of artefactual types and their chronology, and economic concepts have usually served for little more than the classification of cultures into 'hunter–gatherers,' 'pastoralists,' or 'farmers' [Higgs and Vita-Finzi 1972:27].

A major innovation in site catchment analysis was therefore the role given to economy in interpretation of the archaeological record. Vita-Finzi and Higgs (1970:4) are quite clear in stating that attempts to solve the problem of the nature of prehistoric economies "must take into account not only the artefacts but also the possibilities inherent in the site situations themselves." Their study of sites in the Mt. Carmel area of Palestine, as well as the earlier study by Higgs *et al.* (1967) in Epirus, Greece, were attempts to generate testable hypotheses about prehistoric economies from this perspective.

Several other studies had as their primary purpose to reconsider culture–historical reconstructions from the perspective of economies, and in so doing generated hypotheses about those economies by using site catchment analysis. The studies by Graeme Barker (1972, 1973, 1975b) on the Bronze Age of central Italy are a case in point. Barker's analysis sought to refute the standard concept of central Italian prehistory, which postulates "a series of neat cultural phases, each with its economic label, developing with regional variations one after the other" (Barker 1973:359–360), by using, among other data, "the evidence of the location of the sites themselves" (Barker 1973:360). Consideration of the territories of a series of sites (Barker 1972:198, Fig. 10) and their productive potentials led to what Barker (1972:189) described as "a hypothetical reconstruction of related economic networks of sites, within an ecological rather than a cultural framework," as well as to an apparent major revision of at least the "economic labels" of the "neat cultural phases" that characterized the study of central Italian prehistory. The same author's study of early Neolithic sites in Yugoslavia (Barker 1975a), and the study by Dennell and Webley (1975) of Neolithic and Bronze Age sites in southern Bulgaria, both similarly proposed alternative settlement system models to the traditional interpretations, using site catchment analysis to interpret the relation between site location and potential for occupation.

Other studies were less concerned with alternatives to culture–historical scenarios, instead seeking to examine the economic aspects of various cultural units: Webley's (1972) study of Tell Gezer and nearby sites in Palestine; Jarman and Webley's (1975) study of prehistoric sites in Capitanata, Italy; Davidson's (1976) study of several Paleolithic sites in Spain; Jarman's (1972, 1976) examination of prehistoric sites in Italy (the 1972 paper is actually more concerned with presentation of a model than with the substantive results of the analysis); and Ellison and Harriss' (1972) study of prehistoric and early historical sites in southern England all belong to this genre of site catchment studies. This is not to suggest that all these studies are similarly conceived or executed, however. Some rely primarily on site location data (e.g., Webley 1972; Jarman and Webley 1975), whereas others augment the locational data with analysis of faunal remains (e.g., Jarman 1976; Davidson 1976). Ellison and Harriss (1972) were "concerned primarily with the locations of individual sites and with what can be inferred from them" (Ellison and Harriss 1972:913) rather than with reconstruction of economies. To this end, site catchment analysis was the primary line of evidence used, but it was supplemented by other locational techniques for study of land use.

The final major purpose for which site catchment studies have been performed in Europe has been the examination of the environmental context of single sites. For these studies, the term site catchment analysis is hardly appropriate, for neither are they analyses nor are they concerned with catchments in the proper sense of the term. Rather, they are site reports in which the site is related to its natural setting by description of the area within a 5-km (or whatever) radius of the site—that is, the area presumed to provide the majority of resources to the site. Details of the surrounding territory are frequently shown in a drawing and briefly described. Reports by Noy et al. (1973) on Nahal Oren, Israel; by Moore et al. (1975) on Tell Abu Hureyra, Syria; by Fagan (1976) on Gwisho, Zambia; and by Clark (1972) on his reexamination of Star Carr, England, all fall in this category. Clarke's (1972) examination of Glastonbury, England, is similar; here the site exploitation territory was considered in building a model of the Iron Age society represented at the site.

In spite of the explicit concern for the study of the economy, and in spite of the frank regard for behavior and development of laws of human behavior (e.g., Higgs and Jarman 1975:2), many European studies are directed toward clarification of what happened in prehistory rather than with the development of such laws. In all these studies, the assumptions of site catchment analysis and the validity of the distance figures given by Lee, Chisholm, and others are taken as givens, and never have they been subjected to confirmation or disconfirmation. However, Lee's (1969) figures on the distance agriculturalists are willing to travel to tend their fields may be applicable to the societies on which they are based, but they have not yet been shown to have universal validity. It is this almost mechanical use of these figures for delineating the analytic territory that was noted earlier as one of the major problems with site catchment analysis.

American Studies

Site catchment analysis is only beginning to be used by American archaeologists. Some of the analyses in the Americas (especially Rossman 1976; Zarky 1976) have been performed for purposes similar to those of some of the British studies—that is, to examine and quantify the nature of the territory immediately accessible to a site's inhabitants. American archaeology has, however, had a strong tradition of settlement pattern analysis. Beginning with Gordon R. Willey's (1953) studies in the Virú Valley of Peru and continuing up to the present, the settlement pattern concept has been a functional rather than a historical concept. The archaeologist interested in settlement patterns defined a series of site types which can be used for a variety of purposes. One of these is the study of their distribution across the landscape and the explanation of location. Site catchment analysis has been used in American archaeology primarily for modeling the spatial distribution of functionally distinct sites within a settlement system, or for examination of the resource potential of sites thought to have occupied different positions in a settlement system.

Roper's (1975) study of settlement patterns of Woodland sites in central Illinois is an example of the former use of site catchment analysis. A series of very generally defined site types was recorded during a survey of the Sangamon River Valley, and the site catchment data were used to assess the locations of each site. After a statistical analysis was made of these data, Roper was able to postulate a general, but testable, model of Middle and Late Woodland settlement patterns in the valley, and to provide a general test of this model using such limited excavation data as were available, survey data not used in formulation of the site types, and comparative literature.

An example of the latter use is Peebles' (1978) study of Moundville Phase settlement in Alabama. Peebles used soils and their estimated yields to examine resource potential at functionally different sites in the Moundville Phase. His techniques have already been described. Additionally, he related estimated productivity to site size, assuming that there is a relationship between population size and subsistence base, between settlement size and resident population, and between area of scatter and settlement size. The hypothesis was that if a prime criterion for location is agricultural land, then site size should vary with soil productivity. The Pearson product–moment correlation coefficient was used to test the hypothesis. Village–hamlet settlements did show a strong correlation between size and productivity, while the minor ceremonial centers had a rather low relationship (Peebles 1978).

Brumfiel's (1976) test of a population pressure hypothesis in a part of the Valley of Mexico was similarly conceived and executed. The basic argument was expressed as follows:

> We could expect a situation of population pressure to be expressed in a simple correlation between *the relative number of inhabitants at each village* and *the relative productive potential of agricultural land available at each village* [Brumfiel 1976:237, italics in the original].

Brumfiel implicitly made the same assumption as did Peebles but used linear regression to predict site size from productive potential—a measure derived from data on available agricultural land and the fertility of that land (Brumfiel 1976:240).

Browman (1976) used the premises of site catchment analysis as expressed by Higgs and associates (Higgs and Vita-Finzi 1972; Jarman 1972; Jarman *et al.* 1972) to derive predictions about expected spacings of several site types. These predictions are then compared with actual spacings of sites (Browman 1976:471). Using an estimated biomass for the catchment, he then postulated the demographic processes operative in the Jauja–Huancayo basin of Peru at around A.D. 500 (Browman 1976:473–474). This use of the site catchment model, while holding in common with Peebles' and Brumfiel's the incorporation into demographic studies, is the only analysis in which the assumptions of site catchment analysis were used to generate predictions about the form of the archaeological record, and the only study that could be construed to be a test of the validity of those assumptions.

Finally, we might note Hassan's (1975) use of the catchment concept. Hassan's paper is a general discussion of population density, size, and growth rate. In developing the discussion of size, Hassan (1975:38) notes that "population size is a function of the population density and area." Incorporating the catchment concept as a measure of area, he then (1975:39–40) uses it to discuss the relationships between size and density.

It is quite clear that the relationship is variable, suggesting that the attempt to use similar-sized analytic territories in different kinds of places is not only an unrealistic way to proceed in general but is subject to varying degrees of error.

CONCLUSIONS

It has been a major purpose of this chapter to summarize and review the assumptions of site catchment analysis, the techniques employed in its implementation, and the purposes for which it has been performed. It should be clear that there is a wide diversity in purpose and technique. The criterion for selection of papers discussed here was that the authors *said* they were using site catchment analysis or something resembling site catchment analysis. It remains then to come to a conclusion as to exactly what *is* site catchment analysis.

Excluding those reports using a circular territory around a site solely for environmental description purposes, consideration of the remainder of the studies suggests that site catchment analysis is most correctly viewed as a method—that is, a set of techniques for analysis of data (Dunnell 1971:34). Its unity derives from the incorporation of techniques relating site location to resource availability within the territory immediately surrounding a site. It assumes that this territory, which will be of relatively finite size and show seasonal variability, is of primary importance in provisioning the site's residents. How this territory is determined for analysis, however, will depend on whether it is preferable to use an arbitrarily demarcated area (based on either time or distance contours) or to attempt to approximate the area from spacing of the sites. The latter requires slightly more stringent assumptions about the sites analyzed, but provides a better estimation of the behavioral unit (that is, the catchment itself) if it can be shown to be appropriate. The kind of resources analyzed (soil, topography, flora, etc.) will depend on availability of data and the researcher's beliefs about what kinds of resources were important to the community under study. Site catchment analysis is therefore useful with a variety of locational models.

Further, it can be, and has been, used in studies of a variety of types including evaluation of the feasibility of various culture–historical reconstructions (e.g., Barker 1972, 1973, 1975a,b), determination of the feasibility of various forms of economy (e.g., Higgs *et al.* 1967; Vita-Finzi and Higgs 1970), modeling settlement patterns (e.g., Peebles 1978; Roper 1975), and study of demographic processes (e.g., Browman 1976; Brumfiel 1976).

Development of site catchment analysis is, of course, not without problems. These are discussed in the text of this paper.

It is now an infamous fact that archaeologists are prone to borrow methods rather than develop their own. Yet it has also been pointed out by a number of authors that the tendency to do so ignores archaeology's greatest asset—the time depth unavailable to most other social scientists—and it ignores the possibility that the presently known range of cultural expressions does not represent a full range of all societies that have ever existed. The development of site catchment, although it draws on ethnography and geography, has been developed with the consideration of the potentials of the archaeological record. It is to be hoped that the needed development and refinement of the method will occur.

ACKNOWLEDGMENTS

This chapter in its several versions has benefited considerably from the comments of Karen R. Adams, Vorsila L. Bohrer, Sharon L. Brock, Carole L. Crumley, Susan K. Goldberg, Michael B. Schiffer, V. Ann Tippitt, and, of course, the ever-helpful Anonymous Reviewers. Dr. Bohrer and Ms. Adams were kind enough to provide me with copies of several of their unpublished papers as well as to correct my summary of their approach; Christopher S. Peebles provided an advance copy of his Moundville manuscript. Special thanks go to Michael B. Schiffer for inviting me to write this paper. The result of that invitation was not only the opportunity but the necessity to assess more critically a method which I, too, had perhaps rather blindly accepted for several years. My own analyses will never be the same again. The traditions of scholarship require that I absolve all the above-named from liability for remaining errors and shortcomings—a requirement with which I am most happy to comply.

Several very capable colleagues have my undying appreciation for keeping things going, but keeping me involved, informed, and sane, while I completed the final draft of this chapter during the launching of a major field season.

REFERENCES

Adams, K. R.
   1977 Site catchment analysis of wild plant resources in the heavily overgrazed Rio Puerco Valley of New Mexico. Paper presented at the 42nd annual meeting of the Society for American Archaeology, New Orleans.
Barker, G.
   1972 The conditions of cultural and economic growth in the Bronze Age of Central Italy. *Proceedings of the Prehistoric Society* **38**:170–208.
   1973 Cultural and economic change in the prehistory of Central Italy. In *The explanation of culture change: Models in prehistory,* edited by C. Renfrew. Pittsburgh: University of Pittsburgh Press. Pp. 359–370.
   1975a Early neolithic land use in Yugoslavia. *Proceedings of the Prehistoric Society* **41**:85–104.

1975b Prehistoric territories and economies in Central Italy. In *Palaeoeconomy,* edited by E. S. Higgs. London and New York: Cambridge University Press. Pp. 111–175.

Baumler, M.
1976 *An initial prehistoric settlement-subsistence analysis for the Little Blue River Area* (Little Blue Channel-Modification Project, Archaeological Research Design. Report to the U.S. Army Corps of Engineers). Lawrence: Department of Anthropology, University of Kansas. Pp. 11–55.

Browman, D. L.
1976 Demographic correlations of the Wari conquest of Junin. *American Antiquity* **41**(No. 4):465–477.

Brumfiel, E.
1976 Regional growth in the Eastern Valley of Mexico: A test of the "population pressure" hypothesis. *The early Mesoamerican village,* edited by K. V. Flannery. New York: Academic Press. Pp. 234–249.

Cassels, R.
1972a Human ecology in the prehistoric Waikato. *The Journal of the Polynesian Society* **81**:196–247.
1972b Locational analysis of prehistoric settlement in New Zealand. *Mankind* **8**:212–222.

Chisholm, M. C.
1968 *Rural settlement and land use: An essay in location.* Chicago: Aldine.

Clark, J. G. D.
1952 *Prehistoric Europe: The economic basis.* New York: Philosophical Library.
1972 Star Carr: A case study in bioarchaeology. *Addison–Wesley Modular Publications in Anthropology* No. 10.

Clarke, D. L.
1968 *Analytical archaeology.* London: Methuen.
1972 A provisional model of an Iron Age society and its settlement system. In *Models in archaeology,* edited by D. L. Clarke. London: Methuen. Pp. 801–869.
1977a Spatial information in archaeology. In *Spatial archaeology,* edited by D. L. Clarke. New York: Academic Press. Pp. 1–34.
1977b (editor) *Spatial archaeology.* New York: Academic Press.

Davidson, I.
1976 Les Mallaetes and Mondúver: The economy of a human group in prehistoric Spain. In *Problems in economic and social archaeology,* edited by G. de G. Sieveking, I. H. Longworth, and K. E. Wilson. Boulder: Westview Press. Pp. 483–499.

Dennell, R. W., and D. Webley
1975 Prehistoric settlement and land use in southern Bulgaria. In *Palaeoeconomy,* edited by E. S. Higgs. London and New York: Cambridge University Press. Pp. 97–109.

Dunnell, R. C.
1971 *Systematics in prehistory.* New York: Free Press.

Ellison, A., and J. Harriss
1972 Settlement and land use in the prehistory and early history of southern England: A study based on locational models. In *Models in archaeology,* edited by D. L. Clarke. London: Methuen. Pp. 911–962.

Fagan, B. M.
1976 The hunters of Gwisho: A retrospect. In *Problems in economic and social*

archaeology, edited by G. de G. Sieveking, I. H. Longworth, and K. E. Wilson. Boulder: Westview Press. Pp. 15–24.

Findlow, F. J., and S. P. DeAtley
   1974   Prehistoric land use patterns in the Animas Valley: A first approximation. *Anthropology UCLA* **6**(No. 2):1–57.

Flannery, K. V.
   1976a Empirical determination of site catchments in Oaxaca and Tehuacan. In *The early Mesoamerican village,* edited by K. V. Flannery. New York: Academic Press. Pp. 103–117.
   1976b The village and its catchment area: Introduction. In *The early Mesoamerican village,* edited by K. V. Flannery. New York: Academic Press. Pp. 91–95.

Foley, R.
   1977   Space and energy: A method for analysing habitat value and utilization in relation to archaeological sites. In *Spatial archaeology,* edited by D. L. Clarke. New York: Academic Press. Pp. 163–187.

Haggett, P.
   1965   *Locational analysis in geography.* New York: St. Martin's.

Hamilton, W. J. III, and K. E. F. Watt
   1970   Refuging. *Annual Review of Ecology and Systematics* **1**:263–286.

Hassan, F. A.
   1975   Determination of the size, density, and growth rate of hunting–gathering populations. In *Population, ecology, and social evolution,* edited by S. Polgar. The Hague: Mouton. Pp. 27–52.

Higgs, E. S. (editor)
   1975   *Palaeoeconomy.* London and New York: Cambridge University Press.

Higgs, E. S., and M. R. Jarman
   1969   The origins of agriculture: A reconsideration. *Antiquity* **43**:31–41.
   1975   Palaeoeconomy. In *Palaeoeconomy,* edited by E. S. Higgs. London and New York: Cambridge University Press. Pp. 1–7.

Higgs, E. S., and C. Vita-Finzi
   1966   The climate, environment, and industries of Stone Age Greece: Part II. *Proceedings of the Prehistoric Society* **32**:1–29.
   1972   Prehistoric economies: A territorial approach. In *Papers in Economic Prehistory,* edited by E. S. Higgs. London and New York: Cambridge University Press. Pp. 27–36.

Higgs, E. S., C. Vita-Finzi, D. R. Harriss, and A. E. Fagg
   1967   The climate, environment, and industries of Stone Age Greece: Part III. *Proceedings of the Prehistoric Society* **33**:1–29.

Higgs, E. S., and D. Webley
   1971   Further information concerning the environment of Palaeolithic Man in Epirus. *Proceedings of the Prehistoric Society* **37**(Part II):367–380.

Hill, J. N.
   1971   Research propositions for consideration. Southwestern anthropological research group. In *The Distribution of Prehistoric Population Aggregates,* edited by G. J. Gumerman. *Prescott College Anthropological Papers* Arizona: Prescott College Press. (No. 1):55–62.

Hodder, I. R.
   1977   Some new directions in the spatial analysis of archaeological data at the regional scale. In *Spatial archaeology,* edited by D. L. Clarke, New York: Academic Press. Pp. 223–351.

Hodder, I. R. and C. Orton
  1976   *Spatial analysis in archaeology*. London and New York: Cambridge University Press.
Jarman, M. R.
  1972   A territorial model for archaeology: A behavioral and geographical approach. In *Models in Archaeology*, edited by D. L. Clarke. London: Methuen. Pp. 705–733.
  1976   Prehistoric economic development in sub-alpine Italy. In *Problems in economic and social archaeology*, edited by G. de G. Sieveking, I. H. Longworth, and K. E. Wilson. Boulder: Westview Press. Pp. 523–548.
Jarman, M. R., C. Vita-Finzi, and E. S. Higgs
  1972   Site catchment analysis in archaeology. In *Man, settlement, and urbanism*, edited by P. J. Ucko, R. Tringham, and G. W. Dimbleby. Cambridge, Mass: Schenkman. Pp. 61–66.
Jarman, M. R., and D. Webley
  1975   Settlement and land use in Capitanata, Italy. In *Palaeoconomy*, edited by E. S. Higgs. London and New York: Cambridge University Press. Pp. 177–221.
Jochim, M. A.
  1976   *Hunter–gatherer subsistence and settlement: A predictive model*. New York: Academic Press.
King, F. B.
  1978   Additional cautions on the use of the GLO survey records in vegetational reconstruction in the Midwest. *American Antiquity* **43**(No. 1):99–103.
Kroeber, A. L.
  1939   Cultural and natural areas of native North America. *University of California Publications in Archaeology and Ethnology* No. 39
Lee, R. B.
  1969   !Kung Bushman subsistence: An input–output analysis. In *Environment and cultural behavior*, edited by A. P. Vayda. Garden City, N. Y.: Natural History Press. Pp. 47–79.
Moore, A. M. T., G. C. Hillman, and A. J. Legge
  1975   The excavation of Tell Abu Hureyra in Syria: A preliminary report. *Proceedings of the Prehistoric Society* **41**:50–77.
Munson, P. J., P. W. Parmalee, and R. A. Yarnell
  1971   Subsistence ecology of Scovill, a terminal Middle Woodland village. *American Antiquity* **36**(No. 4):410–431.
Noy, T., A. S. Legge, and E. S. Higgs
  1973   Recent excavations at Nahal Oren, Israel. *Proceedings of the Prehistoric Society* **39**:75–99.
Peebles, C. S.
  1978   Determinants of settlement size and location in the Moundville Phase. In *Mississippian settlement patterns*, edited by B. D. Smith. New York: Academic Press. Pp. 369–416.
Roper, D. C.
  1974   The distribution of Middle Woodland sites within the environment of the Lower Sangamon River, Illinois. *Illinois State Museum Reports of Investigations* No. 30.
  1975   Archaeological survey and settlement pattern models in central Illinois. Unpublished Ph.D. dissertation, University of Missouri-Columbia.

Rossman, D. L.
    1976   A site catchment analysis of San Lorenzo, Veracruz. In *The early Mesoameri-can village,* edited by K. V. Flannery. New York: Academic Press. Pp. 95–103.
Schiffer, M. B.
    1975   An alternative to Morse's Dalton settlement pattern hypothesis. *Plains An-thropologist* **20**(No. 70):253–266.
Steward, J. H.
    1938   Basin–plateau aboriginal socio-political groups. *Bureau of American Ethnology Bulletin* No. 120.
Vita-Finzi, C.
    1969a Early man and environment. In *Trends in geography—An introductory survey,* edited by U. Cooke and J. H. Johnson. Oxford: Pergamon. Pp. 102–108.
    1969b *The Mediterranean valleys.* London and New York: Cambridge University Press.
Vita-Finzi, C., and E. S. Higgs,
    1970   Prehistoric economy in the Mount Carmel area of Palestine: Site catchment analysis. *Proceedings of the Prehistoric Society* **36**:1–37.
Webley, D.
    1972   Soils and site location in prehistoric Palestine. In *Papers in economic prehis-tory,* edited by E. S. Higgs. London and New York: Cambridge University Press. Pp. 169–180.
Willey, G. R.
    1953   Prehistoric settlement patterns in the Virú Valley, Peru. *Bureau of American Ethnology Bulletin* No. 155.
Willey, G. R., and P. Phillips
    1958   *Method and theory in American Archaeology.* Chicago: University of Chicago Press.
Wilmsen, E. N.
    1973   Interaction, spacing behavior, and the organization of hunting bands. *Journal of Anthropological Research* **29**(No. 1):11–31.
Wood, W. R.
    1976   Vegetational reconstruction and climatic episodes. *American Antiquity* **41**(No. 2):206–208.
Zarky, A.
    1976   Statistical analysis of site catchments at Ocos, Guatemala. In *The early Mesoamerican village,* edited by K. V. Flannery. New York: Academic Press. Pp. 117–128.

5

Three Locational Models: An Epistemological Assessment for Anthropology and Archaeology

CAROLE L. CRUMLEY

Nearly two decades ago, in an eminently lucid paper, Albert Spaulding (1960) identified what he termed the "dimensions" of archaeology. He defined dimension as "an aspect or property of the subject matter which requires its own special measuring device" (1960:438). As an example, he cited the study of mechanics, where the dimensions are length, mass, and time. He noted that subjects increase in complexity with an increase in the number of dimensions that must be measured in the course of study; thus the study of thermodynamics is more complex than that of mechanics, owing to the added dimension of temperature. Spaulding identified the dimensions of archaeology as form, temporal locus, and spatial locus. Well over half of his discussion of these dimensions and their relationship to the study of archaeology as a whole is devoted to form, reflecting not only his own interest in developing statistically based formal measurement, but also what was at that time the major preoccupation of the field with formal analysis. Although the formal dimension remains the fundament of the necessarily materialist study of archaeology, subsequent inquiry explored the temporal limits of the field and stimulated the development and refinement of many chronometric techniques. Most recently, attention has turned to the spatial dimension (Clarke 1972, 1977b; Hodder and Orton 1976; Parsons 1972; Redman 1973; and numerous

ADVANCES IN ARCHAEOLOGICAL METHOD AND THEORY, VOL. 2

others). This area of study has been termed "spatial archaeology" by David Clarke who defines it as

> the retrieval of information from archaeological spatial relationships and the study of the spatial consequences of former hominid activity patterns within and between features and structures and their articulation within sites, site systems, and their environments: the study of the flow and integration of activities within and between structures, sites and resource spaces from the micro to the semi-micro and macro scales of aggregation. Spatial archaeology deals, therefore, with human activities at every scale, the traces and artefacts left by them, the physical infrastructure which accommodated them, the environments that they impinged upon and the interaction between all these aspects. Spatial archaeology deals with a set of elements and relationships [1977a:9].

Essentially, then, spatial archaeology is a special application of the universal study of objects/points and the relationships among them, which characterizes chemistry as well as comparative literature. What is unique and potentially exciting about such a study in archaeology is that spatial and formal elements and relationships interact through time as process; thus, if we respond to Spaulding's encouragement to develop measuring devices appropriate to the spatial dimension, we shall finally be at the doorstep of a true "processual archaeology."

Yet, despite widespread attention, spatial archaeology boasts no unified theory (Clarke 1977a:5; Crumley 1976:63). One reason for this lack of cohesion is its concurrent development in Britain, where there exists a long tradition of visual display and interpretation of spatial relationships through the influence of the diffusionist school (see Sir Cyril Fox, *The Personality of Britain,* 1932), and in North America, where the spatial dimension has most frequently been measured with tools developed in economic geography. Although some cross-fertilization has taken place, the term locational analysis, as used more frequently in American archaeology, largely reflects the uncritical acceptance by many North American archaeologists of the theoretical assumptions of economic geographers who have developed schemes to identify regional marketing patterns. This concentration on one particular element (markets) and the relationships among them (marketing behavior) is quite appropriate in studies of the Western economy, but such an orientation must be thoroughly examined in terms of its theoretical assumptions and general utility before its successful application in archaeology is assured.

Although some very fine work has been done at what Clarke (1977a:11–15) terms the micro and semimicro scales of aggregation (within structures and within sites), this paper will be concerned only with the macro scale: sites and the relationships between them through time. This is a somewhat broader concern than that of settlement (restricted to habitations) and will integrate functional centers (Crumley 1976:67)—any spot/place/site/location that serves a function or functions not equally available elsewhere—through time and space. Thus, following Spaulding and Clarke, we shall explore the spatial dimension as it relates to both form and time, the macro scale of aggregation, and the theoretical assumptions underlying three macro-level approaches: the gravity model, the central place model, and the regional heterarchy model. The processual implications of these three models' interrelated use will be explored.

INTRODUCTORY CONCEPTS

To evaluate adequately the utility of the three models to be discussed, certain key concepts must be introduced. The first, that of *region,* is of utmost importance, because the macro level of agglomeration is essentially on a regional scale. Although there are inevitable differences of opinion on what constitutes any area termed a region (the Middle East, the Deep South), most geographers would agree that a region is an arbitrary areal classification whose limits are defined by the researcher, for the purpose of studying phenomena within its boundaries (Whittlesey 1954:32ff.; Haggett 1965:241ff.; James 1972:460ff.; Harvey 1973:125). Regions are further subdivided into two categories: the *formal* or *homogeneous* region, emphasizing the homogeneity and uniformity of elements within the regional boundaries, and the *functional* or *nodal* region, emphasizing the interrelatedness of diverse elements within a region (Haggett 1965:242; Kolars and Nystuen 1974:160). Herein, I shall refer to the former as a *homogeneous* region, the latter as a *heterogeneous* region. Homogeneous as well as heterogeneous features characterize any region, and it is within the power of the researcher to stress one or another relative to the study at hand. Thus, certain linguistic characteristics might be described as homogeneous throughout a region, while the physiography of that same region would be characterized as heterogeneous. This is a point to which we must necessarily return in any discussion of regional definition and regional boundaries.

A second important concept, related to that of region and its subdivisions, is *scale.* If you have ever watched an ant labor to cross its landscape, dotted with a variety of features (small pebbles, plants, open expanses), then looked up, aware that the ant's progress is lost in the larger expanse of green lawn, you have experienced the importance of a change in scale. Similarly, any region deemed homogeneous at one scale can surely be found, on closer inspection, to be heterogeneous at a smaller scale. For example, two individuals are both Chicagoans to some-one from St. Louis, but to one another they are from very different areas, the South Side and the North Shore. Chicago is homogeneous at one scale, heterogeneous at another. What effects a change in scale is a change in the elements within a region that are of concern to the re-searcher; is the St. Louisan interested in the Chicagoans' perceptions of the city as a whole (perhaps contrasted with St. Louis), or is the St. Louisan attempting to ascertain the social, political, and economic dis-tinctions within the city of Chicago?

A third concept, related to those of region and scale, is that of *organiza-tional structure*. There are at least two main types: *hierarchical*, in which on the basis of certain factors some elements of the organizational structure are subordinate to others and may be ranked, and *heterarchical*, in which each element possesses the potential of being unranked (relative to other elements) or ranked in a number of different ways, depending on systemic requirements. Minsky and Papert (1972) have used the term heterarchical to characterize computer programs which have the capacity to utilize one another as subroutines. Thus, computer program A may use program B as a subroutine, while in other circumstances B may call A as a subroutine.

This distinction between hierarchical and heterarchical structure can be portrayed in three-dimensional space: connections among elements in a hierarchical structure are most frequently perceived as being vertical (hence such phrases as "filtering down the hierarchy" and "moving up in the hierarchy"), whereas heterarchical structure is most easily envisioned as lateral, emphasizing the number and variety of connections among elements and the varying circumstantial importance of any single element. Thus, an automobile company may be seen as hierarchically organized in terms of corporate decision making, and heterarchically organized in terms of the production of an automobile: into the final product goes the expertise of administrative, research and design, assembly and sales departments. If the unit of study is the automobile, all aspects are equally important. If the study has as its focus departmental efficiency or an interdepartmental softball tournament, however, the departments might be variously ranked.

In like manner, the towns in a region may be viewed as hierarchically organized in terms of administrative functions, and heterarchically or-ganized in terms of marketing: each town, including the administrative capital, contributes a unique good equally important from the standpoint of regional supply and demand, or of variable importance given the problem at hand (for example, obtaining a particular good from the nearest supplier).

The use of the term heterarchy has, to my knowledge, appeared only in the literature of artificial intelligence Minsky and Papert (1972) in connection with computer programming of the mind's functions, but would seem to have widespread utility in spatial studies and elsewhere. The more general of the two varieties of organizational structure is heterarchical; thus hierarchical organization is a type of heterarchical organization.

These three concepts—region, scale, and organizational structure—are in turn related to a fourth: *perception*. Clearly, it is the researcher's perception of the importance of certain factors that determines a region, and, similarly, the scale(s) at which it will be studied. Although it is less well recognized, it is also the perception of structure among elements that determines how they will be studied. This and other concepts introduced will be discussed at length, and their bearing on the three models' utility explored.

SOCIAL PHYSICS MODELS: THE GRAVITY MODEL

Among the most common measuring devices used by regional scientists for studying macro-level agglomeration is a class of models derived from what is termed *social physics*. In order to evaluate the most frequently employed of these, the *gravity model*, it is necessary first to explore the terms *regional science* and *social physics*, and their relationship to the anthropological perspective.

Regional science is a relatively new professional field, founded as a response to the need for an interdisciplinary approach to regional problems (James 1972:522; Haggett 1965:16–17; Isard 1975:5). Unfortunately, the need for the comprehensive involvement of the social sciences in such an endeavor has remained unmet. Other than economic geographers, economists are the most active theoretical and pragmatic social science contributors to regional studies. The resulting world view provided by the field of regional science (Isard 1975:4) is one that most anthropologists and some geographers would find rather naïve (Olsson 1965a, 1970; Haggett 1965; Smith 1976c;6ff.; Olsen 1976:21ff). This perspective also lays open the not-quite-healed wound of the substantivist/formalist debate (Cook 1976).

An example of the manner in which regional scientists interpret social and cultural factors is the concept of social physics (Harvey 1973:48; Olsson 1966:13). Simply stated, social physics applies certain laws derived from the physical sciences to social and cultural aspects of regional studies. In particular, the motivating factors in thermodynamic systems are considered as behaving analogously to those factors that motivate human interaction. Further, the concept of entropy (the mathematical factor that measures unavailable energy in a thermodynamic system) is related to that of information in an economic system. Thus, the loss of information concerning markets or new technology due to imperfect communication is made the analogue of an increase in entropy (James 1972:513) and described by the same mathematical formulae (Wilson 1969).

Anthropologists must applaud the attempt of geographers and regional scientists to ground regional analysis firmly in systems theory (James 1972:512; Olsson 1966, 1970; Harvey 1973:447ff.; Haggett 1965:17; 1972) and to make explicit the nature of hypotheses and explanation, but they are understandably hesitant to employ formulaic relationships derived from a demonstrably "simpler" (in Spaulding's dimensional sense) field in what is clearly a very complex interactional field.

The use of the laws of physics in anthropology is hardly unknown; it was one of the more exciting components of Leslie White's (1949, 1959) attempts to make anthropology more explicit and to search for general laws of human behavior. However, most anthropologists have found White's theories stimulating, but empirically untestable (Harris 1968). White's theories were formulated on the broadest evolutionary scale, at which it would be difficult to devise an appropriate test of any theory.

Operating at a lower level of abstraction, geographers and regional scientists have explored the utility of these social physics models. An extensive literature dealing with the prediction of interaction between communities has been the result. Particularly, they have employed what is termed the gravity model (Olsson 1965a:44ff., 1970:227; James 1972:516). Its premise is as follows: The amount of interaction between two cities is directly proportional to the number of people living in those cities, and inversely proportional to the intervening distance. This relationship may be expressed by the formula

$$I_{ij} = P_i P_j / D_{ij}^b$$

where I_{ij} = the amount of interaction predicted between place i and place j, P_i and P_j = the population of the two places, D_{ij} = the distance separating the two places, and b = an exponent of some chosen value (Haggett 1965:35; Olsson 1970:227)

If such a formula could be demonstrated as applicable to a wide range of cultural interactions, its adoption in anthropology and archaeology would be assured. Not only would patterns of human interaction be explained readily, but they might be predicted with accuracy. The desire to predict site location, or to estimate population or degree of economic activity between sites, is strong among archaeologists; the potential predictive power of the gravity model is perhaps its most attractive feature.

However, some economists and theoretical geographers have expressed reservations concerning the model's utility (e.g., Jackman 1975:18; Harvey 1973:48, 464). Perhaps the most perceptive evaluator of the wholesale employment of social physics models to spatial aspects of interaction is Gunnar Olsson (1965a, 1965b, 1968, 1970). Certain anthropological archaeologists have also reviewed the literature (Plog 1976:257ff.; Johnson 1977). The following discussion will direct the interested reader to successful and unsuccessful examples of the use of the gravity model and to discussions of methods and techniques utilized, but will concentrate on an evaluation of the underlying assumptions of social physics (especially gravity) models and theoretical problems that confront their use in anthropology and archaeology.

Olsson (1965b:26) pinpoints two critical assumptions that underlie the gravity model: that all places are populated by "standard" people with identical needs, tastes, and contacts, and that interaction intensity among centers of population decreases over distance symmetrically in all directions (the distance–decay concept). The first assumption is one made of necessity for all economically derived models, and touches on questions of rationality in economics, and the internal variability of populations. The latter assumption requires that we address these questions and that of boundaries—physical, social, political, and economic—as well.

In regard to rationality in economics, Cook (1976) provides an excellent summary of the substantivist/formalist debate in economic anthropology; it would serve the spatially oriented archaeologist well to become familiar with its salient points. Archaeologists must evaluate a wide variety of quantitative and qualitative evidence to begin modeling the economy of a society; because that evidence is overwhelmingly spatial, the question of what constitutes evidence of one type of economy or another is central to the interpretational process. Most of the literature concerned with the substantivist/formalist debate and its *dénouement* concerns contemporary examples; the archaeologist has the additional dimension of time with which to contend. Adams (1974) and Earle and Ericson (1977) address themselves to this particular problem. Adams presents an especially lucid review treatment of his debate with Polanyi (Polanyi *et al.*, 1957) and others regarding ancient trade, itself a corollary in archaeology to the substantivist/formalist debate in anthropology as a whole. Adams argues that studies of ancient trade have approached the subject too narrowly (that is, on the wrong scale) and urges archaeologists to recognize the multifaceted significance of trade, the importance of analogies drawn from ethnographic and ethnohistoric examples, and the significance of a shifting boundary between trade and intergroup predation. As yet there are few studies of the spatial patterns associated with certain types of economy, but there is some pertinent literature in geography (Feldman 1976). This question must be explored thoroughly before spatial archaeology can advance much further.

A second category of questions raised by the forgoing assumptions of the gravity model is that of internal group variability, perception of boundaries, and individual and group behavior. Many of the critics of the gravity model recognize the importance of noneconomic factors. Jackman (1975:18) remarks that economic (that is, rational) behavior is frequently modified by what he terms "externalities"—those factors outside the economy that affect it—which are not recorded in any measure of marketing behavior. Olsson (1965a:34, 57) urges an inclusion of noneconomic elements in spatial models, and even Isard (1956) admits to the need for a measure of "nontangible" prices (presumably social and political, as well as economic factors that determine price). Olsson (1965a:55) mentions that the addition to the gravity model of age, sex, and other factors affecting an economic system make the model too cumbersome; Haggett (1965:39) also expresses doubt about the model's usefulness in complex situations. On the problem of directionality, Olsson (1965a:36) discusses Hägerstrand's (1957, 1963) analysis of the different "pulls" exerted on rural migrants to the Swedish cities of Linköping and Norrköping, where he found that the smaller place had the greatest influence—that the concept of social physics and the gravity model did not apply. Bylund (1960) makes much the same point: that centers have different attraction values to settlers, based on a variety of factors such as distance from a road, proximity to a church or marketplace, kin relationships, and land use potential. It should be noted, however, that in his successful application he alters one of the classic assumptions of the gravity model, that of a homogeneous plain.

The problem of measuring distance for use in the mathematical formula has been discussed at length in both absolute (Haynes and Enders 1975; Plog 1976; Johnson 1977) and relative (Olsson 1965a:43; Watson 1955; Johnson 1977; Flannery 1968a, 1972; Leone 1968; Cook 1970; Plog 1976) terms. From an absolute point of view, the problems concerned with translating map distance to travel time or costs has been well explored (Ericson 1977; Renfrew 1977; Rowlett and Pollnac 1971; Johnson 1977; Hodder and Orton 1976) and some constructive suggestions made. The more relativistic question concerning perception of distance has had less attention (Olsson 1965:43; Plog 1976:258) but cannot be ignored by the archaeologist considering application of the gravity model. Clearly, some journeys are more sensitive to distance than others (Olsson 1965a:55) and interactions between functional centers are, and have been, carried on for a variety of economic and noneconomic (that is, nonrational) reasons.

Plog (1976:257) argues that if the gravity model is applicable to the present, it is equally applicable to the past; although I would not question his uniformitarianist intent, and a variety of seemingly successful applications do exist in the literature (Morrill 1963; Olsson 1965a:44, 53; Haggett 1965:39; Earle and Ericson 1977; Plog 1976), the difficulty of recovering archaeological information related to perception should be emphasized. Yet just on this point might turn the possibility of inferring perceptual boundaries from archaeological data. Cook (1970:34, 47) notes that the gravity model should work where no social barriers are crossed—that is, at some scale where the region under study is thought to be socially homogeneous. A potentially useful application of the gravity model, then, might be as an initial assessment of two centers' economic interaction. The variance not accounted for by the model might then be more closely examined to determine what other factors might be influencing the economic relations between functional centers.

In a similar search for factors other than distance and population that might affect interaction, Haggett (1965:40) reviews Kariel's (1963) use of the gravity model to study population growth due to migration. Kariel found that his overall level of "explanation" (increase in goodness-of-fit of model) jumped 8 percent when results were adjusted for climatic desirability. The question of the effect of social, economic, political, and natural boundaries on the operation of the gravity model might, then, be approached by employing the model to pinpoint boundaries significant at certain scales of analysis.

The model nonetheless has severe practical limitations in its applicability for archaeological problems; minimally, one must have either artifacts that are sensitive economic indicators (solving the equation for population) or considerable historical evidence of interaction between one center of known and one of unknown location (solving the equation for distance). Such requirements necessitate well-dated sites distributed over a large area.

The difficulty of selecting sensitive economic indicators from archaeological materials has been adequately discussed (S. Plog 1976; F. Plog 1977; Johnson 1977:48; Friedrich 1970; Earle and Ericson 1977). The most salient problem is that, within artifact types, attributes indicative of economic interaction may be difficult to identify and interpret.

The estimation of population for archaeological sites (usually by means of ethnographic or ethnohistoric analogy) is a particularly difficult task. Because few studies of personal and public space have been undertaken to explore the equifinality principle (the concept that similar final results may be achieved with different initial conditions and in different ways), it is with understandable reluctance that most archaeologists approach the use of models that force initial population assumptions. Further difficulties are encountered with the realization that site size does not always reflect population (Crumley 1974) and that only certain portions of the population of a center are involved in the exchange of certain goods (Johnson 1977; Turner 1976). Further, Olsson (1965a) notes that, when used in the equation, population should refer only to that population engaged in the interaction, rather than to the entire population of the center.

A fascinating study by Tobler and Wineberg (1971) using the gravity model and textual evidence solves the equation for distance, producing a "predicted location" map of pre-Hittite Anatolian merchant colonies. However, such complete ethnographic or ethnohistoric information concerning ancient trade is rarely available.

The need to establish contemporaneity for sites used with this model of spatial analysis cannot be overstressed. The degree of accuracy in dating that establishes contemporaneity is also open to question. For example, some sites in the Southwestern United States considered contemporaneous may be dated to within 5–10 years, while Iron Age hillforts in Europe dated to within 50–100 years of one another are considered contemporaneous for the purpose of synchronic spatial analysis.

What may be considered a sufficient area for study is also the subject of debate (Olsson 1966:157; Plog 1976). Disagreement concerns what is termed the "plateau effect" (Olsson 1966:17): within a certain distance close to a community, distance seems to have no effect on interaction intensity (Olsson 1965a:48ff.; Plog 1976:258; Garrison and Marble 1957; Dunn 1954). Estimates (again, for reasons, one suspects, of scale) of the radius of a plateau range from less than 5 miles (Abrams 1943; Chisholm 1968; Davie and Reeves 1939; Marches and Turbeville 1953; Warren 1969) to 300 kilometers (Renfrew 1969:157).

Finally, the synchrony/diachrony question must be raised with the gravity model. Many researchers who are concerned with this model are interested in temporal changes in the system: the manner in which factors (once identified and measured spatially) are affected over time. Given the importance of the concept of equifinality in spatial studies, it is critical to be able to observe the process whereby elements in a system are altered. In the physical sciences, this type of study is termed kinetic; studies concerned with the net change in a system are termed thermodynamic. Perhaps some of the difficulty encountered by archaeologists (particularly those who might wish to apply the gravity model to diachronic studies) is due to the conjoining of systems models with thermodynamically derived spatial models to chart the course of change.

THE CENTRAL PLACE MODEL

The gravity model (GM) structures economic behavior *between* two centers; the central place (CP) model structures economic behavior (particularly retail marketing) *among* many centers, at a regional scale. In the CP model, one encounters more directly the problems associated with regional definition and the bounding of regional systems, many of which stem from assumptions shared with the gravity model.

The CP model has had much more thorough review in both the geographical and anthropological literature than has the gravity model. In keeping with the intent herein to investigate the underlying assumptions of three spatial models, the interested reader is directed toward sources that represent a sampling of the immense literature on the subject (Christaller 1966, 1972; Lösch 1954; Marshall 1969; Berry 1967; Berry and Pred 1965; Haggett 1965; Crumley 1976; Smith 1976d; Johnson 1977). Berry defines central place theory as

> the theory of the location, size, nature, and spacing of . . . clusters of activity, [which] is therefore the theoretical base of much of urban geography and of the geography of retail and service business [1967:3].

If the reader chooses to contrast the CP and GM formulas, Beckman (1958) first expressed the CP model mathematically in the equation $P_{tw} = P_{cw} + kP_{t(w-1)}$. This equation states that the total population served by a center of level w, where $w = 1$, equals its own population plus the total population served by the k centers of the next lower level that it dominates. The CP model was derived by economic geographers for the spatial analysis of retail distribution among centers in a market economy. Its application is most frequently geometric, rather than arithmetic.

Major assumptions of the classic CP model are those of an unbounded, featureless plain and a "closed" economic system. The modified CP model is characterized by three embedded and interrelated assumptions: the dominance of economic factors in the settlement and growth of centers, the rational basis of consumer behavior, and the congruence of the spatial distribution of retail market centers with that of other (noneconomic) factors affecting settlement.

The first two assumptions (those of an unbounded, featureless plain and a closed economic system) apply to the classic scheme (Christaller 1966; Lösch 1954) and have subsequently seen heavy modification (e.g., Hodder and Orton 1976; Olsson 1966; Marshall 1969). As we shall see, however, the theoretical implications of easing these strictures at a methodological level have not been explored. A featureless, unbounded plain is, of course, never actually encountered. There do exist certain homogeneous regions whose boundaries are firmly secured by natural barriers; such is the case for the river valleys ringed by mountains, which constitute many of Skinner's Chinese regions (1977b:211–216). Skinner's definition of region is a homogeneous one, and coincides "with minor exceptions to a physiographic unit" (1977b:211). There is a body of evidence confirming the relationship between successful application of the CP model and physiographically homogeneous regions, particularly river valleys (Johnson 1972:771; Flannery 1976:171ff.; MacNeish 1972; Berry n.d.). Thus, researchers successful in applying the CP model have modified its classic assumptions by substituting for the fabled featureless landscape one characterized by homogeneous distribution of salient physiographic characteristics. It is not surprising that in reality the CP hexagonal lattice adjusts somewhat to physiography, so long as transport costs are not seriously affected.

The charge that the CP model must posit a "closed" economic system (that is, one without external economic input) to operate is refuted by the same studies, successful because of the regions' imposing physiographic boundaries (deserts, mountains) as well. It should be noted, however, that the CP model does indeed reflect only patterns of *retail* (regional) marketing; those undertaking studies of *wholesale* (supraregional) marketing have found CP to be of no utility (Vance 1970:7–9). Central place is, then, a model appropriate at the regional and (in some cases) subregional scales, if the initial regional or subregional definition is of physiographic homogeneity at that scale. Ultimately, one must posit a "closed" system (in terms of boundary definition) to study any system, else one finds oneself studying interactions at the next higher (= larger) systemic level.

The assumption of the dominance of economic factors in the settlement and/or growth of centers, implied by many diachronic applications of the CP model (cf. Morrill 1962, 1963), has serious implications for the archaeologist. Much of our information about the early histories of cities suggests a variety of related factors at work, some economic—keeping in mind the difficulty of that definition—and some not (e.g., Pounds 1971; Netting 1972). The CP model also assumes a hierarchy based on larger and larger scales of dominance in the marketing of certain rank-ordered goods and services, and a positive correlation between the population of retail centers and their relative economic importance. For example, it is assumed that lowest order central places supply ubiquitous goods and services (gas station, post office, etc.), and the next higher-order places supply both these and others (for example, funeral parlor) as well. For the archaeologist, this pyramidal assumption of additional (rather than distinctive) goods and services would imply, for example, that every lowest (fourth) order CP be an agricultural center, that every third-order CP then be both agricultural center and ceramic workshop, that every second-order CP be agricultural center, ceramic workshop, religious shrine, and so forth. Not only does archaeological evidence emphatically *not* yield such explicit site-function evidence on a regional scale, it is clearly *not* the manner in which cities whose histories we understand began. Many (Adams 1974; Skinner 1977a; Crumley 1976) have argued that CP is not applicable to the earliest of urban data, but I would also suggest that it is not the best way to describe the relative importance of modern communities *except* in the study of retail distribution. A number of studies of consumer behavior in CP systems (e.g., Lentnek *et al.* 1975; Murdie 1965) indicate that even in this regard factors unrelated to distance and population are of measurable importance. In archaeology, one is fortunate to have *any* information regarding site function, much less enough to reestablish a would-be CP hierarchy of retail marketing. What one searches for are the relict patterns of a variety of economic and noneconomic interactions, but again the equifinality principle precludes confident use of the CP model in understanding even the market economy of an archaeologically known society.

Crissman (1976a) notes that the CP model was not designed to predict location but to explain (existing) spatial relationships. However, Berry (n.d.) has used the model with some success to guide his search for medieval parishes in southern Burgundy. From a diachronic standpoint, the problem has been recognized and, to some extent, rectified by the application of stochastic growth models to historical situations. For a review of this literature, see Crumley (1976:61–66); Appleby (1976) offers an example of an explanatory, diachronic study. Nonetheless, archaeologists must keep in mind that the CP model only *describes* and *explains* with any degree of certainty centralized, regional economic functions (Olsson 1965b:35). Any prediction of location must be made at peril to regions with functional centers of nonmarket character, and with extreme care to regions with evidence of market centers.

The set of assumptions concerning the operation of a rational market economy, which underlies both CP and formalist economics, has forced many economic anthropologists to reject, in non-Western societies, economists' models based upon marketing behavior (Polanyi 1957; Dalton 1968; Bohannan and Bohannan 1968; Bohannan and Dalton 1965). Smith (1976c:33, 40, Note 21) argues that the market principle has utility in agrarian/preindustrial as well as industrialized societies and is thus an appropriate method cross-culturally and multitemporally. Whether markets (and thereby the so-called "market principle" assumptions of formalist economists) can exist outside Western capitalist contexts is an important question, but its examination is well outside the scope of this study. As Godelier (1972) and Cook (1976:801ff., 842–843) point out, an even more basic question is whether a strictly economic analysis is an appropriate anthropological approach. It is clear that Smith considers the economy a perfectly appropriate focus for the study of interrelationships in society as a whole. With respect to social stratification, she comments (1976b:310, Note 1) that politics, social status, and the like "unnecessarily complicate models of 'elementary' forces." Smith defends this retreat of an anthropologist to the formalist position of most economists on the basis of an adherence to Marxist economic principles (1976b:309–310). However, Godelier casts serious doubt on the ability of strictly materialistic theory to explain relations between production and various other aspects of social life:

> For vulgar materialism, the economy, which it reduces to the relations between technology and environment, "produces" the given society, giving rise to it as an epiphenomenon. This means refusing to see the irreducible differences between the *levels and structures* of social life, the reason for the relative autonomy with which they operate, and reducing all levels to so many functions, either apparent or concealed, of economic activity [1972:*ix–x;* emphasis added].

Godelier's point is that the material economy, although important, is only one aspect of the proper subject matter of anthropologists. Finally, Edel (1969:428–429) makes an important point: the economic process may not be the only system that relates values, technology, and resource ownership. He argues that other, complementary types of analysis are required to understand all the relations within a cultural system. Again, the need for a number of complementary explanatory models on a variety of scales is underscored.

A basic Marxist assumption is that the nature of social organization is determined by the relationship of individuals to the means of production—that the structure of one molds the structure of the other. I would suggest that much of the disagreement outlined above stems from the argument about what constitutes an adequate explanatory model. Leach (1964:5) comments that "the structures which the anthropologist describes are models which exist only as logical constructions in his own mind." Similarly, Lévi-Strauss (1960:53) says it is . . . "hopeless to expect structural analysis to change our way of perceiving concrete social relations. It will only explain them better."

Marx himself was undoubtedly aware of the existence of more than a single, potentially applicable model for social organization. In his rhetorical, social activist role he used a dichotomous model of social organization to dramatize the plight of nineteenth century workers, while in his role as a social scientist he preferred a more moderate, three-class model (Ossowski 1963:75).

In response to Marx, Weber's (1947, 1968) approach to social organization is analytically more differentiated. He discussed class (market situation), status (style of life, sense of honor), power (ability to influence the behavior of others), and ethnicity (perceived common origin) as analytic units, and argues that the organization of complex societies is better approximated by the concept of interest groups. Thus, the Marxist scheme with congruent social and economic hierarchies was not acceptable to Weber because it tended to mask the complexities of intergroup activity. Despite Weber's criticism of the Marxist model, the idea of society-wide social and economic congruity has remained prominent in Western social science.

Subsequently, however, Fallers (1973) and Ossowski (1963) have launched an attack on the prevalent notion of hierarchical socioeconomic stratification, and Fallers has proposed the substitution of the term "inequality." Faller's argument is as follows:

> The term "social stratification," then, has a certain historical appropriateness in contemporary Western societies. I suggest, nevertheless, that it is a poor term for which social scientists might well substitute "inequality." Not only is it quite misleading when applied to the many non-Western societies in which thought and action about inequality center much more upon interpersonal relations of superiority and inferiority; it also *oversimplifies by attempting to capture with a single graphic image the multiple bases of differentiation and equality which exist within Western societies* [1973:29; emphasis added].

Ossowski (1963:176) argues that if one applies different schemes of social organization to different societies, the very choice of a scheme may fix in advance the characteristic features of the society that is to be described. In an attempt to make those interested in social organization aware of the implications of their choice of model, he distinguishes major classes of models (for example, dichotomic, scheme of gradation, nonegalitarian classlessness) and places them in historical and functional perspective. Ossowski's "nonegalitarian classlessness" is essentially Faller's "inequality."

The point of this discussion is that the controlling model of social organization, chosen by most social scientists and inherent in CP—that of hierarchically ordered, class society—is of insufficient utility in the comprehensive social analysis of complex society. One might argue that the freer a society is of role/profession/heritage restraints to social mobility, the less able the class concept is to explain variation. Yet even in societies thought to be restrictive in terms of social mobility (for example, India), there is not only more mobility than is apparent (Dumont 1957), but the caste system can hardly be explained on the basis of a single economic dimension (Harper 1964). Cancian (1974, 1976) has echoed these findings, using a variety of noneconomic measures of individual status in Zinacantan.

In an attempt to link the market economy with an aspect of social organization (marriage) using data from Taiwan, Crissman (1976b) finds the single most powerful correlate of marriage patterns to be simple propinquity. The failure of such an attempt to link the economic relationships of a society as displayed by CP with social organization is most notable because of the regularity with which Taiwanese marketing patterns fit the CP model.

Adams and Kasakoff (1976) are critical of the degree of congruence of endogamous groups and marketing systems. They remark, ''Not only are there endogamous units that do not appear to result from marketing, but the units interlock in several different ways that have yet to be fully elucidated'' (1976:186). Again, it would seem that the spatial, economic CP model cannot sufficiently demonstrate explanatory power in complex society.

Finally, Adams and Kasakoff (1976:186) introduce a question of extreme importance to the critical analysis of CP as exemplified by the work of Smith *et al.* (1976d):

> The failure of these authors to portray the complexity of these systems arises, we feel, from their attempt to view marriage solely from the perspective of marketing. The question to be asked is not ''Does marketing structure marriage?'' but rather ''What does an entire social system, including marketing and marriage, not to mention politics, classes, and religious organizations, look like as a *regional* system?

Smith (1976a:6) comments that regional science was developed for the purpose of generalizing spatial models and making them applicable to social organization. The term *regional system* is defined in Smith (1976a:9) as a ''nodal system . . . [which] include[s] a number of levels of hierarchically organized communities.'' Yet the preceding discussion argues strongly that Smith, many of her contributors, and the majority of regional scientists have made the same fallacious connections: Regional marketing structure equals regional system. They have failed to realize that one cannot begin with the economy and expand the economic model to apply to other aspects of society, but rather one must undertake the more difficult task of choosing a variety of models and systematizing the various results of those applications. Ample evidence has been brought to bear on the point that the explanatory power of a spatial model of formal economic theory (CP) is very weak, and at best must be used with a variety of differently organized noneconomic models to explain any given cultural system. We must turn ourselves to a locational analysis of cultural systems rather than the economic analysis of regions. Regions, defined economically, are not cultural systems.

THE REGIONAL HETERARCHY MODEL

It is clear that many areas of the world might be termed regions, but they do not conform to the homogeneous physiographic requirements of the CP model. In an attempt to formulate an alternative model suitable for regions of diverse physiography, internal divisions, and boundaries, a project has been undertaken in southern Burgundy (France), entitled Spatial Aspects of Continuity and Change in Protohistoric and Historic Gaul (NSF SOC 75-13874, NSF BNS 76-12007, and NSF BNS 76-12007-A01). Since 1974, our research group has accumulated information concerning settlement and land use in the area between 1000 B.C. and the present, with the objective of identifying factors that affect settlement and land use and the goal of better understanding the process involved in regional settlement shifts through time. Although our research is just now moving from the collection to the analysis stage, a model has begun to take shape which may prove useful in other regions of predominantly heterogeneous character.

In addition to the concepts of regional homogeneity/heterogeneity, scale, organizational structure, and perception, two other concepts merit attention in the discussion of this model. Marquardt (n.d.) has underscored the importance of systemic boundaries as appropriate objects for anthropological examination; they are a focus of interest in our study of the history of a regional system. For example, a road or river simultaneously has two functions: it conveys passengers and cargo between points along its length, and it also divides the territory through which it passes. Any border or boundary has aspects of both centrality and peripherality, and this concept is of vital importance in the study of regions through time.

Second, the concept of interregional symbiosis, introduced by Sanders (1956) and elaborated by Flannery (1968b) to represent exchange relationships among environmentally distinct regions, is also of importance to the model. Together, the two concepts—of centrality/peripherality and symbiosis—represent not only the study of points and relationships between points, but also the boundaries that distinguish that unique system of points and relationships from any other such system. The systemic boundaries themselves, then, set the *scale* of the problem under consideration.

Except among European historical geographers (Clout 1977; Pounds, 1973), diachronic regional studies have for the most part relied on simulation or stochastic growth models. We hope to introduce to regional studies the ecological/environmental perspective prevalent in anthropology, and to provide as well a historically documented, period-by-period analysis of the cultural and natural factors influencing settlement and land use in southern Burgundy.

To effect a diachronic, systemic, and processual study of the manner in which boundaries (both of the system as a whole and those within the system) fluctuate, a region with the following characteristics was chosen: (a) physiography that could safely be termed heterogeneous, (b) considerable time depth (over 2000 years of archaeological, historical, and ecological evidence), implying (c) the absence of elements (extensive construction and/or modification of the landscape) destructive to previous spatial configurations. Finally, (d) the area was to be unambiguously defined at the beginning of the period of study.

The territory of the Aedui, a powerful Celtic group which played an important military and economic role in pre- and postconquest Gaul, is particularly suitable for such a study in all respects. This region is not only the homeland of the Aedui, but it also conforms to the French *département* of Saône-et-Loire, which is, in turn, juxtaposed between the Loire and Saône Rivers. At the north and south ends of its eastern boundary are breaks in the Côtes du Challonais and Mâconnais, through which trade, traveling between the Rhône/Saône corridor and the Loire, would be obliged to pass. By means of signal fires, Bibracte (the Aeduan capital, with an estimated population of 40,000) could be notified rapidly of developments in the corridor between the Saône and the Loire. Instrumental in almost every period in the regulation of commerce between Britain, France, and the Mediterranean, this region is distinctive yet extremely diverse (that is, heterogeneous) in terms of its physiography, drainage, climate, subsurface geology, and pedology. Furthermore, preliminary research indicates that it was a distinctive political, social, economic, and demographic region from La Tène (late Iron Age) times until the Middle Ages. The region, bounded in so many ways by such different data, offers a superb opportunity to understand forces of continuity and change in Gaulish society while holding constant (or at least controlling the variation in) the natural environment and such cultural aspects as Roman provincial administration. In addition, it is an area rich in the spatial data critical to the evaluation of relationships between spatial and cultural change.

Physiography, pedology, drainage, climate, and economic resources are tied closely to subsurface geology in the area. One of the main topographic barriers of western Europe is the Massif Central, a result of Plio-Pleistocene uplift orogeny, which, with the Alps, effectively separates the climate of northern Europe from that of southern Europe. The northeastern extent of the Massif Central is represented by the mountains of the Morvan, which dominate the northwest portion of the study region. Extensive faulting in the study area has juxtaposed schists, gneisses, and granites characteristic of the Morvan with deep sedimentary deposits in the valleys of the Saône and the Loire. Faulting has also exposed strata of organic material (lignite, fossiliferrous and oil-bearing shale, etc.) and thus made available resources for producing charcoal and petroleum products. Additionally, the rocks of the Morvan, rich in iron and tin, have been mined at least since the Iron Age (Davies 1935).

Soils in the research area follow these subsurface distinctions. The central part is characterized by ferrous acidic soils, and the "A" horizon is characteristically composed of decayed (plagioclase) granite. Soils in the western, southwestern, and eastern portions of the research area are water-deposited sands, clays, and gravels, and are also acidic.

Drainage and physiography of the region are the result of the extensive northeast–southwest faulting. While the Saône and its tributaries flow roughly south-southeast, the Arroux, its tributaries, and the Semence and Arconce rivers flow southwest and drain into the Loire. In essence, the research area is a "divide" between the Saône–Rhone–North Sea drainage and the Loire–Atlantic drainage.

There are significant distinctions between this central, faulted area and the Saône and Loire river systems in terms of crops grown, amount of pasturage, and natural vegetation. Charollais beef cattle are a major product of the central area, vineyards characterize the east, and cereal crops the west.

The weather of the region also reflects its position between northern (Atlantic) and southern (Mediterranean) Europe; storms come over Mont Dardon from the south-southeast (up the Rhône–Saône corridor) and from the north-northwest (Atlantic–continental). Paleoclimatologists (Brooks 1949; Lamb 1966; Lamb et al. 1966) postulate a warming trend in western Europe at the beginning of the second Iron Age (La Tène), an optimum having been reached in the first centuries A.D. Roman agricultural writers note that crops normally restricted to the Mediterranean climatic zone were successfully grown farther north (Lamb 1966:63), indicating some fluctuation of the temperate/semitropical ecotone.

A wide variety of information concerning climatic conditions, crops, comparative crop yields, field size, imports and exports, property rights, inheritance laws, population size and density, sex ratio, fertility/mortality rates, and the function, nature, and location of human settlement have been obtained from written documents referring to the region. Classical writers and medieval chroniclers give useful quantitative as well as qualitative information.

Evidence for Celtic continuity long after the conquest and the subsequent fall of the Empire in the West has been obtained by using historiographic methods. Historiography is the critical analysis of texts, the analysis of bias, the determination of authorship, and the study of temporal relationships between authors in terms of shared material and changes in the observations at different times. The historiographic method may be employed much as one would analyze a number of modern ethnographies of the same group. Many classical authors were trained, for one reason or another, to be astute observers; some are actually products of a long tradition in Greece of anthropological investigation. Also at the disposal of the contemporary researcher is a long tradition among classical and medieval scholars of textual and contextual criticism. Thus, the historiographic method offers the possibility of observing change in Gaulish groups through time.

A great advantage of the research area is that there exist numerous documents making direct identifiable reference to the Aedui, the Arroux, and Bibracte, Autun, and other locations. The earliest of these documents date from the first centuries B.C. (Crumley 1974), and they continue (with some gaps) through to the present. There is a notable continuity in the location of the seat of political control at the head of the valley of the Arroux (either at Bibracte or at Autun). Augustus' edict of 12 B.C. forced the abandonment of lofty Bibracte and the resettlement of its inhabitants on the valley floor in the new city of Augustodunum (Autun). The continuity of political control between Bibracte and Augustodunum is clearly shown in the pattern of Roman roads serving the area. The loss of Roman control of the region, a result of Burgundian expansion (ca. A.D. 463–476), does not seem to have altered Autun's importance. Although political control was now predominantly ecclesiastical rather than secular, the pattern of dominance of a center at the head of the Arroux valley continued. Not until the rise of Cluny (between Mâcon and Charolles) in the tenth century did the hegemony of Autun wane.

Preliminary analysis of the archeology, history, and ecology of the region leads us to conclude that the region was quite strongly defined during the period 500 B.C.–A.D. 1000. Although political, social, and economic circumstances changed markedly in Gaul during this period, the systemic–spatial boundaries of the region, as outlined above, exhibited a strong continuity. Some factors (for example, the dominance of a city located at the head of the Arroux valley) remained relatively constant. The significance of other factors, such as population, the utilization of and demands for resources, settlement, and routes of trade, is an appropriate focus for our continuing investigation of continuity and change in Gaulish society. The multidisciplinary, multitemporal study of settlement, ecology, and society within this region during a well-documented period of extensive culture change enables us to begin evaluation of the relationships between spatial and cultural continuity and change on a regional scale.

Our initial objective was to collect information enabling us (*a*) to map major physiographic features for the area as a whole, both their extent (boundary and connective studies) and any salient points (such as passes, ore deposits, fords, etc.), and (*b*) to map, for each time period, the available information concerning roads, administrative boundaries, linguistic units, plant communities, etc., and all known functional centers (again, boundary and connective studies).

There have been numerous methodological problems: integration of a wide variety of cultural and natural information, veracity/validity/utility of information, and, most poignantly, problems of scale. For example, so little is known of Celtic rural settlement (Wightman 1975) that the Iron Age excavation and foot survey went on in only a small part of the region (the western side of the Arroux Valley), owing to time and financial restrictions, whereas the data on medieval parishes is so enormous and simultaneously of such spotty coverage that research was undertaken only in about a third of the research area, overlapping the area of Iron Age research and extending to the northwest. Where funds, time, data, or personnel considerations caused such a reduction in scale, a stratified sample was delineated on the basis of physiography, natural vegetation, and any salient cultural features of the period under study (for example, the Celtic road linking Alesia in northern Burgundy with Bibracte, Mont Dardon, and points south). Nonetheless, the strength of the analogies that can be drawn for the region as a whole could conceivably be open to question. We have devised solutions to many of these problems, and hope to contribute to the better understanding of sampling in heterogeneous areas and temperate zones.

Scale, then, is of great importance in the employment of various methods, or, for that matter, various models. Although we have not used the gravity model, it is conceivable that it would be useful in a study of out-migration from the area or of rural marriage patterns in the nineteenth century. Walter Berry (n.d.) has found aspects of the CP model useful in reducing the area of search for the earliest medieval parishes. The medieval parish is not only the religious center for each area, but the market center as well. Berry's study of fourth- to sixth-century, sixth- to eighth-century, and eighth- to tenth-century parishes has shown there to exist by the sixth century a hexagonal lattice of parish centers in the valleys, which becomes more densely packed with the addition of parishes to the area in subsequent periods. He has also shown that the CP model is appropriate to these data *only* in the valleys; highland areas do not exhibit the same geometric regularity. In the highlands, other considerations severely reduce CP's explanatory power. It is my conclusion that the CP model is of utility (*a*) in areas of relatively homogeneous physiography (for example a river valley), and (*b*) when trade *within* the region is of dominant importance in those economic activities being measured (for example, the distribution of ceramics manufactured locally for domestic use). Vance (1970:9) has also advanced the idea that to use CP successfully, the area should have a history of feudalism as well. In his study of interregional trade (wholesaling) he finds that natural (for example, scarcity) and cultural (for example, politics) factors are more important than transport costs. Vance argues for a more comprehensive model of interaction than CP, which he sees as a "special case" both in fact and in conception (1970:9). According to Vance, what is needed is theory based on experience, with that experience acting as a seine to separate the significant detail from the irrelevant fact—a structure derived from an ordered appraisal of historical evidence. It is in that spirit, with anthropological questions in mind, that we have begun this multidisciplinary study of a region through time. Our approach, ironically and appropriately, bears the greatest resemblance to the French school of historical geography (Clout 1977) and most assuredly must be tested elsewhere before its general utility can be assessed.

It is necessary to make explicit the relationship between scale and level of interaction: the smallest macro scale, then, is intra- (among) and inter- (between) community, followed by intra- and interregional, intra- and intercontinental, and ultimately (one supposes) interterrestial. Such interactions as they pertain to economics are better known, and have long been the focus of attention for economic anthropologists. Although there are many noneconomic interactions that take place at the larger scales in the areas of social organization (for example, international activity of elites), linguistics, and the like, very little investigation has been conducted at these scales. Thus, many of the data of utility in forging a more general model are necessarily economic.

In a study designed to test the hypothesized ecological basis of trade and to delineate interregional, intraregional, and local trade, Hughes (1973) utilizes ethnographic, historical, and archaeological data. He finds that long-distance (interregional) trade moves across the strike of the central mountain massif and between areas of the greatest environmental contrasts, and that the centers of more important manufacturing activity (stone quarry, salt spring) are characterized by more frequent movement of persons, more rapid flow of goods, and increased quantities of goods being transported and exchanged, rather than an increase in the density of the network of paths surrounding such centers (1973:113). Hughes also notes the effect of a particular cultural factor in the movement of long-distance trade items: sorcery. Trade moves uphill because of a fear of lowland peoples' expertise in sorcery; highlanders come only to the southern edge of their area, whereas lowlanders quite often travel into the mountains on trading expeditions. Another cultural factor that influences long-distance trade is risk to life and limb; no price is put on time (1973:111). Hughes concludes his study by distinguishing two types of exchange: (*a*) the great ceremonial exchange cycles, which take place within regions of similar resources, and whose desired end is alternating feasting and redistribution among individuals known to one another if not related, and (*b*) long-distance trade, which takes place between regions of different resources among individuals who are frequently strangers to one another. From this we might conclude that heterogeneous regions and boundary areas generally are more likely to be instrumental in long-distance trade networks than homogeneous regions, and that the retail movement of goods and the exchange of services in homogeneous regions expectably might be predictable on the basis of economy alone. Other factors, such as those discussed by Hughes, determine patterns of inter-regional trade, not the least of which are cultural and environmental.

The work of Karl Polanyi and others (Dalton 1957; Hirth 1978; Blanton 1978) concerned with what are termed "ports of trade" or "gateway cities" has served to point out the importance of centers located along natural and cultural borders, but rarely have we seen the borders themselves regarded in terms of their centrality. Berry (n.d.) finds that new parishes in his later periods of study were consistently located on the border between earlier parishes. The excavational history of the site of Mont Dardon gives evidence of its central functions during the Iron Age, Gallo-Roman, and early medieval periods. Today it is a functional center only for picnics and games of *boules,* and its highest point marks the coincidence of the boundaries of three communes. Thus, Mont Dardon is, and has been, both edge and center. We trust that our research will indicate the circumstances under which each has been the case.

A final feature of the regional heterarchy model requires discussion: the heterarchical nature of its pattern of site distribution. The region in Burgundy discussed above emphatically does not exhibit the CP lattice, although when viewed historically, settlement and land use in the region can be seen as responding to certain factors. For example, the Celtic Aedui built their hill forts overlooking the valleys for reasons of military advantage and (one suspects) aesthetics. Subsequently, the Romans abandoned the Celtic highroads in favor of valley roads connecting low-lying Roman towns for transport and other cultural reasons. Place name studies (toponymy) as well as archaeological and historical data confirm this shift in site location. Subsequent dwellers within the region (Franks, Burgundians, contemporary Frenchmen) have added their distinctive pattern of settlement and land use to the landscape. The distribution of modern communities within the region is a result of such superposition. Neither a mathematical (GM) nor a geometric (CP) model is of universal utility, although some areas within the region may retain (for various reasons) the pattern of utilization of a particular period. The period-by-period investigation of factors influencing settlement and land use has necessarily relied on a variety of data, producing a maze of boundaries. These boundaries *do not* necessarily conform to one another, or "nest" within one another. For example, there is no homogeneous measure of individual status in the region even today, and one expects that there has not been in the past, particularly during the heyday of the region in interregional trade (Crumley 1974). Marriage patterns of today reflect the scale at which centers interact: in rural areas, propinquity is still a major factor in choice of a marriage partner, but in cities within the region, linked more firmly with the rest of France and the world, propinquity is not as great a factor as education or occupation. So would it have been in the past.

We have been able to identify this area as a region for certain time periods when the regional boundaries, on the basis of a number of factors, were congruent. When we define a region, we do so because we can comprehend, identify, and select it as a unit in its interrelationships with other units; thus the term "region" has a certain perceptual size; that is, it is defined on a scale at which the researcher believes he or she can distinguish pattern. The failure to recognize this spatial truism is the classic error of Brush (1953) in his study of retail consumer behavior in rural southwestern Wisconsin. To find an appropriate scale of analysis one must search for (*a*) a measure of the connectivity (all scales) of the area under consideration with contiguous areas, and (*b*) areas that exhibit a high degree of overlap of a variety of boundaries. This would be true of both heterogeneous and homogeneous regions. These areas of overlap vary through time, and some boundary areas are more sensitive to change in the regional system as a whole than are others. On the whole, however, it may be said that the major assumption of the regional heterarchy model is that regions must be defined *temporally,* as well as spatially, on the basis of a variety of cultural and natural factors.

Such an assumption underscores the importance of scale, as it frees the researcher of the need to find the same regional systems operating inexorably through time. In many ways, it might cause us to reformulate problems that have not previously been posed as ones of scale; an example is the problem of what constitutes the provincial collapse of the Roman Empire when the scale changed from one of intercontinental interaction to one of regional interaction. In this sense, and perhaps more broadly as well, one can see various sorts of connectivity (roads, trading partnerships, marriage among international elites) as simply communication.

The regional heterarchy model also assumes an open cultural system, for which one must necessarily resort to more complex models of organization (comprising both hierarchies and heterarchies) and regional structure (homogeneous and heterogeneous). Finally, there is the assumption that to understand and identify process, one must actively investigate all relations among the dimensions of study. For archaeologists, those dimensions are form, space, and time. As anthropologists as well, archaeologists must also understand and include the perceptual dimension, the existence of which is a factor in any spatial study, however difficult it might prove to measure. An advantage of the model is that the entirety of settlement and land use data for each period need not be known; however, the need to understand the variety of ways in which a spatial configuration can come into being may well cause archaeologists to turn to the analogous study of spatial aspects of contemporary cultural systems. In sum, the above assumptions make possible the construction of a conceptual framework in which the operation of an open cultural system may be placed.

CONCLUSIONS

The foregoing analyses of the underlying assumptions of the gravity, central place, and regional heterarchy models have had as their focus four concepts: homogeneous/heterogeneous terrain, as such a distinction concerns the study of regions, the hierarchial/heterarchical nature of organizational structures, the notion of scale, and the overarching importance of perception as it operates upon the first three concepts.

The assumptions shared by the gravity and central place models posit a cultural system with the following characteristics: a region that is featureless and (more important) unbounded but nonetheless closed to external stimuli, the economic rationality and lack of variability (along any parameter) of its inhabitants, the dominance of economic factors in the explanation of population agglomerations, and the structural congruence of other cultural factors with those of economics.

The assumptions of the regional heterarchy model posit an open cultural system extending over varied terrain whose boundaries fluctuate through time and space depending on the nature and frequency of communication/connectivity with other cultural systems. The study of such a system can be undertaken only by utilizing a variety of humanistic, social, physical, and natural science techniques and methods such as those developed in the integrated study of anthropology. To an anthropologist trained to observe cross-cultural variability, much of the foregoing may seem to belabor the obvious; however, to my knowledge no one has bothered to contrast the anthropological understanding of cultural system with that of those engaged in the study of regional science. It is not my intention to minimize the latters' contributions, but to integrate more effectively the regional concept into history, anthropology, and the natural sciences. I am not arguing for the abandonment of the gravity and central place models but rather that they should be subsumed, on the basis of effective scale, beneath the RH model. The more general nature of the RH model will enable a more effective linkage with systems theory, while offering the means of conceptualizing a truly dynamic cultural system. To effect this, we must study the *kinetics* of a region—the manner in which the region became what it is—rather than utilizing the "thermodynamic" regional approach, which compares regional time slices without the understanding of the variety of ways in which spatial configurations may have come into being. Victor Turner (1977) argues persuasively that in the understanding of cognitive boundaries lies the understanding of process; perhaps by studying their spatial analogue (boundaries, points, relationships between points) as anthropologists, and adding a fourth dimension—perception—to Spaulding's space–time–form, we can ultimately gain an understanding of process in archaeology.

ACKNOWLEDGMENTS

My colleagues Robert Daniels (Department of Anthropology, University of North Carolina), Thomas Isenhour (Department of Chemistry, University of North Carolina), and Thomas Bell (Department of Geography, University of Tennessee) have patiently read versions of this paper. William Marquardt (Institute of Archeology and Anthropology, University of South Carolina) gave me the term heterarchy for what was then, to me, a nameless concept, and has been instrumental in helping me think through the concepts discussed herein, giving untiringly of his time and freely of his ideas.

REFERENCES

Abrams, R. H.
    1943   Residential propinquity as a factor in marriage selection: Fifty year trends in Philadelphia. *American Sociological Review* **8**:228–294.

Adams, J. W., and A. B. Kasakoff
    1976   Central place theory and endogamy in China. In *Regional analysis,* Vol. II: *Social systems,* edited by C. A. Smith, New York: Academic Press. Pp. 175–187.
Adams, R. McC.
    1974   Anthropological perspectives on ancient trade. *Current Anthropology* **15:**239–258.
Appleby, G.
    1976   The role of urban food needs in regional development, Puno, Peru. In *Regional analysis,* Vol. I: *Economic systems,* edited by C A. Smith, New York: Academic Press. Pp. 147–178.
Beckman, M. J.
    1958   City hierarchies and the distribution of city size. *Economic development and cultural change* (Vol. 6). Pp. 243–248.
Bell, T. L., S. R. Lieber, and G. Rushton
    1974   Clustering of services in central places. *Annals of the Association of American Geographers* **64**(No. 2)**:**214–225.
Berry, B. J. L.
    1967   *Geography of market centers and retail distribution. Foundations of economic geography* series, Englewood Cliffs, N.J.: Prentice-Hall.
Berry, B. J. L., and A. Pred (editors)
    1965   *Central place studies: A bibliography of theory and applications* (Bibliographic Series, No. 1, with Supplement), Philadelphia: Regional Science Research Institute.
Berry, W. E.
    n.d.   New directions in the study of medieval settlement. Manuscript on deposit, University of North Carolina.
Blanton, R. E.
    1978   The origins of Monte Alban. In *Settlement Patterns at the Ancient Zapotec Capital.* New York: Academic Press.
Bohannan, P., and L. Bohannan
    1968   *Tiv economy.* Evanston: Northwestern University Press.
Bohannan, P., and G. Dalton (eds.)
    1965   *Markets in Africa.* Garden City, N.Y.: Natural History Press.
Brooks, C. E. P.
    1949   *Climate through the ages.* (2nd ed.). New York: Dover.
Brush, J. E.
    1953   The hierarchy of central places in southwestern Wisconsin. *Geographical Review* **43:**380–402.
Bylund, E.
    1960   Theoretical considerations regarding the distribution of settlement in inner North Sweden. *Geografiska Annaler* **62:**225–231.
Cancian, F.
    1974   New patterns of stratification in the Zinacantan cargo system. *Journal of Anthropological Research* **30**(No. 3):164–173.
    1976   Social stratification. *Annual Review of Anthropology* No. 9578, 227–248.
Chisholm, M.
    1968   *Rural settlement and land use.* Chicago: Aldine.
Christaller, V.
    1966   *Central places in Southern Germany* (translated by C. W. Baskin), Englewood

Cliffs, N.J.: Prentice-Hall. (Originally published as *Die zentralen Orte in Sud-deutschland*, 1933.)

1972 How I discovered the theory of central places. In *Man, space and environment*, edited by P. W. English and R. C. Mayfield. Oxford University Press: London and New York. Pp. 601–610.

Clarke, D. L.

1972 Models and paradigms in contemporary archaeology. In *Models in archaeology*, edited by D. L. Clarke. London: Methuen, Pp. 47–52.

1977a Spatial information in archaeology. In *Spatial archaeology*, edited by D. L. Clarke. New York: Academic Press. Pp. 1–34.

1977b (editor) *Spatial archaeology*. New York: Academic Press.

Clout, H. D.

1977 The practice of historical geography in France. In *Themes in the historical geography of France*, edited by H. D. Clout. New York: Academic Press. Pp. 1–19.

Cook, S.

1976 Economic anthropology: Problems in theory, method, and analysis. In *Handbook of social and cultural anthropology*, edited by J. Honigmann. Chicago: Rand-McNally. Pp. 795–860.

Cook, T.

1970 Social groups and settlement patterns in Basketmaker III. Unpublished M. A. thesis, Department of Anthropology, University of Chicago.

Crissman, L.

1976a Specific central-place models for an evolving system of market towns on the Changhua Plain, Taiwan. In *Regional analysis*, Vol. I: *Economic systems*, edited by C. A. Smith. New York: Academic Press. Pp. 183–218.

1976b Spatial aspects of marriage patterns as influenced by marketing behavior in West Central Taiwan. In *Regional analysis*, Vol. II: *Social systems*, edited by C. A. Smith. New York: Academic Press. Pp. 123–148.

Crumley, C. L.

1974 Celtic social structure: the generation of archaeologically testable hypotheses from literary evidence. *University of Michigan, Museum of Anthropology, Anthropological Papers* No. 54.

1976 Toward a locational definition of state systems of settlement. *American Anthropologist* **78**:59–73.

Dalton, G.

1968 (editor) *Primitive, archaic, and modern economics: Essays of Karl Polanyi*. Boston: Beacon Press.

Davie, M., and J. R. Reeves

1939 Propinquity of residence before marriage. *American Journal of Sociology* **44**:510–518.

Davies, O.

1935 *Roman mines in Europe*. Oxford: Clarendon Press.

Dumont, L.

1957 Hierarchy and marriage alliance in South Indian kinship. *Occasional Papers of the Royal Anthropological Institute of Great Britain and Ireland* No. 12.

Dunn, E. S.

1954 *The location of agricultural production*. Gainesville: University of Florida Press.

Earle, T. K., and J. E. Ericson (editors)
  1977 *Exchange systems in prehistory.* New York: Academic Press.
Edel, M.
  1969 Economic analysis in an anthropological setting: Some methodological considerations. *American Anthropologist* **71**:421–433.
Ericson, J. E.
  1977 Egalitarian exchange systems in California: A preliminary view. In *Exchange systems in prehistory,* edited by T. K. Earle and J. E. Ericson. New York: Academic Press. Pp. 109–126.
Fallers, L. A.
  1973 *Inequality: Social stratification reconsidered.* Chicago: University of Chicago Press.
Feldman, S. L.
  1976 Location analysis: The historical equilibrium of workers' self-management. *Economic Geography* **52**:24–29.
Flannery, K. V.
  1968a Archeological systems theory and early Mesoamerica. In *Anthropological archeology in the Americas,* edited by B. J. Meggers. Washington, D.C.: Anthropological Society of Washington. Pp. 67–87.
  1968b The Olmec and the Valley of Oaxaca: A model for interregional interaction in formative times. In *Dumbarton Oaks Conference on the Olmec,* edited by E. P. Benson. Washington, D.C.: Dumbarton Oaks. Pp. 79–110.
  1972 The cultural evolution of civilizations. *Annual Review of Ecology and Systematics* **3**:399–426.
  1976 (editor) *The early Mesoamerican village.* New York: Academic Press.
Fox, Sir C.
  1932 *The personality of Britain: Its influence on inhabitant and invader in prehistoric and historic times.* Cardiff: National Museum.
Friedrich, M. H.
  1970 Design structure and social interaction: Archaeological implications of an ethnographic analysis. *American Antiquity* **35**:332–343.
Garrison, W. L., and D. F. Marble
  1957 The spatial structure of agricultural activities. *Annals of the Association of American Geographers* **47**:137–144.
Godelier, M.
  1972 *Rationality and irrationality in economics.* New York: Monthly Review Press.
Hägerstrand, T.
  1957 Migration and area. Survey of a sample of Swedish migration fields and hypothetical considerations on their genesis. In Migration in Sweden: A symposium, edited by D. Hennerberg, T. Hägerstrand, and B. Odering. *Lund Studies in Geography B,* No. 13, 27–158.
  1963 Geographic measurements of migration: Swedish data. In *Human displacements: Entretiens de Monaco en sciences humaines,* edited by J. Sutter. Monaco.
Haggett, P.
  1965 *Locational analysis in human geography.* New York: St. Martin's.
  1972 *Geography: A modern synthesis.* New York: Harper.
Harper, E. B. (editor)
  1964 *Aspects of Religion in South Asia.* Ann Arbor: Association for Asian Studies.
Harris, M.
  1968 *The rise of anthropological theory.* London: Routledge & Kegan Paul.

Harvey, D.
  1973   *Explanation in geography.* London: Arnold.
Haynes, K. E., and W. T. Enders
  1975   Distance, direction, and entropy in the evolution of a settlement pattern. *Economic Geography* **51**(No. 4):357–365.
Hirth, K. G.
  1978   Interregional trade and the formation of prehistoric gateway communities. *American Antiquity* **43**(No. 1):35–45.
Hodder, I. R., and C. Orton
  1976   *Spatial analysis in archaeology.* London and New York: Cambridge University Press.
Hughes, I.
  1973   Stone Age trade in the New Guinea inland. In *The Pacific in transition,* edited by H. Brookfield. New York: St. Martin's. Pp. 97–126.
Isard, W.
  1956   *Location and space economy.* New York: MIT Press and Wiley.
  1975   *Introduction to regional science.* Englewood Cliffs, N.J.: Prentice-Hall.
Jackman, R. A.
  1975   The problem of externalities in a spatial economy. In *Regional science: New concepts and old problems,* edited by E. L. Cripps (London Papers in Regional Science, No. 5). London: Pion.
James, P. E.
  1972   *All possible worlds: A history of geographical ideas.* New York: Odyssey Press.
Johnson, G. A.
  1972   A test of the utility of central place theory in archaeology. In *Man, settlement, and urbanism,* edited by P. J. Ucko, R. Tringham, and G. W. Dimbleby. London: Duckworth, Pp. 769–785.
  1977   Aspects of regional analysis in archaeology. *Annual Review of Anthropology* No. 9603, 479–508.
Kariel, H. G.
  1963   Selected factors areally associated with population growth due to net migration. *Annals of the Association of American Geographers* **53**:210–223.
Kolars, J. F., and J. D. Nystuen
  1974   *Geography.* New York: McGraw-Hill.
Lamb, H. H.
  1966   *The changing climate.* London: Methuen.
Lamb, H. H., R. P. W. Lewis, and A. Woodroffe
  1966   *Atmospheric circulation and the main climatic variables between 8000 B.C. to 0 B.C.: Meterological evidence for world climate from 8000 B.C. to 0 B.C.* London: Royal Meterological Society.
Leach, E. R.
  1964   *Political systems of Highland Burma.* Boston: Beacon Press.
Lentnek, B., S. R. Lieber, and I. Sheskin
  1975   Consumer behavior in different areas. *Annals of the Association of American Geographers* **65**(No. 4):538–545.
Leone, M.
  1968   Neolithic economic autonomy and social distance. *Science* **162**:1150–1151.
Lévi-Strauss, C.
  1960   On manipulated sociological models. In *Bijdragen tot de taal-landen volkenkunde.* Vol. CXVI, no. 1. The Hague.

Lösch, A.
1954 *The economics of location* (translated by W. H. Woglom and W. F. Stolper). New Haven: Yale University Press. (Originally published in 1943.)

MacNeish, R. S.
1972 The evaluation of community patterns in the Tehuacan Valley of Mexico and speculations about the cultural processes. In *Man, settlement, and urbanism,* edited by P. J. Ucko, R. Tringham, and G. W. Dimbleby. London: Duckworth. Pp. 67–93.

Marches, J., and G. Turbeville
1953 The effect of residential propinquity on marriage selection. *American Journal of Sociology* **58**:592–595.

Marquardt, W. H.
n.d. Fundamentally random caterpillars: The influence of statistical ecology on archaeological descriptions of settlement. Paper presented at the symposium *Locational models in archaeology,* Society for American Archaeology, New Orleans, April, 1977.

Marshall, J. U.
1969 *The location of service towns.* Toronto: University of Toronto Press.

Minsky, M., and S. Papert
1972 *Artificial Intelligence Progress Report* (AI Memo No. 252). Cambridge, Mass.: Massachusetts Institute of Technology, Artificial Intelligence Laboratory.

Morrill, R. L.
1962 Simulation of central place patterns over time. *Lund Studies in Geography* **24**:109–120.
1963 The development of spatial distributions of towns in Sweden: An historical–predictive approach. *Annals of the Association of American Geographers* **53**:1–14.

Murdie, R.
1965 Cultural differences in consumer travel. *Economic Geography* **41**:211–233.

Netting, R. McC.
1972 Sacred power and centralization: Aspects of political adaptation in Africa. In *Population growth,* edited by B. Spooner, Cambridge, Mass.: MIT Press. Pp. 219–244.

Olsen, S. M.
1976 Regional social systems: Linking quantitative analysis and field work. In *Regional analysis.* Vol. I: *Economic systems,* edited by C. A. Smith. New York: Academic Press. Pp. 21–61.

Olsson, G.
1965a *Distance and human interaction: A review and bibliography* (Bibliography Series, No. 2). Philadelphia: Regional Science Research Institute.
1965b Distance and human interaction: A migration study. *Geografiska Annaler, Series B* **47**(No. 1):3–43.
1966 Central place systems, spatial interaction, and stochastic processes. *Papers and Proceedings of the Regional Science Association* **18**:13–45.
1968 *Distance, human interaction and stochastic processes: Essays on geographic model building.* Ann Arbor: University of Michigan Press.
1970 Explanation, prediction, and meaning variance: An assessment of distance interaction models. *Economic Geography* **46**(No. 2 Suppl.):223–233.

Ossowski, S.
1963 *Class-structure in the social consciousness.* New York: Free Press.

Parsons, J. R.
  1972   Archaeological settlement patterns. *Annual Review of Anthropology* 1:127–150.
Plog, F.
  1977   Modelling economic exchange. In *Exchange systems in prehistory*, edited by T. K. Earle and J. E. Ericson. New York: Academic Press. Pp. 127–140.
Plog, S.
  1976   Measurement of prehistoric interaction between communities. In *The early Mesoamerican village*, edited by K. V. Flannery, New York: Academic Press. Pp. 255–272.
Polanyi, K., C. Arensburg, and H. Pearson (editors)
  1957   *Trade and market in the early empires*. Glencoe, Ill.: Free Press.
Pounds, J. N.
  1971   The urbanization of the classical world. *Ekistics* 182:22–35.
  1973   *An historical geography of Europe 450 B.C.–A.D. 1330*. London and New York: Cambridge University Press.
Redman, C. L. (editor)
  1973   *Research and theory in current archeology*. New York: Wiley.
Renfrew, C.
  1969   Trade and culture process in European prehistory. *Current Anthropology* 10:151–169.
  1977   Models for exchange and spatial distribution. In *Exchange systems in prehistory* edited by T. K. Earle and J. E. Ericson. New York: Academic Press. Pp. 71–90.
Rowlett, R. M., and R. B. Pollnac
  1971   Multivariate analysis of Marnian La Tène cultural groups. In *Mathematics in the archaeological and historical sciences* edited by F. R. Hodson, D. G. Kendall, and P. Tautu. Edinburgh: Edinburgh University Press. Pp. 46–58.
Sanders, W. T.
  1956   The Central Mexican symbiotic region; A study in prehistoric settlement patterns. In *Prehistoric settlement patterns in the New World*, edited by G. R. Willey. *Viking Fund Publications in Anthropology* No. 23, 115–127.
Service, E. R.
  1960   The law of evolutionary potential. In *Evolution and culture*, edited by M. R. Sahlins and E. R. Service. Ann Arbor: University of Michigan Press. Pp. 93–122.
Skinner, G.
  1977a   Cities and the hierarchy of local systems. In *The city in Late Imperial China*, edited by G. W. Skinner. Stanford: Stanford University Press. Pp. 275–351.
  1977b   Regional urbanization in nineteenth-century China. In *The city in Late Imperial China*, edited by G. W. Skinner. Stanford: Stanford University Press. Pp. 211–249.
Smith, C. A.
  1976a   Analyzing regional social systems. In *Regional analysis*, Vol. II: *Social systems*, edited by C. A. Smith. New York: Academic Press. Pp. 3–20.
  1976b   Exchange systems and the spatial distribution of elites: The organization of stratification in agrarian societies. In *Regional analysis*, Vol. II: *Social systems*, edited by C. A. Smith. New York: Academic Press. Pp. 309–374.
  1976c   Regional economic systems: Linking geographical models and socioeconomic problems. In *Regional analysis*, Vol. I: *Economic systems*, edited by C. A. Smith. New York: Academic Press. Pp. 3–63.
  1976d   (editor) *Regional analysis*, Vol. II: *Social systems*. New York: Academic Press.

Spaulding, A. C.
 1960   The dimensions of archaeology. In *Essays in the science of culture,* edited by
        G. E. Dole and R. Carniero, New York: Crowell. Pp. 437–456.
Tobler, W., and S. Wineberg
 1971   A Cappadocian speculation. *Nature (London)* **231**:40–41.
Turner, B. L.
 1976   Population density in the Classic Maya Lowlands: New evidence for old ap-
        proaches. *Geographical Review* **66**(No. 1):73–82.
Turner, V.
 1977   Process, system, and symbol: A new anthropological synthesis. *Daedalus.*
        Pp. 61–80.
Vance, J. E., Jr.
 1970   *The merchant's world: The geography of wholesaling* (Foundations of Eco-
        nomic Geography Series). Englewood Cliffs, N.J.: Prentice-Hall.
Warren, H.
 1969   Tonque: One pueblo's glaze pottery industry dominated Middle Rio Grande
        commerce. *El Palacio* **76**:36–42.
Watson, J. W.
 1955   Geography—A discipline in distance. *Scottish Geographical Magazine* **71**(No.
        1):1–3.
Weber, M.
 1947   *The theory of social and economic organization,* edited and translated by A. M.
        Henderson and T. Parsons. London and New York: Oxford University Press.
 1968   *Economy and society,* edited by G. Roth and C. Wittich. New York: Bedmins-
        ter Press.
White, L. A.
 1949   *The science of culture.* New York: Farrar, Strauss.
 1959   *The evolution of culture.* New York: McGraw-Hill.
Whittlesey, D.
 1954   Committee Report: The regional concept and the regional method. In *American
        geography, inventory and prospect,* edited by P. E. James and C. F. Jones.
        Syracuse: Syracuse University Press. Pp. 21–68.
Wightman, E. M.
 1975   The pattern of rural settlement in Roman Gaul. *Aufsteig und Niedergang der
        Romischer Welt* **2**(No. 4):584–657.
Wilson, A. G.
 1969   *Entropy in urban and regional modelling* (Working Paper CES-WP-26). Lon-
        don: Center for Environmental Studies.

Archaeologically, What Constitutes an Early Domestic Animal?

STANLEY J. OLSEN

INTRODUCTION

The beginning of the domestication of plants and animals ranks in importance with the first use and control of fire in the process of man's social development.

Defining "domestication" is as diverse a problem as determining the bones of those animals that fall within this category. This is due to the long process involved, negating the pinpointing of animals in the initial stages of the process. It seems reasonable to accept the fact that the events leading from animals that were wild to those that were finally domesticated would follow the process of capture, taming, and controlled breeding (but not necessarily conducted as a well-organized procedure). Animals from either end of the spectrum could probably be identified by one or more of the methods now in use, but what about the first forms that could be considered domestic? Any change from wild, through tame, to domestic would involve such a gradual process, over an undetermined and variable time period, that I seriously doubt if any of the intermediate stages of the process could be satisfactorily isolated and defined (Figure 6.1).

Most, if not all, of the definitions of "domestication" can be challenged

ADVANCES IN ARCHAEOLOGICAL METHOD AND THEORY, VOL. 2

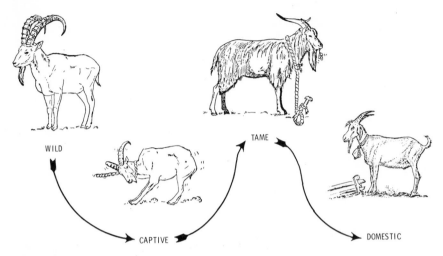

Figure 6.1. Archaeologically, what constitutes a wild/captive/tame or domestic animal? Unknowns: (1) length of time for effects of domestication to be reflected osteologically; (2) number of animal generations required for effects to be reflected osteologically; (3) variability of domestication processes (it does change geographically) used on animals and the osteological effects; (4) aberrant osteological features, present in some wild animals, that mistakenly might be attributed to the effects of domestication.

by citing exceptions to the rule as stated. For example, Bökönyi (1969:219) stated, "I would define the essence of domestication as: the capture and taming by man of animals of a species with particular behavioral characteristics, their removal from their natural living area and the breeding community, and their maintainance under controlled breeding conditions for profit." Many tamed, wild animals will fit this category, from the killer whale (*Orcinus orca*) to many zoo animals. One would hardly consider these as either domestic or on the way to domestication. Zeuner (1963) includes another dimension to the definition by adding symbiosis, in which each partner of the man/animal relationship derives a benefit, although not necessarily equal. He also uses the term slavery as a synonym for domestication. Domestication is a many-faceted process in which there always seem to be exceptions to the simply stated definitions.

Most of the events concerning those animals chosen for domestication and the events leading from wild, through captured, to tamed, and finally domesticated are not found in the archaeological record. We do know that skeletally it is at times possible, given enough material, to separate many species of domestic animals from their wild counterparts. One of the definitions of domestication is that the species will exhibit a morphological change from wild to domestic. The degree of change and where it may occur and be observed is as variable as the animals that are under consideration, although it is the basis for determining most domestic animals.

OSTEOLOGICAL EVIDENCE

For the most part, the varying breeds, or races, or living domestic animals today are distinguished and separated by their varying size and body forms, by the types and color patterns of their pelage or plumage, and in some instances by their horns. Except for the latter, these other separating characters are not generally preserved in animal remains that are recovered from archaeological excavations. Comparisons of morphological features present in bones, mostly fragmentary, must be relied on for identification and interpretation. By far the overwhelming evidence for domestication is from the osteological record.

Even this last statement can be misleading, as the skeletal evidence is by no means complete or at times even adequate. More often than not, the recovered bones are mere scraps or splinters. Even if pieced together (which may, at times, border on the impossible), they usually represent only a few complete elements. The articulated skeleton, or partial skeleton, is a rarity in most sites. The generally incomplete condition of the recovered bones accounts in great part for most of the identifications and interpretations of faunal assemblages being done by workers with a background of vertebrate paleontology where working with incomplete bones and interpreting the identifications is standard practice.

Within the past decade or so we have seen this new subfield in anthropology develop into a full-fledged discipline of zooarchaeology (or archaeozoology in Europe).

Gross Osteological Morphology

Osteologically, how does one differentiate wild animals from those that were eventually selected for domestication, from those captured and tamed wild individuals, and from the first generations of those that eventually became domesticated animals, all of the same species? We know little of the length of time, or the number of animal generations, required to produce changes in bone form or structure that may be used to identify and separate wild from domestic animals of the same species. Meadow and Zeder (1978) state that size reduction and morphological change in domestic animals could have occurred over a period of 30 animal generations (60–150 years), but they could not be separated out of the archaeological record because these authors believe that the smallest temporal units distinguishable are usually no more than 100 years.

One must take into consideration the following questions: To what degree do the various species of animals under consideration vary as individuals? Is there noticeable (or measurable) osteological variation between adult males and females of the same species? Are some of the bones that are being examined representative of extreme variants or aberrant individuals? At times, the terms "larger" or "smaller" are used roughly to separate overlapping populations of similar animals (goats and sheep in particular) that occur within the same area. Take, for example, two well-known and thoroughly studied wild forms of North American deer. The mule deer (*Odocoileus hemionus*) and the white-tailed deer (*Odocoileus virginiana*) occur in the same "overlap" area in the southwestern United States. They can, of course, be separated by the different antlers, but these are present only in the males. The postcranial skeletal elements of the adult mule deer are generally larger overall than the same comparable elements of the white-tailed deer. However, could the bones of a larger-than-average individual of a white-tailed deer be separated from the similar bones of a smaller-than-average mule deer? Would this logic also apply to the wild/domestic sheep and goat problem?

The same observation applies in separating the bones of the bison (*Bison bison*) from those of the domestic cattle (*Bos taurus*) where they occur in early historic sites in western North America. Generally, a large male bison is considerably larger than the large male domestic cattle encountered in colonial sites (there is, of course, little size difference in some modern large domestic cattle). The same is true of large bison cows, which are still larger than large domestic cows. Little difference is noticeable between small bison bulls and large domestic cows. Most experts on bovid anatomy agree that only more or less complete skeletal material will allow for a separation of the two species.

DiPeso (1953) encountered this problem with bovid remains from the Babocomori village trash. When he sent the bones in question to Dr. William Burt, a well-qualified mammalogist, Burt stated that they were "bison (could be cow, but probably not)" (DiPeso 1953:272). During the course of the analysis of the fauna from Quiburi village, a large number of cow bones were encountered, and it was suggested that Dr. Burt reexamine the Babocomori bison (?) bones and compare them with the Quiburi cow bone collection. Subsequently the bones were sent to Dr. Morris Skinner, an authority on bison/cow osteology. These were examined and compared in the Frick Laboratory of the American Museum of Natural History, where an adequate bovid skeletal collection was housed. After his analysis, Skinner concluded that the bones were probably those of a young female bison. He based his decision, with some misgivings, on the criteria of size of horn core for its age and heaviness of mature metacarpal, and in summary he states, "As to the immature dentition we must warn you that anyone willing to state that these specimens are either bison or cow would be out on a long limb if they were confronted with a good comparative collection. It could be neither proved nor disproved" (Skinner 1952).

Most of the published osteological studies on the wild/domestic mammal problem have been related to archaeological excavations in the Near East. This is due to the many early sites that are under investigation in the Fertile Crescent, an area curving from E. Iran, around W. Iraq, N. Syria, S. Turkey, and Palestine. It encompasses one of the centers of the beginnings of agriculture and of the domestication of mammals. Also, the excavations in that area have been quite extensive, being conducted over a considerable period of time, and resulting in the recovery of quantities of faunal material. Unfortunately, it has only been in quite recent times that any importance has been given to saving this excavated bone, and virtually no attempt has been made (except by Reed) to collect and prepare recent animal skeletons from the area for comparison with excavated bones.

Some domestic animal species present very little change from their late Pleistocene ancestors or between wild and domestic forms living at present. Consequently, determining the correct category to which excavated bones belong can more often than not be an impossible task. Equids (horses, asses, zebras) and camelids (camels and llamas), in particular, fall into this category. The taxonomic differences that distinguish and separate the various species of the genus *Equus* have been established mainly on the pattern variations of the occlusal or grinding surfaces of the cheek teeth. For the same reasons as those given for separating some North American deer, so are horses and their near relatives, the asses and onagers, difficult to separate on the basis of postcranial bones alone. It can be most misleading to establish the presence of a domestic horse at an early site when, in reality, it represents a similar-appearing wild form. At times, the validity of the taxonomic position of such an animal can be determined only by a specialist having the required experience gained from working closely with a particular group of animals. An example of this confused assigning of a wild equid to that of a domestic category occurred at a Persian site in an early context at Anau (c. 4800 B.C.). Several isolated bones were listed as belonging to the domestic horse (*Equus caballus*). They were later correctly interpreted as belonging to the onager (*Equus hemionus*), a wild equid of that area (Zeuner 1963).

The small bovids, such as sheep (*Ovis*) and goats (*Capra*), are also difficult to isolate, even on a generic level, and more often than not it is impossible to distinguish between wild and domestic animals of the same species. Reed (1960:129) put it precisely when he said: "The greatest obstacle to an analysis of the origin and spread of prehistoric domestic sheep and goats is my complete disbelief in the validity of most of the published identifications. Sheep and goat skeletons are extra-ordinarily similar and, except for phalanges, metapodials, certain parts of skulls, and horn cores, cannot usually be distinguished."

Reed goes on to state that considerable difficulty arises when the bones of various gazelles and antelope are introduced into the sample, owing to the similarity of all these small artiodactyl bones. He speaks for many zooarchaeologists when he states that the best that can be done at times is to create a sheep/goat grouping for many of the elements, rather than trying to distinguish between wild/domestic animals of certain groups.

This similarity among the same elements of different species is most apparent when one is comparing the lower limb bones or metapodials. It is at times a problem to determine whether the distal end fragment is from a metacarpal (forelimb) or metatarsal (hind limb) of the same species, let alone which species.

The Western Hemisphere has a problem comparable to that found with artiodactyls in the Near East, regarding separating the fragmentary skeletal remains of prehistoric wild/domestic animals. This involves the camelids, of which the llamas are the New World representatives.

The thought of camels generally brings to mind a vision of the great deserts of the Sahara or Mongolia, rather than of North or South America. Actually, these animals, like the horses, originated in the Western Hemisphere and accomplished the major portion of their evolution in North America. The only surviving members of the Camelidae in this hemisphere are the llamas of South America.

Most taxonomists agree, although there is still some controversy, that there are four distinct species of llama. This taxonomic problem is complicated by the close similarity of these forms to one another, and by the fact that osteological comparisons of individuals are made from the skeletons of animals that are partially or completely domesticated and are descended from ancestors with similar backgrounds.

Until this taxonomic controversy is resolved (and it may never be), I shall go along with the following classification of llamas, which is generally accepted.

The four species of llamas that are considered as separate forms are the llama, *Lama glama;* the alpaca, *Lama pacos;* the vicuña, *Lama vicugna* (at times considered a separate genus, *Vicugna*); and the guanaco, *Lama guanicoe*.

The llama and the alpaca are known only in the domesticated state. The vicuña is known only as a wild animal, as is the guanaco. The guanaco is considered by many mammalogists as the ancestral form of the domestic llama. The alpaca is regarded by some animal specialists as being a variety of the vicuña, but in all probability it, too, is derived from the guanaco.

Some modern research workers (Wheeler Pires-Ferreira *et al.* 1976) have hypothesized that since all four species interbreed and produce fertile offspring, they may, in reality, represent but a single species. The problem that arises from this conclusion is that the same logic must then apply to other animals that also meet these standards. For example, the wolf (*Canis lupus*), the coyote (*Canis latrans*), and the domestic dog (*Canis familiaris*) also interbreed and produce fertile offspring. Do we then consider the wolf, dog, and coyote as a single species? I think that this would hardly be justified, nor would most taxonomists follow such a change in classification.

Osteologically, the bones of llamas are not generally distinguishable on a specific level. They are usually listed in site reports, dealing with faunal analysis, as representing a single general group, the Camelidae. At times, the bone fragments may be so similar morphologically that whether they represent llama or deer cannot be determined. They are then simply listed as Camelidae/Cervidae.

When one uses the occurrence of llama bones at a site of known age to establish the beginnings of domestication of this animal, rather shaky results may emerge. For example, how does one really know whether the bones that are excavated represent wild animals that were hunted and killed for food, or whether they represent captured and penned wild animals? How do penned, tamed animals differ osteologically from truly domesticated animals? Not enough evidence is available either for analyzing selective butchering at a kill site or for evaluating the bones of captive animals that remain at a more or less permanent habitation site.

Specific Individual Variation

Reports using single elements or partial bones to establish the presence of most domestic animals should be regarded with suspicion as to their validity. More often than not, the proportions and characters of the skeletons of domestic and wild animals of the same species, and of the same body weight, are nearly inseparable when their bones are compared. It is only through multiple proportional measurements, mainly of the skulls, mandibles, and dentitions, that any close specific assignments can be arrived at with any degree of confidence.

Using the multiple skull characters separating the various species of *Canis* is the only acceptable method of determining which species are present at a site. A series of proportions including relative length of the muzzle, size of teeth relative to total skull size, width of palate, and degree of inflation of the bullae, all have to be taken into consideration. Using only a few width/length measurements of the skull to establish whether a dog or wolf is present in a Near Eastern site may be hazardous. This was emphasized by Clutton-Brock (1969). The wolf of the late Pleistocene in Palestine was the same size as the present-day European wolf, but at the close of the Pleistocene a drastic size reduction occurred, resulting in a dwarfing of these animals by post-Pleistocene times. Kúrten (1965) undertook detailed comparative measurements of numerous wild canids to establish these conclusions.

We do not know enough about the range of variability in either wild or domestic canids to arrive at some of the specific identifications that have appeared in print and that were based on supposedly valid taxonomic characters. The Star Carr canid has been identified as a domestic dog, on the evidence of the crowding and displacement of the teeth, known to be present in the domestic dog but regarded as absent in wolves. However, it is not known whether or not, or how frequently, this condition may occur as an abnormality in wild European wolves.

In the new George C. Page Museum at the Rancho La Brea tar pits in Los Angeles, there is a striking exhibit of 404 dire wolf skulls (*Canis dirus*), all shown together on a translucent backlit wall panel. Here one can view and compare a considerable number of skulls of an extinct canid with little effort. These giant wolves were in no way influenced by man's activities. There is no evidence of any association between the two. However, it is interesting to note that about 25 of the specimens exhibit the "dished" appearance in the rostral area, anterior to the orbits. This character is generally attributed to the domestic dog. It points up the folly of using a single character, or of using fragmentary partial elements, found in canids at least, to push back and establish the presence of domestic dogs at early sites.

Responsibility, in part, for some of the error and confusion in assigning positive, specific designations based on fragmentary and inadequate bones must be borne by the vertebrate paleontologists. Until a few decades ago, a common fault in paleontology was (and to a minor degree still is) to establish a new species taxon for mammals, based at times on a single tooth or on fragmentary jaws, more or less ignoring the possibility that these incomplete specimens might be variants or aberrant individuals of already well-known species.

At times, even complete skulls and skeletons of individuals were assigned new specific taxonomic categories simply because they were from older Pleistocene deposits. For example, the coyote from Rancho La Brea was assigned the new name *Canis orcutti* (Merriam 1910). The living species in that area is *Canis latrans ochropus* (Hall and Kelson 1959). The same is true for the coyote from the Papago Springs Pleistocene cave deposits in Arizona. It was assigned the name *Canis caneloenis* (Skinner 1942). The living coyote of the area is *Canis latrans mearnsi* (Hall and Kelson 1959). Both of these "extinct" canids are within the acceptable individual variation of the living species. Nowak (1973) put both in synonymy with the living coyote (*Canis latrans*) but allowed the specific identifications assigned the fossil forms to remain as subspecific designations. With this I agree.

Occasionally, unfamiliarity with standard, accepted taxonomic rules and procedures account for erroneous interpretations to creep into the published literature. For example, Singh (1974:55) interprets the identification *Canis* sp. from a Levant Neolithic faunal list as "dog species (*Canis* sp.)." In reality, *Canis* sp. indicates that *Canis* is present at that site, but the species is undetermined and could be either wolf, jackal, or dog (Schenk and McMasters 1956). Once a determination is mistakenly carried over as dog, the next author may refer to it as occurring there with no question.

Cross Sections and Chemical Composition of Bone and Horn

Studies of the cross-sectional structures of both horn cores and the lower limb bones of the small bovids have been used to aid in the understanding of the changes that are present in these elements between wild and domestic animals.

The theory that bone structure is modified by external stress, and that the resulting change can be used to distinguish between wild and domestic caprines, was presented by Drew *et al.* (1971) and later enlarged upon by Pollard and Drew (1975) for examining the sectioned bones of domestic and wild llamas.

The method involves viewing petrographic thin sections of bone under cross-polarized light at magnifications of 35–50 times. A full-wave gypsum plate, inserted in the light path, makes it possible to determine alignment of parallel bundles of crystallites of which the mineral substance of bone is composed. Zeder (1978) reviews this work of Drew and others, and also contributes observations of her own with similar experiments. One of the conclusions that she arrived at was that not all research workers feel that bone structure is modified by external stress. Therefore, the foregoing experiments would be open to debate as to their validity in establishing whether a particular bone represented a wild or a domestic animal. The study of the possible use of cross sections of bones for establishing the presence of wild/domestic faunas should be continued, but with more attention being paid to the control of specimens being used.

The use of cross sections of horn cores of goats and sheep as a means of identifying wild or domestic individuals appears to be quite valid if one is considering only animals that are advanced domestics or those that are entirely wild and unaffected by taming or domestication. Hole and his colleagues pointed out: "The horn core is significantly different in the two species involved. The goat (*Capra hircus*) has hollow cores with a keeled front surface, while the wild sheep (*Ovis orientalis*) has cores which are solid except for a few small sinuses, and flat or gently rounded on their front surface" (Hole *et al.* 1969:267).

Dyson (1973:81) interprets the cross-sectional feature of the horn cores of the goats as a text figure. He depicts an almond-shaped section as representing a semidomesticated animal. A laterally flattened section is labeled as representing an animal of many generations of domestication, and a kidney shaped section represents an even longer period of domestication. These examples are from Ali Kosh. Payne (1968) points out that some of these criteria are of doubtful value because the horn core of the wild sheep (*Ovis orientalis*) is two-edged, and a fragment in an archaeological context could be misidentified as belonging to a goat. Horns of ewes of some domestic breeds also show this condition.

Armitage and Clutton-Brock (1976) devised a method of recording the size and form of the horn cores of cattle to determine whether the sex of the animals could be ascertained. Moderate success was claimed for a sample of 80 cores from excavations carried out at Walbrook, England, from early Roman and medieval levels. It may be possible to determine domesticated cattle by using similar statistical analysis if a large enough sample, representing a considerable time span, could be obtained.

Use of various trace elements in bone to ascertain whether domestic or wild populations of animals are present has also been tried, with questionable success. Zeder (1978) has synthesized work already done on trace elements in bone as a means of evaluating the different ecosystems of caprines from the Near East. The levels of calcium, magnesium, and zinc in the bones of Iranian sheep were measured by using atomic absorption spectrophotometry. The results were not conclusive but were considered as more of a demonstration indicating that there may be significant differences in the chemical composition of the bones of animals from different environments. It was determined that perhaps the establishment of levels of elements such as copper, iron, sodium, potassium, selenium, molybdenum, and strontium, among others, may prove to be more informative than those already measured because they might better reflect the nutritional intake and environments of the animals under investigation. At present the data cannot be used to solve the age-old wild/domestic problem.

Sample Size

One of the foremost problems that confronts the analyst who is concerned with determining domestication on the basis of osteological evidence is sample size. What number of bones or animals is to be considered adequate to arrive at meaningful measurements that will aid in the evaluation of a wild/domestic population? Discussions with statisticians regarding minimum numbers of individuals that should be assembled before an acceptable plot can be conducted varied almost with each individual who was consulted. An average of 500 specimens was estimated from all the suggestions. This seems to be an arbitrary figure rather than one based on fact. Perhaps a more realistic figure would be 150 bones, suggested by Evans (1978). Even this relatively lower figure is not generally reached in many archaeological excavations, when you consider, for example, that the presence of the earliest domestic dogs from Jaguar Cave, Palegawra, and Star Carr were established on fragments of one or two individuals.

Perkins (1964:1565) noted this lack of adequate sample size when he stated: "The postcranial skeletons of sheep and goats are remarkably similar, and separation of sheep and goat skeletal material is notoriously difficult unless there is a size difference between the two forms; this is not the case in the Near East. Differences reported in the literature have been based on small samples or on comparison with modern domestic races, and are not reliable." Uerpmann (1978) gives a rather detailed discussion of sample size, as well as individual size variation, for small bovids from Palegawra, Zawi Chemi Shanidar, and some other sites in the Near East.

If the sample is large enough and represents a considerable time span, some meaningful results can be shown. Bökönyi (1974) has plotted measurable variation for both sheep and cattle from European sites that range in age from the Neolithic (c. 7000 B.C.) to the Middle Ages and later (Figures 6.2 and 6.3). By this method of plotting the size differences in metapodials, he demonstrated that considerable variation occurred in the animals once man exerted his influence over them. He started with a more or less stable series of measurements in the Neolithic, which would reflect mainly natural variation, to peaks and lows from the Copper Age, through the Bronze Age, to the Middle Ages. Perhaps the most important point to note in this regard is that change can be observed on a plotted scale only if it is taken over a considerable length of time from a large enough sample.

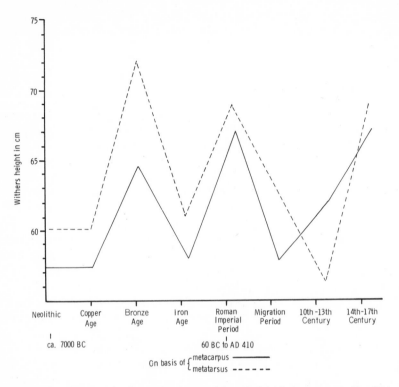

Figure 6.2. Changes in domestic-sheep withers height between early Neolithic and the end of the Middle Ages. (After Bökönyi 1974.)

CULTURAL AND ENVIRONMENTAL EVIDENCE

The cultural association of animals with man, as well as the osteological evidence, has also been utilized in attempts to determine whether the remains represent domestication or whether they represent animals brought to the site from hunting forays. Perkins (1973) cited the high percentage of juvenile goats (*Capra hircus aegagrus*) found at Ali Kosh (7000 B.C.) as being indicative of domestication. He (Perkins 1973) also used the sudden increase in the population of immature sheep (*Ovis aries*) as indicating the beginnings of domestication at Zawi Chemi Shanidar 8870 B.C.). In reaching this conclusion, Perkins assumed that animal breeding by man will result in a greater number of immature forms turning up in trash middens as compared with discarded bones of animals obtained only by hunting.

This hypothesis also embraces the speculation that the number of

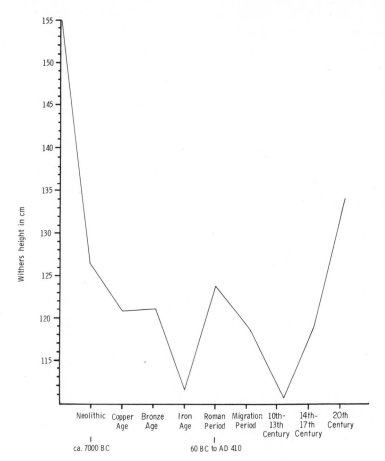

Figure 6.3. Changes in cattle withers height since domestication. (After Bökönyi 1974.)

young, compared with the number of adult goats or sheep, will increase in number from the lower, and hence older, levels of a site as compared with the younger and higher levels in the excavation. Bökönyi (1969) pointed out that at Zawi Chemi Shanidar the percentage difference between young and adult from the top layers to the bottom, which was Mousterian in age, was not significant. No informed scholar would argue for the beginnings of sheep domestication by Neanderthals, so this perplexing bit of nonsupportive evidence for domestication by the percentage method was explained as being due to a special type of selective hunting by the occupants of Shanidar Cave.

The young/adult hypothesis may or may not be a valid avenue to investigate for evidence of early domestication in the Near East. However, I do not think that at this time it is justified to base research conclusions on such a theory until it has been fully tested.

Collier and White (1976) also challenged this assumption that a high percentage of immature animals suggests domestication. They pointed out that a wide variation occurs in the population structure of nondomestic herds of artiodactyls.

What constitutes the young/adult ratio in any wild artiodactyl population in the Near East? For the most part, not enough animals exist in a condition unaffected by man's influence to undertake valid experiments at the present time. Throughout much of the world, areas where game herds abound in sufficient number are rapidly diminishing so that it is doubtful whether satisfactory evidence could ever be obtained to solve this problem by observing living animals. In addition, how could one be certain that any living population of sheep or goats, of any given area, represented a wild group and not one that was already a mixture that included some crossing with feral domestic animals?

Another fact to be considered in evaluating whether the animals under consideration are wild or domestic is whether they were brought back to the area of the present-day site as captive, either to be penned or turned loose in the village. In the case of the wild goat (*Capra hircus aegagrus*), its natural habitat is in hilly, mountainous country, far removed from such sites al Ali Kosh or Tepe Sabz. Yet their remains constitute a high percentage of the recovered animal bones. This suggests that the goats may have been brought in as captives, if not representing domestics, in these two villages. The animals could have been obtained only by someone traveling to their natural range and bringing them back as captives. The same logic regarding natural habitat applies to the occurrence of the wild sheep (*Ovis orientalis*) at these sites, as they also would not be found naturally as far afield as the archaeological sites from which their remains were recovered. Occasionally, supportive evidence such as sheep and goat hoof prints in the now-hardened clay surfaces of village alleys or the remains of stock pen or corral posts and the layers of accumulated animal dung, points to goats and sheep living among village residents, far removed from the animals' natural range.

EVIDENCE FROM ZOOMORPHIC FIGURES

Perhaps because of the unusual place we have given the domestic dog in our culture, its remains spark more interest than do the remains of most of the other domestic animals. There seems to be more competition among faunal workers for the "first" spot for domestic canids from sites the world over. This haste to record a new, and older, domestic dog sometimes leads to uncertainty regarding taxonomic assignment of dog remains and the use of zoomorphic representations interpreted as "dogs" to bolster the scanty skeletal evidence. This is apparent in certain published descriptions that appear to have been based on inadequate material.

In a report relating to the beginning of animal and plant domestication in southwestern Iran (8000 to 9000 B.C.), Hole and others (1969) discuss the recovery of canid remains. The authors mention the difficulty of separating the bones of the southwestern Asian wolf (*Canis lupus pallipes*) from those of the domestic dog, due to the wolf's small size and wide range of its osteological variation. They quote the statement made by Reed in this regard: "One wonders if there exists any good osteological evidence for dogs in southwestern Asia until their skeletons are actually found buried with humans in the Ubaid period in Mesopotamia" (Reed 1961:36–37). Here Reed apparently suggests cultural association, and from his 1960 report would include ceramic figurines and pottery designs interpreted as representing early domestic dogs (Reed 1960). Hole and his colleagues state correctly: "Representations in prehistoric art are always dangerous evidence on which to base zoological conclusions" (Hole *et al.* 1969:314). However, they then proceed to do just that, by depicting shards decorated with zoomorphic figures (Figure 6.4) to suggest what the early dogs of Khuzistan must have looked like. As stated, it is a "dangerous" and perhaps meaningless avenue to pursue. One has only to examine the prehistoric Mimbres art of the southwestern United States for comparable

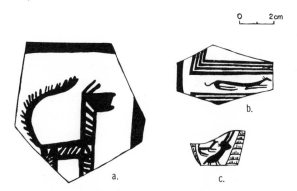

Figure 6.4. Susiana Black-on-buff potshards from sites in Khuzistan, providing data relevant to the faunal analysis: (a) domestic dog with tail curled over back; (b) seluki-like dog; (c) seluki-like dog apparently attacking wild goat or gazelle. (From Hole, Flannery, and Neely 1969.)

examples. The Mimbres people were capable of some beautifully exact animal representations on their ceramic vessels. These include a garfish that is taxonomically correct, even to its rhomboid or ganoid scales. Yet they also produced deer with full-fanned turkey tails or with the heads of fish. Birds were painted having antlers, and jack rabbits were shown with grasshopper hind legs. They also depicted both animals correctly, without these "mutations."

Reed also used ceramic figurines at Jarmo (6700 B.C.) to establish the presence of domestic dogs (*Canis familiaris*). Reed (1959) first regarded the canid remains from Jarmo as wolves and reported that dogs were not present in the midden. He later (Reed 1960) stated that the best evidence for the dog at Jarmo was not biological, but cultural, based on a figurine of a doglike animal (Figure 6.5). However, he was still puzzled, and rightly so, by the absence of any skeletal remains of dogs. In 1961 the evidence, based on clay figurines, was shelved and a supposed dog skull was reidentified, again by Reed (1961), as belonging to the wolf of southwestern Asia (*Canis lupus pallipes*). Finally, in 1970 the large canids from Jarmo were taken out of the wolf category and reinstated, as "they undoubtedly represent dogs and not wolves" (Reed 1969:370). The foregoing change of opinion regarding the specific assignment of the Jarmo canids is understandable to anyone who has worked with the skeletal remains of this family of carnivores for any length of time. However, I believe that the zoomorphic figures of "canids" on the ceramics of Khuzistan and Jarmo are of little value in establishing the presence of domestic dogs in those areas—no more so than the "cloud animals" one sees while lying on one's back and gazing at the summer sky.

SOME EARLY DATES OF DOMESTICATION

I have purposely avoided using the category "first" in connection with listing early dates. First domestication dates, as indicated earlier, are of limited value. They are constantly changing as new excavations are being conducted and more up to date evidence is acquired. They should, of

Figure 6.5. "Dog" figurine from Jarmo. (After Reed 1960.)

course, be recorded if they are to be considered only as progress reports for those students who are not necessarily specialists in animal manipulation and domestication and hence not in constant contact with the newer discoveries as they are being made. There is considerable importance placed on the listing of the age and location of early domestication dates and the evidence from which these dates were determined.

The validity of all early domestic animal identifications, and their associated dates, should be carefully evaluated against the material from which those identifications were arrived at and the conditions under which it was recovered. An assumed determination, based on questionable or inadequate material, should not be accepted.

Some of the more current published dates for the common domestic animals, and their locations, are as follows:

DOMESTIC DOG, *Canis familiaris*. For a number of years, beginning about a decade ago (Lawrence 1967, 1968), the oldest identified domestic dog remains were from Jaguar Cave, Idaho, dated by carbon-14 at 8400 B.C. This animal was determined from several rami and a partial cranium. Turnbull and Reed (1974), working over faunal collections made in 1945–1955 from prehistoric archaeological sites in northeastern Iraq, identified a fragmentary left mandible as belonging to a domestic dog. This was from Palegawra Cave and has been dated by fluorine analysis at about 13,000 B.C. (Flanagan 1975).

It is important to note that although both of these finds possess morphological characters attributed only to the domestic dog, they represent but one or two individuals and disregard the multiple character analysis that should be insisted on for the identification of canids in particular. Of course, the fragmentary nature of the remains dictates this approach to analysis if they are to be regarded at all.

A thorough discussion of dog origins relating to North America, as well as a tabulation of the more important early canid discoveries identified as domestic dog, has appeared in earlier publications (Lawrence 1968; Olsen 1974). In abstract, much of the evidence strongly suggests that earlier ancestors must be sought in Asia and in China in particular (Olsen and Olsen 1977).

A number of ancient dogs have been reported from archaeological sites in the People's Republic of China. A number of domestic dog mandibles have been recovered from the Yang-shao cultural site of Pan-p'o, Shensi Province, having a carbon-14 date of 4865 B.C. Dog remains were also present from the Lungshanoid horizon at Miao-ti-kou II, Honan Province (Ho 1975), as well as at several Lungshanoid and Lung-shan sites. If the increasing interest in archaeological excavations in the People's Republic of China continues at the rate observed over the last few years, it is hoped that other finds of early domestic dogs will be reported. I believe that Asia will prove to be one of the centers of dog domestication.

Chemical dating has established the dog as the earliest domestic animal. This seems logical, even if we were to disregard the scientific dating. Of all the domestic animals having early origins, only the dog would fit into the social patterns of a human hunter–gatherer society. Those that followed would more naturally be associated with the beginnings of agriculture and a sedentary way of life.

DOMESTIC SHEEP, *Ovis aries* and DOMESTIC GOAT, *Capra hircus*. There is some disagreement among domestication specialists as to whether sheep or goats were the earliest artiodactyls to be manipulated by taming and domestication. At any rate, whichever has this dubious honor, they were the first animals chosen after the dog. The habits of these animals, being gregarious and accepting the changes imposed upon them by man, placed them in a position for exploitation. Unlike the dog, the sheep and goats did not compete with man for food. Instead, they utilized grass and leaves for fodder, items not utilized by man for subsistence, and they in turn became available as a food source as well as supplying other needed products of milk, hair or wool, hide, and bone.

A number of occurrences of sheep and goats have been dated and are generally accepted as early dates of domestication by specialists in this field (Reed 1961). Sheep have been found at Zawi Chemi Shanidar (9000 B.C.) and goats at Jericho and Jarmo (7000 B.C.). If the goats recovered from the site at Tepe Ali Kosh are indeed domesticated, then they too may date back about as early as the sheep. Sheep are considered domestic at Jarmo. Sheep remains have been reported from a number of sites in the People's Republic of China (Ho 1975). Those reported from Pan-p'o in Shensi Province are dated at 4865 B.C. However, these may represent wild animals. They also occur at Kao-tui, in Honan Province. The Lungshanoid site of Miao-ti-kou II in Honan Province produced sheep bones dated at 2310 B.C. by the carbon-14 method or 2700 B.C. by using dates provided by analyzing bristlecone pines.

As reported earlier, the problem of osteological identification of most domestic or wild sheep and goats will result in a tabulation of the bones being listed in the general category sheep/goat, *Ovis/Capra*.

DOMESTIC PIG, *Sus scrofa*. Reed (1961) stated that before the Jarmo excavations the earliest domestic pig remains from the Near East were dated at about 4000 B.C. Jarmo animals pushed the date back about three thousand years earlier.

Pigs are reported from Pan-p'o in the People's Republic of China (4865 B.C.) and at Miao-ti-kou I (3880 B.C.) and at Miao-ti-kou II (2310 B.C.) and some other later sites.

Many of the osteological identifications of pigs have been based on molar size and structure. A few observations have been made by zooarchaeologists who noted that there was little morphological difference between pigs associated with early cultural sites and those from Pleistocene horizons having no relationship to man. This one fact alone is justification for including vertebrate paleontologists as analysts for any faunal projects relating to evolutionary patterns of animal growth or the degrees to which animal bones may vary among particular groups of animals. For example, Colbert and Hooijer (1953) in their review of Pleistocene suid remains from Yenchingkou, China, concluded that the size and shape of the teeth correspond with modern specimens of *Sus scrofa*. There was no size difference between the Yenchingkou and modern species. Higham (1975) also noted this for the pigs from Non Nok Tha, Thailand (possibly dating to 3548 B.C.).

DOMESTIC CATTLE, *Bos taurus*. As with sheep and goats, the problem of certifying cattle remains as being "domestic" is hazardous, owing to the great similarity of the bones of the wild and domestic forms. This is particularly true in the early stages of taming and domestication. Bökönyi (1974) gives a rather thorough review and summation of the problem. He states that among the oldest finds of domestic cattle are those from the Pre-pottery Neolithic settlements in Thessaly. This site is on the Balkan Peninsula. Other finds are from Greek Macedonia. Nea Nikomedia has a carbon-14 date of 6200 B.C. There is no carbon-14 date for Argissa Magula in Thessaly, but on the basis of typological comparisons it has been determined to be older than Nea Nikomedia. Unfortunately, all the osteological material is quite fragmentary and the analysis is rather shaky, based on the evidence presented as the "smaller" size of those animals as compared with the wild European *Bos primigenius*.

As with the sheep from the Chinese site of Pan-p'o (4865 B.C.), the cattle may represent wild animals rather than tame or domestic ones. Cattle were also reported from the site of Miao-ti-kou II in Honan Province (2310 B.C.).

DOMESTIC HORSE, *Equus caballus*. The horse is a relatively late newcomer as a domesticated animal. A date of about 3500 B.C. has been recorded for the horse at the Aeneolithic settlement of Dereivka, in the south Ukraine (Bökönyi 1974). At Pan-p'o in Shensi Province, China, the horse has been dated by carbon-14 at 4865 B.C. (Ho 1975). However, it is listed as questionably wild. This is most likely due to the close similarity of the skeletons of ancient finds of *Equus* with those of the still-wild Asian Przewalski's horse.

The earliest occurrence of the horse as a domesticated animal may be earlier in fact than the date at which this event is recorded. This is due to the difficulty of identifying the domestic horse, *Equus caballus*, and separating it from its many early ancestors. The morphological characters that separate wild from domestic animals are so slight and open to argument as to their validity as keys that few experts agree on the taxonomic criteria on which species have been based from the Pleistocene to the present. Where there is a known gap between when the Pleistocene animals died out and the domestic horse appears again, there are, of course, fewer problems with analysis.

I view many of the identifications listed as "domestic horse" with considerable suspicion and doubt. The entire subject of late Tertiary horse evolution and change, and the reasons for assigning taxonomic categories to each group, is a major problem and needs to be evaluated.

I am realist enough to doubt that this will be done in the foreseeable future.

CONCLUSIONS

Much of the foregoing discussion was not intended to heap criticism on faunal workers who analyze Near Eastern vertebrate materials in particular, but rather to point out that, where there is no evident choice of a positive identification on a specific level, it is far better to modify the classification to the widest acceptable taxonomic category. This is particularly true for canids, where divergence within the family Canidae is generally slight, and where morphological characters are not reliable for separating the various species unless they are present as more or less complete skeletons.

Classification is generally based on structural features that can be consistently demonstrated as being valid and reliable for separating animals on a specific or higher taxonomic level. Obviously, a few bones, even when complete, cannot reflect the total variation of a species population. If possible, any determination should be derived from utilizing all the information available from comparative material for the species under consideration from a particular area, as well as that recovered from a specified site. Establishing the presence of any animal, particularly domestic animals at an early site, should be subject to question if those determinations are based on only a few bone fragments.

It is not overstating the problem to emphasize that it is better not to report a specific domestic animal as being present at an early site than to record its presence, only to retract this record later.

REFERENCES

Armitage, P. L., and J. Clutton-Brock
1976 A system for classification and description of the horn cores of cattle from archaeological sites. *Journal of Archaeological Science* **3**:329–348.
Bökönyi, S.
1969 Archaeological problems and methods of recognizing animal domestication. In *The domestication and exploitation of plants and animals,* edited by P. J. Ucko and G. W. Dimbleby. Chicago: Aldine. Pp. 219–229.
1974 *History of domestic mammals in Eastern Europe.* Budapest: Akadémiai Kiadó.
Clutton-Brock, J.
1969 Carnivore remains from excavations of the Jericho Tell. In *The domestication and exploitation of plants and animals,* edited by P. J. Ucko and G. W. Dimbleby. Chicago: Aldine. Pp. 337–345.
Colbert, E. H., and D. A. Hooijer
1953 Pleistocene mammals from the limestone fissures of Szechwan, China. *Bulletin of the American Museum of Natural History* **102** (No. 1):134 pp.
Collier, S., and J. P. White
1976 Get them young? Age and sex inferences on animal domestication. *American Antiquity* **41**:96–102.
DiPeso, C.
1953 The Sobaipuri Indians of the Upper San Pedro River Valley, Southwestern Arizona. *Amerind Foundation* No. 6.
Drew, I. M., D. Perkins, and P. Daly
1971 Prehistoric domestication of animals: Effects on bone structure. *Science* **171**:280–282.
Dyson, R. H.
1973 *The first farmers.* New York: Time-Life Books.
Evans, J. G.
1978 *An introduction to environmental archaeology.* Ithaca: Cornell University Press.
Flanagan, D.
1975 Best friend. In Science and the citizen. *Scientific American* **233**:50–54.
Hall, E. R., and K. R. Kelson
1959 *The mammals of North America.* New York: Ronald Press, 2 vols.
Higham, C.
1975 Non Nok Tha: The faunal remains. *University of Otago, Studies in Prehistoric Anthropology* No. 7.
Ho, P. T.
1975 *The cradle of the East.* Chicago: University of Chicago Press; Hong Kong: Chinese University of Hong Kong.
Hole, F., K. V. Flannery, and J. A. Neely
1969 Prehistory and human ecology of the Deh Luran Plain. *University of Michigan, Memoirs of the Museum of Anthropology* No. 1.
Kúrten, B.
1965 The carnivora of the Palestine Caves. *Acta Zoologica Fennica* No. 107.
Lawrence, B.
1967 Early domestic dogs. *Sonderdruck aus Zeitschrift für Säugetierkunde* **32**(1):47–59.

1968   Antiquity of large dogs in North America. *Tebiwa: Journal of the Idaho State University Museum* 11(2):43–49.

Meadow, R. H., and M. A. Zeder
1978   Approaches to faunal analysis in the Middle East. *Peabody Museum of Archaeology and Ethnology Bulletin* No. 2.

Merriam, J. C.
1910   New mammalia from Rancho La Brea. *University of California, Bulletin of the Department of Geology* 5(25):391–395. Berkeley.

Nowak, M. R.
1973   North American quaternary canis. Ph.D. dissertation in Zoology, University of Kansas. Ann Arbor: University Microfilms.

Olsen, S. J.
1974   Early domestic dogs in North America and their origins. *Journal of Field Archaeology* 1(3 and 4):343–345.

Olsen, S. J., and J. W. Olsen
1977   The Chinese wolf, ancestor of New World dogs. *Science* 197:533–535.

Payne, S.
1968   The origins of domestic sheep and goats: A reconsideration in the light of fossil evidence. *Proceedings of the Prehistoric Society* 34(11):368–384.

Perkins, D.
1964   Prehistoric fauna from Shanidar, Iraq. *Science* 144:1565–1566.
1973   The beginnings of animal domestication in the Near East. *American Journal of Archaeology* 77(3):279–282.

Pollard, G. C., and I. M. Drew
1975   Llama herding and settlement in prehispanic northern Chile: Application of analysis for determining domestication. *American Antiquity* 40(3):296–305.

Reed, C. A.
1959   Animal domestication in the prehistoric Near East. *Science* 130:1629–1639.
1960   A review of the archaeological evidence on animal domestication in the prehistoric Near East. In Prehistoric investigations in Iraqi Kurdistan, edited by R. J. Braidwood and B. Howe. *Oriental Institute of the University of Chicago, Studies in Ancient Oriental Civilization* No. 31, 119–145.
1961   Osteological evidences for prehistoric domestication in southwestern Asia. *Sonderdruck aus "Zeitschrift für Tierzuchtung und Zuchtungsbiologie"* 76(I):31–38.
1969   The pattern of animal domestication in the prehistoric Near East. In *The domestication and exploitation of plants and animals,* edited by P. J. Ucko and G. W. Dimbleby. Chicago: Aldine. Pp. 311–380.

Schenk, E. T., and J. H. McMasters
1956   *Procedure in taxonomy.* Stanford: Stanford University Press.

Singh, P.
1974   *Neolithic cultures of Western Asia.* New York: Seminar Press.

Skinner, M. F.
1942   The fauna of Papago Springs Cave, Arizona, and a study of Stockoceros. *Bulletin of the American Museum of Natural History* 80(6):143–220.
1952   Personal communication to C. DiPeso. Letter in Amerind Foundation files dated January 28.

Turnbull, P. F., and C. A. Reed
1974   The fauna from the terminal Pleistocene of Palegawra Cave, a Zaraian occupation site in Northeastern Iraq. *Fieldiana Anthropology* 66(3):81–146

Uerpmann, H. P.
  1978 Metrical analysis of faunal remains from the Middle East. In Approaches to
        faunal analysis in the Middle East, edited by R. H. Meadow and M. A. Zeder.
        Peabody Museum of Archaeology and Ethnology Bulletin No. 2, 41–45.
Wheeler Pires-Ferreira, J., E. Pires-Ferreira, and P. Kaulicke
  1976 Preceramic animal utilization in the central Peruvian Andes. *Science* **194**:483–
        490.
Zeder, M. A.
  1978 Differentiation between the bones of caprines from different ecosystems in Iran
        by the analysis of osteological microstructure and chemical composition. In
        Approaches to faunal analysis in the Middle East, edited by R. M. Meadow and
        M. A. Zeder. *Peabody Museum of Archaeology and Ethnology Bulletin* No. 2,
        69–84.
Zeuner, F. E.
  1963 *A history of domesticated animals.* London: Hutchinson.

On the Quantification of Vertebrate Archaeofaunas

DONALD K. GRAYSON

During the past two decades or so, the tremendous contribution to knowledge that can be made through the analysis of vertebrate faunas from archaeological sites has been clearly recognized.. Archaeologists, accustomed to thinking in terms of the humans who once occupied the sites they study, have recognized the potentially detailed information on human subsistence to be gained from studying the bony remains of ancient human meals. Equally important, scientists from a wide range of disciplines have recognized that archaeological vertebrates can provide important information on the nature of Quaternary environments, and that such remains can also make valuable contributions to historical biogeography—the attempt to explain why taxa are distributed the way they are distributed "in terms of their history rather than exclusively in terms of their ecology" (Platnick and Nelson 1978:1). As a result, the last two decades have seen a dramatic increase in the volume of literature dealing with vertebrate faunas from archaeological sites. The faunal analysts of earlier generations, who contributed works of extreme importance to the development of modern approaches, would, I think, be pleased to see the attention that is being paid to the field they pioneered.

In this paper, I explore one aspect of the analysis of vertebrate faunas from archaeological sites—the quantification of the abundances of the taxa that constitute such archaeofaunas. Given that there is a wide range of other topics that could be examined under the same title, the contents

ADVANCES IN ARCHAEOLOGICAL METHOD AND THEORY, VOL. 2
Copyright © 1979 by Academic Press, Inc.

of the paper are narrower than the title might imply. I examine only the quantification of taxonomic abundances here because measures of such abundances are basic to most faunal analyses, no matter what their goals. How abundant was taxon A? Was it more abundant than taxon B? How did the abundances of these animals change in relation to each other through time? How did the abundances of these animals change across archaeological sites? Nearly all faunal analyses attempt to answer questions of this sort, regardless of whether the precise problems being addressed relate to human subsistence, climatic change, or historical biogeography. It is virtually impossible to find any faunal analysis that does not present one or more measures of taxonomic abundance. Other issues relating to the quantification of vertebrate faunas may or may not be addressed in any given study, but questions of taxonomic abundance always are. In short, the issue is a basic one. In addition, the general problems involved with constructing an appropriate measure of taxonomic abundance are common to many kinds of counting procedures with which archaeologists must deal. Thus, the issues I explore here are not only basic to faunal analysis, but have wider relevance to archaeology as a whole.

Much recent attention has, in fact, been paid to the nature of the units that are in common use to measure the abundances of taxa represented by faunal remains from archaeological sites (for some general reviews, see Casteel 1976; Chaplin 1971; Payne 1972; Uerpmann 1973a; Ziegler 1973). It has become clear that two major issues must be more fully understood before it will be possible to have faith in any but the simplest kinds of faunal analyses based upon measures of taxonomic abundance: the nature of the units that faunal analysts typically use to measure taxonomic abundance, and the appropriate way to view the variable they are attempting to measure. These are the issues explored in this paper. I shall show that the nature of archaeological faunal data, and of the units used to quantify these data, are often such that taxonomic abundances derived from archaeological vertebrate faunas must be treated as providing nominal or ordinal level information only.

THE UNITS OF QUANTIFICATION

It must be noted at the outset that faunal analysts rarely treat any measure of taxonomic abundance as providing, in and of itself, an absolute measure of the abundance of the taxon involved. Rather, each measure is usually meant to provide information on the abundance of each taxon in relation to the other taxa in the collection. Of the units that have been employed to measure such abundances, three have received the greatest use and greatest analytic attention: the number of identified specimens per taxon, the minimum number of individuals per taxon, and the amount of meat represented per taxon. I shall examine each of these measures in turn.

Counts of Identified Specimens as an Abundance Measure

The number of identified specimens per taxon (NISP) is frequently used as a measure of the abundances of taxa represented within vertebrate archaeofaunas (see, e.g., Ducos 1968, 1975; Gilbert and Steinfeld 1977; Hesse and Perkins 1974; Payne 1975, for studies that either use NISP directly or use measures based upon NISP). [Elsewhere (e.g., Grayson 1974, 1976, 1977c, 1978a), I have used E as the symbol for this measure, derived from "number of identified elements." However, the "number of identified specimens" and the associated NISP clearly have priority and should be employed instead (Casteel and Grayson 1977).]

Even though counts of identified specimens have achieved some popularity as an abundance measure, this unit is the most heavily criticized of all abundance measures in vertebrate faunal analysis. Some of the criticisms leveled at this unit include the following: (1) the unit is affected by butchering patterns; (2) numbers of identified specimens vary from species to species; (3) usage assumes that all specimens are equally affected by chance or deliberate breakage; (4) the unit may be affected by differential preservation; (5) the unit may be affected by collection techniques; (6) entire skeletons may skew abundances based on this measure; (7) the unit may differentially exaggerate sample sizes across taxa; (8) the unit supports fewer analytic procedures than does the unit based on the minimum number of individuals; (9) meat weights are of greater importance in getting at past economies; (10) problems raised by element interdependence invalidate further statistical manipulation; and (11) because of such problems, the unit does not allow valid intersite comparisons. These and other problems are discussed, and the problems involved elaborated, in Binford and Bertram (1977), Bökönyi (1970), Brain (1969), Casteel (1971, 1972), Chaplin (1971), Crader (1974), Daly (1969), Ducos (1968), Gejvall (1969), Grayson (1973, 1977c), Hill (1976), Noe-Nygaard (1977), Payne (1972), Perkins (1964, 1973), Reed (1963), Shotwell (1955, 1958), Thomas (1969), Uerpmann (1973a), and Watson (1972).

Although the number of these criticisms is impressive, it is clear that few are truly fatal to the use of NISP as a measure of taxonomic abundance. Some of the difficulties may be removed through detailed studies of the taphonomy of archaeological faunal assemblages (for instance, numbers 1, 3, and 4), others may be removed through the application of statistical or collection procedures to ensure comparability (for instance, numbers 2, 5, and 6), and still others do not address the validity of the measure (for instance, numbers 8 and 9). The most damaging criticism that can be leveled at the use of numbers of identified specimens is that of potential element interdependence (number 10 and, in part, 7; see Grayson 1973, 1977c). Numbers of identified specimens simply cannot be shown to be independent of one another, given current knowledge: there is no known way of demonstrating which bones and bone fragments necessarily came from different individuals across an entire faunal sample, and thus no way of resolving the patterns of specimen interdependence that must surely characterize many specimen samples. Since the statistical methods used to analyze these samples—from simple counts and percentages to chi-square and beyond—assume not only that the items being manipulated are representative of the sampled population, but also that each item is independent of every other item, the application of such methods to NISP-based counts is inappropriate.

It can, of course, be assumed that each specimen was necessarily contributed by a different individual, as was done explicitly (and appropriately) by Hesse and Perkins (1974) and Gilbert and Steinfeld (1977) and implicitly by all others who use specimen counts, or methods based upon specimen counts, to quantify taxonomic abundances. Clearly, however, this position does not address the underlying problem: assuming that interdependence does not exist does not create independence among the units being counted. Although there certainly may be archaeological faunas for which such an assumption is appropriate, whether or not the assumption is appropriate must be demonstrated in each case in which specimen counts are to be employed. If it seems unreasonable to assume independence among all counted specimens, it might instead be assumed that interdependence is randomly distributed across all taxa. However, given current knowledge, it would be difficult to demonstrate that this assumption is appropriate for any given fauna. In addition, even quick consideration of the very nonrandom effects of, for instance, butchering on skeletal representation suggests that the assumption will rarely be appropriate (see, e.g., Perkins and Daly 1968).

Thus, because of the problem of specimen interdependence, the number of identified specimens per taxon cannot simply be assumed to be an appropriate unit to use as a measure of taxonomic abundance. Instead, the use of this measure must be *demonstrated* to be appropriate for the problem and the fauna at hand. I shall return to this issue later.

Minimum Numbers as an Abundance Measure

The problem of interdependence associated with counts of identified specimens suggests that an alternative unit not affected by this problem be sought for the quantification of taxonomic abundances within vertebrate archaeofaunas. The minimum number of individuals per taxon (MNI) possesses this quality. Because of the way in which minimum numbers are calculated, each calculated "minimum individual" must be independent of every other. Even so, the first well-reasoned introduction of minimum numbers into archaeology was done not to avoid problems of element interdependence, but instead to allow the calculation of a derived measure—meat weights—dependent upon minimum number determination (White 1953). It was no accident that this introduction was made by a paleontologist; identically defined minimum numbers had been in use in paleontology for over 20 years (Howard 1930; Merriam and Stock 1932; Stock 1929) at the time White (1953) transferred the approach to archaeological faunas.

No matter which of the variations of minimum number definitions is employed (e.g., Chaplin 1971; Flannery 1967; White 1953), the basic process is the same. For any taxon within any given set of faunal material, the analyst determines the minimum number of individual animals necessary to account for all the skeletal material identified for that taxon in that set of material. Thus, White (1953:397) recommended that the faunal analyst "separate the most abundant element of the species found . . . into right and left components and use the greater number as the unit of calculation." Common variants of this approach add age and size differences implied by the specimens as criteria in defining minimum numbers. Flannery (1967:157), for instance, expended " 'a great deal of time with small return' to see if all the lefts matched all the rights."

So stated, the basic process of minimum number determination seems quite simple: one excavates a site and retrieves a faunal collection, identifies what can be identified (of course, what can be identified varies across investigators; "identifiable specimens" should always be taken to mean "specimens that a particular investigator was able to identify"), divides the collection into smaller faunal clusters based upon the excavation units employed during retrieval of the fauna, and applies the operational definition of minimum numbers separately to each taxon represented in each of these smaller aggregates of faunal material. The resultant numbers are then manipulated in any further analyses.

Unfortunately, this simple description conceals a serious problem: the values of minimum numbers of individuals that result from this process vary with the way in which the faunal material is divided into the smaller faunal aggregates, which in turn form the basis of minimum number determination. Not only may the use of different approaches to aggregation change the calculated abundances, but those changes in abundance may occur differentially across taxa. I noted this phenomenon several years ago (Grayson 1973); as Casteel (1977) subsequently pointed out, the Russian faunal analyst Paaver had come to the same conclusion some 15 years earlier. Nontheless, the implications of this aspect of the behavior of minimum numbers do not seem to have been adequately understood.

The fact that different aggregation techniques applied to a single faunal collection may produce minimum numbers that are not necessarily comparable can be readily understood through examination of the process of minimum number determination. Recall that, as White (1953) noted, the basic step in minimum number definition is the specification of the "most abundant element" for any given taxon. This specification can be accomplished only after some decision has been made as to precisely how a given faunal collection is to be subdivided into separate analytic units. If all the faunal material from the site is to be treated as a single large aggregate, the most abundant element will be defined once per taxon for that collection. As the collection is divided into smaller and smaller aggregates of faunal material—for instance, by subdividing the collection according to the strata or vertical excavation units from which that collection came—the number of separate specifications of most abundant elements will increase. Thus, dividing a faunal collection into a smaller number of larger faunal aggregates will lead to the definition of smaller absolute minimum number values than will dividing the same collection into a larger number of smaller aggregates.

Were this the only affect of aggregation, there would be relatively little to worry about except for the alteration in sample sizes that different aggregation approaches cause. Minimum numbers are rarely treated as absolute values meaningful in and of themselves: these numbers take on meaning only in relationship to other minimum number values. Thus, except for sample size changes, it would be of no great import if different aggregation methods affected the absolute minimum numbers of individuals as long as all taxa were affected in equivalent fashions. Unfortunately, this is not the case. The changes in minimum number values across taxa that occur when different aggregative approaches are employed differentially affect the calculated minimum number abundances of different taxa. If, for instance, taxon A is twice as abundant as B under one aggregation approach, it is not likely that it will be twice as abundant as B under a different approach to aggregation. This is true because different aggregation methods specify different most abundant elements, and because the most abundant elements for any one taxon will in almost all instances be spatially distributed differently from the most abundant elements of all other taxa. Only if all elements that enter into the calculation of minimum numbers are distributed in identical ways across all aggregative units can different approaches to aggregation fail to differentially alter calculated minimum number abundances among taxa.

A simple example will serve to make this clear. Table 7.1 presents the raw data—counts of identified specimens—for a small faunal collection from, say, a single stratum of an archaeological site. If this material were aggregated by stratum, the right humerus would be specified as the most abundant element for taxon 1, and an MNI of 10 would result. The right femur would be specified as the most abundant element for taxon 2, and an MNI of 15 would result (Table 7.1a). Let us say that this stratum has been divided into three arbitrary levels, and that these levels are chosen as the basis of aggregation. Now, three most abundant elements are chosen for each taxon, and the resultant minimum number totals for the entire stratum are 27 for taxon 1 and 17 for taxon 2 (Table 7.1b). The absolute minimum number counts for each taxon have increased because, by subdividing the single faunal cluster into several smaller ones, the number of elements specified as most abundant has increased. And, the ratios of these taxa to each other have changed dramatically because the spatial distribution of the elements tagged as most abundant differ dramatically between the taxa. It is important to note that the same results would have been obtained had the aggregation units been drawn vertically (as with excavation squares), or had the horizontal units been different possible definitions of natural strata. The effects of aggregation are the same in all these cases.

TABLE 7.1

An Example of the Effects of Aggregation upon Minimum Numbers

1a. Collection from a single stratum:

Taxon	Identified specimens
1	10 right humerus, 9 right radius, 8 right tibia
2	15 right femur, 1 right humerus, 1 right tibia

Taxon 1: MNI = 10
Taxon 2: MNI = 15

1b. Same collection aggregated by arbitrary levels within the stratum:

	Identified specimens	
Level	Taxon 1	Taxon 2
1	10 right humerus	15 right femur
2	9 right radius	1 right humerus
3	8 right tibia	1 right tibia

Taxon 1: MNI = 27
Taxon 2: MNI = 17

A more general statement about the effects of aggregation may be made if we conceive of the distribution of element frequencies as a series of peaks and valleys across aggregation units. For any aggregation unit, it is the peak of the distribution of the most abundant element that defines the minimum number of individuals. If the distributions of elements across taxa are identical in form, then different aggregation approaches will provide different absolute minimum number values, but the ratios of taxa to one another will remain constant. If, on the other hand, the distributions of most abundant elements are not identical in form, and peaks of most abundant elements occur differentially across aggregation units, different aggregation approaches will not only define different absolute taxonomic abundances, but will also alter the ratios of taxa to one another (Figure 7.1).

Thus, two general situations may be specified: that in which the distributions of most abundant elements of all taxa are identical, and that in which the distributions of most abundant elements differ among taxa and

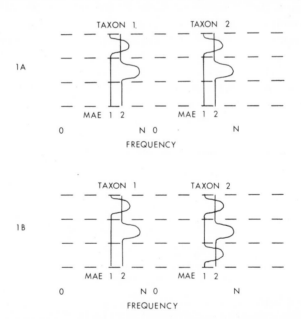

Figure 7.1. Distributions of most abundant elements (MAE) and aggregation effects. Dashed lines represent borders of possible aggregation units. (1A) Distributions of most abundant elements identical; different aggregation methods produce different absolute MNI values but identical ratios of abundance. (1B) Distributions of most abundant elements differ between taxa, with frequency peaks of most abundant elements differentially spaced across aggregation units; different aggregation methods produce different absolute values and different ratios of abundance.

the frequency peaks of those elements are differentially spaced across aggregation units. In the former case, the minimum number abundances of taxa relative to one another will not change when different aggregation approaches are employed. In the latter case, they will.

The nature of these distributions is an empirical issue and must be determined for every case. In fact, much might be learned from analysis of these distributions, above and beyond their value in analyzing their effects upon minimum numbers. Unfortunately, since precise horizontal and vertical locational data are rarely taken for all faunal remains from a site, continuous distributions of elements within a site usually cannot be drawn. However, even with general provenance, distributions of elements across possible aggregation units can be drawn by using the numbers of each identified element per taxon to provide the peaks for each aggregation unit. If the distributions of most abundant elements for all taxa are identical, then minimum numbers may be used without concern for the effects of aggregation on ratios of taxonomic abundance. If the distributions are not identical, they may not be. There is an even quicker way to determine whether or not minimum numbers should be used to provide ratios of taxonomic abundance: calculate minimum numbers by different aggregation units and use those numbers to determine ratios of taxonomic abundance. If the ratios change across aggregation methods, then they are reflecting not only taxonomic abundances within the site, but also differential distributions of most abundant elements across the aggregation units.

How often will the distributions of all most abundant elements be identical across all taxa and across all aggregation units? Unfortunately, it is difficult to see that this will happen with any frequency, except in the trivial instance in which the collection consists of a single taxon. Very little is known about the taphonomy of archaeological faunas, but what is known suggests that there is no reason to expect that element distributions across aggregation units will be identical. The effects of element preservation, butchering techniques, archaeological recovery techniques, the mechanisms that introduce faunal material into sites, and of a host of other, poorly·known variables ensure that these distributions are likely to differ among taxa.

The implications of this situation seem clear: absolute abundances indicated by minimum numbers are dependent upon aggregation method; ratios of taxonomic abundance based upon those numbers are dependent upon the nature of the distribution of most abundant elements within the site. As a result, statistical analyses that assume a ratio scale of measurement (Siegel 1956) can rarely be appropriately applied to minimum number data.

The Effects of Aggregation upon Minimum Number Abundances: An Example

To illustrate the kinds of empirical results that follow from these considerations, I shall examine a single archaeological fauna using minimum number analysis. The fauna to be examined comes from Connley Cave No. 4 (35 Lk 50/4), one of a series of six contiguous rock shelters located in the Northern Great Basin of south-central Oregon. Excavated by the late Stephen Bedwell in 1967, Connley Cave No. 4 provided 1081 mammalian specimens which I was able to identify (Grayson 1977a,b, n.d.) (see Table 7.2). With the exception of a major break in the middle of the sequence, Connley Cave No. 4 contained deposits that, given the resolution of the excavation techniques employed, apparently accumulated continuously through time. The site was excavated by 10-cm arbitrary levels within each of four natural strata; faunal materials were recovered through the use of ¼-inch screens. The entire sequence spans the period

TABLE 7.2

Numbers of Identified Elements by Stratum, Connley Cave No. 4 Mammals[a]

Taxon Stratum:	1	2	3	4	Total
Lepus sp. (1)	7	3	256	388	654
Sylvilagus nuttallii (2)	12	5	75	27	119
Sylvilagus idahoensis (3)			43	34	77
Neotoma cf. *cinerea* (4)	3	3	40	9	55
Thomomys talpoides (5)	4		31	8	43
Bison bison (6)			8	19	27
Sylvilagus sp. (7)	1	1	8	12	22
Cervus canadensis (8)			8	13	21
Ochotona princeps (9)			7	6	13
Odocoileus cf. *hemionus* (10)			10	2	12
Dipodomys ordii (11)		1	4	2	7
Marmota flaviventris (12)			3	2	5
Canis cf. *latrans* (13)			1	4	5
Lynx cf. *rufus* (14)			1	3	4
Vulpes fulva (15)			2	2	4
Microtinae (16)			1	3	4
Erethizon dorsatum (17)			1	2	3
Mustela frenata (18)			2		2
Gulo luscus (19)				1	1
Antilocapra americana (20)			1		1
Ovis canadensis (21)			1		1
Spermophilus beldingi (22)				1	1
					1081

[a] Numbers in parentheses are used to identify taxa in other tables; taxa are presented in order of specimen counts.

11,200–3,000 B.P., with a conspicuous gap in radiocarbon dates between 7,200 and 4,400 B.P. (Bedwell 1969, 1973).

I calculated minimum numbers for this fauna in three different ways. In each instance, the operational definition of minimum numbers was similar to that used by White (1953), in which all elements for a given taxon were separated into right and left components, and the larger of the two values was used as the minimum number of individuals. In addition, patterns of epiphyseal fusion and other age indicators were used as criteria in defining minimum numbers. Size differences among identified specimens were not employed. The three ways in which minimum numbers were calculated for the Connley Cave No. 4 mammals are as follows:

1. All faunal materials were separated by natural stratum and then subdivided by 10-cm units within each stratum. The operational definition of minimum numbers was then applied to each of the aggregates so defined; the resultant values are symbolized as MNI_{10cm}.

2. All faunal materials were grouped according to the natural stratum from which they had come, and the operational definition of minimum numbers was then applied to each of the resulting four clusters of faunal material ($MNI_{stratum}$).

3. The entire sample of faunal material was treated as one large aggregate, and the operational definition of minimum numbers was applied to this single large faunal aggregate (MNI_{site}).

The resultant minimum numbers are shown in Table 7.3.

Examination of this table shows the expected effects of changing aggregation upon minimum number values. Dividing the faunal sample into the largest number of aggregates, each containing a relatively small fraction of the sample, defines the largest minimum number of individuals. Dividing the faunal sample into the smallest number of aggregates, each containing a relatively large fraction of the faunal sample, defines the smallest minimum number of individuals. This situation results from the fact that the most agglomerative approach to aggregation—MNI_{site}—specifies only one element per taxon as most abundant, while more and more most abundant elements are defined as the approach to aggregation becomes increasingly divisive.

The differences between the minimum numbers of individuals determined by the most divisive (MNI_{10cm}) and the most agglomerative methods applied to the Connley Cave No. 4 mammals vary from minor to pronounced. The maximum values that these differences can reach within any given collection are easily determined. The smallest possible minimum number values are obtained when the entire assemblage is

TABLE 7.3

Total Minimum Numbers of Individuals by Aggregation Method, Connley Cave No. 4 Mammals

Taxon[a]	MNI_{10cm}	$MNI_{stratum}$	MNI_{site}
1	72	39	36
2	38	15	10
3	23	8	9
4	23	13	8
5	23	14	13
6	9	2	2
7	12	8	5
8	9	3	2
9	9	7	4
10	5	2	1
11	7	4	4
12	3	3	2
13	5	2	1
14	2	2	1
15	3	2	1
16	3	3	3
17	2	2	1
18	2	2	2
19	1	1	1
20	1	1	1
21	1	1	1
22	1	1	1

treated as a single aggregate, from which minimum numbers are determined. The largest possible minimum number values are obtained when the assemblage is divided into the smallest possible number of units, functionally attained when each element contributes an individual. Thus, the largest minimum number values possible for any given assemblage are equal to the number of identified specimens for that assemblage. Since this is the case, maximum possible differences for minimum number values for all taxa may be calculated by subtracting MNI_{site} from NISP for each taxon. Resultant values for the Connley Cave No. 4 mammals are shown in Table 7.4. Since maximum possible differences in minimum number values necessarily decrease as sample size decreases, the effects of different methods of aggregating faunal data upon absolute values of minimum numbers will be most pronounced for larger samples, and least pronounced for smaller ones. That is, as samples increase in size, the range in values that minimum numbers may take as a result of different aggregation methods increases, and the faith that may be placed in the meaning of absolute minimum number values decreases. This is not the usual behavior of a unit of measurement.

TABLE 7.4

Maximum Possible Differences in Minimum Number Values, Connley Cave No. 4 Mammals

Taxon[a]	MNI_{site}	NISP	Maximum possible MNI difference
1	36	654	618
2	10	119	109
3	9	77	68
4	8	55	47
5	13	43	30
6	2	27	25
7	5	22	17
8	2	21	19
9	4	13	9
10	1	12	?I
11	4	7	3
12	2	5	3
13	1	5	4
14	1	4	3
15	1	4	3
16	3	4	1
17	1	3	2
18	2	2	0
19	1	1	0
20	1	1	0
21	1	1	0
22	1	1	0

The meaning of the values presented in Table 7.4 should be clear. Let us say that we wish to express the abundance of *Lepus* sp. at this site in terms of minimum numbers of individuals. The values that this figure might take range from a minimum of 36 to a maximum of 654. That is, the minimum numbers of this taxon at this site may range through 619 separate values, with the actual value depending upon how the faunal material was aggregated prior to minimum number definition.

Such changes in absolute abundance, which result from different aggregation methods, are in themselves troublesome because they may greatly change the sample sizes with which the faunal analyst is working. Even if the ratios of taxonomic abundances among taxa remain the same when different aggregation methods are used, significance tests applied to the smaller numbers obtained when larger aggregation units are used will give very different exact probabilities compared with those obtained when more divisive approaches are employed. As a result, the meaning of significance tests applied to minimum number values becomes clouded (see also Cowgill 1977).

More serious is the fact that the distribution of most abundant elements will almost always be such as to cause different aggregation methods to differentially alter the absolute abundances of taxa as measured by minimum numbers. It may be predicted that this effect will occur for the Connley Cave No. 4 mammals. The only situation in which this effect will not occur is that in which all most abundant elements are identically distributed across aggregation units. At Connley Cave No. 4, this is not the case. Table 7.5 shows the distribution of most abundant elements for two taxa across levels in stratum 3 of this site. Clearly, most abundant elements are not identically distributed in this instance; with the exception of those cases in which sample sizes are extremely small, this is true in other cases as well. Accordingly, it is to be expected that different aggregation methods will differentially alter taxonomic abundances based upon minimum numbers of individuals at this site.

Table 7.6 shows these expected results for selected pairs of the five taxa represented by the greatest numbers of identified specimens at Connley Cave No. 4. No ratios of abundances are identical across aggregation

TABLE 7.5

Distribution of Most Abundant Elements within Stratum 3 for Two Connley Caves No. 4 Mammals

Stratum 3 level	Taxon 4	Taxon 5
24	1 right mandible	—
25	—	—
26	6 right mandible	4 right innominate
27	2 right mandible	3 right femur
28	—	1 left innominate
29	2 right mandible	1 left femur
30	2 left mandible	1 right innominate
31	1 maxilla	—
32	1 right innominate	1 left mandible

TABLE 7.6

The Effects of Aggregation upon Abundance Ratios Based upon Minimum Numbers: Selected Pairs of Connley Cave No. 4 Mammals

Taxon pair	Abundance ratios		
	MNI_{10cm}	$MNI_{stratum}$	MNI_{site}
1–2	1.89	2.60	3.60
2–3	1.65	1.88	1.11
3–4	1.00	0.62	1.13
4–5	1.00	0.93	0.62

methods, and many are widely disparate. Expectations based upon considerations of the distribution of elements across aggregation units are correct. At Connley Cave No. 4, little faith can be placed in the ratios of taxonomic abundance indicated by minimum numbers. And the same is true for any fauna for which most abundant elements are not identically distributed across aggregation units.

Finally, it is important to note that the differentially altered absolute abundances caused by the effects of aggregation methods upon minimum numbers may dramatically alter the outcome of any significance test applied to minimum number data. Assume, for instance, that we are interested in knowing whether the abundance of *Lepus* sp. changed significantly, compared with the abundance of all other mammals, between Connley Cave No. 4 strata 3 and 4. The choice of MNI_{10cm} as the measure of abundance would provide a χ^2 value of .01, and would lead to the conclusion that the abundance of this genus did not change significantly between these two strata. If $MNI_{stratum}$ were chosen as the abundance measure, a χ^2 value of 3.58 would result and, depending upon the significance level chosen, might or might not lead to the conclusion that the changes were significant. If NISP (the maximum possible minimum number value) were chosen, a χ^2 value of 49.64 would result, and the conclusion that these changes were extremely significant would necessarily follow (see Table 7.7).

And, lest some of the significance of this example be missed, I shall note that the kinds of phenomena I have discussed here would have been seen if horizontal excavation units or different possible natural stratigraphic divisions been used instead of arbitrary levels as the aggregation units.

TABLE 7.7

Comparing Taxonomic Abundances between Strata: Connley Cave No. 4 *Lepus* sp.[a]

	Abundance of *Lepus* sp. (A) and all other mammals (B) by analytic approach					
	MNI_{10cm}		$MNI_{stratum}$		NISP	
Stratum	A	B	A	B	A	B
3	25	53	14	48	256	247
4	37	76	23	37	388	150

[a] Comparison using:
MNI_{10cm}: $\chi^2 = 0.01$, $p > .90$.
$MNI_{stratum}$: $\chi^2 = 3.58$, $.10 > p > .05$.
NISP: $\chi^2 = 49.64$, $p < .001$.

Minimum Numbers as Ordinal Measures

Methodological considerations lead to the conclusion that the effects of aggregation upon minimum numbers are such that we can have faith neither in the absolute abundances these numbers indicate, nor in the ratios of taxonomic abundance they provide. As a result, minimum numbers may rarely provide more than ordinal level data on taxonomic abundances. Often, they may not provide even this.

In order to show that minimum numbers may provide valid ordinal level data on taxonomic abundance, it is necessary to show the conditions under which rank orders of taxonomic abundance are not affected by aggregation methods. A general answer to this question may most easily be obtained by examining the distribution of taxonomic abundances within archaeological faunas. For all archaeofaunas that I have examined, this distribution is decidedly nonnormal. Most taxa are represented by a very few individuals, whereas only a relatively small number of taxa are represented by a large number of individuals; Casteel (n.d.) has shown that this situation is a general one. A few examples of this distribution are shown in Figures 7.2 through 7.4.

The reasons for the frequency with which this distribution occurs relate to the factors that deposit animals in archaeological sites, as well,

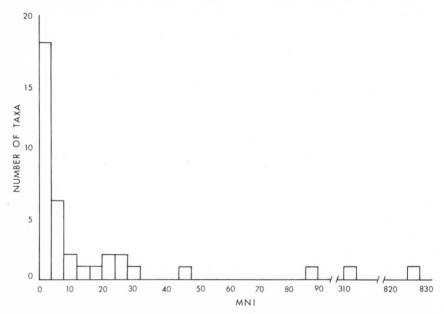

Figure 7.2. The distribution of abundance in some vertebrate archaeofaunas: Tick Creek mammals. (From Parmalee 1965.)

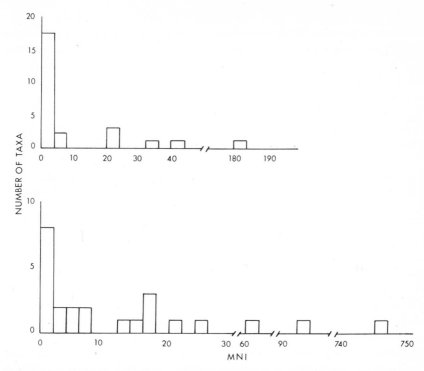

Figure 7.3. (top). The distribution of abundance in some vertebrate archaeofaunas: Eschelman mammals. (From Guilday, Parmalee, and Tanner 1962.)

Figure 7.4. (bottom). The distribution of abundance in some vertebrate archaeofaunas: Buffalo mammals. (From Guilday 1971.)

perhaps, to the techniques archaeologists use to recover them. Those relatively few animals that are present in great abundance are likely those that represent economically important taxa retrieved by the human occupants of the site; the relatively numerous taxa that are present in lower numbers are likely those that represent economically unimportant taxa, or taxa that are present for natural, not cultural, reasons (Thomas 1971), or taxa whose abundances have been reduced by collecting techniques. No matter what the reason for the distribution, it does serve to increase the probability that the use of different aggregation methods to calculate minimum numbers will not greatly rearrange the rank orders of taxonomic abundances. At the upper end of the distribution of taxonomic abundances, where relatively few taxa are represented by relatively large samples, different taxa tend to be widely separated in abundance. Accordingly, alterations in absolute abundances caused by different aggregation methods are not likely to rearrange ordinal abundances. At the lower end of the distribution, where a relatively large number of taxa are represented by small samples, changes in absolute abundances due to aggregation methods will primarily cause increases or decreases in ties of ranks, not reversals of rank orders of abundance. Although increases or decreases in ties of rank orders will most certainly affect ordinal level analytic techniques, it is also true that taxa at this end of the distribution are so poorly represented that it is questionable whether the abundances of these taxa should be quantified in any but a nominal sense. Indeed, at this end of the distribution, classifications based upon biological taxonomy are often used only to create larger classes of taxa based on nonphylogenetic criteria, which are then manipulated as a unit—for instance, "mesic" versus "xeric" rodents (e.g., Grayson 1977c). Once this is done, those taxa represented by relatively small samples now become shifted toward the upper end of the distribution of taxonomic abundances and, as a result, become less prone to having their rank orders altered as a result of the effects of different methods of faunal aggregation.

Thus, the general nature of the distribution of abundances in archaeological faunas is often such that the rank orders of taxonomic abundances based upon minimum numbers *may* remain stable across aggregation units, even though absolute abundances will be differentially changed by these methods. However, as with the distribution of most abundant elements across aggregation units, the question of the nature of the distribution of taxonomic abundances in an archaeological fauna is an empirical one. There is no theoretical reason why such a distribution cannot be of any given form in any instance. The only way the distribution of abundances can be determined for any faunal collection is by examining those abundances. For any distribution, the greater the separation between the abundances of different taxa, the less will be the chance that different aggregation methods will affect rank orders of taxonomic abundance. There are other ways to judge whether or not aggregation methods affect rank orders of abundance; these I shall discuss below. But, unless the distribution of abundances is such that taxa (or other faunal classes) are widely separated in abundance, there is little reason to think that aggregation methods will not alter rank orders of taxonomic abundance based upon minimum numbers.

The Effects of Aggregation upon Minimum Number-Based Rank Orders of Abundance: An Example

Different aggregation methods may or may not affect rank orders of taxonomic abundance derived from minimum number counts, depending upon the magnitude of the effect these methods have in differentially altering absolute taxonomic abundances, and depending upon the distribution of taxonomic abundances in the faunal collection. How do the different aggregation methods affect rank order abundances of the Connley Cave No. 4 mammals?

Examination of the distribution of taxonomic abundances of these mammals shows that, as with the sites illustrated in Figures 7.2 through 7.4, most taxa are represented by relatively few individuals (as measured by MNI_{10cm}), while a few are represented by a relatively large number of individuals (Figure 7.5). From this distribution, it may be expected that ordinal rearrangements, as measured by a rank order correlation coefficient, will occur, and that this rearrangement will primarily affect less abundant taxa by increasing the number of tied ranks.

The rank orders of taxonomic abundance produced by MNI_{10cm}, $MNI_{stratum}$, MNI_{site}, and NISP are shown in Table 7.8. Clearly, these rank orders do not remain stable across different aggregation methods: both inspection of rank orders and Kendall's tau values show that some ordinal rearrangement has occurred. Table 7.9 shows the rank order of ordinal rearrangements of taxonomic abundances, from least to greatest, for all pairs of measures used to quantify the abundance of the Connley Cave No. 4 mammals, as indicated by Kendall's tau coefficients. Not surprisingly, the rearrangements are least between those sets of measurements derived from the most similar approaches to aggregating faunal data prior to minimum number definition, and greatest between those pairs based upon the least similar approaches to aggregation. Thus, those approaches that divide the collection into the largest number of faunal aggregates (NISP, which represents the maximum possible number of individuals, and MNI_{10cm}) show relatively minor ordinal rearrangements between

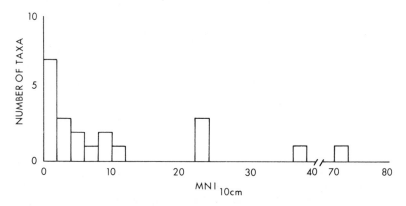

Figure 7.5. The distribution of abundance of the Connley Cave No. 4 mammals.

TABLE 7.8

Rank Orders of Abundance from All Abundance Measures: Connley Cave No. 4 Mammals

Taxon	MNI_{10cm}	$MNI_{stratum}$	MNI_{site}	NISP
1	1	1	1	1
2	2	2	3	2
3	4	5.5	4	3
4	4	4	5	4
5	4	3	2	5
6	8	15	11.5	6
7	6	5.5	6	7
8	8	10	11.5	8
9	8	7	7.5	9
10	11.5	15	18	10
11	10	8	7.5	11
12	14	10	11.5	12.5
13	11.5	15	18	12.5
14	17	15	18	15
15	14	15	18	15
16	14	10	9	15
17	17	15	18	17
18	17	15	11.5	18
19	20.5	20.5	18	20.5
20	20.5	20.5	18	20.5
21	20.5	20.5	18	20.5
22	20.5	20.5	18	20.5

themselves, and the same is true for those approaches that divide the collection into the smallest number of aggregates ($MNI_{stratum}$ and MNI_{site}). The magnitude of rearrangement increases as increasingly agglomerative approaches are compared with increasingly divisive ones.

Nonetheless, all Kendall's tau values are associated with exact probabilities of less than .001. In no cases do these values exceed those that might occur from resampling the same population using the same aggrega-

TABLE 7.9

Rank Order of Rearrangements of Ordinal Taxonomic Abundances for All Pairs of Abundance Measures, Connley Cave No. 4 Mammals

Measurement pair	Kendall's tau
MNI_{10cm} with NISP	.9471, $p < .001$
$MNI_{stratum}$ with MNI_{site}	.8878, $p < .001$
MNI_{10cm} with $MNI_{stratum}$	.8167, $p < .001$
MNI_{10cm} with MNI_{site}	.7714, $p < .001$
$MNI_{stratum}$ with NISP	.7620, $p < .001$
MNI_{site} with NISP	.7114, $p < .001$

tion method; the values indicate that the same population of rank-ordered variates is being sampled by each aggregation method. The predictions I made concerning ordinal abundances in this fauna seem correct.

Some Methodological Comments on Ordinal Level Manipulation of Minimum Number Counts

(This section should be skipped by those interested only in the more general aspects of minimum number analysis.)

The nature of minimum numbers of individuals is such that they can rarely be used as the basis of ratio scale analyses of taxonomic abundances. Because of the nature of the distribution of taxonomic abundances in most archaeological faunas, minimum number counts may often be used to provide ordinal level data on taxonomic abundance. However, this is not necessarily true, as I have noted. There undoubtedly are situations in which different aggregation methods will produce markedly different rank orders of taxonomic abundance as measured by a rank order correlation coefficient. These situations may, in fact, occur fairly frequently. As a result, whether or not minimum numbers may be treated as providing ordinal level data on taxonomic abundance must be treated as an empirical question to be answered anew with each application.

Thus, before ordinal level statistical procedures are applied to a set of minimum number values that have been transformed to ranks, it is necessary to demonstrate that ranks remain invariant across those aggregation procedures that are appropriate to the questions being asked. Two possible definitions of "invariant" may be used in this context: (a) that there are no changes whatsoever in rank order between the most and least divisive aggregation methods used in minimum number definition; (b) that there are changes in rank orders between these methods, but that these changes are not statistically significant when measured by a rank order correlation coefficient.

The following comments on testing for invariance, and on treating situations in which invariance does not occur, may be used in conjunction with either of these two definitions.

Working with one's own data, it is simple to test for rank order invariance. Given that only a relatively small series of ways of aggregating faunal material will be appropriate for testing any hypothesis about that material, one can test for rank order invariance by comparing the rank orders produced by the most divisive aggregation approach with those produced by the most agglomerative approach. If rank orders are invariant between the most divisive and most agglomerative aggregation methods, then the selected set of rank orders may be used in further manipulations, since these rank orders have been shown to be left unchanged by the most extreme aggregation methods appropriate to the problem.

The situation in which a researcher can recalculate minimum numbers by different aggregation methods is much less common than the situation in which that person wishes to compare data sets for which minimum numbers cannot be recalculated (for examples of such situations, see studies in Freeman 1973; Strauss 1977). I can suggest two simple ways by which the assumption of invariance may be shown to be reasonable in these settings:

1. Prepare a frequency diagram of taxonomic abundances based upon minimum numbers of individuals. If most taxa are represented by a very few individuals, while only a few are represented by many specimens or individuals, and these few are widely separated in abundance, then the assumption of invariance is supported. Recall that it is wisest either to combine those taxa represented by small samples into larger analytic units, or to treat those taxa as attributes of the faunal collection that may be either present or absent, but whose abundances may not be counted.

2. For each faunal assemblage that is to be compared, prepare one set of rank orders of taxonomic abundances based upon minimum numbers, and a second set based upon specimen counts. Since specimen counts represent maximum possible minimum number values, invariance between the most divisive possible aggregative approach (that which would provide NISP) and the more agglomerative aggregation approach provided by minimum numbers will lend support to the assumption of invariance. This method provides stronger support for the assumption of invariance as the method of aggregation used to calculate the reported minimum numbers becomes increasingly agglomerative. For instance, the assumption is given more support if one is comparing rank orders based upon specimen counts with those based upon $MNI_{stratum}$ than if one is comparing rank orders based upon specimen counts with rank orders based upon MNI_{10cm}. This is true simply because ordinal rearrangements will be greatest between those aggregation methods that are least similar. The less similar the aggregation methods used in the test for invariance, the stronger will be the support for the assumption of invariance.

What can be done if rank orders are not invariant across aggregation methods? One can, of course, treat the taxa represented as attributes that may be either present or absent. But it is also possible that the differences in rank orders are not so great as to alter the outcome of tests with which they are to be used. To see if this is so, determine the rank orders of taxonomic abundances that result from using the least and most divisive approaches to faunal aggregation appropriate to the problem at hand.

Calculate the test statistic for each set of resultant rank orders compared with each of the other set of rank orders involved in the test. If all probabilities fall below, or all fall above, the adopted significance level, the problem is resolved: the rank orders are not invariant, but this does not matter, since the outcome of the test is not altered. [See Bradley (1968) for a similar approach to resolving zero differences or tied observations in single data sets.]

Minimum Numbers as Maximally Ordinal Counts: A Final Methodological Argument

I have argued that the effect of aggregation methods upon minimum numbers is often such as to restrict the use of this measure to providing at best ordinal level data on taxonomic abundances, and that the settings in which minimum numbers may be treated as ordinal in scale must be empirically determined in each instance. There is also a second reason why minimum numbers should not be treated as providing more than ordinal level information on taxonomic abundance. Minimum numbers of individuals mean precisely what the name states: the *minimum* number of individual animals needed to account for the faunal material in some aggregation unit. The actual abundances that any given minimum number may represent will vary from that minimum number to some unknown higher figure. As a result, the actual distances between minimum numbers are unknown: it is not possible to say that an MNI of, for instance, 40 reflects twice as many individuals as an MNI of 20, or that equal minimum number values for different taxa reflect equal actual abundances. Recall that in both interval and ratio scales the distances between any pair of measured units must be known (see, e.g., Siegel 1956; Stevens 1946, 1951; Suppes and Zinnes 1963). Since the actual distances between minimum numbers are not known, these values can never provide valid measures that are more than ordinal in scale.

The question becomes one of whether minimum numbers can provide even ordinal level information on taxonomic abundances. It is obvious that an MNI of 10 for some given taxon might result from the presence of 30 animals in the faunal aggregate, whereas an MNI of 20 for a different taxon might result from the presence of only 25 animals in that aggregate. Thus, it is not necessarily true that minimum numbers will provide ordinal level information on taxonomic abundances.

The appropriate way to view a minimum number is by seeing that number as the lowest figure possible in a distribution of numbers of individual animals. For any minimum number, N, the actual number of animals that N may represent has a frequency distribution that begins at N and continues upward to NISP. In any given case, N may represent a greater number of actual individuals than the next higher number in the series. However, the greater the separation between calculated minimum number values, the less the chance that those values will fail to reflect the rank order of actual abundances. Thus, taxa that are similar in abundance will *probably* not have their ordinal abundances accurately reflected by minimum number values: those ordinal abundances may, in fact, be randomly rearranged. On the other hand, taxa whose abundances are well separated will *probably* have their ordinal abundances accurately reflected by minimum number counts. This, of course, is precisely the situation in which I concluded, for other reasons, that minimum numbers might be used to provide ordinal level data anyway. Again, it is seen that minimum numbers may be used to provide ordinal abundances for taxa whose sample sizes are well separated, but not for those whose sample sizes are similar, and that the situations for which this is true must be empirically determined. And, again, it is seen that minimum numbers may not be used as the basis of ratio scale analyses of taxonomic abundance.

The Relationship of MNI and NISP

Earlier in this paper, I noted that the number of identified specimens per taxon must be *demonstrated* to be an appropriate measure of taxonomic abundance for the problem and fauna at hand. It is now possible to explore NISP as a measure of taxonomic abundance more fully.

I shall begin by noting again that the number of identified specimens can be seen as the maximum possible minimum number of individuals for a given taxon in any set of faunal material, the upper end of a distribution of estimated abundance whose lower end is marked by MNI. As a result, the relationship of any given NISP value to the actual abundance that the analyst is trying to measure is similar to the relationship of MNI to that actual abundance in an important way: the exact relationship between the number of identified specimens and the actual abundance being measured is in most cases unknown, beyond the fact that that abundance must be equal to or less than the NISP value. Accordingly, NISP values cannot be assumed to provide an abundance measure that is greater than ordinal in scale.

Can specimen counts be assumed to provide ordinal level information on taxonomic abundance? Recall that the major problem affecting these counts is that of potential interdependence of identified specimens. The effect of interdependence upon specimen counts is much the same as that of aggregation upon minimum numbers: both have the potential of differentially altering measured taxonomic abundances. In the case of minimum numbers, such differential alteration will occur unless most abundant elements are identically distributed across aggregation units. In the case of specimen counts, differential alteration will occur unless all specimens are independent of one another, or interdependence is randomly distributed across taxa. As a result, specimen counts probably accurately reflect ordinal taxonomic abundances in the same settings in which minimum numbers may do this. Taxa whose abundances are well separated will *probably* have their ordinal abundances accurately reflected by specimen counts, whereas this will *probably* not be the case for taxa that are similar in abundance.

Thus, both minimum numbers and specimen counts may be seen to operate in similar ways in similar settings as measures of taxonomic abundance. This helps explain why, in the case of Connley Cave No. 4, rank orders of taxonomic abundance based upon specimen counts did not differ significantly from those based upon minimum numbers. Can the relationship between minimum numbers and specimen counts be made more precise than this?

In an earlier article, which looked in detail at the relationship between the number of identified specimens per taxon and the minimum number of individuals defined from them, I showed that the relationship of the ratio MNI/NISP to NISP for any given fauna was of the form

$$MNI/NISP = \alpha NISP^{\beta} \qquad (1)$$

in which α and β are constants that must be empirically determined for any given fauna (Grayson 1978a; see also Grayson 1978b).

Casteel (n.d.) has recently explored these relationships in detail. He has noted that since equation (1) describes the relationship between MNI/NISP and NISP, then it is also true that MNI must be a function of NISP:

$$MNI = \alpha NISP^{\beta+1} \qquad (2)$$

As a result, MNI values for any series of taxa can be predicted quite accurately from specimen counts for those taxa. Although I suspect that much can be learned from studying the variability in MNI values which is not predicted by NISP, the point I wish to make here is that specimen counts provide much the same information on taxonomic abundances as do minimum numbers (see Ducos 1968, 1975; Gejvall 1969; Poplin 1976; Shotwell 1958, for further discussions of the relationship between MNI and NISP).

What, then, should be concluded about these measures of taxonomic abundance? First, it must be concluded that until we know more about the relationship between minimum numbers, specimen counts, and the actual abundances faunal analysts are trying to measure, neither MNI nor NISP can usually be assumed to provide greater than ordinal scale information on taxonomic abundances. Second, whether ordinal scale measurement has been achieved with either of these measures must be examined in each instance these measures are employed. I have suggested some procedures with which this demonstration might be made. Third, since counts of identified specimens per taxon provide much the same information on ordinal scale abundances as is provided by minimum numbers, there would seem little reason to employ minimum number analysis unless there is some special and convincing reason for doing so (see also Casteel n.d.; Ducos 1968, 1975). Finally, it is clear that our understanding of these measures has barely scratched the surface of their complexities. High on the list of priorities of problems to be solved must be the search for a means of discovering the patterns of interdependence among all specimens within a fauna. Once such a method has been discovered, many of the kinds of problems I have examined here will simply disappear.

Meat Weights as an Abundance Measure

Rather than counting specimens or minimum individuals, the weight of meat represented per taxon might be used as a measure of taxonomic abundance. Most frequently, meat weights have been derived in order to assess the relative contribution of taxa to subsistence in terms of their mass. The reasons for proceeding in this fashion are simple. If, for instance, bison and mice are each represented by one specimen, and therefore one individual, in a faunal collection, both counts of specimens and of minimum individuals will treat them as equally frequent, although their contribution to the diet of the individuals involved would not have been so. The weight of meat per taxon has been used to avoid this difficulty. Meat weights may also be used to estimate the relative composition of a prehistoric fauna in terms of its biomass, or weight per unit area. However, as I shall discuss below, the difficulties involved in inferring the composition of a prehistoric fauna from the remains that happen to accumulate in an archaeological site are so great that such studies have been avoided by those working with archaeological faunas, although they have been attempted in paleontology (Guthrie 1968).

Several ways of calculating the weight of meat per taxon represented by the bones in a faunal aggregate have been used. In each method, some measure thought to be correlated with meat weight in a known way is used to derive those weights through the use of some simple functional relationship. The commonly used measures are the weight of bone per taxon and the minimum number of individuals per taxon. In addition, measurements of single bones have been used to calculate the weights of the individuals from which those bones came. I shall briefly discuss each of these methods.

The use of the weight of bone per taxon to derive meat weights is quite common (see, e.g., Cook and Treganza 1950; Kubasiewicz 1973; Reed 1963; Uerpmann 1973a,b). In this method, the weight of bone per taxon is assumed to be a fixed percentage of the meat weight for that taxon; bone weight is therefore multiplied by the appropriate factor to obtain meat weight. All these methods have assumed that meat weight is a simple linear function of bone weight, and that the major difficulty in applying this approach lies in determining the correct factor for converting bone to meat weight. Casteel (1978), however, has shown that bone weights and meat weights in individuals are not related in a simple linear fashion, but are instead related curvilinearly. Thus, rather than using an equation of the form

$$Y = \alpha X \qquad (3)$$

where Y = the predicted meat weight of the taxon involved,
X = the weight of bone identified for that taxon, and
α = a constant to be determined empirically
to predict meat weight from bone weight, the actual relationship for individuals is of the form

$$Y = \alpha X^{\beta} \qquad (4)$$

where Y = the predicted meat weight of an individual of the taxon involved,
X = the bone weight of that individual, and
α and β are constants to be determined empirically.

Because the relationship between bone weight and meat weight for an individual is curvilinear, one cannot simply use a single constant (α) to convert one to the other. For instance, using the appropriate equation for pigs, Casteel (1978) showed that bone weight varied from 82% to 2% of meat weight (total tissue weight minus bone weight) as the weight of bone varied from 100 to 100,000,000 grams. Casteel (1978) also noted that equation (4) applies to individuals, not to composite aggregates of faunal material. Because this is so, the equation cannot be applied to such aggregates. Only when all the bones involved are from a single individual would it be appropriate to use such an equation to predict meat weight from bone weight. Alternatively, one could assume that all bones in the aggregate came from a single individual, but such an assumption is clearly inappropriate. Casteel (1978) concludes, as did Chaplin (1971) before him, that this method of inferring meat weight from bone weight must be rejected as invalid.

If this method is inadequate, then the minimum number of individuals per taxon might be used to determine meat weights per taxon. In this method, the minimum number value for a taxon is multiplied by the average weight of a modern individual of that taxon, and the resultant figures are then used in further analyses (e.g., Parmalee 1965; Smith 1975; Stewart and Stahl 1977; White 1953). It should be evident that meat weights so derived will suffer from the same problems that affect the minimum number values upon which they are based. In most cases, the approach can provide at best ordinal data on the "dietary contributions" of taxa in terms of meat weights. In addition, and as is recognized by most individuals using the approach, this method ignores variation in the sizes of the animals represented in the faunal aggregate, thus compounding difficulties resulting from the use of minimum numbers of individuals. As a result, it is difficult to have faith in the results obtained from this approach (for other critiques of this method, see Casteel 1976; Guilday 1970; Kubasiewicz 1973). If accurate meat weights for selected individuals are required, then a third approach might be employed. In this approach, equations are established that relate a measure of bone size to meat weight (or, if one wishes, to some other criterion of body size) for each taxon involved. Once these equations have been established, they are used to predict the weights of individuals represented by archaeological specimens. Noddle (1973) has begun to apply this approach to various elements from modern cattle; Casteel (1976) has done the same for fish. The advantages of this approach for predicting the weights of individual animals are sizable, since the resultant values are quite accurate, assuming the equations derived from modern vertebrates are applicable to their archaeological counterparts (Noddle 1973). Of course, this approach does not allow the analyst to determine meat weights for all individuals in a faunal aggregate, since there is usually no way of knowing which specimens came from different animals. If the most abundant element is used to control for this problem, then difficulties relating to aggregation once again emerge. Although the method does have the potential of providing accurate meat weights for individual animals whose body size is of interest (see, e.g., Casteel 1974), it would not seem to provide a means of accurately assessing total meat weight per taxon in a faunal aggregate, nor has it been proposed to be used in this fashion.

In sum, of the two methods that have been commonly used to estimate the weight of meat per taxon represented by the bones within a faunal aggregate, that based upon bone weights is invalid, and that based upon minimum numbers of individuals can usually provide no better than ordinal level information on meat abundances, at least given our current understanding of minimum numbers. The third method, based upon measurements of individual bone specimens, is accurate, but can be applied only to individuals, not to entire faunal aggregates. Thus, an appropriate way of measuring relative taxonomic abundances in terms of meat weight does not seem to be available.

THE NATURE OF THE UNDERLYING VARIABLE

To this point, I have treated the problems relating to the measurement of the abundances of taxa that make up a vertebrate archaeofauna as problems that relate only to the behavior of the units of measurement. There is, of course, much more to the issue than this. Not only do we need to understand the behavior of the units of quantification we employ, we also need to understand the nature of the variables we are trying to measure. If those variables can appropriately be measured by using ratio scales, then we are justified in seeking ratio scale measures to accomplish this goal. If, however, the variables of interest are nominal or ordinal in scale, we must use only nominal or ordinal measures. These considerations have received detailed attention in many disciplines (e.g., Cronbach 1960; Stevens 1951), including some areas of archaeological research (e.g., Spaulding 1977). They have, however, received surprisingly little attention in vertebrate faunal analysis.

Broadly construed, there have been two main uses of vertebrate faunal analysis in archaeology: the study of past environments, and the study of past human subsistence systems. The goals of these two uses of faunal data differ, although both kinds of studies are often conducted within the same analytic framework. Those interested in studying past environments through the use of archaeological faunas are primarily interested in using those faunas to monitor the nature of biotic communities in general, and of vertebrate communities in particular, in the area surrounding the site. On the other hand, those interested in studying past human subsistence systems are primarily interested in monitoring the taxa employed as energy sources within those systems.

A major distinction that must be drawn between these two approaches relates to the nature of the faunal sample with which each set of practitioners must operate. Those who are using archaeological faunas to probe past environments are using a complex sampling scheme to reach their goal. The variable of interest in this setting is the abundance of different taxa in the environment at some point in the past. Because it is impossible to sample those taxa directly, points in the environment at which remains of those animals accumulated are sampled. That is, taxa present in the environment are sampled through accumulation in archaeological sites, and those sites are then sampled by the archaeologist. There are numerous techniques available for ensuring that the sample retrieved from the site is representative, but there are no ways available for discovering the relationship between the faunal accumulation and what was in the environment at the time the sample accumulated. Even if ratios of taxonomic abundances within the archaeological fauna were accurately specified, the meaning of those ratios would be unclear. As a result, manipulating counts of taxonomic abundance as actual counts implies much greater precision in the archaeological faunal record than that record actually provides in this setting.

There can be no doubt that the taxa present in a collection may be treated as nominal data, as attributes that can be either present or absent. Even though taxonomic abundances may mean little in the paleoenvironmental setting, the animals that are present must have been in the area surrounding the site of deposition, with rare exceptions resulting from human activities. Thus, it is usually valid to draw paleoenvironmental inferences from the kinds of taxa represented in vertebrate archaeofaunas (see e.g., Anderson 1968; Guilday 1958, 1961; Parmalee 1968, 1971). But troubles abound once an attempt is made to go beyond such nominal scale analysis. If the taxa represented in an archaeofauna are present because of some mechanism that differentially sampled the surrounding environment, then the kinds of taxa present in the fauna may not reflect proportions of habitats surrounding the site, but may instead reflect the nature of the accumulating mechanism. As a result, even ordinal level analyses of past environments from these taxa may be invalid. At the most, counts of taxa may indicate whether there was more of one habitat type than another in the area surrounding the site, but will rarely if ever indicate how much more. Of course, if counts of taxa can at best provide ordinal level information concerning past environments, there can be little reason to think that quantifying the abundances of each of these taxa can provide more robust information. It follows from all these considerations that, given current knowledge of the ways in which archaeological faunas accumulate, paleoenvironmental inferences may at best be ordinal in scale, and may often be nominal in scale only.

The situation changes when the faunal component of subsistence systems becomes the target of investigation. Here, the population to be sampled is usually conceived of as being the faunal accumulation within the site itself. Since the population about which inferences are to be drawn is the faunal accumulation itself, the question of the relationship between taxonomic abundances in the environment and in the sample does not usually arise, and a representative sample of the target population can be obtained through normal archaeological sampling procedures. Of course, other categories of problems exist. One of the most crucial of these relates to what is, and what is not, "cultural" bone (Thomas 1971). In many, perhaps most, cases it is virtually impossible to make such distinctions given current knowledge. In rockshelters, for instance, a myriad of predators and scavengers may add to faunal accumulations; that fraction which is due to human predation may be impossible to identify. Even nominal level measurements are affected by this problem and, as a result, it may not be possible to make any statements about human subsistence from such data. If distinctions between cultural and natural bone can be drawn, then the variable of interest becomes the abundance of economically important taxa in the faunal accumulation. Because these taxa are being directly sampled, their absolute abundances are more directly interpretable than the abundances of animals analyzed for their paleoenvironmental significance. Butchering patterns, activities of scavengers, and other variables that alter the taxonomic abundances of economically important animals will cloud the meaning of those abundances, but such problems are less severe once uncoupled from the sampling difficulties encountered by paleoenvironmental work. I emphasize that I am not saying that it is easier to reconstruct prehistoric subsistence systems than it is to reconstruct prehistoric environments. Not only may it be impossible to routinely separate cultural from natural bone, but many parts of prehistoric subsistence systems are simply gone from the record; the definition of the problems we are trying to solve must take this into account. What I am saying is that when the analyst wishes to count the abundances of vertebrate taxa within a site as a means of inferring aspects of prehistoric subsistence, it becomes appropriate to envisage those abundances as potentially ratio level in scale. Here, a ratio-scale measure of taxonomic abundance may be required.

In both paleoenvironmental and economic analytic settings, it is clear that the problems relating to the formation of archaeological faunas are vast in both number and scope. It will matter little if we have the methods needed to measure taxonomic abundances if we do not know what the resultant numbers mean. In vertebrate faunal analysis in archaeology, I suggest that we often do not.

CONCLUSIONS

Quantification of the abundances of the taxa represented within vertebrate archaeofaunas is a basic step in the analysis of such faunas: it is difficult to find any faunal report in which some measure of taxonomic abundance is not presented. Specimen counts and minimum numbers are almost always used to provide that measure. Yet, faunal analysts have a long way to go before abundance counts become readily interpretable.

First, the possible meanings of taxonomic abundance must be understood. In paleoenvironmental reconstruction using faunal data, this issue is an exceedingly complex one because the relationship between the fauna analyzed and the fauna that was in the surrounding environment is almost always unknown. As a result, although the presence of certain taxa in an archaeofauna will provide information on what kinds of habitats were most likely present in the area surrounding the site, and can certainly provide data on what animals were present in that area, the abundances of those taxa are as likely to reflect the usually unknown mechanisms of accumulation as they are to reflect some known environmental parameter. Clearly, data on how such faunas accumulate are needed. The problems are less severe when the analytic goal of faunal analysis is the understanding of prehistoric human subsistence systems. In this case, the target and the sampled populations are usually identical, and the absolute abundances of taxa represented within the sample become more directly interpretable *as long as* those taxa present as a result of human activities can be distinguished from those that are not.

Second, given that taxonomic abundances may be interpreted in the way in which they are to be interpreted, and that an appropriate scale of measurement has been selected, the nature of the possible measures of abundance must be understood. The most commonly used measure of abundance, the minimum number of individuals, is affected by a wide range of difficulties. Because the relationship between minimum numbers of individuals and the actual number of individuals in a faunal aggregate is never known, and because of the effects of aggregation itself, minimum numbers cannot provide a valid measure of taxonomic abundance that is greater than ordinal in scale. In addition, the settings in which this measure may provide even an ordinal scale measure of abundance must be empirically determined in every case. By comparing rank orders of abundance that result from different aggregation methods, it is possible to control for the effects of aggregation upon those ranks. However, it is much more difficult to control for the fact that the relationship between minimum numbers of individuals and the actual number of individuals for any given faunal aggregate is usually unknown. Here, all that can be said is that the greater the separation between minimum numbers, the greater are the chances that ordinal scale abundance will be accurately reflected by these numbers. This problem cannot be satisfactorily resolved until the relationship between actual taxonomic abundances within an archaeofauna and the abundances indicated by minimum numbers is understood. Until that time, all we can really be sure of is that actual abundances lie somewhere between the minimum provided by minimum numbers and the maximum provided by counts of identified specimens. These considerations are, I think, damaging to the traditional use of minimum numbers as a measure of taxonomic abundance within archaeological faunas.

Counts of identified specimens are plagued by the problem of interdependence, the potential effects of which are similar to the potential effects of aggregation upon minimum numbers. Accordingly, many of the caveats that apply to minimum numbers also apply to specimen counts. These counts cannot usually be shown to provide a measure of taxonomic abundance that is greater than ordinal scale, and the settings in which they will provide even this must be determined empirically. However, the situations in which it is likely that minimum numbers will provide ordinal scale information are the same as those in which it is likely that specimen counts will provide such information. In addition, the minimum number of individuals for a series of taxa is a function of the number of identified specimens for those taxa. As a result of all these factors, when ordinal scale taxonomic abundances can be obtained, they can be obtained directly from specimen counts.

I have simplified some of the problems involved in the quantification of taxonomic abundances by couching these problems in terms of the four measurement scales defined by Stevens (1946, 1951). If a measure of taxonomic abundance can be shown to produce ordinal scale results, it is possible that the distances between taxa, as quantified by either minimum numbers or specimen counts, have some meaning, even if the actual distances are not known. If so, then an ordered-metric scale, in which not only rank orders but also some indication of the relative magnitude of differences between those ranks are known, may be constructed (see, e.g., Blalock 1974). It is, perhaps, in this poorly examined realm that the interrelationship between measures of taxonomic abundance and measurement scales may be most appropriately explored until methods for solving the problem of interdependence of specimens have been developed.

It is clear that much needs to be done before it can be concluded that an acceptable measure of taxonomic abundances within vertebrate archaeofaunas is available. Much more work also needs to be done in order to understand the processes that lead to the formation of those faunas. Although a start has been made in this direction (see Binford and Bertram 1977, and references therein; for paleontological approaches, see Behrensmeyer 1975, 1978; Clark and Guensburg 1970; Dodson 1971;

Wolff 1973; see also references in Munthe and McLeod 1975), there is far to go before these processes are even dimly understood. Until such an understanding is reached, there is little reason to think that taxonomic abundances from any but the simplest vertebrate archaeofaunas will be easily interpretable. Unfortunately, although it is clear that the processes that lead to the formation of vertebrate archaeofaunas can be identified, it seems clear as well that it will be exceedingly difficult, if not impossible, to infer the processes that led to the accumulation of any given archaeofauna from the bones that constitute that fauna in such complex settings as those provided by rock shelters. Nonetheless, the limits will not be known until they are reached, and such studies are crucially important if the analysis of vertebrate faunas from archaeological sites is to make lasting contributions to either archaeological or biological knowledge.

ACKNOWLEDGMENTS

The assistance of Drs. R. W. Casteel, Robert C. Dunnell, and M. B. Schiffer during preparation of this paper is gratefully acknowledged. Analysis of the Connley Caves fauna was supported by the American Philosophical Society. I thank M. L. Johnson and E. Kritzman (Puget Sound Museum of Natural History, University of Puget Sound), J. L. Patton (Museum of Vertebrate Zoology, University of California), and S. Rohwrer and R. M. Free (Thomas Burke Memorial Museum, University of Washington) for the help they provided during the analysis of the Connley Caves material.

REFERENCES

Anderson, E.
    1968   Fauna of the Little Box Elder Cave, Converse County, Wyoming. The carnivora. *University of Colorado Studies in Earth Sciences* **6**:1–59.
Bedwell, S. F.
    1969   Prehistory and environment of the pluvial Fort Rock area of south central Oregon. Unpublished Ph.D. dissertation, Department of Anthropology, University of Oregon.
    1973   *Fort Rock Basin: Prehistory and environment.* Eugene: University of Oregon Books.
Behrensmeyer, A. K.
    1975   The taphonomy and paleoecology of Plio-Pleistocene vertebrate assemblages east of Lake Rudolf, Kenya. *Bulletin of the Museum of Comparative Zoology, Harvard University* **146**:473–578.
    1978   Taphonomic and ecologic information from bone weathering. *Paleobiology* **4**:150–162.
Binford, L. R., and J. B. Bertram
    1977   Bone frequencies—And attritional processes. In *For theory building in archaeology,* edited by L. R. Binford. New York: Academic Press. Pp. 77–153.

Blalock, H. M., Jr. (editor)
   1974   *Measurement in the social sciences.* Chicago: Aldine.
Bökönyi, S.
   1970   A new method for the determination of the minimum number of individuals in animal bone material. *American Journal of Archaeology* **74**:291–292.
Bradley, J. V.
   1968   *Distribution-free statistical tests.* Englewood Cliffs, N.J.: Prentice-Hall.
Brain, C. K.
   1969   The contribution of Namib Desert Hottentots to an understanding of australopithecine bone accumulations. *Scientific Papers of the Namib Desert Research Station* No. 39.
Casteel, R. W.
   1971   Differential bone destruction: Some comments. *American Antiquity* **36**:466–469.
   1972   Some biases in the recovery of archaeological faunal remains. *Proceedings of the Prehistoric Society* **38**:383–388.
   1974   Use of Pacific salmon otoliths for estimating fish size, with a note on the size of late Pleistocene and Pliocene salmonids. *Northwest Sceince* **48**:175–179.
   1976   *Fish remains in archaeology and paleo-environmental studies.* New York: Academic Press.
   1977   Characterization of faunal assemblages and the minimum number of individuals determined from paired elements: Continuing problems in archaeology. *Journal of Archaeological Science* **4**:125–134.
   1978   Faunal assemblages and the "weigemethode" or weight method. *Journal of Field Archaeology* **5**:71–77.
   n.d.   A treatise on the minimum number of individuals index: An analysis of its behaviour and a method for its prediction. Manuscript on deposit, Department of Archaeology, Simon Fraser University.
Casteel, R. W., and D. K. Grayson
   1977   Terminological problems in vertebrate faunal analysis. *World Archaeology* **9**:235–242.
Chaplin, R. E.
   1971   *The study of animal bones from archaeological sites.* New York: Seminar Press.
Cronbach, L. J.
   1960   *Essentials of psychological testing* (2nd ed.). New York: Harper.
Clark, J., and T. E. Guensburg
   1970   Population dynamics of *Leptomeryx fieldiana: Geology* **16**:411–451.
Cook, S. F., and A. E. Treganza
   1950   The quantitative investigation of Indian Mounds. *University of California Publications in American Archaeology and Ethnology* **40**:223–262.
Cowgill, G. L.
   1977   The trouble with significance tests and what we can do about it. *American Antiquity* **42**:350–368.
Crader, D. C.
   1974   The effects of scavengers on bone material from a large mammal: An experiment conducted among the Bisa of the Luangwa Valley, Zambia. In Ethnoarchaeology, edited by C. B. Donnan and C. W. Clewlow, Jr. *University of California Archaeological Survey Monograph* No. IV:162–173.
Daly, P.
   1969   Approaches to faunal analysis in archaeology. *American Antiquity* **34**:146–153.

Dodson, P.
1971 Sedimentology and taphonomy of the Oldman Formation (Campanian), Dinosaur Provincial Park, Alberta (Canada). *Palaeogeography, Palaeoclimatology, Palaeoecology* **10**:21–74.

Ducos, P.
1968 L'origine des animaux domestiques en Palestine. *Publications de l'Institut de Préhistoire de l'Université de Bordeaux* No. 4.
1975 Analyse statistique des collections d'ossements d'animaux. In *Archaeozoological studies,* edited by A. T. Clason. Amsterdam: North-Holland Publishing. Pp. 35–44.

Flannery, K. V.
1967 The vertebrate fauna and hunting patterns. In *The prehistory of the Tehuacan Valley* (Vol. 1), edited by D. S. Byers. Austin: University of Texas Press. Pp. 132–178.

Freeman, L. G.
1973 The significance of mammalian faunas from Paleolithic occupations in Cantabrian Spain. *American Antiquity* **38**:3–44.

Gejvall, N.-G.
1969 *Lerna, a pre-classical site in the Argoilid,* Vol. 1: *The Fauna.* Princeton: American School of Classical Studies at Athens.

Gilbert, A. S., and P. Steinfeld
1977 Faunal remains from Dinkha Tepe, northwestern Iran. *Journal of Field Archaeology* **4**:329–351.

Grayson, D. K.
1973 On the methodology of faunal analysis. *American Antiquity* **38**:432–439.
1974 The Riverhaven No. 2 vertebrate fauna: Comments on methods in faunal analysis and on aspects of the subsistence potential of prehistoric New York. *Man in the Northeast* **8**:23–39.
1976 A note on the prehistoric avifauna of the Lower Klamath Basin. *Auk* **93**:830–833.
1977a A review of the evidence for early Holocene turkeys in the Northern Great Basin. *American Antiquity* **42**:110–114.
1977b On the Holocene history of some Northern Great Basin lagomorphs. *Journal of Mammalogy* **58**:507–513.
1977c Paleoclimatic implications of the Dirty Shame Rockshelter mammalian fauna. *Tebiwa: Miscellaneous Papers of the Idaho State University Museum* No. 9.
1978a Minimum numbers and sample size in vertebrate faunal analysis. *American Antiquity* **43**:53–65.
1978b Reconstructing mammalian communities: A discussion of Shotwell's method of paleoecological analysis. *Paleobiology* **4**:77–81.
n.d. Mt. Mazama, climatic change, and Fort Rock Basin archaeofaunas. In *Volcanism and human ecology,* edited by P. D. Sheets and D. K. Grayson. New York: Academic Press (in press).

Guilday, J. E.
1958 The prehistoric distribution of the opossum. *Journal of Mammalogy* **39**:39–43.
1961 Prehistoric record of *Scalopus* from western Pennsylvania. *Journal of Mammalogy* **42**:117–118.
1970 Animal remains from archaeological excavations at Fort Ligonier. *Annals of the Carnegie Museum* **42**:177–186.

1971 Biological and archaeological analysis of bones from a 17th century Indian village (46 Pu 31), Putnam County, West Virginia. *West Virginia Geological and Economic Survey Report of Archaeological Investigations* No. 4.

Guilday, J. E., P. W. Parmalee, and D. P. Tanner
1962 Aboriginal butchering techniques at the Eschelman Site (36 La 12), Lancaster County, Pennsylvania. *Pennsylvania Archaeologist* **32**:59–83.

Guthrie, R. D.
1968 Paleoecology of the large-mammal community in interior Alaska during the late Pleistocene. *American Midland Naturalist* **79**:346–363.

Hesse, B., and D. Perkins, Jr.
1974 Faunal remains from Karataş-Semayük in southeast Anatolia: An interim report. *Journal of Field Archaeology* **1**:149–160.

Hill, A.
1976 On carnivore and weathering damage to bone. *Current Anthropology* **17**:335–336.

Howard, H.
1930 A census of the Pleistocene birds of Rancho La Brea from the collections of the Los Angeles Museum. *Condor* **32**:81–88.

Kubasiewicz, M.
1973 Spezifische Elemente der Polnischen archäozoologischen Forschungen des letzen Vierteljahrhunderts. In *Domestikationsforschung und Geschichte der Haustiere*, edited by J. Matolsci. Budapest: Akadémiai Kiadó. Pp. 371–376.

Merriam, J. C., and C. Stock
1932 The Felidae of Rancho La Brea. *Carnegie Institution of Washington, Publication* No. 422.

Munthe, K., and S. A. McLeod
1975 Collection of taphonomic information from fossil and recent vertebrate specimens with a selected bibliography. *PaleoBios* No. 19.

Noddle, B.
1973 Determination of the body weight of cattle from bone measurements. In *Domestikationsforschung und Geschichte der Haustiere*, edited by J. Matolsci. Budapest: Akadémiai Kiadó. Pp. 377–389.

Noe-Nygaard, N.
1977 Butchering and marrow fracturing as a taphonomic factor in archaeological deposits. *Paleobiology* **3**:218–237.

Parmalee, P. W.
1965 The food economy of Archaic and Woodland peoples at the Tick Creek Cave Site, Missouri. *Missouri Archaeologist* **27**:1–34.
1968 Cave and archaeological faunal deposits as indicators of post-Pleistocene animal populations and distribution in Illinois. *University of Illinois College of Agriculture, Special Publication* **14**:104–113.
1971 Fisher and porcupine remains from cave deposits in Missouri. *Illinois Academy of Science, Transactions* **64**:225–229.

Payne, S.
1972 On the interpretation of bone samples from archaeological sites. In *Papers in economic prehistory*, edited by E. S. Higgs. London and New York: Cambridge University Press. Pp. 65–81.
1975 Faunal changes at Franchthi Cave from 20,000 B. C. to 3,000 B. C. In *Archaeozoological studies*, edited by A. T. Clason. Amsterdam: North-Holland Publishing. Pp. 120–131.

Perkins, D., Jr.
1964 Prehistoric fauna from Shanidar, Iraq. *Science* **144**:1565–1566.
1973 A critique on the methods of quantifying faunal remains from archaeological sites. In *Domestikationsforschung und Geschichte der Haustiere*, edited by J. Matolsci. Budapest: Akadémiai Kiadó. Pp. 367–370.
Perkins, D., Jr., and P. Daly
1968 A hunter's village in Neolithic Turkey. *Scientific American* **219**(5):96–106.
Platnick, N. I., and G. Nelson
1978 A method of analysis for historical biogeography. *Systematic Zoology* **27**:1–16.
Poplin, F.
1976 Remarques théoriques et pratiques sur les unités utilisées dans les études d'ostéologie quantitative, particulièrement en archéologie préhistorique, *Union Internationale des Sciences Préhistorique et Protohistorique, IXème Congrès, Thèmes Spécialisés B*:124–141.
Reed, C. A.
1963 Osteo-archaeology. In *Science in archaeology*, edited by D. Brothwell and E. S. Higgs. London: Thames & Hudson. Pp. 204–216.
Shotwell, J. A.
1955 An approach to the paleoecology of mammals. *Ecology* **36**:327–337.
1958 Inter-community relationships in Hemphillian (Mid-Pliocene) mammals. *Ecology* **39**:271–282.
Siegel, S.
1956 *Nonparametric statistics for the behavioral sciences*. New York: McGraw-Hill.
Smith, B. D.
1975 Toward a more accurate estimation of the meat yield of animal species at archaeological sites. In *Archaeozoological studies*, edited by A. T. Clason. Amsterdam: North-Holland Publishing. Pp. 99–106.
Spaulding, A. C.
1977 On growth and form in archaeology: Multivariate analysis. *Journal of Anthropological Research* **33**:1–15.
Stevens, S. S.
1946 On the theory of scales of measurement. *Science* **103**:677–680.
1951 Mathematics, measurement, and psychophysics. In *Handbook of experimental psychology*, edited by S. S. Stevens. New York: Wiley. Pp. 1–49.
Stewart, F. L., and P. W. Stahl
1977 Cautionary note on edible meat poundage figures. *American Antiquity* **42**:267–270.
Stock, C.
1929 A census of the Pleistocene mammals of Rancho La Brea, based on the collections of the Los Angeles Museum. *Journal of Mammalogy* **10**:281–289.
Strauss, L. G.
1977 Of deerslayers and mountain men: Paleolithic faunal exploitation in Cantabrian Spain. In *For theory building in archaeology*, edited by L. Binford. New York: Academic Press. Pp. 41–76.
Suppes, P., and J. L. Zinnes
1963 Basic measurement theory. In *Handbook of mathematical psychology*, edited by R. D. Luce, R. R. Bush, and E. Galanter. New York: Wiley. Pp. 1–76.
Thomas, D. H.
1969 Great Basin hunting patterns: A quantitative method for treating faunal remains. *American Antiquity* **34**:393–401.

1971 On distinguishing natural from cultural bone in archaeological sites. *American Antiquity* **36**:366–371.

Uerpmann, H.-P.

1973a Animal bone finds and economic archaeology: A critical study of "osteoarchaeological" method. *World Archaeology* **4**:307–322.

1973b Ein Betrag sur Methodik der wirtschaftshistorischen Auswertung von Tierknochenfunden aus Siedlungen. In *Domestikationsforschung und Geschichte der Haustiere,* edited by J. Matolsci. Budapest: Akadémiai Kiadó. Pp. 391–396.

Watson, J. P. N.

1972 Fragmentation analysis of animal bone samples from archaeological sites. *Archaeometry* **14**:221–227.

White, T. E.

1953 A method for calculating the dietary percentages of various food animals utilized by aboriginal peoples. *American Antiquity* **18**:393–399.

Wolff, R. G.

1973 Hydrodynamic sorting and ecology of a Pleistocene mammalian assemblage from California (U.S.A.). *Palaeogeography, Palaeoclimatology, Palaeoecology* **13**:91–101.

Ziegler, A. C.

1973 Inference from prehistoric faunal remains. *Addison-Wesley Module in Anthropology* No. 43.

8

The Role of Archaeometry in American Archaeology: Approaches to the Evaluation of the Antiquity of *Homo sapiens* in California

R. E. TAYLOR and LOUIS A. PAYEN

INTRODUCTION

Archaeologists have assumed as their intellectual domain a time frame spanning more than a million years and a geographic perspective that includes all those identifiable localities where human behavior has left physical expression. The major reordering of research priorities that has taken place in archaeology over the last two decades has added enlarged responsibilities by calling on archaeologists to delineate both the course and the cause of the evolution of hominid cultural systems. Obviously, the primary data base of archaeological study is the physical evidence of human behavior. However, it is a truism to recall that the artifact component of that record constitutes only one segment of the total ecological posture that is reflected at each site locus. Contemporary approaches to an understanding of the evolution of hominid behavior are now looking to the need to isolate the intersecting biophysical as well as cultural vectors that have determined the direction which that behavior has taken (Leone 1973).

ADVANCES IN ARCHAEOLOGICAL METHOD AND THEORY, VOL. 2

In general, American archaeologists traditionally have been educated primarily as specialists in the collection, analysis, and interpretation of the artifact component and related cultural features of the prehistoric record. Although there obviously are wide divergences in theoretical and conceptual viewpoints, generally there is an accepted core of knowledge assumed to be common to most researchers trained in the American anthropological tradition. With few notable exceptions, this common core of expertise has not generally included experience in the collection and interpretation of the biophysical components of the archaeological record. Until recently, those who prepared for a career in archaeology were not likely to possess sufficient background in one of the sciences or mathematics to the degree that would be required to pursue basic research in technical studies of archaeological materials. Despite this, over the last two decades it appears that American archaeologists have become convinced of the crucial role that physical and natural science-based analysis of data recovered from archaeological localities can play in expanding their understanding of the evolution of cultural behavior (cf. Butzer 1971, 1975). Although notable achievements can certainly be traced back before World War II, the beginnings of a consistent trend can be seen developing in the middle 1950s. Advancements over the last three decades unfortunately have been piecemeal and uneven, but one has the sense that a consensus has been achieved concerning the need for a comprehensive biophysical/ecological perspective in the analysis of the archaeological record for any time period or region.

One might ask what generic term could be employed to apply to the total range of natural and physical science-based studies that are employed in archaeological research. In the English-speaking world, the term *archaeometry* has been utilized as such a designation. Several alternative terms could readily be employed—for example, analytic archaeology or archaeological science. However, by usage and tradition, archaeometry probably is the most appropriate term to designate the subdiscipline within archaeology concerned with the application and interpretation of natural and physical science data within an archaeological context.

Because of the varied history of archaeometric studies in American archaeology, we thought it would be useful to define and characterize this subdiscipline while offering proposals that might contribute to enhancing its future contributions in New World archaeological studies. We shall focus particularly on the structure of one of its component areas, archaeochronometrics. Finally, we shall offer a specific case study to illustrate the role that archaeometric data can play in clarifying important archaeological questions.

STRUCTURE AND ROLE OF ARCHAEOMETRY

The word *archaeometry* was coined by Sir Christopher Hawkes as the name for the bulletin of the Research Laboratory for Archaeology and the History of Art at Oxford, which began publication in 1958 (M. J. Aitken, personal communication). Its more general and inclusive usage developed out of the widespread distribution of this journal. The narrow and even, to some, archaic denotative meaning of the second element of the word (-metry = "process of measuring" from the Greek *meitron,* a measure) has now been superseded by the current emphasis on archaeometry's role of providing an interface between the archaeologist and the collaborating physical or natural scientist. Perhaps its most valuable contribution has been in the matching of archaeological problem and perspective with the physical scientist's priorities, capabilities, and interests.

The most comprehensive compendium and review of physical and chemical methods employed in archaeological studies is *Science in Archaeology* (Brothwell and Higgs 1969). Its sixty-one chapters are divided into seven sections concerned with (*a*) dating methods, (*b*) paleoenvironmental studies (including paleoclimatic, soil, and floral and faunal analyses), (*c*) osteology, (*d*) microscopic and radiographic studies, (*e*) petrographic and spectrographic analyses of artifacts, (*f*) statistical concepts, and (*g*) remote sensing techniques. Elsewhere (Taylor 1976:7), it has been suggested that archaeometric studies might be divided into four broad subdivisions: (*a*) archaeological chronology or archaeochronometrics, (*b*) archaeological analytics (physical and chemical analyses of artifact materials), (*c*) paleoenvironmental/paleoecological reconstructive studies, and (*d*) archaeological remote sensing applications. A possible additional category would involve data manipulation and processing methods (for example, mathematical modeling, statistical analyses, and data retrieval techniques). Since such a category reflects an increase in the quantification of archaeological data in general rather than any specific archaeometric application, it was thought inappropriate to include it as a fifth subdivision. Rather, quantitative and statistical sophistication as provided from the point of view of a mathematician should be considered a wholly separate but equally vital need in the education of an archaeologist.

As Butzer (1975:106) has noted, interdisciplinary studies have enjoyed at least verbal acclaim among archaeologists for several decades. In New World archaeology, a number of major projects over the last twenty years have utilized teams of specialists from diverse disciplinary backgrounds. Studies conducted as part of the Boylston Street Fishweir (Johnson 1942), the Tehuacan Valley Archaeological and Botanical Project (MacNeish

1967), and the Tule Springs Early Man Project (Wormington and Ellis 1967) are good examples of this orientation. At the same time, over the last ten years, we have seen a rapid increase in the number of analytic techniques of potential relevance in archaeological studies. Various instrumental methods have been developed that can use smaller amounts of sample material while providing a much expanded corpus of analytic data. Certainly the pace of instrumental and technical refinement shows no sign of abating, but it might be emphasized that in archaeometric studies generally, the problem is no longer a lack of technical capacity and expertise. Currently, the issue of greatest priority is the efficient organization and delivery of the resources presently available in pursuit of solutions to archaeological problems. Proposals for a more effective and efficient application of archaeometric resources as an integral part of general archaeological research designs have been made over the last decade (cf. Taylor 1970, 1976; Butzer 1975; MacNeish 1978). The proposals offered were drawn from these sources.

Earlier we noted that one of the most valuable roles that the archaeometric specialist can play is in providing an interfacing function between the interests and priorities of the natural/physical scientist and those of the field research archaeologist. Perhaps the most important point to make is that data provided by physical science colleagues to further the aims of archaeological research can be of optimum quality when these studies are *collaborative* in the fullest sense of the word. It seems extremely counterproductive for a physical scientist's involvement in an archaeological project to be limited to that of providing "miscellaneous services" to the archaeologist after the conclusion of field studies. The best time to consult with an archaeometric or a physical science colleague is at the very beginning of the initial planning for an archaeological field research program, whether reconnaissance or excavation is to be employed. The degree and level of complexity to which an archaeometric component for a given archaeological field study should be developed depend on the goals of the study. Even during the initial development of the archaeological research design, however, it might be helpful for an archaeometric specialist to review a draft: Questions and issues perhaps not apparent to the archaeologist could be raised. Normally it would be expected that a potential for interdisciplinary research would become apparent to the archaeometrist but in a field that he would not be competent to assess. It would then be his responsibility to consult with other appropriate specialists. After a review of the interdisciplinary potential of the archaeological study, the archaeometrist could then provide recommendations to the archaeologist as to the range of collaborative studies that would be appropriate depending on the size and aims of the field studies.

If the input of an archaeometrician/archaeologist could be designed into the initial stages of a given archaeological study, then a number of the problems noted in previous discussions of this issue could be avoided. Archaeologists will have established on-going, long-term collaborative relationships with appropriate scientific specialists either directly or through the intermediate offices of an archaeometrician having a parallel interest in the region, time frame, or problems of relevance to the specific archaeological study. In cases where it might be urged that the size, duration, and scope of the archaeological study is too restricted to permit or justify the inputs of an archaeometric component, an appropriate strategy would be to develop an overall general plan on a regional basis with which individual, smaller-scale projects could be articulated insofar as the collection and interpretation of an incremental corpus of archaeometric data would be concerned. The visit of those involved in collaborative analytic studies to the sites while field work is in progress would be the rule and not the exception. Such on-the-ground interactions would benefit both the archaeologist and the physical science specialist in that both would become cognizant of the practical as well as the theoretical contexts of the various studies. It is hoped that field directors would be willing under such conditions to modify their survey or excavation strategies in the interest of obtaining particular types of samples collected according to criteria suggested by the scientific specialist(s).

An additional problem involves the reporting of the results of the collaborative research studies. One would hope that such results in the primary archaeological site report or monograph would not be assigned to the rear of the document in the form of a seldom-consulted appendix. It seems rather unproductive for technical data to be developed and reported in total isolation from the main theme of the general archaeological synthesis. It also seems reasonable to propose that the principal investigator clearly understand the significance of the physical science data in terms of the interpretation of cultural behavior at the sites being studied. If the director of the excavations does not feel that he is prepared to evaluate the technical data in such a context, then this might be done in collaboration with the principal archaeometric colleague or following a meeting of all contributing scientific specialists. Depending on the length and complexity of the field study, it might be helpful if a conference of participants in the research could be held, perhaps in connection with an appropriate national meeting to review research progress and to allow the various collaborators to view their studies in the context of the whole project. If one is dealing with a series of smaller projects spaced over a number of years, it might be appropriate to schedule periodic reviews of the status of the technical inputs to the study on a regional basis to give archaeologists in a given area opportunity to query interested scientific specialists in terms of progress that has been made and problems that still need to be resolved.

One of the factors that may have been partially responsible for the delays in the implementation of an interdisciplinary orientation in American archaeological research is the lacuna in technical training in graduate programs. In the late 1970s, it seems reasonable to suggest that major Ph.D. degree-granting departments consider as a minimum the development of a course that deals with the subject matter of archaeometry. In several institutions, those trained primarily in Quaternary geology, physical geography, palynology, zoology, biology, or chemistry have made major contributions in assisting archaeology graduate programs to provide their students with an interdisciplinary perspective. In other departments, the primary appointment is an anthropologically trained archaeometrist. Whatever the vehicle by which students are exposed to interdisciplinary concerns in the conduct of field studies, it is hoped that the next decade will witness a generation of American archaeologists cognizant of the full range of analytic resources available in the pursuit of a more precise knowledge of the human past.

Implicit in this discussion is the assumption that an appropriate level of support for archaeometric studies will be available. In the past, it has been unfortunately true that some funding agencies and even archaeologists saw support for "technical studies" as a frill and even as a "nonarchaeological" expense that could be eliminated if funding limits were imposed. However, since the development of a capacity to perform archaeometric studies involves a relatively major investment in instrumental resources and competent technical assistance, budget support for such research cannot be turned on and off without severely limiting or even destroying its viability and effective operation. The lack of longer-term predictable support for archaeometric studies also contributes to the "service function" mentality that previously characterized relationships between some archaeologists and potential physical science collaborators. Reduced funding, which to the archaeologist might mean a limitation in the length of field season or a modification of sampling strategy, would severely cripple the analytic component of the study, often to the level where a judgment would have to be made whether the project is worth doing at all. If the level of support is below a critical threshold level, a collaborating scientist, who usually is already heavily involved in projects more central to his own research, can logically conclude that the archaeologist in charge of the project considers the role of the scientific studies to be of low priority.

Happily, it appears that the major funding agency for archaeological research in the United States, the anthropology program of the National Science Foundation, is now (1979) in the process of reevaluating policies with reference to the support of archaeometric studies and their relationship to the quality of archaeological data. Because of the support and interest of the NSF and other funding and professional organizations such as the National Endowment for the Humanities, such professional organizations as the newly formed Society for Archaeological Sciences, the archaeological geology section of the Geological Society of America, and the archaeological chemistry division of the American Chemical Society, we can look forward to a highly productive period over the next decade in archaeometric-oriented studies.

ARCHAEOLOGICAL CHRONOLOGY

Of archaeometry's four subdivisions, that of archaeochronometrics has achieved some of the most dramatic and easily observable results. Archaeological studies within the American anthropological tradition are unique in that, as social scientists, archaeologists are equipped to study the evolution of hominid behavior in a temporal framework exceeding a million years. Data obtained through archaeological study provide the only direct evidence we possess for ascertaining the relevant variables responsible for the course and characteristics of our biological and cultural evolution over more than 98% of its course. The documentation of the temporal relationships of episodes in this evolutionary history is the task of the group of archaeometrists dealing with physical dating methods applicable in archaeological contexts.

In the history of New World archaeology, chronological structures have been developed basically in two phases. The foundation studies, beginning late in the nineteenth century, employed strategies such as artifact cross-dating and seriation and, as derived from geology, stratigraphic interpretations. In the case of seriation or cross-dating, artifacts themselves were looked to as containing elements that could be utilized to infer temporal relationships. For later time periods, in regions such as Mesoamerica, ethnohistoric documentation, including native calendric records, rounded out the mechanisms for the determination of archaeological chronological reconstructions (Nicholson 1978).

Although initiated with the development of dendrochronology and its application to United States Southwestern archaeology, the second mode or approach received its major impetus with the development and application of the radiocarbon method following World War II. The ability to independently assign specific time frameworks to archaeological materials began to significantly alter the basis on which much of the chronology-building in New World archaeology was approached. The validity of the radiocarbon determinations and the accuracy of the results of the application of other physical methods as they were subsequently introduced could not be directly evaluated on the basis of the traditional expertise possessed by most archaeologists. Although standard archaeological dating strategies (artifact cross-ties, etc.) still formed the infrastructure on which prehistoric chronology was developed, the real time values, when applied to archaeological materials, increasingly began to reflect the availability of radiocarbon or other geophysical and geochemical dating methods (Taylor 1978; Willey 1978:516).

Table 8.1 lists the physical dating methods currently employed in archaeological chronology (Taylor 1976, 1978). These methods have been divided into operational and experimental, and time placement and time/relative placement within each of the primary categories. Relative placement methods provide sequential relationships lacking siderial time equivalents, whereas time placement methods (including those sometimes labeled as "absolute" dating methods) provide potential calendric time equivalents. The basis of the difference between time and relative placement lies in the physical or chemical mechanisms employed. Fixed-rate processes yield time placement results, whereas calibrated or noncalibrated variable-rate processes yield time or relative placement, depending on the accuracy and precision of the calibration process. The references listed in Table 8.1 provide sources for general review of the status of each method in terms of its use in archaeological chronology.

By a significant margin, radiocarbon data continue to carry a major share of the load in the determination of prehistoric chronology for many areas of the New World. Dendrochronology, obsidian hydration, thermoluminescence, and the still-experimental amino acid racemization method trail behind ^{14}C in their applicability in routine dating applications. The dominant position of the ^{14}C method, measured in terms of the number of researchers and facilities, does not, of course, reflect its importance in archaeology or even geology as much as the significance of ^{14}C data in geophysical, geochemical, and environmental studies. A number of the major contributions in the radiocarbon field have been principally justified and supported in relationship to their significance in studying geophysical or geochemical mechanisms. For example, the existence of

TABLE 8.1

Classification of Archaeological Geochronometric Methods

Status	Type	Basis	Method	Reference
Operational	Time placement	Radiometric	Radiocarbon	Taylor (1979)
			Potassium–argon	Curtis (1975)
			Fission-track	Fleischer (1975)
			Uranium–actinum series	Fleming (1976)
		Biological	Dendrochronology	Bannister and Robinson (1975)
	Relative placement	Geophysical	Archaeomagnetism	Tarling (1975)
		Geologic	Varve	Butzer (1971)
		Chemical	Obsidian hydration	Ericson (1975)
			FUN (fluorine, uranium, nitrogen)	Butzer (1971)
Experimental	Time placement	Radiometric	Thermoluminescence	Fleming (1976)
			Electron spin resonance	Ikeya (1978)
			Alpha-particle recoil	Garrison et al. (1978)
	Time/relative placement	Chemical	Amino acid racemization	Bada and Helfman (1975)
			Fluorine diffusion	Taylor (1975)

"calibration curves" for ^{14}C values is, to a great degree, a result of studies originally concerned with documenting changes in the intensity of earth's dipole geomagnetic field during the Holocene (Taylor 1978).

Although the determination of chronology in prehistoric studies is not an end in itself, without an understanding of chronological relationships among archaeological units, sites, and localities, generalizations and inferences that seek to abstract aspects of behavior from the archaeological record may be rendered irrelevant and meaningless. Broad-scaled "processual analysis" assumes as valid the basic chronologies employed. In fact, archaeometric studies in general might be regarded as a means of providing more stable and secure foundations on which both middle-range and "higher" levels of inference and abstraction about the evolution of human biological and cultural systems can be developed and evaluated.

To illustrate one role that basic archaeometric strategies can play in an evaluation of significant archaeological and paleoanthropological issues, we shall examine the data relating to claims for the antiquity of *Homo sapiens* in an area of western North America. A series of reports presented over the last 20 years have proposed that artifacts excavated from several California sites should be assigned ages ranging up to several hundred thousand years. Skeletal remains of anatomically-modern *Homo sapiens* recovered from several California localities have been assigned ages ranging up to 70,000 years on the basis of published radiocarbon and amino acid racemization determinations. If supported, their presence in such a time frame could contribute to a major restructuring of current views concerning both the genetic and cultural relationships among populations of our species in both the Old and the New World.

ARCHAEOLOGY AND GEOCHRONOLOGY OF EARLY MAN SITES IN CALIFORNIA

The area circumscribed by the modern political boundaries of California has provided a strangely disproportionate number of alleged sites and skeletal remains with Pleistocene or early Holocent age assignments (Heizer 1953). As far back as 1851, in what may be the first published account of an archaeological find in California, a geologist, J. B. Trask, reported the recovery of portions of a human skeleton from a natural limestone cavern in a context that, to him, was "strongly presumptive of high antiquity" (*Daily Alta California*, December 1851; reprinted in Wallace 1951:30–31). The immediate context of this and other discoveries was the large-scale excavation activities occasioned by the California gold rush. When the Sierra Nevada mines began to penetrate the deep auriferous gravels, skulls and "artifacts" began to appear. Several reports associated cultural materials, such as mortars and metates, with the remains of mastodons (Bancroft 1883:687–713; Heizer 1948, 1952).

The earliest widely publicized Early Man find was the Calaveras skull, rhapsodized over by Bret Harte in the 1860s. In 1866, J. D. Whitney, a geologist conducting a survey of California, came into possession of a skull reported to have been recovered in deposits that were then labeled as Pliocene (Brewer 1866; Whitney 1867, 1879:267–277). This claim caused considerable comment and interest in both American and European scientific circles. Although there was strong evidence that the whole episode was the result of a mining camp joke, Hrdlicka (1907:121–128) later took the time to point out its modern affinities. By early in the twentieth century, the validity of this and most other Auriferous Gravel Man sites had been rejected on the basis of both skeletal morphology and artifactual evidence by the first generation of professional American archaeologists (Holmes 1899, 1901; Sinclair 1908).

Since that time, the number of California localities where human skeletal remains (Table 8.2, Figure 8.1) or alleged artifact materials (Table 8.3, Figure 8.2) of proposed early Holocene or Pleistocene age had been recovered had climbed to twenty-nine. With respect to the skeletal materials, the proposed ages range from terminal Pleistocene (Rancho La Brea and Arlington Springs) to the 70,000-year assignment given to the Sunnyvale female. Of the fifteen samples listed in Table 8.2, four have previously been removed from serious consideration on the basis of either radiocarbon values or differential fluorine concentration measurements. These include the Calaveras, Moaning Cave, Stanford (I), and Tranquility skeletons. With a single exception, those remaining samples *with proposed ages in excess of 15,000 years* fall into two groups: the two bone collagen radiocarbon-dated skeletons in the 17,000- to 24,000-year range, and amino acid racemization-dated skeletons from four sites falling in the 25,000- to 70,000-year range. The one exception is the Yuha burial with published radiocarbon and uranium series determinations of caliche that the excavators propose also date the human bone sample. We shall comment on the Yuha materials separately.

The fourteen California localities (Table 3) with proposed cultural deposits of suggested Pleistocene age constitute a much more problematical group of samples. Suggested ages for the largely lithic materials offered as evidence range from the terminal Pleistocene to greater than 100,000 years for the Calico and Texas Street sites. Previously, four sites have been definitely or provisionally removed from the list. These include the various "Auriferous Gravels" sites, Buchanan Canyon, Potter Creek, and Samwel Cave sites. The Buchanan Canyon materials have been tenta-

TABLE 8.2

California Localities with Published References to Human Skeletal Remains of Suggested Early Holocene or Pleistocene Age

Map reference (Figure 8.1)	Locality	Proposed age[a]	Material data	Basis of age estimate	Status in this paper[c]	References
1	Arlington Springs (Santa Rosa Island)	10,000 ± 200	Soil organics	Radiocarbon	S	Orr (1962); Irwin (1975)
2	Batiquitos Lagoon (W-99)	45,000	Bone	Racemization	I	Bada and Helfman (1975)
3	Calaveras[b]	Pliocene (recent)	—	Geologic (fluorine content)	R	Whitney (1879) (Irwin 1975)
4	Del Mar (W-34A)	41,000–48,000	Bone	Racemization	I	Bada et al. 1974; Bada and Helfman (1975)
5	Diablo Canyon	9320 ± 140	Bone	Radiocarbon	S	Greenwood (1972); Irwin (1975)
6	Laguna Beach	>14,800, 17,150 ± 1470	Bone	Radiocarbon	SR	Berger and Libby (1969); Berger et al. (1971)
7	Los Angeles (Baldwin Hills)	>23,600 26,000	Bone Bone	Radiocarbon Racemization	SR	Bowden and Lopatin (1936); Berger et al. (1971); Bada et al. (1974)

250

8	Moaning Cave[b]	12,000–50,000 (1400 ± 250)	—	Geologic (radiocarbon)	R	Orr (1952) (Broecker et al. 1960)
9	Mostin	10,260 ± 340	Carbonate	Radiocarbon	SR	Ericson and Berger (1974)
10	Rancho La Brea	9,000 ± 80	Bone	Radiocarbon	S	Merriam (1914); Berger et al. (1971)
11	Scripps (W-2) (W-12A)	44,000 27,000–39,000	Bone Bone	Racemization Racemization	I I	Bada et al. (1974); Bada and Helfman (1975)
12	Stanford (I)[b]	Early Holocene (5130 ± 70)	— Bone	Geologic (radiocarbon)	R	Heizer and McCown (1950) (Irwin 1975)
13	Sunnyvale	70,000(?)	Bone	Racemization	I	Bada and Helfman (1975)
14	Tranquility[b]	Pleistocene (2550 ± 60)	— Bone	Paleontological (radiocarbon)	R	Hewes (1943) (Berger et al. 1971)
15	Yuha	22,000	Carbonate	Radiocarbon, geologic; ^{230}Th	I	Bischoff et al. (1976); Payen et al. (1978)

[a] Ages expressed as specific values in years before present or, in the case of radiocarbon values, in radiocarbon years before present.

[b] Original age assignment cited. Revised age assignments in parentheses.

[c] S, Proposed age supported; SR, proposed age supported with reservations (see text); I, evidence incomplete; R, proposed age rejected.

251

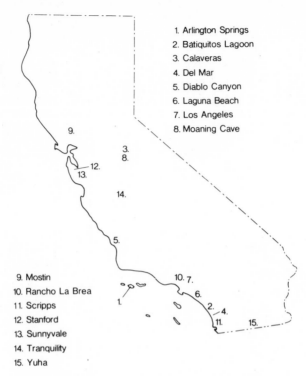

1. Arlington Springs
2. Batiquitos Lagoon
3. Calaveras
4. Del Mar
5. Diablo Canyon
6. Laguna Beach
7. Los Angeles
8. Moaning Cave

9. Mostin
10. Rancho La Brea
11. Scripps
12. Stanford
13. Sunnyvale
14. Tranquility
15. Yuha

Figure 8.1. Map of localities listed in Table 2.

tively assigned an age of approximately 5000–7000 years based on the still highly experimental fluorine diffusion profile measurement method (Taylor 1975). The Farmington materials have been provisionally retained despite the radiocarbon data indicating an age of a few thousand years. On the basis of geological and geomorphological data, Ritter *et al.* (1976) seem to have made a convincing argument that the radiocarbon determinations were made on samples not associated with the lithic-bearing horizon in the Farmington locality.

Studies at the Potter Creek and Samwel Cave sites had originally been carried out between 1902 and 1905 by a University of California (Berkeley) team led by a paleontologist, John C. Merriam. These initial studies were specifically designed from the beginning to investigate the antiquity of man in Western North America. In fact, both caves were chosen because they represented the closest speleological analogues to the Upper Paleolithic cave sites in the Dordogne Valley of southwestern France. Despite massive excavational exposures employing excellent horizontal and vertical stratigraphic controls, the original excavations revealed only

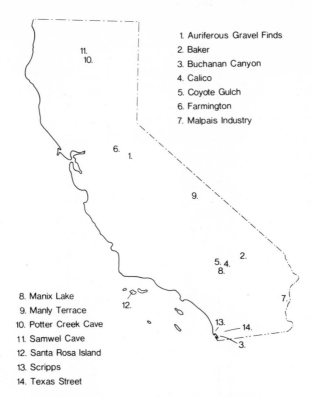

1. Auriferous Gravel Finds
2. Baker
3. Buchanan Canyon
4. Calico
5. Coyote Gulch
6. Farmington
7. Malpais Industry

8. Manix Lake
9. Manly Terrace
10. Potter Creek Cave
11. Samwel Cave
12. Santa Rosa Island
13. Scripps
14. Texas Street

Figure 8.2. Map of localities listed in Table 3.

a highly tentative association of possible artifact materials with an extremely rich Pleistocene fauna. Recent radiocarbon and obsidian hydration studies of the artifact materials themselves have revealed that the culture-bearing levels in both caves seem to date to only the last few thousand years (Payen and Taylor 1976; Payen *et al.* 1978a).

One of the most interesting features of the remaining twenty-one localities is that for those sites with suggested ages in excess of 15,000 years only the Laguna Beach and Yuha skeletons were reported to have been found together with artifact materials. When the Laguna Beach skeleton was originally discovered in 1933, it was reported to be in association with a "well-developed midden containing stone chips." Unfortunately, only the bone samples were retained (Berger *et al.* 1971).

With the exceptions noted, the proposed California Pleistocene archaeological and skeletal occurrences exhibit a basic problem confronting all serious students of the movement of *Homo sapiens* into the Western Hemisphere. Simply stated, the issue can be divided into the following

TABLE 8.3

California Localities with Published References to Cultural Associations of Suggested Pleistocene Age

Map reference (Figure 8.2)	Locality	Proposed age[a]	Physical evidence offered	Basis of age estimate	Status in this paper[c]	References
1	Auriferous gravels[b]	Tertiary; Pliocene (recent)	Lithics	Geologic (typological)	PR	Whitney (1879) (Holmes 1901)
2	Baker	9,000–11,000	Lithics	Typological	I	Glennan (1974)
3	Buchanan Canyon[b]	Pre-Wisconsin (probably La Jollan age)	Lithics	Typological (fluorine diffusion)	PR	Minshall (1974) (Taylor 1975)
4	Calico	30,000->200,000 >34,000	Lithics Hearth(?)	Geologic Radiocarbon	AR	Leakey et al. (1968); Haynes (1973); Berger and Libby (1969); Berger (1972) Simpson (1961)
5	Coyote Gulch	Late Pleistocene	Lithics	Typological	I	Simpson (1961)
6	Farmington	7000–~100,000 (1660 ± 220; 1170 ± 70; 1195 ± 75)	Lithics	Geologic, typological (radiocarbon)	I	Treganza and Heizer (1953); (Ritter et al. 1976)
7	Malpais Industry	Pleistocene	Lithics	Geologic, typological	I	Rogers (1939); Hayden (1976)

254

	Site	Age	Material	Method	Status	Reference
8	Manix Lake	>20,000 14,250 ± 1000; 19,300 ± 400	Lithics	Typological, radiocarbon	I	Simpson (1958); Berger and Libby (1967); Fergusson and Libby (1962)
9	Manly Terrace	~20,000	Lithics	Geologic	I	Clements and Clements (1953)
10	Potter Creek Cave[b]	Later Quaternary (1910 ± 150; 1915 ± 150; 2010 ± 150)	Lithics	Geologic, paleontological (radiocarbon)	PR	Sinclair (1904) (Payen and Taylor 1976)
11	Samwel Cave[b]	Later Quaternary (few thousand years)	Lithics	Geologic, paleontological (obsidian hydration)	PR	Furlong (1906) (Payen et al. 1978a)
12	Santa Rosa Island	11,000 ± 160->40,000	Lithics, Hearths(?)	Radiocarbon	I	Orr (1968); Berger (n.d.)
13	Scripps	21,500–34,000	Hearths(?)	Radiocarbon	I	Carter (1957); Rubin and Suess (1955); Hubbs et al. (1962)
14	Texas Street	35,000–~100,000	Lithics(?) Hearths(?)	Geologic Radiocarbon	AR	Carter (1957); Broecker and Kulp (1957)

[a] Ages expressed as specific values in years before present or, in the case of radiocarbon values, in radiocarbon years before present.
[b] Original age assignment cited. Revised age assignments in parentheses.
[c] PR, Pleistocene age rejected; AR, artifact status rejected; I, evidence incomplete.

questions: (*a*) Are the alleged artifacts demonstratively the product of human manufacture? and (*b*) what age assignment is to be placed on acceptable evidence of human behavior or directly on the *Homo sapiens* skeletal samples? The issue of the age would seem to be the most tractable archaeometric problem. Let us briefly consider this aspect of the question, first for the skeletal samples.

DATING CALIFORNIA PLEISTOCENE SKELETAL MATERIALS

Until the advent of the radiocarbon method, except for attempts to use fluorine and nitrogen values as temporal indices, estimations of age for bone samples thought to be of pre-Holocene age were based largely on indirect means, through geological or paleontological considerations, including the degree of morphological affinity to modern Native American populations. In the early part of this century it was assumed that any Pre-Holocene age *Homo sapiens* populations in the New World would exhibit morphological characteristics similar to those observed on skeletal samples of *Homo* of similar age in Europe. Beginning in the 1950s, fluorine and nitrogen concentrations in bone were used to indicate the degree of contemporaneity of suites on bone samples from similar depositional contexts. It was on the basis of its fluorine content, for example, that the Calaveras skull controversy was definitively laid to rest (Irwin 1975; cf. Heizer 1974).

One would have assumed that the advent of the radiocarbon method would have provided a means of directly dating bone samples of proposed Pleistocene age. Unfortunately, initially it was assumed that bone would constitute a poor sample type because of its low organic carbon content and generally porous structure. (It should be noted that *burned* bone was highly recommended. However, the actual sample was derived from the carbonized skin and tissue, not from the bone structure itself). Radiocarbon determinations obtained on bone that utilized the carbonate fraction (the total acid-leached carbonates) did indeed yield extremely anomalous results. It was not until techniques were developed in the 1960s for extracting the "collagen" (typically the acid-insoluble) fraction that attitudes about the possibility of obtaining reliable ^{14}C data on bone samples began to be modified. When this approach was applied to human bone samples from California localities, a new chapter in the debate concerning the antiquity of *Homo sapiens* in the New World was opened.

As noted in Table 8.2, two collagen-based radiocarbon dates on bone from California have yielded values in excess of 15,000 years. The Laguna Beach sample had been excavated in 1933 during grading operations leveling a street bed in Laguna Beach, a coastal suburb south of Los Angeles. Over the next three decades, the skull and other bone fragments were shown to a number of authorities in both America and Europe with inconclusive results. It was clear, however, that morphologically the skull was essentially indistinguishable from those of contact-period Native American populations (Berger *et al.* 1971; Stewart 1969:255). A similar type of discovery was made in 1936 during storm drain excavations carried out by WPA crews in the Baldwin Hills section of west-central Los Angeles. Portions of a heavily mineralized cranium and fragments of a humerus were recovered. Despite efforts to obtain additional samples, no cultural remains or other skeletal materials were located (Lopatin 1940). A few months later the remains of a mammoth were found at the same depth but about 379 meters distant from the first find (Clements 1938). Later, fluorine and nitrogen chemical analyses indicated that the mammoth and human samples were of similar age (Heizer and Cook 1952:298–299).

To date, there has not been unanimous acceptance of the validity of these collagen-based ^{14}C values. Although the initial study by Berger reported satisfactory agreement between bone collagen and associated charcoal ^{14}C values, contamination of the bone organics by noncollagenous organics in Pleistocene samples remained a possibility (Haynes 1967), and several investigators have subsequently suggested methods to ensure that a pure *in situ* collagen fraction was extracted from bone samples (Krueger 1965; Sellstedt *et al.* 1966; Longin 1971; Protsch 1973; Hassan and Ortner 1977). There seems to be general agreement, however, that with careful processing techniques, reliable bone collagen ^{14}C values can be obtained on bone samples of Holocene age. Table 8.4 illustrates such results on two samples of bone from the same burial in a central California archaeological site. In both cases, the carbonate, "collagen" (=acid-insoluble), and total amino acid fraction of the bone were measured for their ^{14}C content (Taylor and Slota 1979). These data again illustrate the early view that the carbonate fraction in bone yields highly unreliable results. In this case, the carbonate ^{14}C "ages" are nearly 2000 years younger than the "ages" of the collagen and amino acid fractions. Except as an indication that each bone had been subject to a similar degree of exchange with groundwater carbonates, the apparent ^{14}C age of the carbonate fraction is clearly spurious. By contrast, the values obtained on all organic fractions are statistically identical and seem to reflect the actual age of the burial based on archaeological criteria including radiocarbon values on charcoal from other sites of the same phase.

Although carefully prepared acid-insoluble fractions of Holocene-age bone can yield reliable radiocarbon values, it is also clear that as one

TABLE 8.4

Radiocarbon Determinations on the Carbonate, Collagen, and Amino Acid Fractions of Human Bone Samples from a Prehistoric Burial in Northern California (Site SJo-112, Burial 36)

Sample number	Sample type	Organic carbon yield (%)	$\delta^{13}C$ (%)[a]	Corrected ^{14}C age[b]
UCR-449A	Carbonate	—	8.42	930 ± 140
UCR-449B	Collagen	6.95	−19.89	2765 ± 155
UCR-449C	Amino acids	1.26	−21.41	2930 ± 150
UCR-450A	Carbonate	—	−9.43	830 ± 100
UCR-450B	Collagen	6.49	−20.24	2835 ± 140
UCR-450C	Amino acids	1.12	−21.29	2960 ± 140

[a] Expressed with respect to PDB standard. Error on values ±0.2‰.
[b] Expressed with respect to 0.95 NBS oxalic acid standard ($t\frac{1}{2}$ = 5568 years) normalized to −25.00‰ $\delta^{13}C$.

considers the radiocarbon dating of Pleistocene-age bone samples, potential difficulties immediately loom up. Most important, the organic content of bone, in the 20–25% range for modern samples, usually decreases drastically in Pleistocene-age bone. With decreases in the amount of *in situ* organics, the potential percentage contribution of migrating organics significantly increases and contamination problems can become acute. Unfortunately, there are at present no well-documented criteria that can be objectively employed to determine if the collagen fraction of a bone sample has been subjected to geochemical effects that have significantly altered the organic composition and thus the $^{14}C/^{12}C$ ratio in the bone. The difficulties in obtaining reliable ^{14}C values on Pleistocene bone organics should not be underestimated. Although work goes on in an attempt to isolate the geochemical indicators that would permit the identification of samples that can be expected to yield anomalous radiocarbon results, the prudent view has been expressed by Gordon Willey, who recently stated that "the collagen dating of human skeletons [in California] is suggestive—but no more—of very early habitation in the area" (Willey 1978:528).

In 1973, a relatively new physical dating technique was applied to a series of human bone samples from California (Bada *et al.* 1974). Aspartic acid racemization values for a suite of bone samples from the San Diego area yielded a range of ages from 27,000 to 48,000 years (Del Mar, Scripps, and Batiquitos Lagoon). Two years later, a 70,000-year age was reported on a sample from Sunnyvale, near San Jose, California (Bada and Helfman 1975). Simply stated, the amino acid racemization technique is based on the fact that the amino acids present in the proteins of most living organisms consist only of the L-amino acids. Over time, L-amino acids undergo slow racemization, which produces corresponding D-amino acids. Fossil materials have been found to contain both L- and D-amino acids, with the D/L amino acid ratios increasing with the age of the sample. Of the various amino acids, aspartic acid has been the most widely used in fossil bone dating, in part owing to the fact that it has one of the fastest racemization rates of the stable amino acids. At 20°C in bone, the half-life (that is, the time it takes the D/L ratio to reach 0.33) of aspartic acid is approximately 15,000 years. Thus, for most mid-latitude localities such as those found in California, aspartic acid racemization rates are much slower than the decay rate of radiocarbon and therefore can be used to date bones that are too old to be dated by radiocarbon. Also, because of the sensitivity of most amino acid analyzers, the amount of bone required is much less than that required by standard ^{14}C counting techniques.

Since racemization is a chemical reaction, the rate of the reaction is obviously temperature-dependent. Therefore, in order to attempt to date a bone by using racemization, it is necessary to evaluate the average temperature to which the bone has been exposed. Typically, this temperature has been evaluated by means of a procedure in which the *in situ* rate of amino acid racemization for a particular site or region is indirectly calculated by measuring the extent of racemization in a bone that has been previously dated, most often by the radiocarbon technique. After such a "calibration" step has been carried out, it is assumed that other bones in this same general region can be dated by their extent of amino acid racemization, using as a rate constant that calculated in the dated sample. For example, the rate of aspartic acid racemization used to calculate the amino acid age of the Del Mar, Scripps, and Batiquitos Lagoon skeletons was calculated by using the collagen-based ^{14}C determination on the Laguna skeleton.

Several geochemists have expressed skepticism as to the validity of an approach that assumes that temperature is the only variable that must be considered in converting the D/L aspartic acid ratio to "dates." Hare (1974) has suggested that leaching by groundwater action can cause order of magnitude changes in the measured amino acid ratios in samples derived from natural environments. Bender (1974) has insisted that the rate of racemization depends on the state of the amino acid (free amino acids racemize about an order of magnitude more rapidly than those bound as peptides). On the other side, Bada and Helfman (1975) have noted that differences in modern mean annual temperatures between sites is reflected also in similar differences in calculated paleotemperature data deduced from calibrated amino acid ratios in fossil bones from these sites.

On this basis, it is argued that if factors other than time and temperature were generally important, such concordances in data would not occur. Also, the concordance of the D/L aspartic acid calibrated ages with radiocarbon values is pointed to as confirming that time and temperature are the principal parameters affecting racemization ratios in bone.

It is clear that, to date, nothing approaching a clear consensus has been achieved as to the general validity of the values assigned to bones of alleged Pleistocene age, based on either their radiocarbon or their amino acid racemization values. The range of views expressed by those concerned with the problem range from guarded optimism that future studies will establish specific criteria by which an objective evaluation of the validity of the values produced can be accomplished, to outright disbelief in the validity of the vast majority of the published ^{14}C and amino acid values as applied to bone, based on the view that few if any such samples could be represented as even minimally approaching a closed geochemical system.

The nature of the evidence offered to demonstrate the Pleistocene age of the Yuha burial, the most recent addition to the catalogue of proposed "early humans" in California, sets it apart from the rest of the skeletal samples so far considered. In 1971, a local community college conducting an archaeological field class in the Yuha Desert region of the Imperial Valley excavated a shallow, semiflexed burial covered by a rock cairn containing several lithic artifacts (Childers 1974). The archaeological context of the burial normally would occasion no special comment, as the type of internment was known from several other localities in the region. These other cairn burials had been dated on the basis of artifact typology and radiocarbon determinations to approximately the last 5000 years (Wilke 1978). The presence of ceramic associations in the immediate vicinity of the burial suggested a late prehistoric context. A morphological study of the crania suggested a close similarity to the La Jollan cranial samples (cf. Rogers 1977; Schulz 1978). Radiocarbon determinations carried out on the caliche removed from the external surface of the bones and a cairn boulder yielded values of approximately 22,000 radiocarbon years B.P. On the basis of additional carbonate radiocarbon determinations made on soil samples from adjacent localities and the application of a modified [230]Th method to the carbonate encrustation on the boulder, it was stated that a minimum age of 22,000 years B.P. "seems to be positively affirmed" for the Yuha burial (Bischoff et al. 1976). This declaration was accompanied by the assertion that, unlike the evidence relating to any other human remains dated prior to 12,000 years ago in the Western Hemisphere, the geology and stratigraphy of the site had been fully documented in detail (Childers 1974; Barker et al. 1973).

Serious objections to both the quality of the dating evidence and the

geologic and archaeological context of the burial site based on independent observations have been made by Payen *et al.* (1978b). They point
out the well-known problems in interpreting ^{14}C values due to the difficulties in determining initial carbon isotope ratios and the degree of isotopic
exchange that has occurred in the deposit after implacement by such
factors as dissolution and reprecipitation (cf. Geyth *et al.* 1971; Bartlett
1951; Brothwell and Burleigh 1977). Examination of the geomorphology
and pedology of the burial locality indicates a complex carbonate environment and history. Both the degree of soil development and the land
form on which the burial rests appear totally inconsistent with the
suggested age. The presence of relatively unweathered lithics and pottery,
coupled with the fact the site is located in the general proximity of an
ethnographically known trail system, is suggestive of a late-period temporary camp. Proposals that a direct radiocarbon determination be made on
the extensive postcranial materials available from the burial has as yet not
been implemented by those responsible for curating the sample. Until such
data are available, the proposed Pleistocene-age assignment of the Yuha
burial can, at best, be regarded as highly premature.

Our view of the status of each of the fifteen California localities with
proposed human skeletal remains of suggested early Holocene or Pleistocene age has been indicated in column six of Table 2. The Pleistocene
assignment of four skeletons have been rejected previously. The proposed
dates assigned to the Arlington Springs, Diablo Canyon, and Rancho La
Brea specimens seem to be supported. The reported ages assigned to the
Laguna Beach, Los Angeles (Baldwin Hills), and Mostin samples are
supported with reservations. These reservations reflect continuing concern regarding the integrity of the organic fraction used in the ^{14}C
analyses. Such reservations can be removed when criteria now being
developed to identify potential contamination factors are fully developed.
Because of the current problems surrounding the use of the amino acid
racemization method on bone, we propose the listing of the Batiquitos
Lagoon, Del Mar, Scripps, and Sunnyvale skeletons under the category of
evidence incomplete. Until such a time as a direct ^{14}C measurement is
available for the Yuha skeleton, we also propose listing it under the
incomplete-evidence category.

EVALUATING CALIFORNIA PLEISTOCENE CULTURAL MATERIALS

We can now turn to the issues surrounding the corpus of data for the
pre-Holocene occupation of California based on physical evidence other
than skeletal samples. This primarily involves an evaluation of reported

instances of chipped lithics that, on geologic or typological grounds, have been designated artifacts and have also been assigned an age of 10,000 to more than 200,000 years. As noted previously, the total number of localities that currently merits consideration is ten (Table 8.3). Unlike the skeletal samples, where the issue of human origin is *a priori* moot, the principal question is whether certain chipped rock samples are the product of human or natural processes. In four instances, a parallel question involves a determination of the nature of features labeled hearths.

In general, the incidence of negative judgments concerning the artifactual character of a given lithic assemblage, at least for California, seems to correlate positively with the increasing age assignment of the proposed artifact sample. There has, as yet, been little dispute concerning the artifact characterization of lithic samples for sites dated up to approximately 10,000–15,000 years. Once past this temporal boundary, however, there is an increasing reluctance to accept human agency as responsible for the chipping process observed on many lithic objects offered as artifacts. Obviously, the question or issue of age of a lithic sample is irrelevant, insofar as the archaeologist is concerned, if the sample is not to be considered to have received its form as a result of human agency. Three California localities seem to stand out as type sites with respect to this issue. These localities include the Calico, Texas Street, and Santa Rosa Island (a number of sites *not* including Arlington Springs).

Currently, probably the best known of the proposed California Pleistocene-age localities is the San Bernardino County Regional Park Calico Early Man Site, as a State of California highway information sign states on the nearest freeway off-ramp (Schuiling 1972). This site is located in the eastern Mohave Desert near Yermo, California. Beginning in 1948, attention was directed to the general area by an amateur archaeologist, Ritner Sayles, who conducted surface surveys of sites situated around the Manix Lake Basin. These studies were continued by Ruth D. Simpson of the San Bernardino County Museum of Natural History. Artifact materials assumed to be associated with high stands of Pleistocene Lake Manix were grouped together and defined as the Manix Lake Lithic complex. Radiocarbon determinations on tufa materials adhering to a group of boulders at the highest extent of the lake yielded values of 15,000–20,000 years (map reference 8 on Table 8.3 and Figure 8.2).

In 1963, during one of his many visits to southern California, L. S. B. Leakey designated an area where subsurface excavations should be conducted. The criteria utilized for the selection of a specific area was that it be conducted in a fan deposit deep enough to "contain archaeological materials and geological data" (Simpson 1972:35). Meticulous excavations supervised by Ruth Simpson over a 6-year period in two Master Pits and a series of trenches and several off-site excavations revealed about 10 meters of sedimentary deposits. Out of the literally hundreds of thousands of chipped lithic fragments removed from the excavated areas, a little more than 600 have been designated as core tools and, along with about 1500 "flakes," have been divided into a number of standard functional lithic categories—for example, choppers, chopping tools, and gravers. An alleged hearth feature was also located. Examination of the remnant magnetism of one of the rocks composing this feature supported the suggestion that it had been subjected to heating (Berger 1972).

The age of the lithic assemblage and hearth feature has been the subject of considerable debate. Radiocarbon values obtained on soil carbonates and a tusk fragment indicated an age in excess of 40,000 years (R. Berger, personal communication). The staff geologist for the Calico project argued for an age of the fan deposit and associated lithics of about 50,000–75,000 years. Many geologists and geomorphologists who have examined the profiles insist that a more probable minimum age would be on the order of several hundred thousand years, with the possibility that portions of the fan are several million years old. If indeed the Calico materials turn out to be of human origin, then this site could be one of the earliest in both the Old and New Worlds.

The problem of identifying the effects of human as opposed to natural fracturing processes in the evaluation of alleged simple or "crude" chipping technologies is as old as the beginnings of serious prehistoric studies in Europe in the mid-nineteenth century. Whether one refers to the chipped flints from Upper Oligocene deposits found near Thenay, France, or the better-known Eolith controversy, the issue of natural versus human origins for various chipped rock fragments occupied the attention of many eminent late nineteenth- and early twentieth-century European and English archaeologists. This problem receded in importance, however, as archaeologists turned their attention to collections and cultural contexts where such a controversy was an obvious non-issue. However, in situations such as that encountered at Calico, it is important to determine if there indeed exists an analytic method that can be objectively applied, and that would distinguish between fortuitously fractured lithics (geofacts) and those produced through conscious flaking by human agency (artifacts). In the absence of such a procedure, the issue of the artifact/geofact characterization of proposed tools from several California localities remains in the realm of mere opinion and consensus.

Some four decades ago, in connection with the Old World Eolith problem, Alfred Barnes proposed a relatively objective method that, when applied to a series of flaked stone, could, he insisted, distinguish between natural fracture and controlled flaking (Barnes 1939). He argued that the critical variable was what he called the "angle platform-scar," which is equivalent to the so-called beta angle of many contemporary lithic studies (Wilmsen 1970:14). Barnes' original data consisted of 2600 beta-angle measurements made on 16 accepted Paleolithic industries and 900 specimens of naturally fractured stones from seven localities. His measurements seemed to show that populations of human-chipped stones are characterized by a low frequency of obtuse beta angles (<25% over 90°), whereas natural fracturing seemed to be characterized by a much higher frequency of obtuse angles.

Barnes' original paper has drawn a certain amount of comment and criticism (Carter 1957:329, 1967; Speth 1972:54). However, there has been no general acceptance, due in part, perhaps, to the assumption that single-variable approaches to such an obviously complex issue (Speth 1972) were doomed to failure. However, in cases where the method has been employed and the results published or reported (e.g., Asher and Asher 1965; Kumiko Ikawa-Smith, personal communication), the basic validity of the approach seems to have been supported. To determine if any meaningful and critical data would be forthcoming by an examination of the distribution of beta angles on the disputed California Pleistocene lithic assemblages, one of us (L.A.P.) conducted a set of studies that continued in the tradition of the experiments of Barnes and the Ashers (Payen 1979; n.d.).

The renewed experiment was based on more than 14,000 measurements on 54 sample collections of controlled (artifact) and uncontrolled (geofact) fracturing (Tables 8.5 and 8.6). Twenty-nine lots were measured representing known controlled flaking (Table 8.5). These include 13 prehistoric quarry-shop samples (preforms and roughouts), 14 prehistoric tool assemblages, and 2 ethnographic examples. A total of 7375 beta angles was obtained from 1548 specimens. Angles ranged from 32° to 146°. Sample means are variable, ranging from 61° to 85°. The weighted mean for all samples is 72°, with a standard deviation of 13°. Thus, roughly two-thirds of the angle measurements fall between 59° and 85°. The actual percentage of obtuse angles present in each sample lot ranges from 0 to 17%, with the typical sample having about 6% greater than 90°. This compares well with Barnes' results on his Paleolithic series, which range from 1 to 18%.

Twenty-five sample lots were measured representing uncontrolled fracturing (Table 8.6). Four samples represent internal force fracturing, usually a result of temperature changes. Two are of geologic origin and are examples of the so-called pot-lid spalling often observed on desert pavements. The other two were produced experimentally by heating chalcedony with a blow-torch and then plunging it into ice water. The remainder, 21 sample lots, are examples of various external or mechanical fracturing. Seven are of geologic origin and include examples of flint recovered from glacial till and Eocene jasper pebbles broken by slumping into underlying karst. Eight samples were collected from roadways and mines where vehicles and heavy equipment caused breakage. Finally, six samples were produced under controlled experiment by investigators at the San Bernardino County Museum; these include dropping a 50-pound boulder onto a block of chalcedony, shattering with dynamite, tumbling for 12 hours, crushing with an 8-ton roadroller, and passing through mechanical rock crushers. A total of 7057 platform-scar angles, or apparent fracture angles, was obtained from 1246 specimens. It should be noted that in several classes of fracture no true platforms are present, such as in the pot-lid spalling samples. Here the lowest angle between the scar and the adjacent surface was measured.

Angles in the uncontrolled fracture samples range from 30° to 154°, the typical sample ranging from 40° to 114°. Sample means range from 84° to 99° and represent less variability than was observed in the controlled series. The weighted mean for all samples is 88°, with a deviation of 17°, or roughly two-thirds of the angles falling between 71° and 105°. The actual percentage of obtuse angles in each sample ranges from 33% to 62%, but averages around 42%. This is within the expected range predicted by Barnes, but is somewhat below his actual observation for natural lots, which was from 53% to 76% over 90°. Comparison of the controlled and uncontrolled series in Figure 8.3 clearly indicates that two kinds of fracturing exhibit different flake-angle distributions. A statistically significant difference is observed, which suggests the Barnes test does indeed distinguish between populations of conscious and fortuitous flaking (Payen 1979).

Lithic samples were taken from nine populations of fractured chalcedony segregated by the excavators at Calico (Table 8.7). Two samples were obtained from the apparent source in Mule Canyon, where chalcedony is interbedded in Miocene lake sediments of the Barstow Formation four miles west of the site area. One sample was taken from the desert pavement adjacent to the outcroppings, the other from stone shattered *in situ* where the beds have been faulted and warped. Five hundred angles were obtained from each sample lot.

Another series comprises two lots that represent the Manix Lake Industry, an assemblage found on the surface of the Calico foothills and thought to be associated with a former stand of Pleistocene Lake Manix dated around 19,700 radiocarbon years ago (Simpson 1958, 1960, 1972:33–35). One Manix sample was drawn from site SBCM-1508, a quarry shop. The other sample represents ovate bifaces thought to be finished implements.

TABLE 8.5

Controlled Fracture: Measurement of Beta Angles on Known Artifact Sample Lots

Sample	Type[a]	Material	Number of specimens	Number of angles	Range	Mean	σ	%>90°
Gold Lake (California)	QS	Basalt	78	700	31–136°	67.4°	14.6°	5
Davies Canyon (California)	QS	Basalt	88	450	36–125°	71.6°	16°	9
Humbug Valley (California)	QS	Basalt	29	150	40–112°	70.8°	15.1°	5
Modoc Glass Mt. (California)	QS	Obsidian	44	600	29–132°	64°	16.1°	5
Borax Lake (California)	QS	Obsidian	46	200	39–121°	71.4°	12°	7
Flint Ridge (Kentucky)	QS	Flint	21	200	40–113°	67.4°	14.5°	7
McCullough Farm (Ohio)	QS	Flint	28	100	36–104°	68.9°	14.7°	5
Scioto River (Ohio)	QS	Flint	11	100	45–115°	71°	12.5°	5
Wyandotte (Indiana)	QS	Flint	27	200	39–140°	68.5°	13.8°	7
Flint Ridge (Ohio)	QS	Flint	23	100	42–104°	73.7°	12.2°	7
Flint Ridge (Illinois)	QS	Flint	8	100	38–100°	65.8°	14.7°	7
Peoria (Oklahoma)	QS	Chert	12	186	33–128°	73.6°	15.2°	10
Ben Bolt (California)	QS	Chert	15	100	45–130°	73.8°	16°	13
Clovis (New Mexico)[b]	TA	Chert	64	64	34–96°	66.8°	11.6°	2
Folsom (Colorado)[b]	TA	Chert	594	594	35–99°	69.9°	10.2°	2
San Dieguito I (C) (California)	TA	Chert, basalt	20	135	40–114°	71.7°	11.9°	4
San Dieguito I (SE) (Arizona)	TA	Rhyolite	20	180	45–111°	72.2°	11°	5

Site	Type[a]	Material						
San Dieguito II (SE) (Arizona)	TA	Chert, rhyolite	27	259	44–112°	74.1°	10°	7
San Dieguito II-III (SW) (California)	TA	Felsite	36	377	40–105°	70°	11.1°	3
San Dieguito II-III (C) (California)	TA	Chert, basalt	18	188	42–110°	73.6°	11.6°	4
Pinto Basin (California)	TA	Jasper, chert	13	100	40–87°	61.5°	9.4°	0
La Jolla Complex (California)	TA	Metavolcanic, quartzite	41	260	35–103°	77.8°	10.4°	17
Amargosa Complex (California)	TA	Jasper, chert	31	250	48–101°	71.3°	10°	3
Early Horizon (C) (California)	TA	Chert	73	600	32–127°	71.1°	15.5°	9
Mill Creek, Late (California)	TA	Basalt	43	250	38–121°	76.8°	13.3°	12
Solvieux (France)	TA	Flint	94	600	49–124°	80.7°	10.7°	12
Denbigh (Alaska)[b]	TA	Chert	32	32	62–101°	85.1°	7.8°	6
T. Orcutt-Karok (California)	E	Obsidian	11	200	35–92°	64.6°	11.2°	0.5
Karok Wealth Blade (California)	E	Obsidian	1	100	50–81°	64.2°	7.5°	0

[a] QS = quarry shop; TA = tool assemblage; E = ethnographic.
[b] Data drawn from Wilmsen (1970).

TABLE 8.6

Uncontrolled Fracture: Measurement of Beta Angles on Known Nonartifact Sample Lots

Sample	Type[a]	Material	Number of specimens	Number of angles	Range	Mean	σ	%>90°
Tahoe City (California)	G	Basalt	13	100	42–122°	86.4°	18.4°	43
Cerro Pinto (Baja California)	G	Rhyolite?	20	183	36–154°	98.8°	23.3°	62
Heat–cold (SBCM)	Ex	Chalcedony	24	100	30–147°	89°	23.5°	47
Heat (SBCM)	Ex	Chalcedony	13	70	48–131°	92.5°	16.8°	57
Olentangy till (Ohio)	G	Flint	9	63	57–135°	90.1°	18.9°	50
Westerville till (Ohio)	G	Flint	27	161	31–144°	87°	19.1°	40
Big Walnut Cr. till (Ohio)	G	Flint	60	343	36–143°	91.3°	18.2°	47
Scioto till (Ohio)	G	Flint	70	275	43–142°	88.2°	15.8°	41
Sardine Pk. talus (California)	G	Jasper	50	250	43–133°	86.4°	18.4°	39
Black Rock talus (California)	G	Basalt	20	115	33–142°	90.3°	19.5°	47
Springfield karst (California)	G	Jasper	91	500	42–146°	91.4°	17.9°	50
Truckee (California)	RB	Basalt	40	400	42–142°	84.6°	14.9°	34
High Rock (Nevada)	RB	Obsidian	82	400	43–156°	85.8°	15°	33
Volcano (California)	RB	Rhyolite	74	500	48–154°	88.8°	15.1°	43
Midhills (California)	RB	Opal, chert	40	250	46–134°	87.2°	16.7°	42
English Mt. (California)	RB	Chert	102	650	38–140°	87.1°	14.6°	35

Baker (California)	RB	Rhyolite	42	270	37–145°	85.9°	18.3°	40
Marble Cliff (Ohio)	RB	Flint	65	350	56–142°	90.3°	15.1°	46
Lancha Plana (California)	RB	Chert	136	1000	37–151°	87.4°	19.2°	41
Dropping 50-pound boulder (SBCM)	Ex	Chalcedony	49	200	46–137°	87.2°	16.9°	45
Blasted with dynamite (SBCM)	Ex	Chalcedony	41	200	45–138°	92.5°	17.2°	51
Tumbled 12 hours (SBCM)	Ex	Chalcedony	18	100	40–139°	90.7°	20.6°	53
Eight-ton roadroller (SBCM)	Ex	Chalcedony	52	200	50–137°	89.3°	15.7°	45
Telesmith cone crusher (SBCM)	Ex	Chalcedony	84	300	45–136°	83.6°	17°	32
Telesmith gyratory crusher (SBCM)	Ex	Chalcedony	24	77	36–123°	87.2°	20°	40

[a] G = geologic; Ex = experimental; RB = road breakage.

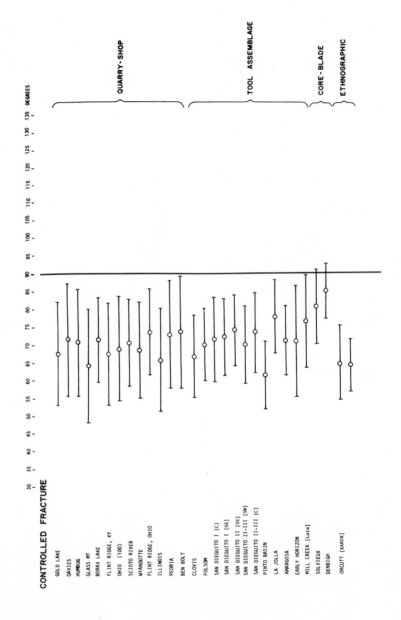

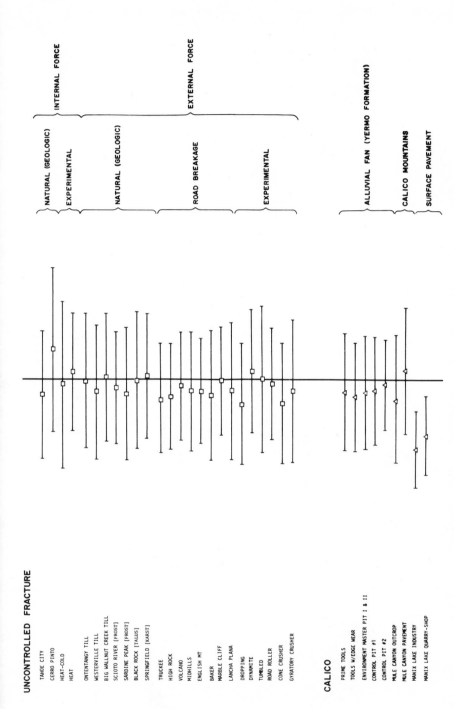

UNCONTROLLED FRACTURE

NATURAL (GEOLOGIC)
INTERNAL FORCE
EXPERIMENTAL

TAHOE CITY
CERRO PINTO
HEAT-COLD
HEAT

ONTENTANGY TILL
WESTERVILLE TILL
BIG WALLNUT CREEK TILL
SCIOTO RIVER [FROST]
SARDINE PEAK [FROST]
BLACK ROCK [TALUS]
SPRINGFIELD [KARST]

NATURAL (GEOLOGIC)

TRUCKEE
HIGH ROCK
VOLCANO
MIDHILLS
ENGLISH MT

ROAD BREAKAGE

BAKER
MARBLE CLIFF
LANCHA PLANA
DROPPING
DYNAMITE
TUMBLED
ROAD ROLLER
CONE CRUSHER
GYRATORY CRUSHER

EXPERIMENTAL

EXTERNAL FORCE

CALICO

ALLUVIAL FAN (YERMO FORMATION)

PRIME TOOLS
TOOLS W/EDGE WEAR
ENVIRONMENT MASTER PIT I & II
CONTROL PIT #1
CONTROL PIT #2
MULE CANYON OUTCROP

CALICO MOUNTAINS
MULE CANYON PAVEMENT

SURFACE PAVEMENT
MANIX LAKE INDUSTRY
MANIX LAKE QUARRY-SHOP

Figure 8.3. Plot of β (flake angles) for data listed in Tables 5, 6, and 7.

271

TABLE 8.7

Calico Samples: Measurement of Beta Angles on Sample Lots Recovered and Excavated from Calico Locality

Sample	Type[a]	Material	Number of specimens	Number of angles	Range	Mean	σ	%>90°
Prime tools	—	Chalcedony	83	593	30–140°	86.7°	16.5°	36
Tools with edge wear	—	Chalcedony	74	494	45–154°	85.5°	15.3°	34
Environment Master Pits I & II	—	Chalcedony	302	1250	34–145°	86.5°	16°	36
Control Pit 1	—	Chalcedony	84	300	40–131°	87.2°	15°	37
Control Pit 2	—	Chalcedony	47	166	52–128°	88.8°	12.8°	41
Mule Canyon outcrop	G	Chalcedony	73	500	31–145°	84.4°	17.7°	36
Mule Canyon pavement	G	Chalcedony	90	500	48–151°	92.8°	17.8°	52
Manix Lake Industry	TA	Chalcedony	85	600	42–120°	70.9°	10.7°	3
Manix Lake quarry	QS	Chalcedony	93	1000	38–124°	73.7°	11.2°	6

[a] G = geologic; TA = tool assemblage; QS = quarry shop.

These were found embedded in the desert pavement and are generally covered with desert varnish. One thousand platform-scar angles were measured for the quarry, and 600 for the implements.

The final series represents flaked stone recovered by controlled excavation in the Yermo formation. Measured lots include a sample of 1250 angles on fractured siliceous cobbles and boulders in the material stockpiled from Master Pits I and II. Platform-scar angles (593 measurements) were taken on 83 of the so-called prime tools selected by L. S. B. Leakey as unquestionable examples of human craftsmanship, and a similar sample of 494 angles was taken on pieces said to exhibit edge damage or modification resulting from use (Clay Singer, personal communication 1978). Also from the Yermo deposit are two additional samples that represent the silicate rocks from Test Pits 1 (300 angles) and 2 (166 angles), both thought to have been excavated beyond the limits of the occupation area.

Examination of Table 8.7 indicates that Manix Lake Industry samples clearly differ from the various lots from Mule Canyon and those recovered from the Yermo sediments. There is no significant statistical difference between the series selected as artifacts and those specimens from the Master Pit excavations that were rejected as not being artifacts and the material recovered from the outlying test pits (significance level set at .01). All appear to have been drawn from the same population. When the Calico series is compared with the controlled and uncontrolled series (Figure 8.3), it is evident that the Manix samples fall within the expected range for human workmanship as defined by Barnes. Compare, for example, the Manix Industry mean of 71° (deviation between 60° and 82°) with the weighted mean of 72° (deviation between 60° and 85°) for controlled fracture.

Turning to the alleged artifacts from the Yermo deposit, it is clear that they fall within the range of the uncontrolled fracture series (Figure 8.3). For example, compare the prime tool mean of 87° (deviation between 70° and 103°) with the weighted mean for the uncontrolled fracture series of 88° (deviation between 71° and 105°). Statistically, there is no significant difference between the alleged Calico tools and the uncontrolled fracturing sample. [See Payen (1979) for a detailed discussion of the statistical tests applied.] With the exception of the two Manix Lake assemblages, the application of the Barnes approach suggests that all the samples of chipped stone offered as evidence of human occupation at the Calico Early Man Site represents the effects of natural fracture processes—that is, the Calico tools are geofacts. We are proposing that this procedure empirically seems to be a valid method distinguishing between artifacts and geofacts. We offer these specific data for the purpose of eliciting independent studies by other workers to confirm or reject the validity of the technique or the procedures used to arrive at the conclusions offered.

At present, we are offering no suggestions concerning the nature of the hearth feature reported by the Calico excavation team. Several suggestions have been put forth to account for similar occurrences at other sites, but there do not seem to be sufficient data to determine whether any of these explanations are applicable for the Calico situation.

We can comment only briefly on the characteristics of the other two sites where artifacts have been reported with age assignments in excess of 20,000 years. The Texas Street site in the Mission Valley area of metropolitan San Diego was proposed as representing an area of human occupation during the Third Interglacial by George Carter as early as 1950 (Carter 1950, 1952, 1954). At Texas Street, Carter has recovered crude broken and chipped quartzite pebbles in geologic contexts which he insists could have been deposited only during the previous interglacial period. As at Calico, the issue turns, however, not on the age but on the artifact characteristics of the fractured pebbles. A preliminary analysis of the distribution of beta angles on a sample of material from the Texas Street site has indicated that all materials so far studied were fractured by natural processes (Payen 1979).

The Woolley Mammoth site is only the most recent addition to the roster of proposed sites identified on Santa Rosa Island, one of the Channel Islands lying some 30 miles off the Southern California coast. Since the beginning of the twentieth century, paleontologists have collected dwarf mammoth remains from various areas of the island, and peculiar red-baked circular fire areas have been reported, sometimes in close proximity to localities where the mammoth materials had been recovered. Philip C. Orr of the Santa Barbara Museum of Natural History was the first to suggest that these fire areas were the product of human activity; however, the earliest human bone fragments, dated at about 10,000 years, were recovered from the Arlington Springs site (Orr 1968). Indications of much greater age, however, were forthcoming when more of the fire areas were dated up to the limit of the ^{14}C method at about 40,000 years (Orr and Berger 1966; Berger and Orr 1966).

In 1975, a local geologist, John Woolley, discovered a large fire area that had been exposed in three-dimensional perspective as a result of natural erosional processes in a narrow gully. When excavated by Rainer Berger, this feature contained a fire-reddened area about 3 meters in diameter. Along its circumference mammoth bones and chipped lithics labeled as tools (cores, scrapers, and a pick) were recovered. The feature itself was located some 14 meters above the present mean ocean level and about 8 meters below the present land surface. Three samples of charcoal from the feature were dated at greater than 40,000 years (Berger n.d.). At present, further radiocarbon determinations utilizing isotopic enrichment and mass spectrometric techniques are underway. A study of the lithic samples is also planned (R. Berger, personal communication).

Our view of the status of each of the fourteen California localities with published references to cultural materials of proposed Pleistocene age has been indicated in column six of Table 3. Four localities (Auriferous-Gravels sites, Buchanan Canyon, Potter Creek Cave and Samwel Cave) have previously been rejected on the basis of dating evidence. To this list we wish to add Calico and Texas Street on the basis of our rejection of the artifact character of the chipped lithics offered as evidence. We believe that there is insufficient evidence to firmly reject or accept any of the other eight localities listed in Table 3. At the same time, additional data from Manix Lake and Santa Rosa Island, particularly the Woolley Mammoth Site, should be soon forthcoming. Such data should clarify the status of both of these localities.

CONCLUSION

It is an historical fact that unsupported claims of great human antiquity arise more frequently in California than in any other part of the New World. Whether the infamous hoax of the Calaveras skull set this local phenomenon in train, or whether the Golden State produces more archaeological freaks, or whether the citizens of that element of the Union are simply uncommonly gullible, we do not know. But the situation does exist and is likely to continue, and therefore it becomes an integral consideration in practicing and evaluating archaeology in California. Other states probably have their own special archaeological anomalies (Hester *et al.* 1975).

Rather than seeing the "Early-Man" orientation in California archaeology as an example of uncommon gullibility, we would suggest that, in large part, the problem may be one of failure to apply consistently already-existing archaeological and archaeometric techniques and methodologies. It seems clear that the specific issues we have been considering are fundamental to any critical undertaking of Pleistocene cultural studies in California. It seems vacuous to attempt to discuss the nature of, for example, California Pleistocene settlement patterns or resource exploitation systems when the quality of the data base appears to be so fundamentally deficient. Certainly if one can demonstrate neither the artifact character nor the temporal assignment of much of the evidence offered, it is questionable if any meaningful "higher-level" studies would be appropriate.

Earlier we noted that one important role of archaeometric studies is that of providing basic data to which archaeologists can turn when considering more broadly based inferences about cultural development and process. It might be useful to recall the sequence of development of the data base and conceptual frameworks of other academic disciplines with longer histories than that possessed by American archaeology. In several physical sciences in the late seventeenth and eighteenth centuries, attempts to provide broad inferences about the behavior of "matter" were generally uniformly barren of demonstrable results until basic foundation structures such as the periodic nature of the elements became available. Although there are obvious differences with respect to approaches to the data that characterize the physical sciences as opposed to, for example, archaeology, both have in common the need for a consensus on certain fundamental understandings as a prerequisite for advances in the understanding of the operations of more complex or abstract systems.

Our brief examination of the evidence supporting or refuting claims of great antiquity for *Homo sapiens* in California provides one of the more obvious examples of the need for professional archaeological studies to confront and deal with foundation issues before proceeding to consider more general or theoretical issues. The use of archaeometric data at an appropriate level is one important component of these studies that is currently available. We have previously suggested that the most effective implementation of archaeometric studies takes place in an environment in which there is a recognition that archaeology itself, by the nature of its subject matter, is already a highly interdisciplinary field of study. Any archaeometric component of a given archaeological project provides a more comprehensive and formal structure within which a complete archaeological study can proceed.

In this context, it is important to emphasize again that the size or scope of a project should not inhibit the successful implementation of archaeometric studies. What is required is a regional research design into which small-scale projects could be fitted on an incremental basis. To this must be added continuing communication and consultation among archaeological field researchers and those archaeometricians interested in regional issues. It is the genuine commitment to the interdisciplinary characteristic of archaeology, rather than its scope or budget, that will make this type of research effective and productive.

We have offered several specific suggestions as to procedures that might be employed in developing a more effective utilization of existing archaeometric resources. These include the need to consult with archaeometric specialists early in the planning for an archaeological research program, the potential benefits to be accrued if a draft of the archaeological research design could be reviewed from the perspective of an archaeometric specialist, the value to those involved in collaborative studies or visits to sites while field work is in progress, and the need to understand the implication of the technical data in terms of the general archaeological issues being studied.

When we turn to the specific questions surrounding the proposed Pleistocene occupation in California, we believe that the role of archaeometric studies will continue to be critical. It is hoped that some clear consensus will emerge relative to the artifact characteristics of the large sample of chipped lithic materials as well as the temporal assignment of a number of the sites noted in Tables 8.2 and 8.3. We especially await with interest the evaluation of the Barnes method as applied to the disputed lithic samples, with those disputing the validity of the results presented here providing comparable data. Also, studies are currently underway and planned to resolve many of the questions surrounding the accuracy of the collagen-based ^{14}C and amino acid racemization values on bone.

REFERENCES

Asher, R., and M. Asher
   1965   Recognizing the emergence of man. *Science* **147**:243–250.
Bada, J. L., and P. M. Helfman
   1975   Amino acid racemization dating of fossil bones. *World Archaeology* **7**:160–173.
Bada, J. L., R. A. Schroeder, and G. F. Carter
   1974   New evidence for the antiquity of man in North America deduced from aspartic acid racemization. *Science* **184**:791–793.
Bancroft, H. H.
   1883   *The native races of the Pacific States of North America,* Vol. IV: *Antiquities.* San Francisco: Bancroft.
Bannister, R., and W. J. Robinson
   1975   Tree-ring dating in archaeology. *World Archaeology* **7**:210–225.
Barker, M. A., E. Burton, and W. M. Childers
   1973   *A preliminary report on a burial excavated in the Yuha Desert of Imperial County, California.* Riverside, Calif.: United States Department of Interior, Bureau of Land Management.
Barnes, A. S.
   1939   The differences between natural and human flaking on prehistoric flint implements. *American Anthropologist* **41**:99–112.
Bartlett, H. H.
   1951   Radiocarbon datability of peat, marl, caliche, and archaeological materials. *Science* **114**:55–56.
Bender, M. L.
   1974   Reliability of amino acid racemization dating and paleotemperature analyses on bone. *Nature (London)* **252**:378–379.
Berger, R.
   1972   An isotopic and magnetic study of the Calico site. In *Pleistocene Man at Calico,* edited by W. C. Schulling. San Bernardino, Calif.: San Bernardino County Museum Association. Pp. 65–69.

n.d.   The Woolley Mammoth site: Santa Rosa Island, California. In *Peopling of the New World,* edited by J. Ericson, R. E. Taylor, and R. Berger. Socorro, N.M.: Ballena Press (in press).

Berger, R., and W. F. Libby
   1967   UCLA radiocarbon dates VI. *Radiocarbon* **9:**477–504.
   1969   UCLA radiocarbon dates IX. *Radiocarbon* **11:**194–209.

Berger, R., and P. C. Orr
   1966   The fire areas on Santa Rosa island, California, II. *Proceedings of the National Academy of Sciences U.S.A.* **56**(6):1678–1682.

Berger, R., R. Protsch, R. Reynolds, C. Rozaire, and J. R. Sackett
   1971   New radiocarbon dates based on bone collagen of California paleoindians. *Contributions of the University of California Archaeological Research Facility* **12:**43–49.

Bischoff, J. L., R. Merriam, W. M. Childers, and R. Protsch
   1976   Antiquity of man in America indicated by radiometric dates on the Yuha burial site. *Nature (London)* **261:**128–129.

Bowden, A. O., and I. A. Lopatin
   1936   Pleistocene Man in southern California. *Science* **84:**507–508.

Brewer, W. H.
   1866   Alleged discovery of an ancient human skull in California. *American Journal of Science* **42:**424.

Broecker, W. S., and J. L. Kulp
   1957   Lamont radiocarbon measurements IV. *Science* **126:**1324–1334.

Broecker, W. S., E. A. Olson, and P. C. Orr
   1960   Radiocarbon measurements and annual rings in cave formations. *Nature (London)* **185:**93–94.

Brothwell, D., and R. Burleigh
   1977   On sinking Otavalo Man. *Journal of Archaeological Science* **4:**291–294.

Brothwell, D., and E. Higgs (editors)
   1969   *Science in archaeology* (2nd ed.). Thames & Hudson.

Butzer, K. W.
   1971   *Environment and archaeology: An ecological approach to prehistory* (2nd ed.). Chicago: Aldine.
   1975   The ecological approach to archaeology: Are we really trying? *American Antiquity* **40:**106–111.

Carter, G. F.
   1950   Ecology-geography-ethnology. *Scientific Monthly* **70**(2):73–80.
   1952   Interglacial artifacts from the San Diego area. *Southwestern Journal of Anthropology* **8**(4):444–456
   1954   An interglacial site at San Diego, California. *The Masterkey* **28**(5):165–174.
   1957   *Pleistocene Man at San Diego.* Baltimore: Johns Hopkins Press.
   1967   Artifacts and naturifacts: Introduction. *Anthropological Journal of Canada* **5**(1):2–5.

Childers, W. M.
   1974   Preliminary report on the Yuha burial, California. *Anthropological Journal of Canada* **12**(1):2–9.

Clements, T.
   1938   Age of the "Los Angeles Man" deposits. *American Journal of Science* **36:**137–141.

Clements, T., and L. Clements
  1953 Evidence of Pleistocene Man in Death Valley, California. *Bulletin of the Geological Society of America* **64:**1189–1204.
Curtis, G. H.
  1975 Improvements in potassium-argon dating: 1962–1975. *World Archaeology* **7:**198–209.
Ericson, J. E.
  1975 New results in obsidian hydration dating. *World Archaeology* **7:**151–159.
Ericson, J. E., and R. Berger
  1974 Late Pleistocene American obsidian tools. *Nature (London)* **249:**824–825.
Fergusson, G. J., and W. F. Libby
  1962 UCLA radiocarbon dates I. *Radiocarbon* **4:**109–114.
Fleischer, R. L.
  1975 Advances in fission track dating. *World Archaeology* **7:**136–150.
Fleming, S.
  1976 *Dating in archaeology.* New York: St. Martin's.
Furlong, E. L.
  1906 The exploration of Samwel Cave. *American Journal of Science* **22:**235–247.
Garrison, E. G., C. R. McGimsey, III, and O. H. Zinke
  1978 Alpha-recoil tracks in archaeological ceramic dating. *Archaeometry* **20:**39–46.
Geyth, M. A., J. H. Benzler, and G. Roeschmann
  1971 Problems of dating Pleistocene and Holocene soils by radiometric methods. In *Paleopedology, origin and nature and dating of paleosoils,* edited by D. H. Yaalon. Jerusalem: Israel University Press.
Glennan, W. S.
  1974 The Baker site (SBr-541). *Pacific Coast Archaeological Society, Quarterly* **10:**17–34.
Greenwood, R.
  1972 9000 years of prehistory at Diablo Canyon, San Luis Obispo County, California. *Occasional Papers, San Luis Obispo County Archaeological Society* No. 7.
Hare, P. E.
  1974 Amino-acid dating of bone—The influence of water. *Carnegie Institution of Washington, Yearbook* **73:**576–581.
Hassan, A. A., and D. J. Ortner
  1977 Inclusions in bone material as a source of error in radiocarbon dating. *Archaeometry* **19:**131–135.
Hayden, J. D.
  1976 Pre-althermal archaeology in the Sierra Pinacate, Sonora, Mexico. *American Antiquity* **41:**274–289.
Haynes, C. V., Jr.
  1967 Carbon-14 dates and Early Man in the New World. In *Pleistocene extinctions: The search for a cause,* edited by P. S. Martin and H. E. Wright, Jr. New Haven: Yale University Press. Pp. 267–286.
  1973 The Calico site: Artifacts or geofacts? *Science* **181:**305–309.
Heizer, R. F.
  1948 A bibliography of ancient man in California. *University of California Archaeological Survey, Report* No. 2.
  1952 A survey of cave archaeology in California. *University of California Archaeological Survey, Report* No. 15, paper 15.

1953   Sites attributed to Early Man in California. *University of California Archaeological Survey, Report* No. 22, paper 21.

1974   Some thoughts on hoaxes and flakes. *Bulletin of the Texas Archaeological Society* **45**:191–196.

Heizer, R. F., and S. F. Cook
1952   Fluorine and other chemical tests of some North American human and animal bones. *American Journal of Physical Anthropology* **10**(3):289–303.

Heizer, R. F., and T. D. McCown
1950   The Stanford skull, a probable Early Man from Santa Clara County, California. *University of California Archaeological Survey, Report* No. 6, 1–20.

Hester, T. R., R. F. Heizer, and J. A. Graham
1975   *Field methods in archaeology* (6th ed.). Palo Alto, Calif.: Mayfield Publishing.

Hewes, G. W.
1943   Camel, horse and bison associated with human burials and artifacts near Fresno, California. *Science* **97**:328–329.

Holmes, W. H.
1899   Preliminary revision of the evidence relating to Auriferous Gravel Man in California. *American Anthropologist* **1**:107–121, 614–645.

1901   Review of the evidence relating to Auriferous Gravel Man in California. *Smithsonian Institution Annual Report for 1899* pp. 419–472.

Hrlicka, A.
1907   Skeletal remains suggesting or attributed to Early Man in North America. *Bureau of American Ethnology, Bulletin* No. 33.

Hubbs, C. L., G. S. Bien, and H. E. Suess
1962   La Jolla natural radiocarbon measurements II. *Radiocarbon* **4**:204–238.

Ikeya, M.
1978   Electron spin resonance as a method of dating. *Archaeometry* **20**:148–158.

Irwin, H. T.
1975   United States of America. In *Catalogue of fossil hominids*, Part III: *Americas, Asia, Australia,* edited by K. P. Oakley, B. G. Campbell, and T. I. Molleson. London: Trustees of British Museum. Pp. 31–45.

Johnson, F. (editor)
1942   *The Boylston Street Fishweir (No. 2).* Andover, Mass.: Papers of the Robert S. Peabody Foundation for Archaeology.

Krueger, H. W.
1965   The preservation and dating of collagen in ancient bones. *Proceedings, 6th International Conference on Radiocarbon and Tritium Dating* **Conf-650652**:332–337.

Leakey, L. S. B., R. D. Simpson, and T. Clements
1968   Archaeological excavations in the Calico Mountains, California: Preliminary report. *Science* **160**:1022–1023.

Leone, M. P.
1973   Issues in anthropological archaeology. In *Contemporary archaeology; a guide to theory and contributions,* edited by M. P. Leone. Carbondale: Southern Illinois University Press. Pp. 14–27.

Longin, R.
1971   New method of collagen extraction for radiocarbon dating. *Nature (London)* **230**:241–242.

Lopatin, I. A.
1940   Fossil man in the vicinity of Los Angeles, California. *Proceedings, Sixth Pacific Science Congress* **4**:177–181.

MacNeish, R. S.
1967 An interdisciplinary approach to an archaeological problem. In *The prehistory of the Tehuacan Valley* (Vol. 1), edited by D. S. Byers. Austin: University of Texas Press. Pp. 14–24.
1978 *The science of archaeology?* North Scituate, Mass.: Duxbury Press.

Merriam, J. C.
1914 Preliminary report on the discovery of human remains in an asphalt deposit at Rancho La Brea. *Science* **40**:198–203.

Minshall, H. L.
1974 Early Man site at Texas Street and Buchanan Canyon in San Diego, California. *Anthropological Journal of Canada* **12**:18.

Nicholson, H. B.
1978 Western Mesoamerica: A.D. 900–1520. In *Chronologies in New World archaeology*, edited by R. E. Taylor and C. W. Meighan. New York: Academic Press. Pp. 285–329.

Orr, P. C.
1952 Excavation in Moaning Cave. *Santa Barbara Museum of Natural History, Bulletin* No. 1.
1962 The Arlington Springs site, Santa Rosa Island, California. *American Antiquity* **27**:417–419.
1968 *Prehistory of Santa Rosa Island.* Santa Barbara, California: Santa Barbara Museum of Natural History.

Orr, P. C., and R. Berger
1966 The fire areas on Santa Rosa Island, California, I. *Proceedings of the National Academy of Sciences U.S.A.* **56**(5):1409–1416.

Payen, L. A.
1979 The pre-Clovis of North America: temporal and artifactual evidence. Unpublished Ph.D. dissertation, University of California, Riverside.
n.d. Artifacts or geofacts at Calico: Application of the Barnes test. In *Peopling of the New World*, edited by J. E. Ericson, R. E. Taylor, R. Berger, and N. M. Socorro. Ramona, California: Ballena Press (in press).

Payen, L. A., M. C. Hall, and M. D. Kelley
1978a Radiocarbon and obsidian hydration studies of Samwel Cave. *Abstracts, Fifth Biennial Meeting, American Quaternary Association, Edmonton* p. 231.

Payen, L. A., C. H. Rector, E. W. Ritter, R. E. Taylor, and J. E. Ericson
1978b Comments on the Pleistocene age assignment and associations of a human burial from the Yuha Desert, California. *American Antiquity* **43**:448–453.

Payen, L. A., and R. E. Taylor
1976 Man and Pleistocene fauna at Potter Creek Cave, California. *Journal of California Anthropology* **3**:51–58.

Protsch, R. R.
1973 The dating of upper Pleistocene Subsaharan fossil hominids and their place in human evolution with morphological and archaeological implications. Unpublished doctoral dissertation, University of California, Los Angeles.

Ritter, E. W., B. W. Hatoff, and L. A. Payen
1976 Chronology of the Farmington complex. *American Antiquity* **41**:334–341.

Rogers, M. J.
1939 Early lithic industries of the lower basin of the Colorado River adjacent desert areas. *San Diego Museum Papers* No. 3, 1–75.

Rogers, S. L.
1977 An early human fossil from the Yuha Desert of Southern California: Physical characteristics. *San Diego Museum Papers* No. 12.

Rubin, M., and H. E. Suess
  1955 United States Geological Survey radiocarbon dates II. *Science* **121**:481–488.
Schuiling, W. C. (editor)
  1972 *Pleistocene Man at Calico.* Bloomington, Calif.: San Bernardino County Museum Association.
Schulz, P. D.
  1978 Review of S. L. Rogers, An early human fossil from the Yuha Desert of southern California: Physical characteristics. *Journal of California Anthropology* **5**:137–138.
Sellstedt, H., L. Engstrand, and N.-G. Gejvall
  1966 New application of radiocarbon dating to collagen residue in bones. *Nature (London)* **212**:572–574.
Simpson, R. D.
  1958 The Manix Lake archaeological survey. *The Masterkey* **32**:4–10.
  1960 Archaeological survey of the Eastern Calico Mountains. *The Masterkey* **34**(1):25–35.
  1961 Coyote Gulch: Archaeological investigations of an early lithic locality in the Mohave Desert of San Bernardino County. *Archaeological Survey Association of Southern California* Paper No. 5, 1–38.
  1972 The Calico Mountains Archaeological Project. In *Pleistocene Man at Calico,* edited by W. C. Schuiling. San Bernardino, Calif.: San Bernardino County Museum Association. Pp. 33–43.
Sinclair, W. J.
  1904 The exploration of the Potter Creek Cave. *University of California Publications in American Archaeology and Ethnology* **2**(2):1–27.
  1908 Recent investigations bearing on the question of the occurrence of Neocene Man in the auriferous gravels of the Sierra Nevada. *University of California Publications in American Archaeology and Ethnology* **7**(2):107–131.
Speth, J. D.
  1972 Mechanical basis of percussion flaking. *American Antiquity* **37**:34–60.
Stewart, T. D.
  1969 Laguna Beach man re-examined in the light of direct C-14 dating. *Proceedings, American Association of Physical Anthropologists* **31**(2):255–256.
Tarling, D. H.
  1975 Archaeomagnetism: The dating of archaeological materials by their magnetic properties. *World Archaeology* **7**:185–197.
Taylor, R. E.
  1970 Chronological problems in West Mexican archaeology: A dating systems approach to archaeological research. Unpublished Ph.D. dissertation, University of California, Los Angeles.
  1975 Fluorine diffusion: A new dating method for chipped lithic materials. *World Archaeology* **7**:125–135.
  1976 Science in contemporary archaeology. In *Advances in obsidian glass studies,* edited by R. E. Taylor. Park Ridge, N.J.: Noyes Press. Pp. 1–21.
  1978 Dating methods in New World archaeology. In *Chronologies in New World archaeology,* edited by R. E. Taylor and C. W. Meighan. New York: Academic Press. Pp. 11–27.
  1979 Radiocarbon dating: An archaeological perspective. *Archaeological chemistry II,* edited by G. F. Carter. Washington, D.C.: American Chemical Society. Pp. 33–69.

Taylor, R. E., and P. Slota
  1979 Fraction studies in marine shell and bone for radiocarbon dating. In *Advances in radiocarbon dating,* edited by R. Berger and H. Suess. Berkeley: University of California Press. Pp. 422–432.
Treganza, A. E., and R. F. Heizer
  1953 Additional data on the Farmington complex: A stone implement assemblage of probably early post-glacial date from central California. *University of California Archaeology Survey, Report* No. 22, 28–38.
Wallace, W. J.
  1951 Archaeological deposits on Moaning Cave, Calaveras County. *University of California Archaeological Survey, Report* No. 12.
Whitney, J. D.
  1867 Notice of a human skull, recently taken from a shaft near Angels, Calaveras County. *Proceedings of the California Academy of Science* 3:277–278.
  1879 The auriferous gravels of the Sierra Nevada of California. *Memoirs of the Harvard Museum of Comparative Anatomy* 6:258–288.
Wilke, P. J.
  1978 Cairn burials of the California deserts. *American Antiquity* 43:444–448.
Willey, G. R.
  1978 A summary scan. In *Chronologies in New World archaeology,* edited by R. E. Taylor and C. W. Meighan. New York: Academic Press. Pp. 513–563.
Wilmsen, E. N.
  1970 Lithic analysis and cultural inference: A Paleo-Indian case. *Anthropological Papers of the University of Arizona* No. 16.
Wormington, H. M., and D. Ellis
  1967 Pleistocene studies in Southern Nevada. *Nevada State Museum Anthropological Papers* No. 13.

Paleoethnobotany in American Archaeology

RICHARD I. FORD

For a half-century American archaeologists have been encouraged to save plant remains from their sites for botanically trained scientists to identify and to interpret. The results of these collaborative efforts have enabled the reconstruction of the prehistoric environment and have produced an understanding of the place of plants in the lifeways of extinct cultures. Archaeobotanical data have mutually benefited the cooperating disciplines.

However, much of the potential of archaeological plant materials for anthropological interpretations of prehistory remains to be implemented. In part this situation is caused by the variety of plant remains and finished vegetable artifacts, which only well-trained specialists can interpret with competence. In part it results from the different perspectives botanists and archaeologists use to interpret archaeobotanical data. This review will explore the significance of botanical evidence for an analysis of the dynamic functioning of a prehistoric culture in relation to its environment. To accomplish this the history of paleoethnobotany will be reviewed briefly from a perspective of the theoretical orientation of previous research. Procedures employed to recover various categories of archaeological plants, the botanical techniques used to identify them, and the potential significance of these data will be discussed. Finally, recent research will be examined from a perspective that advocates a close association between paleoethnobotany and anthropological theory.

ADVANCES IN ARCHAEOLOGICAL METHOD AND THEORY, VOL. 2

THEORETICAL PERSPECTIVE

Paleoethnobotany lacks a unifying theory. Its methods are principally derived from botanical sciences, and its contributions are determined by botanical questions or specific archaeological problems. The absence of an explicit theory has resulted in a number of conventions or "styles" of paleoethnobotanical reporting. One approach simply lists the scientific *identifications* of plant material, with little elaboration. A second presents the *phylogenetic relationships* of crop plants and their determinant role in human affairs. A third resorts to *diffusion* as an explanation for the distribution of economically significant domesticated species. A fourth acknowledges *ecological relationships* and the mutual interactions among groups and various plant communities. A fifth relies upon *ethnographic analogy* for interpretations of plant uses in the past. A final procedure uses plants to define *subsistence–settlement patterns* and the season(s) a site was occupied. Naturally, the quality of the data and the interests of the investigator structure how archaeological plants are interpreted, and, of course, a paleoethnobotanical report can entail more than one approach. Nevertheless, because such diverse standards of analysis by specialists are acceptable, it is inevitable that archaeologists must sometimes publish a final report as a separate appendix or chapter—a final report that may have no immediate relevance to the original archaeological objectives.

Paleoethnobotany is an important adjunct to anthropological archaeology. If the study of the ethnobotany of living peoples is a guide to the past, plants from archaeological sites are a by-product of specific human cognitive patterns of behavior and the accidental inclusions from the local plant environment. Plants are not selected at random by members of any known culture, and they probably were not by the prehistoric peoples of North America. They are named, classified, and collected according to the rules and beliefs of each culture. The context for the use of each plant is culturally prescribed, and the associated artifacts and resulting plant debris reflect that activity for the archaeologist. In some instances, however, nothing may be preserved archaeologically of these activities except the microscopic evidence left from decayed or burnt plants.

Paleoethnobotany, then, is the analysis and interpretation of the *direct* interrelationships between humans and plants for whatever purpose as manifested in the archaeological record. Its objective is the elucidation of cultural adaptation to the plant world and the impact of plants upon a prehistoric human population, not simply the recognition of useful plants, and its subject is all archaeologically known cultures, including so-called civilizations. Perhaps more than any other class of archaeological data, including artifacts, plant evidence expresses most aspects of past societies and their involvement with both external social and natural environments. Again, if modern ethnobotanical studies can provide research assumptions about prehistory, virtually every facet of archaeologically revealed cultural life undoubtedly had one or more plants associated with it.

Figure 9.1 presents a heuristic model with utility for paleoethnobotanical research. To appreciate the relationships among the cultural categories and environmental sectors, one must recognize that humans are culture-dependent, biological animals. They live in populations whose biological needs are satisfied by extracting resources from the natural environment. Their nutritional requirements can be estimated from archaeological evidence of population size and perhaps its demographic characteristics. When these figures are compared with the nutritional composition of plant foods of known or potential use from the reconstructed floral environment, they can provide approximations of the quantity of certain species needed to satisfy them. The resultant figures can be compared with the availability of particular plant species in the local environment. After this assessment is completed, the paleoethnobotanist may conclude that provisioning the population was rather easy; that because of the periodicity of several species, several alternative plant food resources should be considered; or that the local environment could not adequately provide a dependable subsistence base and thus exchange of surplus with other societies should be investigated. By this means the impact of a prehistoric population on the plant environment can be established and the consequences of an increase in the size of the human population can be appreciated.

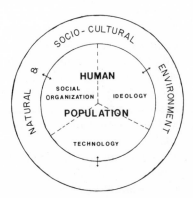

Figure 9.1. A model of the complex interactions between a human population and its environments.

The technological components of a culture usually depend upon a variety of plants both in the production of utensils and as the materials constituting the final product. Their identification and geographical distribution are useful for understanding a number of prehistoric industries such as textile production. At the same time some of the more mundane aspects of prehistoric life had potential for dramatically altering the landscape. For example, the amount of wood needed to build and to maintain a village and the fuel for heating and cooking can be approximated on the basis of archaeological evidence, and the impact of their procurement compared with the availability and abundance of these plants recognized from charcoal, pollen, and phytoliths. Thus, in order to satisfy human material wants, the technological subsystems of a culture can be modeled and tested with archaeological evidence.

The material correlates of a social organization should be detectable with plant evidence. A local kin-group may be recognized from its refuse, which may contain cultivars, such as corn, differing phenotypically from those of its neighbors because of inbreeding or land tenure arrangements. Similarly, sodalities organized across kin lines may have had distinctive plant symbols and medicines that left residue. In more complex societies, social status may determine access to exotic goods or types of firewood enabling the archaeological recognition of classes from the floral evidence. More difficult to detect, perhaps, are the remains of critical rites that individuals undergo and that use plants to simulate death and rebirth and to symbolize changes in social status. Plants functioning in these social contexts would not leave obvious recoverable evidence, but they are so prevalent in these situations that it may be quite rewarding for the archaeologist to seek their remains.

Plants have been crucial to the religious life of most cultures; indeed, they are often the metaphor for life itself. Calendrical rites are signaled by changes in the life cycles of important plants. Moreover, the balance in nature between humans and noncorporal beings is maintained or reconstituted with the use of medicinal plants. Communication with these beings is also facilitated with tobacco and other psychoactive plants, which may transport the human spirit to the spiritual world. These relationships are most difficult to interpret without ethnographic analogies; nonetheless, they may be reconstructed with archaeobotanical remains where no other kind of evidence is available.

The external social environment affects a human population through warfare, marriage, and exchange. Plants may be indicative of all three transactions if groups from different environmental settings are involved. Agricultural produce, for example, may be stolen, given to distant kinsmen, or traded for nonlocal materials. Village specialization in local raw materials for utensils, medicines, or ceremonial accoutrements may stimulate exchange in plants from one ecological zone to another. In other instances, an intervillage exchange network traversing a similar natural environment may encourage specialization in certain plant products such as textiles, baskets, arrows, and tobacco by one village, which are then conveyed to others. These external cultural relationships cause differential exploitation of the plant world, a situation that may appear as dissimilar assemblages in the archaeobotanical record.

Naturally, evidence for these potential relationships will not remain in every site, but the possibility must be acknowledged. Unless such evidence is sought and its importance for cultural reconstruction recognized, valuable information about past lifeways can easily be dismissed as beyond the archaeologist's grasp for ''lack of evidence.''

In the interpretation of prehistoric plants as they affected the people and culture, the determinateness of biological factors is frequently stressed. The previous discussion indicates that there is a dynamic interaction in the functioning of a culture. However, this does not resolve the limitations that biology imposes upon a culture. Figure 9.2 illustrates the relationship of culture and nature as interpreted by ethnobotanists. Certainly, nature, or in this case plant biology, imposes constraints on a culture, but the choice of a plant is by no means dictated strictly by its biological properties to the exclusion of human cognition. To contrast the extremes of the continuum, certainly firewood is selected on the basis of its availability, inherent heat value, and combustibility (that is, production of

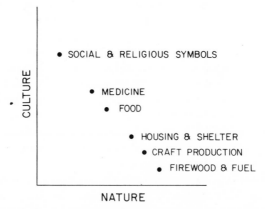

Figure 9.2. How plants are used is determined by cultural definitions and biological constraints.

ash, soot, smoke, etc.). Yet, not every potential fuel is used, and the selection of wood depends upon cultural specification and classification. At the other end are plants symbolizing social relations or procreating a sacred ambiance. Ethnographically, a certain purple-blossomed daisy (*Erigeron divergens*) is important in some Pueblo rituals of seasonal transition. Several purple-flowered plants grow in the local environment, but in this example, the human intellect has imbued only one of them with cultural meaning. A similar dialogue between nature and culture occurs for all other categories. The choices of certain plants for medicinal use are partially explicable because of their biochemical constituents, but they must also fit a cultural classification and logic. Furthermore, the chemical properties of food are detectable by Western scientific experimentation and are usually quite beneficial. Nevertheless, what is eaten (and not everything nutritious is), how it is prepared, and under what circumstances it is consumed are defined by cultural principles.

In each situation a culture defines appropriate plant resources, and the behavioral consequence of their extraction modifies to some degree the structure and composition of the local plant communities. Human activities directed by prescribed rules may have an unintended impact on the plants. Hence, preparing a corn field or simply living in an encampment may alter the soil, the make-up of a plant community, or the entire ecosystem.

To understand how plant populations withstand exploitation, one must have detailed knowledge of their biology. Three major forces affect plant variability, viability, and productivity: human selection, animal predation, and insect herbivory, and nonbiological natural phenomena. Generally, human and animal utilization is predictable and attuned to the phenology of each species. The role of humans in their dynamic interaction with plants is best comprehended by ascertaining what rules they follow, including the methods used, and when they collect the plants. Their actions are then compared with the natural parameters of each environmental factor determining plant growth and reproduction. On the other hand, physical forces, particularly climatic events, are unpredictable and generally are more detrimental to plant survival than are the other two. The occurrence in the past of natural environmental processes can be determined by means of archaeobotanical evidence, such as tree rings and pollen. In all their manifestations plant remains are indispensable for monitoring prehistoric local environments and for reconstructing processes of cultural adaptation to the natural world. The potential of paleoethnobotany as an aid to the interpretation of past cultures has barely been realized.

HISTORICAL PERSPECTIVE

Pre-1930 Findings

The history of ethnobotany and the development of modern archaeology are inseparable. Indeed, many research problems in contemporary American archaeology were anticipated decades ago by ethnobotanists. The initial use of the term ethnobotany was, in fact, a direct consequence of an examination of archaeological plants from Mancos Canyon, Colorado.

Following the World's Columbian Exposition in Chicago in 1893, the dried plants from the prehistoric cliffdweller exhibit were sent to Dr. John W. Harshberger, a botanist at the University of Pennsylvania. On December 4, 1895, in a lecture presenting the results of his labors to the University Archaeological Association, he designated the study of vegetable products employed for various purposes and the plants used by primitive and aboriginal people as ethnobotany (Harshberger 1896). Up to this time the study of American Indian uses of plants was appreciated in ethnology and botany but had no apparent importance to American archaeology. Harshberger's research, however, was preceded by half a century in Western Europe, and although he was unaware of it, de Rochebrune even anticipated him when he referred to his identification of vegetation from Ancón, Peru, as *ethnographie botanique* (de Rochebrune 1879).

The pioneering efforts of European botanists who collaborated with archaeologists and the theoretical basis for much of their research went unrecognized and unappreciated in America. Alphonse deCandolle in his *Géographie Botanique Raisonée* (1855) discussed the origins of domesticated plants and recognized that archaeology could contribute to the history of crops. He expanded the scope of his coverage to include some archaeological evidence in 1882 (deCandolle 1884). Meanwhile, domesticated plants were central to evolutionary ideas espoused by Darwin, Spencer, and Morgan. With theoretical guidance from these renowned biologists and early anthropologists and with the worldwide expansion of archaeology, European botanists analyzed plant remains from Swiss lake dwellings, Egyptian tombs, Pompeii, and even the arid Peruvian coast.

The recovery of plants from contexts characterized by exceptional preservation encouraged botanical research. The long-submerged berries, apples, cereal, wooden and bone tools, etc., from the Swiss lakes gave Oswald Heer (1865) an unprecedented opportunity to describe the vegetable economy of these Neolithic people and to examine cereal grains from a developmental perspective. Elsewhere, aridity maintained ancient remains for the botanist. Unger (1860) and Schweinfurth (1887) received dried plants from Egypt to identify. Similar circumstances of preservation and the excavations by *huaceros* produced voluminous materials from Peru. Saffray identified plants accompanying a mummy exhibited at the Centennial Exposition in Philadelphia (Saffray 1876). De Rochebrune (1879) and Wittmack (1880–1887) had an extensive quantity of materials from Ancón, which they identified by proper scientific name and ordered according to ethnographically known categories of usefulness. Harshberger (1898) analyzed similar plants from Peru, but despite his leadership in the field of ethnobotany and the example established by European botanists, the excavation goals of American archaeologists did not change.

Prior to 1930, ethnobotany was well established among American ethnologists, botanists, and explorers. Lists of utilitarian plants accompanied most ethnographies, and detailed tribal ethnobotanies published during this period are classics. Despite the legacy of this invaluable information for interpretation of archaeological plants, archaeologists were simply not accustomed to recover botanical remains. Occasionally, obvious examples of basketry, wooden artifacts, or desiccated corncobs from dry shelters in the Southwest and mountainous areas of the East were kept, but far more "trash" was simply dumped out. Charred debris was rarely conspicuous enough for attention. There were a few notable exceptions, of course. At Mills' request, J. H. Schaffner, a botanist, identified charred plant parts from the Baum Village in Ohio (Mills 1901). Young (1910) identified plants in human feces from Salts Cave, Kentucky. Holmes studied textiles from mounds and shelters (Holmes 1896) and their impressions on pottery (Holmes 1884). Kidder and Guernsey (1919) saved plants from northern Arizona, which they sent to specialists. Otherwise, little of ethnobotanical value remains from the early scientific excavators in North America.

Post-1930 Developments

Certainly omission of paleoethnobotany from the history of American archaeology before 1930 is explicable, but not afterward (see Willey and Sabloff 1974). The events of this decade, highlighted by Volney H. Jones' Newt Kash Hollow report (1936), are antecedent to archaeological interests for the next half-century.

In 1930 Carl E. Guthe, then chairman of the National Research Council Committee on State Archaeological Surveys, explicitly recognized the significance of excavated plant evidence and issued an open invitation to archaeologists to submit their vegetable remains to the Museum of Anthropology at the University of Michigan for identification (Guthe 1930). This service was provided by Melvin R. Gilmore, a distinguished ethnobotanist who joined the Museum's curatorial staff in 1929. At first only a few specimens arrived, but in short order sizable quantities from throughout the United States were received. Volney Jones became Gilmore's assistant in 1931, but because of Gilmore's failing health, Jones assumed almost exclusive responsibility for the identification of archaeological plants and for the reports issued by the Ethnobotanical Laboratory.

In addition to the establishment of this program, other research activities stimulated interest in archaeobotanical remains. Gilmore's studies of the vegetable debris from the Ozark Bluff Dwellers led him to postulate the possibility of the domestication of native plant species by these prehistoric people (Gilmore 1931). Shortly thereafter, Wakefield and Dellinger (1936) examined the dietary implications of plant parts recovered from feces from a desiccated Ozark Bluff Dweller body. Elsewhere interest in the food economy of prehistoric people was heightened by Hough (1930), as he attempted intuitively to estimate the relative dietary contribution of cultivated and collected wild plants in the prehistoric pueblos. These research directions—origins of agriculture and prehistoric diets—coincided with the successful completion at Showlow, Arizona, of a dendrochronological sequence in the Southwest (Douglass 1929). Prehistoric plant evidence could no longer be ignored.

Jones' research inaugurated a distinct field of ethnobotany. Before 1930 a few archaeologists submitted unusual plant specimens from excavations to botanists for identification. Kidder and Guernsey, for example, sent prehistoric squash parts to F. W. Waugh of the Canadian Geological Survey, maize to G. F. Will in Bismarck, North Dakota, and to G. W. Collins, a geneticist with the U. S. Bureau of Plant Industry, and small seeds to W. E. Safford with the same agency. Unlike these economic botanists and even Gilmore, Jones emphasized more than just botanical identifications and possible uses. He placed the remains in an environmental and cultural context, which likened his reports to what today is called cultural ecology. Jones established a standard for interpreting archaeobotanical evidence unmatched by botanical specialists until the 1960s when, with the example set by Bohrer (1962) and Yarnell (1964), two of his students, this kind of interpretation became more common.

His Newt Kash Hollow report (Jones 1936) demonstrated the potential of plant remains in archaeological interpretation, and confirmed Guthe's belief that a significant body of evidence was being discarded. This publication illustrates clearly the innovative techniques for handling archaeological plant remains and the knowledge of ethnobotany, anthropology, and plant ecology he brought to his identifications and interpretations. A variety of dried plant parts came from this large shelter in Kentucky, including bluestem grass beds, human feces, and cultigens. The grass suggested to Jones that a prairie environment preceded the forest of the 1930s. The coprolites were soaked in detergent and their contents carefully sorted and identified. The results argued for the presence of domesticated native plants, notably sumpweed, sunflower, maygrass, and goosefoot. Remains from the midden also supported this conclusion, especially because the known tropical introductions, squash and gourd, were present. Subsequently, the goosefoot has been reinterpreted (Asch and Asch 1977), but the others are regarded as native plants manipulated by prehistoric people. By today's standards this report and many others by him are more pleasing to read than are the site reports to which they are appended.

The ethnobotany Jones and Gilmore practiced went beyond the uses of plants specified by Harshberger's definition. This semantic discrepancy was rectified by Jones when he defined ethnobotany as the study of the interrelations of primitive man and plants (Jones 1941:220), and included archaeological plants as part of its domain. To his mind ethnobotany is more than the economic uses of plants to satisfy utilitarian needs; it also incorporates ecological relationships, religion, philosophy, and notions of primitive botany.

Despite these advances and contributions to archaeological understanding, the study of floral remains was secondary to other archaeological evidence. By introducing an anthropological perspective to botanical identifications, Jones helped to establish a distinct American archaeological tradition. Universal appreciation of this development did not follow, however, until the 1950s with the publication of *Excavations at Star Carr* (Clark 1954). Even though comparable interdisciplinary research had focused on wood and pollen from the Boylston Street fishweir (Johnson 1942) in Boston, it was Clark's effective demonstration of environmental archaeology that caught the attention of American archaeologists. More than ever before, biological remains of all kinds were now submitted to the few practicing specialists.

The crisis of quantity, which would soon swamp laboratories, was anticipated by Walter W. Taylor in 1956 when he convened a conference to discuss the identification of nonartifactual materials. At this meeting both Jones (1957) and Cutler (1957) addressed the history of botanical identifications in the United States and the assistance required of the archaeologist if specialists were to issue prompt and informative reports.

As American interest in environmental and subsistence reconstructions using floral remains increased, multinational research teams began to direct concerted attention to the beginnings of plant domestication. In fact, the term *palaeoethnobotany* was introduced by Helbaek (1959) as a consequence of his participation in the multidisciplinary projects in the Near East directed by Robert J. Braidwood. In Mexico, first in Tamaulipas and later in Tehuacan, Richard S. MacNeish (1958, 1961) excavated evolutionary sequences of plant species that were given to economic botanists to interpret. The vast influx of plant evidence produced by the long-term, large-scale projects required the services of many botanical specialists to conduct the analyses; no longer could one handle with authority the array of archaeological plant evidence ranging from numerous species to many types of remains.

Crop plants commanded little attention in American archaeology or botany until the late 1930s and 1940s (Ames 1939). Cultigens recovered from archaeological sites were identified, but they received special note only when unexpected or new occurrences were recognized (e.g., Steen and Jones 1941; Vestal 1938). Unlike Europe, where ideas about the origin of agriculture stimulated the retrieval of archaeological plants, the theoretical contributions of Spinden (1917), which focused on arid lands, and of Sauer (1936, 1952), which looked toward humid lowlands as the locality for initial domestication, were not investigated systematically by archaeologists until decades after their publication. Meanwhile, evolutionary biology and the development of crop plants became central issues for some botanists, and confirmation of their ideas concerning the origin of New World agriculture demanded archaeological evidence.

Maize was long recognized by archaeologists as indispensable to pre-Columbian civilizations, but its origin and diffusion remained unresolved in 1939, when Mangelsdorf and Reeves (1939) published their initial tripartite hypothesis for the emergence of modern maize from an ancestral wild pod corn. Previously, even Harshberger (1893) and other botanists had addressed these issues (Mangelsdorf 1974), but it was the direct relevance of the Mangelsdorf and Reeves hypothesis that stimulated archaeological interest and brought botanical specialists to recognize the significance of archaeobotanical remains for their research. At the same time Anderson (Anderson and Cutler 1942) introduced the racial concept into the classification of corn and applied it to maize in existing collections (e.g., Brown and Anderson 1947) and to corn grown by living Indians (Anderson and Carter 1945). By defining morphological attributes on cobs and kernels, races could be identified in archaeological collections and the diffusion of prehistoric corn could be traced (Anderson and Blanchard 1942; Anderson 1948; Jones 1949; Jones and Fonner 1954; Cutler 1952). Publication of *Races of Maize in Mexico* (Wellhausen *et al.* 1952) provided named races, which apparently corresponded to archaeological varieties, and diffusion of races from Mexico could be outlined with greater precision (e.g., Cutler 1966; Cutler and Blake 1971; Galinat and Gunnerson 1963). The diffusion of races by this approach has not been universally accepted, and other models for local developments have been presented (Jones 1968; Winter 1973).

In order to discover the temporal and spatial relationships among populations of archaeological corn, a detailed understanding of cob and kernel anatomy and morphology are requisite. Nickerson (1953) provided such a procedural description for examining races of maize, and Galinat has treated archaeological maize with a careful eye for anatomical and genetic variation (Galinat and Ruppé 1961; Galinat 1965, 1974).

Archaeological excavations in dry shelters produced the evidence botanical specialists were seeking. Bat Cave in New Mexico gave Mangelsdorf the opportunity to examine several stages in his hypothesized evolutionary sequence in maize (Mangelsdorf and Smith 1949; Mangelsdorf et al. 1967a), and introduced Smith (1950) to the variety of archaeological plants, which he has continued to analyze (Smith 1967). The archaeological investigations by MacNeish in Tamaulipas (MacNeish 1958) and in Tehuacan (MacNeish 1961) yielded a great wealth of desiccated plant materials that at the time appeared to support Mangelsdorf's theory (Mangelsdorf et al. 1967b), although Mangelsdorf (1974:49) subsequently has rejected his interpretation of the earliest maize while continuing to object to Beadle's position that teosinte (Zea mexicana) is the ancestor of corn (Beadle 1977). The wealth of desiccated plant materials from MacNeish's efforts was also invaluable to studies of cucurbits, beans, and other plants.

Whitaker and Cutler have long provided individual and collaborative interpretations of cucurbits from archaeological sites. Whitaker has been particularly concerned with the presence of bottle gourds in the New World (Whitaker 1948; Whitaker and Bohn 1950; Whitaker and Carter 1954), and along with Cutler with the domestication and importance of all cucurbits in the Americas (Whitaker and Bird 1949; Whitaker et al. 1957; Cutler and Whitaker 1961; Whitaker and Cutler 1965, 1971). More recently, Heiser, who earlier established his reputation among archaeologists for his studies on the evolution and aboriginal domestication of the sunflower (Heiser 1949, 1955; Heiser et al. 1969), following Whitaker, has examined the prehistory and taxonomic relationships of the bottle gourd in the tropics (Heiser 1973).

Beans have been studied extensively by Kaplan. His seminal investigations of prehistoric cultivated beans in the Southwest (Kaplan 1956) led him to an examination of even more species through his work with

MacNeish's Mexican materials (Kaplan and MacNeish 1960; Kaplan 1965; Sauer and Kaplan 1969).

Stephens, a recognized authority on the evolution of New World cotton (Hutchinson *et al.* 1947), benefited from the discovery of significant remains of *Gossypium* by MacNeish (Smith and MacNeish 1964), which enabled him to extend his studies back in time (Smith and Stephens 1971) and to synthesize the results of his research for both continents (Stephens 1970, 1973).

Grain amaranths are the particular interest of Sauer. His ethnobotanical and taxonomic studies (1950a, 1967) have provided valuable information from southwestern Pueblos (Sauer 1950b) and from archaeological contexts (Sauer 1969).

In contrast to Europe, where archaeobotanical research is over a century old, the relative youthfulness of North American paleoethnobotany is illustrated by the fact that the leading pioneer (Jones) and most of the botanical specialists who have provided plant identifications for archaeologists or who have documented the basic stages in the domestication of individual species of North American crop plants are still practicing scientists. Since the early 1960s, their ranks have been augmented by many younger colleagues, and together they have produced a prodigious number of reports (see the general summaries by Smith *et al.* 1966; Munson 1966; Cutler and Blake 1973; Nickel 1978).

Problem Orientation

The major research issues addressed by paleoethnobotany parallel its historical division: prior to 1930 the problems received descriptive answers; after 1930 the complexity of the data demanded processual explanations. Analysis of the earliest floral remains were applied to the solution of botanical and historical problems, including the uses of plants, the origin of agriculture, and migrations. Those recovered after 1930 have been interpreted according to anthropological interests, with emphasis on environmental reconstruction, human adaptations, and recently prehistoric ideology and information processing.

1. *Uses of Plants.* Until recently this was, by earlier definition, the paramount concern of ethnobotany. The first items dredged from the Swiss lakes raised the question of their use and importance to an extinct society. Subsequently, the study of foodstuff and related technological items from archaeological contexts have consumed the attention of botanical specialists. In the past 50 years utilitarian and materialist interests have shifted from a description of the plants and the potential uses to their

significance in the total economy and their extraction from the natural environment.

2. *Origin of Agriculture.* With the discovery of the first archaeological plants, deCandolle's ideas about agricultural origins and the spread of various crop plants could be tested. Even in the absence of the theoretical models that guide contemporary research, an outline of crop development emerged in the Old World by the turn of the century. Today, of course, modern genetics, better chronological controls, and the meticulous excavation of numerous sites combine for a more detailed explanation of agricultural origins than was possible previously.

3. *Migrations.* In Europe the migration of ethnic groups has been a dominant theme. Simultaneously, the emergence of diffusion as an explanation for cultural similarities led botanical specialists to examine plant remains for clues to past homelands and introductions into new habitats. In American archaeology migrations have not been a consuming problem, but cultural contacts have. Botanical evidence is important for discovering long-distance interactions as well as for outlining networks of trade and exchange.

4. *Environmental Reconstruction.* Recognition of environmental changes did not become critical until the exposure of acceptable Early Man sites with extinct fauna and the development of dendrochronology. With the addition of palynology and charcoal analysis, changes in the natural environment could be discovered and short-term fluctuations affecting a single culture could be determined.

5. *Human Adaptations.* With the acceptance of Jones' definition of ethnobotany came an explicit recognition that ecological interactions were basic to human–plant relations. These were rarely investigated until the biological needs of human populations were quantified and the ability of the local vegetation and crops to satisfy them was determined. From this assessment potential subsistence problems may be discovered, alternative strategies proposed, and the dynamics of the interactions better understood.

6. *Prehistoric Ideology.* This paleoethnobotanical interest could not be investigated until archaeologists modified their excavation procedures from single soundings to the exposure of large areas of a site and the recovery of plants from them. Consequently, differential spatial use of plants and their deposition could be discovered and related to possible beliefs and classifications of plants within functional categories.

Each of these paleoethnobotanical problems is equally important to archaeology and general anthropology. They will be discussed in detail following a description of archaeobotanical evidence and techniques.

ARCHAEOBOTANY

Depositional Environment

Archaeobotany is the study of plant remains derived from archaeological contexts. These remains may be examined from a number of perspectives, including paleoethnobotany, and they may solve problems unrelated to human activities and volition, notably biological evolution and paleoclimatology. Archaeobotany refers to the *recovery* and *identification* of plants by specialists regardless of discipline; paleoethnobotany implies their *interpretation* by particular specialists.

The archaeological record is incomplete, and since most parts of plants are perishable, unlike more durable artifacts, floral evidence is low on the survival scale. The seven biases in archaeological data enumerated by Collins (1975) apply to plant fragments. What endures through time is a differential assemblage based upon the prehistoric cultural pattern of disposal, the nature of the material, and the geochemical history of the archaeological deposit. The probability that uncharred material dropped on open soil will become part of the archaeological record is quite remote, owing to the decomposition processes of soil flora, arthropods, and chemical action. With the disappearance of soft tissue, perhaps a resistant phytolith may survive. Charcoal has a better chance for incorporation in the record, and plant parts deposited in oxygen- or bacteria-inhibited environments have the best prospects of long-term preservation Croes 1976. In any case, those that do endure still may not be exposed by the archaeologist!

The physical environment of every deposit selects differentially for the preservation of particular archaeobotanical evidence. Generally, the least destructive environments are anaerobic aquatic and permanently dry situations. The latter, however, are not always conducive to pollen preservation, and the former may still waterlog and distort tissue beyond recognition. Loss in other contexts is more acute. In soils with a pH below 5.5, pollen, spores, and phytoliths are well preserved, but soil acid and wetting are detrimental to charred materials. Unless the site is very recent or material is deeply buried in an arid locality, uncharred plant remains do not last long, and their presence should be treated with suspicion.

The activity of soil organisms and geologic processes have a continuous impact on an archaeological deposit. Seeds fall down soil cracks, worms displace quantities of charred fragments, and burrowing animals relocate a variety of objects. These disturbances are most conspicuous in rock shelters, but are probably more pervasive in open sites.

In addition to environmental factors, the pattern of cultural activities on a site produces a nonrandom distribution of remains. The location of plant preparation, consumption, and disposal results in a mosaic of plant parts. Munson *et al.* (1971) discuss the differential preservation of subsistence items. Those with dense, inedible waste products—for example, nutshells, corncobs, and fruit stones—are often prepared near a fire—the waste may even be used for fuel—and have an excellent chance of preservation in the archaeological record. A second group consisting of plants with dense but edible structures—for example, seeds, grain, and nut meats—may be charred accidently during preparation. Recent excavations in dry shelters indicate that food processing does not often occur adjacent to fires and very little food debris actually comes into contact with fire. The last group includes edibles with soft tissue and a high water content. These greens and tubers leave little waste and are rarely burned; only unpredictable calamities preserve them for the archaeologist. Even after the favorable deposition of plant remains, later human activities at a site may disturb the deposits of earlier occupants. Such eventualities further diminish the quality of supposedly *in situ* archaeobotanical data.

Beyond this list are plant remains from a variety of uses. Included are tools, storage facilities, and domestic structures, which in open sites are not preserved unless a catastrophe such as a major fire or the Ozette mudslide (Gleeson and Grosso 1976) occurs. Other plant parts, including pollen, spores, and opal, are not dependent upon fire for their preservation, but they necessitate special techniques of recovery. Unfortunately, the destruction of plant evidence through archaeological ignorance is still all too frequent.

Artifacts may also preserve plant parts. Sun-dried adobe bricks may include plant temper and pollen. After soaking the bricks, European-introduced plants have been recovered from California missions (Hendry 1931) and from Awatovi (Jones, personal communication). Fired clay daub and pottery also bear impressions of plants and vegetable artifacts (Schiemann 1932). Holmes (1884) initiated the study of textiles in the Eastern United States by examining their impressions on pottery. Dr. Doreen Ozker and I have identified an egg gourd seed (*Cucurbita pepo* var. *ovifera*) from a seed cast inside a Schultz Thick sherd, ca. 500 B.C., from Saginaw, Michigan. Elsewhere, prehistoric dent corn from Mississippian corncribs has been verified from baked mud dauber nests. In other contexts copper and other mineral salts preserve textiles and pollen (King *et al.* 1975). Again, these are unusual opportunities for the archaeologist and paleoethnobotanist, which, fortunately, are contrary to the differential and continuous loss of prehistoric plant evidence occurring at most sites.

Nature of Evidence

Archaeobotanical evidence is classified into three categories: macroremains, microremains, and chemical evidence. This practical classification derives from the methods of recovery and techniques of identification.

Macroremains are visible to the unaided eye and require no more than low-power magnification for their identification. (It is misleading to call them macrofossils, since few, if any, plants from American sites are fossilized.) Materials in this category include wood and wood products, nuts, wild plant seeds and fruit stones and pips, cultigens, and artifacts made from plants. Aside from artifacts, soft plant tissue, and coprolites from anaerobic contexts, most of these result from burning in an oxygen-reduced environment. Rarely are they truly carbonized—that is, reduced to pure carbon. Instead, they are caramelized, or charred, and can actually be further reduced.

Microremains are microscopic in size and require a high-power compound microscope for their identification. Pollen, spores, plant opal (phytoliths), calcium oxalate crystals, and other idioblastic inclusions compose this category.

Chemical evidence derives from the soil or from residues on artifacts. The soil contains the chemical compounds left from the decomposition or complete combustion of plants. In addition, since plants contain a number of trace elements (Stiles 1946), they are sometimes detectable on stone tools, in cooking or storage receptacles, and in pipes and other special-purpose utensils. The consumption of chemical isotopes in vegetable food can be discovered in human bone.

Methods of Recovery and Identification

Archaeobotanical evidence is helpful for determining field strategy as well as being indispensable for reconstructing past cultures. In both cases preplanning and consultation with botanical specialists in advance are essential for the maximization of archaeobotanical potential. Bohrer and Adams (1977) have described in detail the procedures they require for the recovery and documentation of botanical remains from Salmon Ruin in New Mexico. Their data retrieval system can be adapted to other field programs. As they point out, the documentation of plant samples must be complete and accurate. Large excavation projects benefit by employing a paleoethnobotanist in the field to coordinate the recovery and field processing of the remains. This saves invaluable time, prevents confusion later, and provides an effective feedback in the field so that field strategy may be altered if necessary.

In the field a botanical specialist can assist with the location of sites and the recognition of features in excavations. The identification of growing plants whose presence often correlates with human disturbance can aid in locating prehistoric sites and even agricultural fields (e.g., Berlin *et al.* 1977). During excavation, root molds, rodent burrows, and postmolds are recognized by differences in soil chemistry, which a botanist or geologist can help detect (e.g., van der Merwe and Stein 1972).

The actual recovery of floral remains from a site requires extensive logistic preparation. Each category of evidence necessitates a different recovery procedure. Since Struever (1968) popularized flotation for separating charred macroremains from their soil matrix, a number of techniques for processing bulk samples under various field conditions have been advanced (Jarman *et al.* 1972; Schlock 1971; Stewart and Robertson 1973; Limp 1974; Watson 1976; Minnis and LeBlanc 1976). Recently, Keeley (1978) has described the relative efficiency of several flotation techniques, and Keepax (1977) has warned about sources of contamination of the sample. Given the near-universal adoption of flotation, two critical pieces of information should be reported by the excavator. The first is the standard volume of the soil sample, usually 1 or 2 liters. The second is the aperture of the sieve used to trap light fraction material. Because not all charred plant parts float and in arid sites where calcium carbonate permeates the material as little as 10% may float, the smallest screen size indicates what may have been missed.

Not all soil need be processed with water, particularly if it is from a dry shelter where it has rarely, if ever, been wet. If the matrix will pass through nested geologic screens, this dry technique is preferred. Breakage is reduced, and the exfoliation of charcoal that sometimes follows wetting is avoided. Once again, screen sizes should be specified.

The extensive use of water separation (flotation) has created a crisis in the laboratory. What takes days to float in the field takes months to sort in the laboratory. A single kilogram of charred material may take from 20 minutes to several hours to sort, depending upon the sample and the experience of the technician (Keeley 1978). A variable-power binocular dissecting microscope (7–30×) is employed to sort samples into morphological categories: charcoal and bark, nuts, seeds, fruit stones, individual cultigens, amorphous plant material, etc. Common misidentified items in these samples are round, seedlike nodules or concretions (.5–10 mm in diameter) of iron or manganese that form in the soil. A simple laboratory test will demonstrate their inorganic composition (Alford *et al.* 1971).

Others include insect feces and small rodent pellets, which are sometimes mistaken for seeds.

Improved laboratory procedures are attempting to cope with the massive volume of flotation samples. Rane Curl, a chemical engineer, in cooperation with paleoethnobotanists at the University of Michigan, has experimented with a technique to reduce laboratory processing time by filling the void fraction space in clean, charred plant samples with oil and then floating them in zinc chloride. The results to date indicate that nuts, seeds and cultigens, hardwood charcoal, and conifer charcoal can be separated from one another in a distillation column.

Since archaeobotanical remains are initially sorted into homologous parts and not into taxonomic species, a voucher collection must reflect this difference. A standard herbarium rarely maintains a collection of those parts of the plant that were useful to prehistoric people, and certainly a curator does not want the collections cannibalized for comparative purposes. Consequently, separate voucher collections of potential archaeological plant parts obtained from taxonomically identified plants must be assembled and maintained. In addition, these collections of wood, seeds, fibers, etc., must contain charred materials to enable recognition of distortion and shrinkage caused by fire. Although adequate guides to wood and seed identification are available, they are based upon fresh specimens. An inexperienced person should use them only with caution, and all identifications should be verified by comparison with a documented reference collection.

The condition of archaeobotanical remains often renders them delicate to handle and difficult to identify. Several techniques ameliorate these problems. Fragile charred pieces can be strengthened through the alteration of their carbon crystal structure by carbonizing them at 1200°C in nitrogen, or their microanatomical features can be cast for examination with peels of synthetic resin or embedded for microtome sectioning and microscopic identification (Glauert 1965). For all categories of evidence, the scanning electron microscope (SEM) is indispensable for making identifications of even the most fragmentary scraps.

Once the genera or species are identified, their population characteristics have to be described. In each instance attributes and measures of morphological variation are recorded and compared with a reference collection that reflects the normal range of variation in a local population. The extent of the description depends upon the scope of the investigation. For the paleoethnobotanist, seed morphology and size, for example, may indicate the extent of human intervention in a plant population's growth (Baker 1972). Sculpture on the testae of some species may vary according to the season they were harvested and even as a result of human interference in the plant's life cycle (Robert Bye, personal communication, 1978). In other cases, the range of variation in a population of corncobs may result from climatic stress or farming practices that did not eliminate competing plants in the fields. Merely tabulating the presence or absence of identified taxa may omit important information about human–plant interactions in the past. Furthermore, ethnobotanical studies have demonstrated that cultures are not adapted to particular life zones or microenvironments but rather to individual species (e.g., Ford 1968). The importance of a species depends upon the way it is defined by a particular culture as well as by its physical–chemical properties, number, and distribution. By assuming as part of the analysis that the taxon is the unit of interaction with a culture, then knowledge of a plant's anatomy, physiology, and natural history may, in part, dictate the form of individual tools, tool assemblages, and even the location of sites themselves.

Further insight about the relations between an archaeological culture and identified plants is obtained through reference to ethnobotanical studies of ethnographic peoples who are familiar with these plants. Because this information simply provides hypotheses for testing, these data do not have to pertain to groups in the same culture area as the site. Inconsistencies and paucities in the reporting of ethnographic and botanical details require that a wide range of publications should be consulted. These analogies may suggest material correlates for the use of plants that can be investigated with similarly associated archaeological remains excavated from a site. A superb example of this contextual procedure is found in the Tonto National Monument report (Bohrer 1962).

Perhaps the least satisfactory aspect of archaeobotanical analysis is the statistical treatment of the data. Literally millions of pollen grains, seeds, and charcoal are counted and weighed annually. Most of these data are tabulated in charts now awaiting further study. Even with the standardization of data, however, these numerical frequencies do not necessarily indicate the importance of a plant. As stated previously, many factors contribute to the differential preservation and distribution of vegetable evidence on a site. Under these circumstances, between-site comparisons of numerical frequencies are quite meaningless. One solution is to disregard tests of significance comparing sites, and instead to consider the economic activities represented by the plant remains (Dennell 1976). Another is to index the number of independent samples containing a taxon relative to the total number of samples examined. In this manner relative comparisons can be made without the biases imposed by absolute counts.

Despite the difficult task of determining the overall importance of plants on the basis of relative frequencies, metric descriptions of the populations of economically significant annual seed taxa should be presented. For seeds and grain at least medians, means, ranges, and standard deviations are required. These data enable comparisons of similarities and differences between populations. Measures of diversity within large assemblages and the patterning of these data have been sought with factor analysis, but such treatment is uncommon (e.g., Marquardt 1974; Blakeman 1974). It is apparent that the statistical analysis of archaeobotanical data will receive extensive attention within the next few years.

Paleoethnobotanical Interpretations of Archaeobotanical Data

Wood/Charcoal

Wood is helpful to the paleoethnobotanist for dating, environmental reconstructions, and cultural interpretations. The identification of archaeological wood specimens, especially if they are charred, is done with a key in conjunction with a synoptic collection of modern samples. Most textbooks of dendrology have identification keys to today's economically important species. Hough's *Encyclopedia of Wood* plates constitute a very convenient resource, and Paulssen (1964) provides insights for working with small pieces of charcoal.

The principles underlying dendrochronology are the bases for dendroclimatology. This approach to climatic reconstructions provides seasonal climatic patterns, local trends, and long-term changes (Fritts 1976). When the specific parameters of seasonal patterns of precipitation in the past are compared with the growth and reproduction requirements of subsistence annuals, the climatic impact on a prehistoric culture can be appreciated better than by other, more general methods.

Wood appearing in the archaeological record is culturally patterned. Charcoal from a site is an unnatural assemblage. Firewood was not collected at random or in the proportion of the species in the natural environment; some are preferred for particular purposes to the exclusion of others, such as their heat value (Graves 1919); some are overrepresented because the species are better self-pruners. In ancient Mesoamerica class differences are indicated by charcoal. The upper class burned oak and pine charcoal prepared by villagers from mountainous areas, while the lower classes collected fagots from within a few kilometers of their residences. Elsewhere, fuel collected from cleared agricultural fields, and wood from reforestation is an indicator of changes made in the landscape by the prehistoric people themselves (Minnis and Ford 1977). Wood is basic for tools, boats, and shelters. In the latter case, as Dean

(1970) has demonstrated at Kiet Siel, building sequences determined by dendrochronology offer excellent evidence for prehistoric population dynamics, estimates of size and growth, and concomitantly the distance traveled for obtaining building materials. The combined archaeobotanical evidence of charcoal, pollen, and witness tree records (F. B. King 1978) provides an exceptional basis for reconstructing the prehistoric arboreal environment and the cultural manipulation of it.

Nuts

Schopmeyer (1974) is commonly referred to by botanical specialists for information and bibliographic references about the biology of nut-bearing trees and about their reproductive histories. It is a useful guide to the identification of nutlike remains only if the fragments are large and retain surface markings.

Nuts were used mostly for food, and must be considered for their nutritional value and availability. The dietary importance of all nut species cannot be compared. Their caloric value separates them into groups. One group—hickory, pecan, walnut, butternut, hazelnut, and pine—has an average of 600 calories per 100-gram edible portion. A second group—chestnut and acorn—averages half this amount. The taste of acorns varies according to the amount of tannic acid, and if ethnographic evidence is a guide, the flavor of nuts varies from one tree to the next, and those with better taste will be sought. With these facts in mind, one can appreciate that estimating the carrying capacity for nuts is perilous. Most published figures are averages or maximal for cultivated, not "wild," trees, and they rarely account for the number of climatic, biological, and cultural factors that make the time intervals between good masts unpredictable. Estimates of nut yields are useful for interpretation, but models based on these figures alone are poor predictors of archaeological population adaptations.

In order to cope with yearly variation in yield, prehistoric populations adopted complementary strategies. In the eastern deciduous forest in particular, alternative nut species were collected because their yields are not synchronized. When only a few species were available, populations had to have access to a large territory or to alternative areas widely separated in space to counteract local disparities in nut production. For mobile bands this was a viable option, but for larger, more sedentary groups, bulk storage from year to year was necessary. If nuts are kept in a cool, dry habitat, such as an insulated pit, a bag, or a special granary, they will last throughout most of a year. A second cultural means was to boil the nut meat and to save the oil in containers for later use as food or as a lubricant (Battle 1922). In any case, in cultures where nuts were important they did partially dictate human population distribution, settlement pattern, and the form of utensils for their preparation and storage.

Occasionally masts were sufficiently great that the surplus could be burned as fuel. What have appeared to be burnt caches of nuts prepared for eating may be, in fact, a technological use complementary to firewood.

Seeds

Archaeological seeds constitute the one category of plant remains that individuals without botanical training believe they can master. After learning to recognize a seed (see above for pitfalls), one must be able to distinguish uncharred from charred seeds, because anaerobic bacteria will give testae a dark and carbonized appearance (Brunton and Morant 1937). Gunn (1972) provides useful instruction for making comparative collections and identifications. Several seed manuals for North America are well-illustrated (Martin and Barkley 1961; Delorit 1970; Montgomery 1977), although a good reference collection remains indispensable. Neergaard (1978) is an excellent resource for seed biology. Seeds have long been invaluable for reconstructing archaeological food patterns and, more recently, past landscapes and land use.

Wild seeds and fruits were essential to Native American diets. Fruits were a source of energy and an important source of vitamins and minerals. Edible seeds provided about 300 calories per 100-gram edible portion and a complete protein when supplemented with other foods complementing their deficient amino acids. These plant products varied in quantity produced from one season to the next. Wild rice (*Zizania aquatica*), an annual grass popularly thought to be in endless supply, varied in its availability from year to year because of climatic events and the adverse effects of natural predators. The dietary significance of wild rice and other wild food plants ranged from one season to the next as snacks, seasonal supplements, staples, and surplus commodities (Figure 9.3). A snack food is simply an edible seed or fruit produced in insufficient quantity to sustain more than a segment of the total population for more than a couple of meals or between-meal interludes. Not all members of a population have an opportunity to consume these foods. Dietary supplements exemplified by condiments and spices are in sufficient supply to provide some to the entire population for at least a short period of time. Seasonal staples are harvested in a quantity that will sustain a population for several weeks to several months. Storable staples will last for several seasons at least. Given this perspective, one appreciates the problems different frequencies of plant remains pose for interpretation: the taxa identified in two similar assemblages of archaeological seeds may actually represent entirely different dietary patterns. In the case of fruits, as an example, their

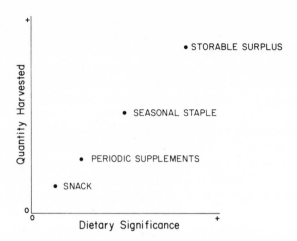

Figure 9.3. The importance of edible plant products depends upon the amount available. A given plant may qualify for a different category from one year to the next.

hard, durable pits, which have a high archaeological survival rate, may by their numerous presence give a false impression of their nutritional contribution, which was often as a snack food.

Seeds from weedy plants can cause special problems for explaining their occurrence in a site deposit. Some were the accidental disposal of edible seeds in a fire, but others result from natural dispersal of volunteer weed seed throughout a site, including hearth areas. Although this background seed fall may not assist with the reconstruction of subsistence patterns, it is helpful as an indicator of the local vegetation at the time the site was occupied and of the nature and extent of human disturbance to the immediate plant community.

Domesticated Plants

Domesticated plants are totally dependent upon humans for their reproduction and their very existence. The evidence left by various cultigens depends upon the anatomy of each species, but all are invaluable for understanding cultural dynamics.

Aside from stalks and husks found in dry locations, remains of corn usually consist of charred kernels, cobs, and detached cupules. Since dried cobs were frequently used for fuel, they are found in greater frequency than are kernels or the remains of other cultigens. This disposal pattern is most fortunate for the paleoethnobotanist, however, because cobs are aids to discovering growing conditions and farming practices. Traditionally, corn has been analyzed by classifying the remains into races, especially those found in Mexico (Wellhausen *et al.* 1952). A normative approach such as this does not consider phenotypic variation within and between populations. Kernel row number and cob length are plastic genetic traits, and when corn is grown under stressful conditions, the number of rows may be reduced and the cob itself will be shorter. Even when maize is grown under ideal conditions, the presence or absence of tiller and abnormal cobs is indicative of field practices. In some cultures these were never collected. Furthermore, land tenure and ritual practices, which culturally isolated gene pools within a village, may produce detectable differences in populations of archaeological cobs. As cultures changed in prehistory, the importance of subsistence resources did as well. Consequently, the evolution of corn from a seasonal security resource to an agricultural staple (Ford 1977) witnessed the aboriginal selection of traits related to increased productivity. Such changes now appear to be a result of cultural preference and selection rather than a product of the diffusion of new races of maize.

The remains of other cultigens do not present the same paleoethnobotanical opportunities. Owing to their methods of preparation and chemical composition, beans are not well preserved by charring, and their distinctive varietal colors are lost through burning. Different species can be distinguished from their morphology or by statistical comparison when size is diagnostic. Since various species of beans have individual growth requirements, their identification may have implications for interpreting other archaeological evidence. Bottle gourds and cotton likewise had interesting positions in prehistoric economics. Gourd vessels and rattles and cotton textiles and cordage are found in sites well beyond the areas where climatic conditions favored their growth. The discovery of their seeds is the best indicator that they were cultivated locally. The summer squash (*Cucurbita pepo*) was raised for its edible seeds and for use as vessels. In the Eastern United States at least, this function of the rind appears to have been more important when it was first introduced. When pottery containers became commonplace, then cultural selection was for a soft, fleshy pumpkin, which could be eaten. The nature of the remains through time reflects this change in cultural emphasis.

Pollen and Spores

Pollen analysis was used in the service of archaeology in Europe long before it became commonplace in the United States. Although Sears examined pollen from barrow pits associated with sites in the Southeast and pollen was used for environmental reconstructions at the Boylston Street fishweir (Johnson 1942) and in Mexico (Deevey 1944), the extent of its archaeological significance was not appreciated until the controversy surrounding the fossil maize pollen from the Valley of Mexico and its role in the story of the evolution of corn (Barghoorn *et al.* 1954). A background and introduction to palynological procedures are to be found in Faegri and Iversen (1975), and a more technical discussion and bibliography are available in Muir and Sarjeant (1977).

Pollen and spores constitute the most ubiquitous archaeobotanical evidence on any prehistoric site. Wind-pollinated flowering plants disperse pollen in quantity, whereas pollen from insect-pollinated plants is probably present in only trace amounts unless introduced by human populations. Spores from nonflowering plants such as fungi are often found in soil even if pollen has been destroyed by chemical, fungal, or bacterial action. Both are helpful for reconstructing past environments, for establishing relative chronologies, and for providing a rare glimpse into rituals and sacred symbols (Bryant 1978).

The value of pollen for reconstructing vegetation depends, in part, upon the surface receiving it. Lakes, bogs, and large, open surfaces catch pollen from vegetation covering a broad region, and will give a general assessment of that area (Tauber 1965). Pollen preserved in most archaeological soils is more restricted in origin, has been filtered by overstory vegetation, and is a better index of local plant communities. Because prehistoric people usually did not disturb hundreds of hectares by burning and land clearance, pollen trapped on sites is more likely to reflect human impact than is a regional pollen spectrum. Taken together, however, both catchment types can give an indication of the density of tree cover if absolute counting techniques are employed. Pollen is also useful for outlining broad climatic patterns, as Schoenwetter (1970) has demonstrated for the Colorado Plateau. Since regional pollen sequences are comparable, a pollen profile from a lakeside site or burial can provide a nondestructive means of relative dating (cf. Black and Eyman 1963).

Many cultural activities included collecting insect pollinated flowers for food, medicine, and ceremonies. By carefully sampling a site, particularly storage areas (Hill and Hevly 1968), and by washing the surfaces of grinding tools or storage vessels, it is possible to discover potential medicinal plants and foodstuff from the residual pollen and spores. Likewise, sodality-sponsored rituals include flowers particularly symbolic of them, and these ceremonial activities someday might be recognized by their unnatural pollen assemblage. Copper salts from metal objects will fossilize perishables in direct contact and will preserve pollen of potential cultural value as well (King *et al.* 1975).

To date, little has been done with spores from North American sites. Fungi were used for food, medicine, and technological purposes, and in the absence of other evidence, spores may reveal use of these plants in the past. Since spore-producing plants are also part of the detritus cycle, they can indicate something of decaying garbage and the physical decomposition of a site after abandonment. Although spores have been used in archaeological interpretation in Europe (Dimbleby 1967; vanGeel 1976), their potential still has not been realized.

Tissue and Fibers

Unfortunately, many of the dietary items and utilitarian artifacts used by archaeological cultures are unavailable to archaeologists. These are the fleshy tissues and soft parts of edible plants and fibers from quids, textiles, basketry, and cordage. Charred objects, casts, and impressions (except on pottery surfaces) from open sites are exceptional finds. Leaves, buds, and fleshy food did have an important place in prehistoric subsistence, especially on a seasonal basis, but their actual contribution remains speculative. Fibers and plant materials that were converted into clothing, sandals, baskets, bags, snares, etc., are recovered from dry shelters; several exceptional interpretive reports describe their cultural importance (e.g., Cosgrove 1947, Jennings 1957; Bohrer 1962; Jones and Fonner 1954; Haury *et al.* 1950; Watson 1974). Regrettably, the botanical identifications of many perishable items have been ignored for lack of laboratory facilities or have been misidentified (for example, *Apocynum*, Indian hemp is often mistaken for the processed fibers of *Yucca*).

Knowledge of these plants enables paleoethnobotanists to describe their habitats and phytogeography, to postulate the season they were collected, and to indicate the methods needed to prepare them, based upon their anatomical and physiological composition. Recognition of basketry and textile techniques provides a chronological indicator (e.g., Adovasio 1970, 1974; Kent 1957). The anthropological study of their manufacture and stylistic differences is a key to intercommunity trade and exchange, and to social units found within a site (e.g., Adovasio 1970, 1978; Adovasio and Gunn 1977; Croes 1977; Kent 1957; Rudy 1957; Tuohy and Rendall 1974).

Coprolites

The biological and cultural significance of desiccated human paleofeces was recognized by Wakefield and Dellinger (1936) and by Jones (1936), who reconstituted them in a solution of trisodium phosphate. Callen, however, rediscovered this technique and further advanced coprolite analysis in the early 1960s (Callen and Cameron 1960; Callen 1963). Subsequently, coprolites were actively sought, and their inspection produced the best evidence for what people actually ate, insight into daily activities, and better information about the season of site occupation (Bryant 1974c) in the Great Basin (Heizer 1967; Fry 1976), in Texas

(Bryant 1974b), and in Kentucky (Yarnell 1969). Martin and Sharrock (1964) first recognized the potential of pollen preservation in paleofeces, and because of the complementary pollen and macroremains, palynological analysis is now routinely conducted with coprolites (Napton and Kelso 1969; Riskind 1970; Schoenwetter 1974; Bryant 1974a; Cowan 1978). In other words, in archaeobotanical terms they are a composite of all categories of plant evidence, and their analysis demands an exceptional reference collection (Heiser and Napton 1969; Bryant 1974c).

Although human paleofeces are often outnumbered by animal scats in sites where they are preserved, those that are found yield unparalleled data. The diet of the site's occupants for a very short period of time, as represented by a coprolite, can be quantified, and less well-preserved foods like leaves, buds, and bark can be recognized. Cowan (1978) has suggested that their composition may even be evidence for an inadequate supply of food. Their pollen content may also indicate the season of the year of habitation, although pollen can still be ingested from plants long after it has been shed. By combining evidence from food plants and pollen, some specific details of the local plant communities can be discovered.

Scats from animals have received inadequate attention (Fonner 1957). Those excavated from archaeological sites are commonly left by dogs that have scavenged human garbage and, consequently, may contain items such as small bird bones, which are otherwise missing from archaeological debris. They also yield well-preserved pollen accidently ingested by the animal on its daily round. Scats from herbivores that occupied a site simultaneously or serially with humans contain plant tissue from the local vegetation, which because of their restricted grazing territories are very representative of local plants.

Plant Crystals

Phytoliths or plant opals form in the epidermal cells of leaves and then remain in the soil after the organic parent material decays. Although their variability usually restricts identification to taxonomic levels above the genus, nonetheless they hold potential for certain types of archaeological investigations (Rovner 1971). The quantity and variety of phytoliths from soil taken at a site indicate the general nature of the local vegetation (Wilding 1968). These data are complementary to pedological and pollen studies. More specific is the opportunity they afford for the recognition of economic plants. Since monocotyledonous leaf blades and culms contain quantities of silicate opals, if they were used, their phytoliths may be detectable. Pearsall (1978) has identified maize phytoliths from coastal Ecuador from contexts unconducive to the survival of other corn parts.

Thatch, bedding, mats, and baskets, now long gone, may be rediscovered in the form of concentrations of rather homogeneous phytoliths.

Other types of crystalline inclusions are located in other plant structures and should receive attention. Calcium oxalate and stone cells are found in tubers and fruits and could be evidence for their use in prehistory, especially when derived from paleofeces (Bryant and Williams-Dean 1975).

Plant Residues

In many archaeological situations recoverable plant remains are unavailable, but chemical residues left by a plant on an artifact can be analyzed and the plant or group of plants to which it belongs can be identified. Residues have been examined on tools, in pots, and from smoking pipes. Several chemical tests are applicable to determine if a plant was processed or consumed in some manner (Briuer 1976). Lack of evidence does not disprove that a plant was not used, because these stains are rare, and even when they are present the amount may be insufficient. The function of stone tools may be approached from an examination of the chemical residues left by a plant (Briuer 1976; Shafer and Holloway 1977; Wylie 1975). When a specific compound is known to be detectable from a plant whose use is suspected, then more exact tests can be employed. The alkaloids in tobacco, for example, are detectable with gas chromatography (Raffauf and Morris 1960), and the presence of nicotine in a Basketmaker III pipe confirms that at least tobacco was burned in it (Jones and Morris 1960). Although the anatomical structures of charred food adhering to cooking pots can rarely be identified, the presence of phosphate ions (Duma 1972) and other chemicals can prove that organic material was prepared in the vessel. Undoubtedly, much more can be done with residues if chemists can be convinced of the utility of this research.

Skeletal Evidence

The human skeleton preserves considerable information about vegetable contributions to the diet. To date the most detailed studies concern strontium and carbon isotopic analyses. Strontium passes through the food chain in ever-decreasing amounts. Herbaceous plants contain the most, and from these plants grazers add it to their systems. If plants were a primary food in a human diet, then the bones would have a greater strontium content than those of meat eaters. Of course, age, sex, maturation, and local environmental conditions are factors to be controlled, but for adult skeletons valuable anthropological information can be obtained.

Different dietary patterns between sexes, households, and classes of individuals within a population can be detected (Brown 1973).

The significance of maize in the prehistoric North American diet has been an abiding problem for archaeologists. Strontium analysis is one approach to an answer, but carbon isotopic research provides a more direct means. Corn is a tropical grass with a carbon pathway differing considerably from plants evolving in temperate areas, and as such it has a higher $^{13}C/^{12}C$ value. The amount of this isotope in the human skeleton is relative to the contribution of corn to the diet (Vogel and van der Merwe 1977). Because many edible weed taxa of tropical origin such as *Chenopodium* and *Portulaca* have similar carbon pathways to corn, more experimental research is needed before this technique can be applied generally. Nonetheless, it holds considerable promise for resolving arguments related to the evolution of subsistence patterns.

Other sources of indirect evidence for the preparation and consumption of plants by prehistoric populations are human teeth and bones. Tooth wear can suggest grit in the diet resulting either from a type of food such as tubers or from the grinding of plant material, and significant numbers of dental caries may indicate a diet that included corn or other cooked starch. Skeletal pathologies may indicate deficiencies in some mineral possibly provided by a plant. Teeth and bones can also evidence growth arrest lines resulting from nutritional stress, its frequency, and possible problems associated with the inadequate provisioning of the population (Blakely 1977).

PALEOETHNOBOTANICAL INTERPRETATIONS

At this juncture in the history of paleoethnobotany in the United States, no single study has utilized all the categories of archaeobotanical evidence discussed in this review. Recently, however, several exemplary reports have appeared addressing the critical problems of traditional concern to paleoethnobotany.

Useful Archaeological Plants

The identification and interpretation of utilitarian plants continues as a basic interest to paleoethnobotanists. Aside from subsistence plants, archaeological tools and artifacts made from plants have received limited attention, in part because they are uncommon finds and in part because studies by technologists working before 1930 remain adequate. The major exception to this generalization is in the field of textiles (M. E. King 1978) and basketry (Adovasio 1978), where new analytic techniques and interpretations have been advanced. Kent (1957) has published detailed descriptions of woven textiles from the Southwest and has described their technological evolution and areal distribution. Her work now permits the temporal placement of textiles and their trade relationships. Scholtz (1976) has provided an update to the analysis of ties and cordage in the East, which goes back almost 100 years to Holmes' (1896) pioneering endeavors.

On the other hand, prehistoric food plants have received considerable attention, and numerous published studies permit regional subsistence patterns to be discerned and processual examinations of individual sites to be undertaken. The uses of cultigens, nuts, seeds, and fruits in the Great Lakes drainage have been compiled by Yarnell (1964). Ford (1977) has synthesized changes in food webs in the postglacial Eastern United States (Figure 9.4). For thousands of years additional plant foods were added to the diet, including cultigens, without major displacements, until 1000

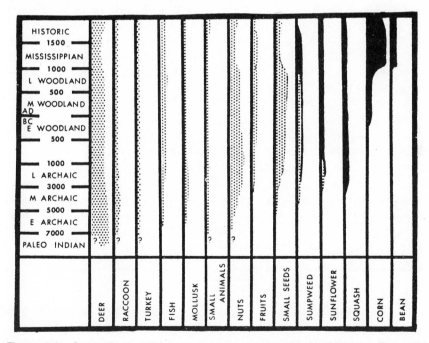

Figure 9.4. Generalized subsistence pattern changes in the Midwest. The solid graphs represent domesticated plants; the stippled graphs are wild-plant and animal foods. (Revised from Ford 1977.)

years ago when the pattern changed drastically. At this time a major subsistence shift occurred with a change from gathering numerous species of wild seeds and nuts and gardening squash and corn to a field system of agriculture based on corn as the staple.

Throughout prehistory, with or without extensive plant husbandry, the complex problems in scheduling and gathering foods with unpredictable and variable annual yields had to be resolved. Those associated with the harvest of climax forest products have been investigated at the Koster site in Illinois (Asch *et al.* 1972), and the possible solutions resorted to by sedentary agriculturalists are discussed by Bohrer (1970), Ford (1977), and later in this chapter.

Origins of Agriculture

The relevance of archaeobotanical plants to support ideas about the development of farming and the domestication of plants was long ago advocated by deCandolle (1884). Since his time, extraordinary effort has been devoted to this task. But the genetic modification of plants— although very important—is actually only one step along a continuum of human–plant interactions, which starts with the gathering of wild foods. Edible foods may be *harvested* without humans deliberately affecting the plant population's survival. Unintended consequences may occur, however, which benefit or alter the plant population: seeds are dispersed, competitors are trampled, and manipulation itself may enhance the population (Harlan and deWet 1964). Other plants may be collected after they have been *tended* in some manner. Although no detectable genetic changes occur, humans have intervened in the growth cycle of the plant population, enhancing its competitive advantage and chances for reproductive success. The next step after tending is transplanting or storing and dispersing seeds to assure their availability for germination. These *cultivated* plants may develop morphological changes such as seed coat variation indicative of this intensive human manipulation in their growth, but they are viable and unaltered when humans are not involved. *Domesticated* plants are dependent upon humans for their very existence. They are a cultural artifact resulting from human selection for certain genetically controlled features that would be disadvantageous under natural conditions.

The first domesticated plants entered the United States from Mexico by independent routes into the Southeast and the Southwest. For illustrative purposes the crop history in the East will be summarized. By 4500 years ago, apparently preceding the Southwest, squash (*Cucurbita pepo*), possibly represented by two varieties, and the bottle gourd (*Lagenaria siceraria*) were being grown by preceramic Archaic-period gardeners in Missouri (Chomko and Crawford 1978), in Kentucky (Marquardt and Watson 1977), and in Tennessee (J. Chapman, personal communication 1978). The current status of the evidence indicates that these tropical cultivars preceded the eventual domestication of the native sumpweed and sunflower and possibly the cultivation of maygrass and goosefoot.

Sunflower and sumpweed are annual composites that experienced a series of selective changes by prehistoric people, resulting in larger seeds and greater yield, and that were dispersed from habitats where they grew naturally to distant places where human protection was required. In the case of the sumpweed a new variety was developed by these prehistoric farmers, *Iva annua* var. *macrocarpa* (Blake 1939; Black 1963; Yarnell 1972). It, however, was apparently abandoned after White contact and is extinct today. The sunflower also underwent stages in human interference in its annual growth cycle beginning with simple tending to assure population continuity, to selection for larger achenes and disks, and finally to planting in fields. In contrast to sumpweed, it was adopted by Europeans and is an important crop in the world economy (Heiser 1955; Yarnell 1976).

Several additional plants were manipulated during the Late Archaic and Woodland periods, but there is no evidence for their domestication. Asch and Asch (1977) have documented the case for the cosmopolitan goosefoot, *Chenopodium bushianum,* and conclude that although humans encouraged it and even disseminated it, no obvious genetic changes resulted. Maygrass (*Phalaris caroliniana*) was recognized by Jones (1936) growing disjunct from its modern range of distribution without any morphological changes resulting from its apparent cultivation. The planting of these indigenous species may have taken place in the context of squash gardens which supplemented nuts and other harvested wild plant foods (Figure 9.4). Giant ragweed (*Ambrosia trifida*) was once considered as a possible cultivated plant in the East, but after an examination of geographic clinal variation in its seed size, Payne and Jones (1962) concluded that wild stands were probably being harvested.

The horticultural plants in the East were augmented a little more than 2000 years ago by corn introduced from the Southwest and 1000 years later by common beans. With the addition of these crops cultural changes already in progress were amplified, and domesticated plants soon dominated the subsistence economy. Accompanying these developments was a shift from ecologically complex gardens to field agriculture and the origin of anthropogenic local ecosystems with their promise of greater predictability than in natural areas, but with new problems of risk and crop loss to which Mississippian cultures had to adapt (Ford 1974).

Environmental Reconstruction and Land Use

Pollen and macroremains have been used to reconstruct past environments and alterations brought about by human activities. For determining the composition of the floral environment a combination of pollen, charcoal, and seeds is essential, because some species are not represented if only one kind of archaeobotanical evidence is employed.

The most significant transformation of the landscape occurred with the evolution of field agriculture as a technological subsystem. The dependence of corn upon the proper temperature and moisture at critical times in its growth cycle has assisted interpretations of land use studies in the Southwest. Schoenwetter and Dittert (1968) used pollen to determine rainfall patterns in the Navajo Reservoir area and to relate them to changes in settlement patterns. Soil moisture produced by winter-dominant storms enabled more widespread agricultural settlements than was possible when summer storms prevailed. Wherever farming was practiced, the preparation and abandonment of fields resulted in a mosaic of successional plant communities and a greater concentration of economically important plants than were present in the mature forest. Recent studies by Minnis and Ford (1977) and by Ford and others on Black Mesa in Arizona demonstrate that the introduction of corn as a technological system to higher elevations encouraged dense stands of ruderal plants, which were harvested to supplement staple crops. The result was a greater useful biomass than existed before human disturbance. Aside from pinyon nuts and juniper berries, virtually all the seeds recovered from these higher elevation sites—pigweed, goosefoot, Indian ricegrass, wolfberry, cholla cactus—derive from plants that grew in cleared corn fields or on abandoned agricultural land.

Human Population Adaptations

Despite the success and promise of research into the dynamics of human–plant interrelationships, results are limited unless a reasonable reconstruction of the size and demographic characteristics of the prehistoric human population is available. Without these estimates, speculations about the amount of various plant resources required to sustain or to shelter the population are unrealistic. Furthermore, more exact nutritional assessments of native food plants based upon their aboriginal methods of preparation are necessary before one can determine how a population's subsistence needs were met. Once these data are available, then possible problems encountered by a population when various plant foods were unavailable or limited in quantity relative to the number of prehistoric community members (Figure 9.3) are better appreciated by the archaeologist.

Estimates of the population residing at Arroyo Hondo near Santa Fe, New Mexico, enabled Wetterstrom (1976) to calculate its nutritional requirements and to model how they might be satisfied with different combinations of crop and gathered wild plant foods. After reconstructing the prehistoric environment from macroremains and limited pollen data, she calculated the consequences to the staple crops if their productivity were severely stressed. From the results, she predicted that wild plants were a hedge against possible nutritional privation, but even with these plant foods occasional nutritional deficiencies should be expected. Her data confirmed that the very plants she postulated would be gathered in quantity were present in the macroremains and that an examination of human bone and teeth revealed signs of growth arrest and other evidence for periodic nutritional problems. From the results of her analysis, she obtained a better understanding of the strategies prehistoric people used for coping with variability in plant productivity.

Cultural Contacts

One of the traditional promises of paleoethnobotany has been that migrations, trade, and social intercourse could be traced through the floral remains from archaeological sites (Pickersgill 1972). The premise is that if a plant evolved in one area and is found elsewhere, then some form of migration or contact occurred. Although this seems logical enough, providing explanations for continental plant distributions is difficult. Plant evidence per se has not demonstrated any migrations in North America, but it has revealed apparent contacts for which the cultural processes remain to be explained beyond diffusion.

Direct evidence for long-distance contacts between Mexican cultures and the prehistoric United States have long been sought by archaeologists. Similarities in artifacts, architecture, and styles suggested contact without proof of interaction. Plants have substantiated that these contacts occurred in both the Southwest and the Southeast. In the Southwest four species of squashes, at least the same number of different beans, cotton, and amaranth were introduced at various times from Mexico, where their ancestral populations are found. In the Southeast the list is less impressive but equally significant. Several thousand years after the initial arrival of tropical domesticates two additional plants were introduced. Tobacco (*Nicotiana rustica*) was raised prehistorically in the East (but not in the Southwest) as well as in eastern Mexico, close to its place of origin. Likewise, some form of culture contact with Mexico brought *Chenopodium nuttalliae,* a grain chenopod, to the Ozark shelter area (Gilmore 1931).

Paleoethnobotanical interpretations can suggest patterns of exchange, even though an anthropological understanding of how it transpired may still elude us. An example is provided by the wide distribution of cotton textiles in the Southwest (Kent 1957). Since cotton requires a long growing season and more water than many site areas where finished products are found can provide, trade from sites where the seeds have been excavated and from several possible production centers, notably Canyon de Chelly (Magers 1975) and Hohokam sites, should be investigated. The distribution of bottle-gourd ceremonial rattles and vessels presents a similar problem.

Ideology, Information, and Decisionmaking

Perceptions by prehistoric people about the organization, operation, and maintenance of the world are the least obvious in the archaeological record. Yet, because they underpin the beliefs and rules that guide human behavior toward and decisions about the plant world, they should not be ignored. Excavated plant remains are patterned and can suggest an ethnotaxonomy of certain categories of plant utilization. For example, in the upper Rio Grande valley some prehistoric puebloans preferred pinyon pine wood over all others for indoor cooking and heating, and they used juniper for outdoor burning. This pattern contrasts a spatial order—inside versus outside—and it forms a concomitant functional taxonomy of firewood preferences.

Ethnographic accounts of North American Indians present insights that should be testable with archaeobotanical data. Hall (1976, 1977), who is attempting to understand the basic structure of prehistoric Midwestern cultures from the meaning given to material objects by ethnographically known people, has found that plants are indispensable to his quest. The color of leaves, the pungent quality of their smoke, etc., are qualities that had cultural value. Aspects of time and space have plant associations as well. Throughout the continent the four cardinal directions have sacred meaning, order cultural activities including the procurement of plants, and are symbolized by colors and often by specific plants and animals. Plants may represent seasonal changes or signal the start of communal activities, and their general condition can be a barometer to the state of nature. Because of their intimate knowledge of plant morphology, biology, and natural history, paleoethnobotanists can assist in explaining why certain plants may receive special attention, and they can help to design the research necessary for discovering if these generalizations had analogous significance in the past.

The results of such research endeavors are not mere abstractions and are important for understanding prehistoric cultural adaptations. The plants that fulfill the subsistence requirements of a human population compose a system of interrelationships. The potential availability of each culturally defined plant will vary from season to season and from year to year. The condition of the plant population is determined by environmental factors, and assuming the same processes operate today as in the past, a reconstruction of the environment at the time a site was occupied can be represented as a series of probability statements about the problems each plant posed for the prehistoric people. The information about the plant as interpreted by the human population dictated what course of action to follow. Again, by simulating these relationships feedback decisions can be proposed that may have been relevant to the archaeological situations under investigation. If the status of a particular plant population was adequate, it might have been harvested; if it was not, then an alternative plant may have been selected, or it may have become necessary to consume more stored food than usual. Bohrer (1970) hypothesized the Hohokam ecosystem from Snaketown archaeobotanical data and noted that the harvest of corn could be jeopardized if run-off and rainfall were inadequate at certain times of the year. A correction for a poor yield of corn as suggested by ethnographic examples drawn from the Pima and Papago is to harvest more saguaro cactus fruits and seeds and mesquite pods than under normal conditions. There are occasions, however, when a simple feedback loop dictating how, when, and where to gather a plant or when to concentrate on an alternative still did not satisfy a population's needs. Under these circumstances other kinds of regulatory mechanisms, frequently ceremonial in nature, operated.

Ceremonial activities can also be viewed as a means for coping with environmental vicissitudes as they are in the ethnographic present (Ford 1968). When crops fail, then rituals propitiating the appropriate spirits might be initiated. At other times ceremonials are held to celebrate a bountiful harvest and to thank the gods for their assistance. Some of these ceremonial activities serve to regulate natural environmental interactions by dictating what wild plant can or cannot be collected, when to start preparing agricultural fields, or when to harvest the crop. Each decision will impact upon the plant communities by scheduling the human exploitation of resources, often for the benefit of the plants and ultimately the people. Other ceremonies of thanksgiving include offerings of food, which are shared communally and may overcome disparities in the yield from one field to the next. Ceremonial objects, such as those described recently from Chetro Ketl (Vivian *et al.* 1978), are sometimes found archaeologically, but how they relate to a ceremonial organization, ceremonial activities, and human adaptation to a sometimes capricious environment is difficult to decipher. The simulation of potential ecological and information relationships in the past may suggest an answer.

Beliefs concerning appropriate behavior toward plants in the local ecosystem have implications for the composition of the plant communities. An example of preferential selection of pinyon and juniper firewood was described above. Under these circumstances it appears that more pinyon would have been burned annually than juniper, and this differential use of firewood varieties must have affected the availability of each. Recognition of these firewood categories suggests the archaeological examination of the logistics of gathering firewood and the environmental consequences of the prolonged collecting of certain species by a sedentary community. Changes brought to the landscape by prehistoric activities were variable in their magnitude, significance, and length of time to develop, but through them all the people had to adjust to a landscape that they created.

The investigation of ideological aspects of archaeological cultures has implications for the evolution of plants themselves. A testable proposition illustrating the general importance of color symbolism and the specific colors of corn kernels in the Southwest can be suggested. The four cardinal directions are represented in prehistoric pueblo art and have ritual significance in the modern pueblos along with a color of maize representing each direction, red, white, blue, and yellow. A common explanation for the evolution of a productive maize agriculture in this area is the successive diffusion of more advanced races of corn from Mesoamerica. An alternative hypothesis is that it evolved in the Southwest as a result of the integration of maize into the ritual system in Pueblo II times, and the selection for homogeneous kernel colors representative of the cardinal directions that was necessary for ceremonials. Such a cultural basis for the selection of specific phenotypic traits would also affect the arrangement of the fields and the maintenance of the growing crops in order to satisfy ritual obligations for ceremonial presentations of pure-colored cornmeal. The latent consequence of these activities is a more stable gene pool, less variability in the corn population, and a more productive yield.

A final research interest in anthropology to which paleoethnobotany can contribute is an understanding of cultural differences in the use of essentially the same plant environment. Because of their respective values, needs, and technology two cultures may evidence entirely different preferences for even the most mundane plant resources. Along the San Juan River west of Shiprock, New Mexico, for example, prehistoric

Pueblo cultures gathered fuel from the saltbush and sagebrush communities which grew surrounding their village. Juniper occurred sparingly at best near the sites. In contrast, the historic Navajo who occupied virtually the same locations burned juniper to the exclusion of the locally abundant shrubs. This may be accounted for by their use of steel axes, the availability of wagons and horses, and perhaps the cultural importance they attribute to juniper. Whatever the explanation, the contrast in cultural preference was left in the archaeobotanical record.

INTEGRATION OF PALEOETHNOBOTANY AND ARCHAEOLOGY

Paleoethnobotany has entered an era when technical advances and the accumulation of new evidence have never been more rapid. Each summary of the field, both in the United States and Europe, underscores its unprecedented developments (cf. Dimbleby 1967; Yarnell 1970; Renfrew 1973). More efficient data storage and retrieval systems are required for the codification and dissemination of archaeobotanical data, especially those contained in hundreds of unpublished contract archaeology reports, but progress is being made in this direction (see Field 1977).

Another major trend is the continued growth of multidiscipline research of archaeological sites and the importance archaeobotanical remains have for these projects. The pioneering examples set by Braidwood and Mac-Neish have been followed in the United States by Struever in the lower Illinois Valley and particularly the massive flotation program at Koster (Asch *et al.* 1972), by Watson and her associates in the Mammoth Cave area (1969, 1974), by Shafer and Bryant (1977) at Hinds Cave in Texas, by the work at Antelope House in Arizona (Rock and Morris 1975), and by Daugherty at Ozette in Washington, to mention but a few. On a smaller scale, most archaeological projects, if they do nothing else with plants, do employ flotation, and send the charred remains to specialists.

However, multidiscipline participation is not the same as interdisciplinary research. Effective communication among scientists is essential if the research objectives of the archaeological project are to be attained. This is accomplished when the problems under investigation are clearly stated, and in addition to other goals, each specialist contributes to their solution. Goodyear (1975), in his description of the Hecla project, proposes questions about prehistoric subsistence activities and land use that would enable a botanical specialist to recommend specific categories of plant data that should be recovered to resolve his problems. Research such as this with explicit questions and hypotheses is the foundation for interdisciplinary cooperation.

As the objectives of archaeology focus on broader issues of cultural integration and evolution, paleoethnobotany will make an even more profound contribution to anthropological archaeology than it has in the past. The methods and theory are available to the task; what is required for this realization is effective research administration. Unfortunately, it is still too common to find plant remains shipped to specialists with few instructions months after the termination of excavations. Under these conditions, the interests of the specialist dictate the content of the report, and the final site report is a collection of appendices from each participant. Cooperative research should strive for an integrated interpretation of prehistory. Paleoethnobotany has expanded its horizons to the benefit of this archaeological goal. Innovative techniques are producing exciting answers to traditional as well as new problems in both archaeology and botany. The interdependence of these disciplines, if matched by mutual understanding and cooperation, will result in ever-more-significant advances of anthropological importance.

ACKNOWLEDGMENTS

An initial draft of this manuscript benefited immeasurably from the critical comments and insightful suggestions provided by Dr. Vaughn Bryant and Karen Cowan Ford and by the anonymous paleoethnobotanists who reviewed it. The published version was prepared while I was a Weatherhead Scholar at the School of American Research. I appreciate the support of the School and the assistance of the reviewers.

REFERENCES

Adovasio, J. M.
   1970   The origin, development and distribution of Western Archaic textiles. *Tebiwa: Journal of the Idaho State University Museum* **13**:1–40.
   1974   Prehistory of North American basketry. *Nevada State Museum Anthropological Papers* **16**:100–145.
   1978   *Basketry technology.* Chicago: Aldine.
Adovasio, J. M., and J. Gunn
   1977   Style, basketry, and basketmakers. In *The Individual in Prehistory*, edited by J. N. Hill and J. Gunn, New York: Academic Press. Pp. 137–153.
Alford, J. J., J. E. Bundschuh, and F. C. Caspall
   1971   A simple field test for the detection of manganese in Quaternary deposits. *American Antiquity* **36**:475–477.
Ames, O.
   1939   *Economic Annuals and Human Cultures.* Cambridge: Botanical Museum of Harvard University.
Anderson, E.
   1948   Racial identity of the corn from Castle Creek. In Archaeology of Castle Park, Dinosaur National Monument, Robert F. Burgh and Charles R. Scoggin. *University of Colorado Studies, Series in Anthropology* No. 2, 91–92.

Anderson, E., and F. D. Blanchard
 1942 Prehistoric maize from Canyon del Muerto. *American Journal of Botany* **29**(10):832–835.
Anderson, E., and G. F. Carter
 1945 A preliminary survey of maize in the southwestern United States. *Annals of the Missouri Botanical Garden* **32**:297–318.
Anderson, E., and H. C. Cutler
 1942 Races of *Zea mays:* I, Their recognition and classification. *Annals of the Missouri Botanical Garden* **29**:69–86.
Asch, D. L., and N. B. Asch
 1977 Chenopod as cultigen: A re-evaluation of some prehistoric collections from eastern North America. *Midcontinental Journal of Archaeology* **2**:3–45.
Asch, N. B., R. I. Ford, and D. L. Asch
 1972 The paleoethnobotany of the Koster site: The Archaic horizons. *Illinois State Museum Report of Investigations* No. 24.
Baker, H. G.
 1972 Human influences on plant evolution. *Economic Botany* **26**(1):32–43.
Barghoorn, E. S., M. K. Wolf, and K. H. Clisby
 1954 Fossil maize from the Valley of Mexico. *Harvard University, Botanical Museum Leaflets* **16**:229–240.
Battle, H. B.
 1922 The domestic use of oil among the southern aborigines. *American Anthropologist* **24**:171–182.
Beadle, G. W.
 1977 The origin of *Zea mays.* In *Origins of agriculture,* edited by C. A. Reed, The Hague: Mouton. Pp. 615–635.
Berlin, G. L., J. R. Ambler, R. H. Hevly, and G. G. Schaber
 1977 Identification of a Sinagua agricultural field by aerial thermography, soil chemistry, pollen/plant analysis, and archaeology. *American Antiquity* **42**:588–600.
Black, M.
 1963 The distribution and archaeological significance of marsh elder, *Iva annua* L. *Papers of the Michigan Academy of Science, Arts, and Letters* **48**:541–547.
Black, M., and C. E. Eyman
 1963 The Union Lake skull, a possible early Indian find in Michigan. *American Antiquity* **29**:39–48.
Blake, S. F.
 1939 A new variety of *Iva ciliata* from Indian rock shelters in the South–Central United States. *Rhodora* **41**:81–86.
Blakely, R. L. (editor)
 1977 Biocultural adaptation in prehistoric America. *Southern Anthropological Society Proceedings* No. 11.
Blakeman, C. H., Jr.
 1974 The late prehistoric paleoethnobotany of the Black Bottom, Pope and Massac Counties, Illinois. Ph.D. dissertation, Department of Anthropology, Southern Illinois University, Carbondale.
Bohrer, V.
 1962 Nature and interpretation of ethnobotanical materials from Tonto National Monument. Archeological studies at Tonto National Monument, Arizona. *Southwestern Monuments Association Technical Series* **2**:75–114.

1970 Ethnobotanical aspects of Snaketown, a Hohokam village in southern Arizona. *American Antiquity* **35**:413–430.

Bohrer, V. L., and K. R. Adams
1977 Ethnobotanical techniques and approaches at Salmon ruin, New Mexico. *Eastern New Mexico University Contributions in Anthropology* No. 8.

Briuer, F. L.
1976 New clues to stone tool function: Plant and animal residues. *American Antiquity* **41**:178–484.

Brown, A. F. B.
1973 Bone strontium content as a dietary indicator in human skeletal populations. Unpublished Ph.D. dissertation, Department of Anthropology, University of Michigan, Ann Arbor.

Brown, W. L., and E. Anderson
1947 The northern flint corns. *Annals of the Missouri Botanical Garden* **34**(1):1–28.

Brunton, G., and G. Morant
1937 *Mostagedda and the Tasian culture.* London.

Bryant, V. M., Jr.
1974a Pollen analysis of prehistoric human feces from Mammoth Cave. In *Archeology of the Mammoth Cave area,* edited by P. J. Watson. New York: Academic Press. Pp. 203–209.
1974b Prehistoric diet in Southwest Texas: The coprolite evidence. *American Antiquity* **39**(3):407–420.
1974c The role of coprolite analysis in archeology. *Bulletin of the Texas Archeological Society* **45**:1–28.
1978 Palynology: A useful method for determining paleoenvironments. *Texas Journal of Science* **30**:25–42.

Bryant, V. M., Jr., and G. Williams-Dean
1975 The coprolites of man. *Scientific American* **232**(1):100–109.

Callen, E. O.
1963 Diet as revealed by coprolites. In *Science in archaeology,* edited by D. Brothwell and E. Higgs. New York: Basic Books. Pp. 186–194.

Callen, E. O., and T. W. W. Cameron
1960 A prehistoric diet revealed by coprolites. *The New Scientist* **8**(190):35–40.

Chomko, S. A., and G. W. Crawford
1978 Plant husbandry in prehistoric eastern North America: New evidence.for its development. *American Antiquity* **43**:405–408.

Clark, J. G. D.
1954 *Excavations at Star Carr: An early Mesolithic site at Seamer, near Scarborough, Yorkshire.* London and New York: Cambridge University Press.

Collins, M. B.
1975 Sources of bias in processual data: An appraisal. In *Sampling in archaeology,* edited by J. W. Mueller. Tucson: University of Arizona Press. Pp. 26–32.

Cosgrove, C. B.
1947 Caves of the Upper Gila and Hueco areas in New Mexico and Texas. *Papers of the Peabody Museum of American Archaeology and Ethnology, Harvard University* **24**(2):1–181.

Cowan, C. W.
1978 Seasonal nutritional stress in a Late Woodland population: Suggestions from some Eastern Kentucky coprolites. *Tennessee Anthropologist* **3**(2):117–128.

Croes, D. R. (editor)
1976 The excavation of water-saturated archaeological sites (wet sites) on the

Northwest Coast of North America. *National Museum of Man Mercury Series, Archaeological Survey of Canada* No. 50.

Croes, D. R.
    1977   Basketry from the Ozette Village archaeological site: A technological, functional, and comparative study. Ph.D. dissertation in Anthropology, Washington State University, Pullman.

Cutler, H. C.
    1952   A preliminary survey of plant remains. In Mogollon cultural continuity and change, the stratigraphic analysis of Tularosa and Cordova Caves, P. S. Martin *et al. Fieldiana: Anthropology* **40**:461–479.
    1957   Botany. In The identification of non-artifactual archaeological materials, edited by W. W. Taylor. *National Academy of Sciences–National Research Council, Publication* No. 565, 39–40.
    1966   Corn, cucurbits and cotton from Glen Canyon. *University of Utah Anthropological Papers* No. 80, 1–62.

Cutler, H. C., and L. W. Blake
    1971   Travels of corn and squash. In *Man across the sea,* edited by C. L. Riley, J. C. Kelly, C. N. Pennington, and R. L. Rands. Austin: University of Texas Press.
    1973   *Plants from archeological sites east of the Rockies.* St. Louis: Missouri Botanical Gardens.

Cutler, H. C., and T. W. Whitaker
    1961   History and distribution of the cultivated cucurbits in the Americas. *American Antiquity* **26**(4):469–485.

Dean, J. S.
    1970   Aspects of Tsegi Phase social organization: A trial reconstruction. In *Reconstructing prehistoric Pueblo societies,* edited by W. A. Longacre, Albuquerque: University of New Mexico Press. Pp. 140–174.

deCandolle, Alphonse
    1884   *Origin of cultivated plants.* London: Kegan Paul, Trench.

Deevey, E. S., Jr.
    1944   Pollen analysis and Mexican archaeology. An attempt to apply the method. *American Antiquity* **10**(2):135–149.

Delorit, R. J.
    1970   *An illustrated taxonomy manual of weed seeds.* River Falls, Wis.: Agronomy Publications.

Dennell, R. W.
    1976   The economic importance of plant resources represented on archaeological sites. *Journal of Archaeological Science* **3**:229–247.

de Rochebrune, A. T.
    1879   Recherches d'ethnographie botanique sur la flore des sepultures péruviennes d'Ancón. *Actes de la Société Linnéenne de Bordeaux* **3**:343–358.

Dimbleby, G.
    1967   *Plants and archeology.* New York: Humanities Press.

Douglass, A. E.
    1929   The secret of the Southwest solved by talkative tree rings. *National Geographic Magazine* **56**:736–770.

Duma, G.
    1972   Phosphate content of ancient pots as indication of use. *Current Anthropology* **13**:127–130.

Faegri, K., and J. Iversen
    1975   *Textbook of pollen analysis.* Copenhagen: Munksgaard.

Field, B. S.
  1977   Development of a system for the processing, storage and retrieval of ethnobotanical data. *Department of Geography, University College, London, Occasional Papers* No. 32.
Fonner, R. L.
  1957   Appendix B, b-c. Mammal feces from Danger Cave; Juke Box Cave. In Danger Cave, by Jesse D. Jennings. *Memoirs of the Society for American Archaeology* **14**:303–304.
Ford, R. I.
  1968   *An ecological examination of the population of San Juan Pueblo, New Mexico.* Ph.D. dissertation, Anthropology, University of Michigan. Ann Arbor: University Microfilms.
  1974   Northeastern archaeology: Past and future directions. *Annual Review of Anthropology* **3**:385–413.
  1977   Evolutionary ecology and the evolution of human ecosystems: A case study from the midwestern U.S.A. In *Explanation of prehistoric change,* edited by J. N. Hill. Albuquerque: University of New Mexico Press. Pp. 153–184.
Fritts, H. S.
  1976   *Tree rings and climate.* New York: Academic Press.
Fry, G. F.
  1976   Analysis of prehistoric coprolites from Utah. *University of Utah Anthropological Papers* No. 97.
Galinat, W. C.
  1965   The evolution of corn and culture in North America. *Economic Botany* **19**(3):350–357.
  1974   The domestication and genetic erosion of maize. *Economic Botany* **28**:31–37.
Galinat, W. C., and J. H. Gunnerson
  1963   Spread of eight-rowed maize from the prehistoric Southwest. *Harvard University Botanical Museum Leaflets* **20**:117–160.
Galinat, W. C., and R. J. Ruppé
  1961   Further archaeological evidence on the effects of teosinte introgression in the evolution of modern maize. *Harvard University Botanical Museum Leaflets* **19**:163–181.
Gilmore, M. R.
  1931   Vegetal remains of the Ozark Bluff-Dweller culture. *Papers of the Michigan Academy of Science, Arts, and Letters* **14**:83–102.
Glauert, A. M.
  1965   The fixation and embedding of biological specimens. In *Techniques for electron microscopy,* edited by D. H. Kay. Philadelphia: F. A. Davis Co.
Gleeson, P., and G. Grosso
  1976   Ozette site. In The excavation of water-saturated archaeological sites (wet sites) on the Northwest Coast of North America, edited by D. R. Croes. *National Museum of Man Mercury Series, Archaeological Survey of Canada* **50**:13–44.
Goodyear, A. C., III
  1975   Hecla II and III, as interpretive study of archeological remains from the Lakeshore project, Papago Reservation, south central Arizona. *Arizona State University, Anthropological Research Paper* No. 9.
Graves, H. S.
  1919   The use of wood for fuel. *United States Department of Agriculture Bulletin* No. 753.

Gunn, C. R.
    1972   Seed collecting and identification. In *Seed biology* III, edited by T. T. Kozlowski. New York: Academic Press.
Guthe, C. E.
    1930   Identification of botanical material from excavations. *National Research Council, Division of Anthropology and Psychology, Circular* No. 6.
Hall, R. L.
    1976   Ghosts, water barriers, corn and sacred enclosures in the eastern woodlands. *American Antiquity* **41**:360–364.
    1977   An anthropocentric perspective of eastern United States prehistory. *American Antiquity* **42**:499–518.
Harlan, J. R., and J. M. deWet
    1964   Some thoughts on weeds. *Economic Botany* **18**(1):16–24.
Harshberger, J. W.
    1893   Maize: A botanical and economic study. *Contributions from the Botanical Laboratory of the University of Pennsylvania* **1**(2):1–134.
    1896   The purposes of ethnobotany. *American Antiquarian* **17**:73–81.
    1898   Uses of plants among the ancient Peruvians. *Bulletin of the Museum of Science and Art* **1**:1–4.
Haury, E. W., *et al.*
    1950   *The stratigraphy and archaeology of Ventana Cave, Arizona.* Albuquerque: University of New Mexico Press.
Heer, O.
    1865   Die pflanzen der pfahlbauten. *Neujahrsblatt für Naturforsch. Gesellschaft Zürich* **68**:1–54.
Heiser, C. B., Jr.
    1949   Study in the evolution of the sunflower species *Helianthus annuus* and *H. bolanderi. University of California Publications in Botany* **23**:157–208.
    1955   The origin and development of the cultivated sunflower. *American Biology Teacher* **17**:161–167.
    1973   Variation in the bottle gourd. In *Tropical forest ecosystems in Africa and South America: A comparative review,* edited by B. J. Meggers, E. S. Ayensu, and W. D. Duckworth. Washington: Smithsonian Institution Press. Pp. 121–128.
Heiser, C. B., D. M. Smith, S. B. Clevenger, and W. C. Martin, Jr.
    1969   The North American sunflowers (*Helianthus*). *Memoirs of the Torrey Botanical Club* **22**(3).
Heizer, R. F.
    1967   Analysis of human coprolites from a dry Nevada cave. *University of California Archaeological Survey Report* No. 70.
Heizer, R. F., and L. K. Napton
    1969   Biological and cultural evidence from prehistoric human coprolites. *Science* **165**(3893):563–568.
Helbaek, H.
    1959   Domestication of food plants in the Old World. *Science* **130**:365–373.
Hendry, G. W.
    1931   The adobe brick as a historical source. *Agricultural History* **5**:110–127.
Hill, J. N., and R. H. Hevly
    1968   Pollen at Broken K Pueblo: Some new interpretations. *American Antiquity* **33**:200–210.

Holmes, W. H.
    1884   Prehistoric textile fabrics of the United States derived from impressions on pottery. *Annual Report of the Bureau of Ethnology, 3rd, 1881–1882.* Pp. 393–425.
    1896   Prehistoric textile art of eastern United States. *Annual Report of the Bureau of Ethnology, 13th, 1891–1892.* Pp. 3–46.

Hough, W.
    1930   Ancient Pueblo subsistence. *Proceedings of the 23rd International Congress of Americanists.* Pp. 67–69.

Hutchinson, J. B., R. A. Silow, and S. G. Stephens
    1947   *The evolution of Gossypium.* London: Oxford University Press.

Jarman, H. N., A. J. Legge, and J. A. Charles
    1972   Retrievals of plant remains from archaeological site by froth flotation. In *Problems in economic prehistory,* edited by E. S. Higgs. London and New York: Cambridge University Press. Pp. 39–48.

Jennings, Jesse D.
    1957   Danger Cave. *Memoirs of the Society for American Archaeology* No. 14.

Johnson, F. (editor)
    1942   The Boylston Street fishweir. *Papers of the Robert S. Peabody Foundation for Archaeology* No. 2.

Jones, V. H.
    1936   The vegetable remains of Newt Kash Hollow shelter. In Rockshelters in Menifee County, Kentucky, edited by W. S. Webb and W. D. Funkhouser. *University of Kentucky Reports in Archaeology and Anthropology* 3:147–165.
    1941   The nature and status of ethnobotany. *Chronica Botanica* 6:219–221.
    1949   Maize from the Davis site: Its nature and interpretation. In The George C. Davis site, Cherokee County, Texas, by H. Perry Newell and Alex D. Krieger. *Society for American Archaeology, Memoir* No. 15.
    1957   Botany. In The identification of non-artifactual archaeological materials, edited by W. W. Taylor. *National Academy of Sciences–National Research Council Publication* No. 565, 35–38.
    1968   Corn from the McKees Rocks village site. *Pennsylvania Archaeologist* 38(1–4):81–86.

Jones, V. H., and R. L. Fonner
    1954   Plant materials from sites in the Durango and LaPlata areas, Colorado. In Basket Maker II sites near Durango, Colorado, by Earl A. Morris and Robert F. Burgh. *Carnegie Institution of Washington Publication* 604:93–115.

Jones, V. H., and E. A. Morris
    1960   A seventh-century record of tobacco utilization in Arizona. *El Palacio* 67:115–117.

Kaplan, L.
    1956   The cultivated bean of the prehistoric Southwest. *Annals of the Missouri Botanical Garden* 43:189–251.
    1965   Archeology and domestication in American *Phaseolus* (beans). *Economic Botany* 19:358–368.

Kaplan, L., and R. S. MacNeish
    1960   Prehistoric bean remains from caves in the Ocampo region of Tamaulipas, Mexico. *Harvard University Botanical Museum Leaflets* 19:33–56.

Keeley, H. C. M.
    1978   The cost-effectiveness of certain methods of recovering macroscopic organic

remains from archaeological deposits. *Journal of Archaeological Science* **5**:179–183.

Keepax, C.
1977 Contamination of archaeological deposits by seeds of modern origin with particular reference to the use of flotation machines. *Journal of Archaeological Science* **4**:221–229.

Kent, K. P.
1957 The cultivation and weaving of cotton in the prehistoric southwestern United States. *Transactions of the American Philosophical Society* **47**(3).

Kidder, A. V., and S. J. Guernsey
1919 Archeological explorations in northeastern Arizona. *Bureau of American Ethnology Bulletin* No. 65.

King, F. B.
1978 Additional cautions on the use of the GLO survey records in vegetational reconstructions in the Midwest. *American Antiquity* **43**:99–103.

King, J. E., W. E. Klippel, and R. Duffield
1975 Pollen preservation and archaeology in eastern North America. *American Antiquity* **40**:180–190.

King, M. E.
1978 Analytical method and prehistoric textiles. *American Antiquity* **43**:89–96.

Limp, W. F.
1974 Water separation and flotation processes. *Journal of Field Archaeology* **1**:337–342.

MacNeish, R. S.
1958 Preliminary archaeological investigations in the Sierra de Tamaulipas, Mexico. *Transactions of the American Philosophical Society* **48**(6):1–210.
1961 *First annual report of the Tehuacán archaeological–botanical project.* Andover, Mass.: Robert S. Peabody Foundation for Archaeology.

Magers, P. C.
1975 The cotton industry at Antelope House. *Kiva* **41**(1):39–47.

Mangelsdorf, P. C.
1974 *Corn, its origin, evolution and improvement.* Cambridge, Mass.: Harvard University Press.

Mangelsdorf, P. C., and R. G. Reeves
1939 The origin of Indian corn and its relatives. *Texas Agricultural Experiment Station Bulletin* **574**:1–315.

Mangelsdorf, P. C., and C. E. Smith, Jr.
1949 New archaeological evidence on evolution in maize. *Harvard University Botanical Museum Leaflets* **13**:213–260

Mangelsdorf, P. C., H. W. Dick, and J. Cámera-Hernández
1967a Bat Cave revisited. *Harvard University Botanical Museum Leaflets* **22**:1–31.

Mangelsdorf, P. C., R. S. MacNeish, and W. C. Galinat
1967b Prehistoric wild and cultivated maize. *The prehistory of the Tehuacan Valley* Vol. 1. Environment and subsistence. Austin: University of Texas Press. Pp. 178–200.

Marquardt, W. H.
1974 A statistical analysis of constituents in human paleofeces specimens from Mammoth Cave. In *Archeology of the Mammoth Cave area,* edited by P. J. Watson. New York: Academic Press. Pp. 193–202.

Marquardt, W. H., and P. J. Watson
  1977 Current state research: Kentucky shellmound archaeological project. *Southeastern Archaeological Conference Newsletter* No. 19, 4.
Martin, A. C., and W. D. Barkley
  1961 *Seed identification manual.* Berkeley: University of California Press.
Martin, P. S., and F. W. Sharrock
  1964 Pollen analysis of prehistoric human feces: A new approach to ethnobotany. *American Antiquity* **300**(2):168–180.
Mills, W. C.
  1901 Plant remains from the Baum village site. *Ohio Naturalist* **1**(5):70–71.
Minnis, P. E., and R. I. Ford
  1977 Analysis of plant remains from Chimney Rock Mesa. In Archaeological investigations at Chimney Rock Mesa: 1970–72, by Frank W. Eddy. *Memoirs of the Colorado Archaeological Society* **1**:81–91.
Minnis, P. E., and S. A. LeBlanc
  1976 An efficient, inexpensive arid lands flotation system. *American Antiquity* **41**:491–493.
Montgomery, F. H.
  1977 *Seeds and fruits of plants of eastern Canada and northeastern United States.* Toronto: University of Toronto Press.
Muir, M. D., and W. A. A. Sarjeant (editors)
  1977 *Palynology.* Stroudsburg, Pa.: Dowden, Hutchinson and Ross.
Munson, P. J.
  1966 An annotated bibliography of archaeological maize in eastern North America. *Pennsylvania Archaeologist* **36**(1–2):50–65.
Munson, P. J., P. W. Parmalee, and R. A. Yarnell
  1971 Subsistence ecology of Scovill, a terminal Middle Woodland village. *American Antiquity* **36**:410–431.
Napton, L. K., and G. Kelso
  1969 Preliminary palynological analysis of Lovelock Cave coprolites. Archaeological and paleobiological investigations in Lovelock Cave, Nevada. *Kroeber Anthropological Society Special Publications* No. 2, 19–27.
Neergaard, P.
  1978 *Seed pathology.* New York: Halsted (Wiley).
Nickel, R. K.
  1978 The study of archaeologically derived plant materials from the Middle Missouri Subarea. *Plains Anthropologist* **28**(78–2):53–58.
Nickerson, N. H.
  1953 Variation in cob morphology among certain archaeological and ethnological races of maize. *Annals of the Missouri Botanical Garden* **40**(2):79–111.
Paulssen, L. M.
  1964 *Identification of active charcoals and wood charcoals.* Copenhagen: Munksgaard.
Payne, W. W. and V. H. Jones
  1962 The taxonomic status and archaeological significance of a giant ragweed from prehistoric bluff shelters in the Ozark Plateau. *Papers of the Michigan Academy of Science, Arts, and Letters* **47**:147–163.
Pearsall, D. M.
  1978 Phytolith analysis of archeological soils: Evidence for maize cultivation in Formative Ecuador. *Science* **199**:177–178.

Pickersgill, B.
    1972 Cultivated plants as evidence for cultural contacts. *American Antiquity* **37**:97–104.
Raffauf, R. F., and E. A. Morris
    1960 Persistence of alkaloids in plant tissue. *Science* **131**:1047.
Renfrew, J. M.
    1973 *Paleoethnobotany.* New York: Columbia University Press.
Riskind, D. H.
    1970 Pollen analysis of human coprolites from Parida Cave. *Papers of the Texas Archeological Salvage Project* **19**:89–101.
Rock, J. T. and D. P. Morris (editors)
    1975 Environment and behavior at Antelope House. *Kiva* **41**(1):1–132.
Rovner, I.
    1971 Potential of opal phytoliths for use in paleoecological reconstruction. *Quaternary Research* **1**:343–359.
Rudy, S. S.
    1957 Textiles. In Danger Cave, by Jesse D. Jennings, *Memoirs of the Society for American Archaeology* **14**:235–264.
Saffray, Dr.
    1876 Les antiquities péruviennes à l'exposition de Philadelphia. *La Nature* **4**:401–407.
Sauer, C. O.
    1936 American agricultural origins: A consideration of nature and culture. In *Essays in anthropology in honor of A. L. Kroeber,* edited by Robert H. Lowie. Berkeley: University of California Press.
    1952 *Agricultural origins and dispersals.* Bowman Memorial Lectures Series 2. American Geographical Society.
Sauer, J. D.
    1950a The grain amaranths: A survey of their history and classification. *Annals of the Missouri Botanical Garden* **37**(4):113–125.
    1950b Amaranths as dye plants among the Pueblo peoples. *Southwestern Journal of Anthropology* **6**(4):412–415.
    1967 The grain amaranths and their relatives: A revised taxonomic and geographic survey. *Annals of the Missouri Botanical Garden* **54**:103–137.
    1969 Identity of archaeological grain amaranths from the Valley of Tehuacan, Puebla, Mexico. *American Antiquity* **34**(1):80–81.
Sauer, J. D., and L. Kaplan
    1969 *Canavalia* beans in American prehistory. *American Antiquity* **34**(4):417–424.
Schiemann, E.
    1932 Entstehung der kulturpflanzen. *Handbuch der Verebungwissenschaft* **3**.
Schlock, J. M.
    1971 Indoor water flotation: A technique for the recovery of archaeological material. *Plains Anthropologist* **16**:228–231.
Schoenwetter, J.
    1970 Archaeological pollen studies of the Colorado Plateau. *American Antiquity* **35**:35–48.
    1974 Pollen analysis of human paleofeces from Upper Salts Cave. In *Archeology of the Mammoth Cave area,* edited by P. J. Watson. New York: Academic Press. Pp. 49–58.

Schoenwetter, J., and A. E. Dittert, Jr.
  1968   An ecological interpretation of Anasazi settlement patterns. In *Anthropological archaeology in the Americas,* edited by B. J. Meggers. Washington: Antopological Society of Washington. Pp. 41–66.
Scholtz, S. C.
  1976   Prehistoric plies: A structural and comparative analysis of cordage, netting, basket and fabric from bluff shelters. *Arkansas Archaeological Survey, University of Arkansas Museum Publications in Archaeology, Research Series* No. 9.
Schopmeyer, C. S. (Technical Coordinator)
  1974   Seeds of woody plants in the United States. *Agricultural Handbook* No. 450. United States Department of Agriculture.
Schweinfurth, G.
  1887   Die letzten botanischen entdeckungen in den gräbern Aegyptens. *Botanische Jahrbücher für Systematik, Pflanzengeschichte und Pflanzengeographie* **8.**
Shafer, H. J., and V. M. Bryant, Jr.
  1977   Archaeological and botanical studies at Hinds Cave, Val Verde County, Texas. *Texas A and M University Anthropology Laboratory Special Series* No. 1.
Shafer, H. J., and R. G. Holloway
  1977   Organic residue analysis and stone tool function from Hinds Cave, Val Verde County, Texas: A progress statement. In Archaeological and botanical studies at Hinds Cave, Val Verde County, Texas, H. J. Shafer and V. M. Bryant, Jr. *Texas A and M University Anthropological Laboratory Special Series* No. 1, 103–128.
Smith, C. E., Jr.
  1950   Prehistoric plant remains from Bat Cave. *Harvard University Botanical Museum Leaflets* **14**:157–180.
  1967   Plant remains. In *The prehistory of the Tehuacan Valley,* Vol. 1: *Environment and subsistence,* edited by D. S. Byers. Austin: University of Texas Press. Pp. 220–256.
Smith, C. E., Jr., and R. S. MacNeish
  1964   Antiquity of American polyploid cottons. *Science* **143**:674–675.
Smith, C. E., Jr., and S. G. Stephens
  1971   Critical identification of Mexican archaeological cotton remains. *Economic Botany* **25**(2):160–168.
Smith, C. E., *et al.*
  1966   Bibliography of American archeological plant remains. *Economic Botany* **20**(4):446–460.
Spinden, H. J.
  1917   The origin and distribution of agriculture in America. *Proceedings of the Nineteenth International Congress of the Americas,* pp. 269–276.
Steen, C. R., and V. H. Jones
  1941   Prehistoric lima beans in the Southwest. *El Palacio* **48**(9):197–203.
Stephens, S. G.
  1970   The botanical identification of archaeological cotton. *American Antiquity* **35**:367–373.
  1973   Geographical distribution of cultivated cottons relative to probable centers of domestication in the New World. In *Genes, enzymes and populations,* edited by A. M. Srb. New York: Plenum.
Stewart, R. B., and W. Robertson
  1973   Application of the flotation technique in arid lands. *Economic Botany* **27**(2):114–116.

Stiles, W.
    1946   *Trace elements in plants and animals.* New York: Macmillan.
Struever, S.
    1968   Flotation techniques for the recovery of small-scale archaeological remains. *American Antiquity* **33**:353–362.
Tauber, H.
    1965   Differential pollen dispersion and the interpretation of pollen diagrams. *Danmarks Geol. Unders* 11. Raekke **89**:1–69.
Tuohy, D. R., and D. L. Rendall
    1974   Collected papers on aboriginal basketry. *Nevada State Museum, Anthropological Papers* No. 16.
Unger, F.
    1860   Botanische streifzüge auf dem gebiet der culturgeschichte. *Sitzungsberichte der Kaiserlichen Akademie der Wissenschaften in Wien, Mathematisch-Naturwissenschaftliche Klasse* **38**.
van der Merwe, N. J., and P. H. Stein
    1972   Soil chemistry of postmolds and rodent burrows: Identification without excavation. *American Antiquity* **37**:245–254.
vanGeel, B.
    1976   Fossil spores of Zygnemataceae in ditches of a prehistoric settlement in Hoogkarspel (The Netherlands). *Review of Palaeobotany and Palynology* **22**:337–344.
Vestal, P. A.
    1938   *Cucurbita moschata* found in Pre-Columbian mounds in Guatemala. *Harvard University Botanical Leaflets* **6**(4):65–69.
Vivian, R. Gwinn, D. N. Dodgen, and G. H. Hartmann
    1978   Wooden ritual artifacts from Chaco Canyon, New Mexico: The Chetro Ketl collection. *Anthropological Papers of the University of Arizona* No. 32.
Vogel, J. C., and N. J. van der Merwe
    1977   Isotopic evidence for early maize cultivation in New York State. *American Antiquity* **42**:238–242.
Wakefield, E. G., and S. C. Dellinger
    1936   Diet of the bluff dwellers of the Ozark Mountains and its skeletal effects. *Annals of Internal Medicine* **9**:1412–1418.
Watson, P. J.
    1976   In pursuit of prehistoric subsistence: a comparative account of some contemporary flotation techniques. *Midcontinental Journal of Archaeology* **1**:77–100.
Watson, P. J., *et al.*
    1969   The prehistory of Salts Cave, Kentucky. *Illinois State Museum, Reports of Investigations* No. 16.
Watson, P. J. (editor)
    1974   *Archeology of the Mammoth Cave area.* New York: Academic Press.
Wellhausen, E. J., L. M. Roberts, and E. Hernandez X., in cooperation with P. C. Mangelsdorf
    1952   *Races of maize in Mexico: Their origin, characteristics and distribution.* Cambridge, Mass.: Bussey Institution, Harvard University.
Wetterstrom, W. E.
    1976   *The effects of nutrition on population size at Pueblo Arroyo Hondo, New Mexico.* Ph.D. dissertation, University of Michigan. Ann Arbor: University Microfilms.

Whitaker, T. W.
  1948   *Lagenaria:* A Pre-Columbian cultivated plant of the Americas. *Southwestern Journal of Anthropology* **4**(1):49–68.
Whitaker, T. W., and J. B. Bird
  1949   Identification and significance of the cucurbit materials from Huaca Prieta, Peru. *American Museum Novitiates* **1426**:1–15.
Whitaker, T. W., and G. W. Bohn
  1950   The taxonomy, genetics, production, and uses of the cultivated species of *Cucurbita. Economic Botany* **4**(1):52–81.
Whitaker, T. W., and G. F. Carter
  1954   Oceanic drift of gourds: experimental observations. *American Journal of Botany* **41**(9):697–700.
Whitaker, T. W., and H. C. Cutler
  1965   Cucurbits and culture in the Americas. *Economic Botany* **19**:344–349.
  1971   Prehistoric cucurbits from the Valley of Oaxaca. *Economic Botany* **25**:123–127.
Whitaker, T. W., H. C. Cutler, and R. S. MacNeish
  1957   Cucurbit materials from three caves near Ocampo, Tamaulipas. *American Antiquity* **22**(4):352–358.
Wilding, L. P.
  1968   Biogenic opal in soils as an index of vegetative history in the Prairie Peninsula. In The Quaternary of Illinois, edited by R. E. Bergstrom. *University of Illinois, College of Agriculture, Special·Publication* No. 14, 96–103.
Willey, G. R., and J. A. Sabloff
  1974   *A history of American archaeology.* San Francisco: Freeman.
Winter, J. C.
  1973   The distribution and development of Fremont maize agriculture: Some preliminary interpretations. *American Antiquity* **38**(4):439–451.
Wittmack, L.
  1880–1887
         Plants and Fruits. In *Necropolis of Ancón in Peru,* by W. Reiss and A. Stübel, Chapter 13.
Wylie, H. G.
  1975   Tool microwear and functional types from Hogup Cave, Utah. *Tebiwa: Journal of the Idaho State University Museum* **17**(2):1–31.
Yarnell, R. A.
  1964   Aboriginal relationships between culture and plant life in the upper Great Lakes region. *Anthropological Papers, Museum of Anthropology, University of Michigan* No. 23.
  1969   Contents of human paleofeces. In The prehistory of Salts Cave, Kentucky, edited by P. J. Watson. *Illinois State Museum Report of Investigations* No. 16.
  1970   Palaeo-ethnobotany in America. In *Science in archaeology* (2nd ed.), edited by D. Brothwell and E. Higgs. New York: Praeger. Pp. 215–228.
  1972   *Iva annua* var. *macrocarpa:* extinct American cultigen? *American Anthropologist* **74**:335–341.
  1976   Early plant husbandry in eastern North America. In *Culture change and continuity,* edited by C. E. Cleland. New York: Academic Press. Pp. 265–273.
Young, B. H.
  1910   The prehistoric men of Kentucky. *Filson Club Publication* No. 25.

Subject Index

S

Sampling, cross-cultural method and, 46–50
Seeds, paleoethnobotany and, 307–308
Site catchment analysis
  methods, 122–130
  nature of, 120–122
  reasons for doing
    American studies, 133–135
    European studies, 130–133
Skeletal evidence, paleoethnobotany and, 313–314
Skeletal materials, Pleistocene, dating of, 256–261
Social physics models, for archaeology and anthropology, the gravity model, 145–150
Societies, past, relating our society to, 13–15
Spores, paleoethnobotany and, 309–311

T

Technology, social context of, 17–18, 23–28
  measurement or reflexive phase, 19–23

popular culture phase, 18–19
Tissue, paleoethnobotany and, 311

V

Variable, underlying, nature of, 227–229

W

Warfare, kinship and, 56–57
Wood, paleoethnobotany and, 305–306

Y

Yale school, hologeistic studies and, 42–43

Z

Zoomorphic figures, evidence for early domestic animals from, 188–190